Brazil

LATIN AMERICAN HISTORIES

JAMES R. SCOBIE, EDITOR

James R. Scobie: Argentina: A City and a Nation, SECOND EDITION

Charles C. Cumberland: Mexico: The Struggle for Modernity

Rollie E. Poppino: Brazil: The Land and People, SECOND EDITION

Brazil

THE LAND AND PEOPLE

SECOND EDITION

ROLLIE E. POPPINO

ILLUSTRATIONS BY
CARYBÉ AND POTY

New York · Oxford University Press · 1973

Foreword to the Second Edition

Substantial portions of the first edition of this study have been outdated by the rapid pace of demographic and economic expansion in Brazil during the past five years. The population—larger by at least ten million persons—continues to pour into the cities in unprecedented numbers, making Brazil for the first time a predominantly urban nation. The recovery and sustained growth of the economy—unmatched in Latin America and rivalled in few countries anywhere in the world—are now often described as the "Brazilian miracle." A veritable revolution is under way in the system of education throughout the country, and a bold new venture to settle and develop the vast Amazon basin has been undertaken as a national crusade to equip the Brazilian people to meet the challenges of a modern industrial society and economy.

This new edition incorporates data and observations reflecting these changes. Some new material has been included in the first chapter, The Land, but the principal additions are to be found in the concluding chapters, The Industrial Revolution, and The New Society. The political chronology has been updated to include significant recent events, and a representative listing of new works in English has been added to the bibliography.

I wish to thank the many Brazilian friends who assisted me in the collection of materials for this edition, and shared with me their insights into the significance and portent of development in Brazil since 1967.

Davis, California   R. E. P.
April 1973

Foreword

The rising interest in Brazilian studies in the United States over the past several years has pointed up the need for a short history of Brazil from its colonial origins to the present. To date the field has been left largely to the translator, the anthropologist, the sociologist, the economist, and more recently to the student of politics. For the most part the relatively few historians of Brazil writing in English have directed their attention to the colonial era, the empire, the republic, or to limited topics within these broader areas. It is hoped that the present volume may serve as an introduction for the general reader and as a frame of reference for these more specialized studies.

Brazil: The Land and People reviews the evolution of the society and economy of Portuguese America since 1500. Approximately one-half of the volume is devoted to the colonial period, with emphasis on trends of continuing importance and on developments that helped to shape the Brazilian mentality. The discussion of the national period focuses on the decades since about 1870. The first chapter describes the physical and cultural regions of the half-continent. Subsequent chapters deal with patterns of exploration and settlement, the successive cycles of the plantation and mining economies, the Africans and Europeans who peopled the land, the introduction and development of manufacturing industries, and the impact of the industrial economy on the number, distribution, and aspirations of the Brazilian people. A political chronology and statistical tables are provided for reference. The annotated bibliography is designed as a guide to further study.

This work is the product of twenty years of research in the history of Brazil. Many of the materials and ideas incorporated in it were acquired in the course of research in Brazil in 1950-51, 1957, 1958, and 1963. The visits to Brazil and extensive travel within the country were made possible by the generosity of the Henry L. and Grace Doherty Foundation, the *Fundação pelo Desenvolvimento da Ciência na Bahia,* the Department of State, the Social Science Research Council, and the faculty research and fellowship programs of the University of California. The manuscript could not have been completed without the unflagging support of the director and staff of the university library. Above all, I am indebted to many Brazilian friends and colleagues for their enthusiastic assistance and encouragement.

Davis, California   R. E. P.
June 1967

Contents

Maps

Tables 370-74

Brazil

Introduction

Nearly half a millennium has gone by since the first Portuguese explorer set foot on the continent of South America. In that time Brazil has evolved into a distinctive segment of the New World—*in* Latin America but not wholly *of* it. The surface similarities between Portuguese and Spanish America imposed by geographic proximity, the common Latin origin of the dominant cultures, similar political and economic ties with Europe, and comparable experiences in conquering and displacing the native population, have sometimes overshadowed real differences between the Brazilians and their Spanish American neighbors. The most striking contrast, in fact and potential, is the vast size and political unity of Brazil. While the Spanish empire in America disintegrated into eighteen separate nation-states, Portuguese America remained intact to become physically a giant among the independent nations of the world.

Language differences pose an effective barrier between the Brazilians and other peoples of the Western Hemisphere, preventing easy awareness and understanding of each other. The use of a minor European tongue—spoken outside Brazil only in Portugal and the remnants of its overseas empire—perpetuates a degree of cultural isolation today that

3

is comparable to the physical isolation of colonial Brazil before 1808. At the same time it reinforces the self-conscious distinctiveness of the Brazilians, and may help to preserve characteristics that are a source of national pride.

Informed Brazilians are aware and approve of the national preference for compromise to avert the spilling of blood, and point proudly to the thousands of miles of frontier established without violence. Yet, their heritage in this respect is not unlike that of Spanish-, English-, and French-speaking residents of the hemisphere. A great deal of blood was shed in wresting the land from its aboriginal occupants, preserving it from European rivals, and maintaining its political unity. Brazilian non-violence is a comparatively recent development.

The Portuguese conquerors were no less willing than their Spanish counterparts to despoil subject peoples of accumulated treasures and to exploit the mineral wealth of their new domain. But the easy road to riches was long denied them in Brazil. While Spaniards were encountering Indian civilizations and unprecedented quantities of silver and gold in Mexico and Peru, the Portuguese in the New World found only scattered forest peoples, dyewood, and fertile soil. Of necessity Brazil became an agricultural colony nearly two centuries before its fabulous trove of gold and diamonds was revealed. The plantation culture and economy which still prevail in much of the country were firmly implanted long before the dreams of the gold seekers were rewarded. But the discovery of the mines which rescued Brazil from economic stagnation when hope was waning—and similar experiences with coffee in the nineteenth century and with rubber and cacao in the twentieth—have inspired in the Brazilians unlimited confidence in the miraculous bounty of the land. No matter how great the need or discouraging the outlook, the land will provide for its people.

These people, and their tolerance for each other, are perhaps the chief distinction of Brazil today. Although cultural fusion and miscegenation are not unique to Brazil, the peculiar blend of African and Portuguese strains, with admixtures of other European, Indian, Levantine, and Oriental blood and customs, has produced an ethno-cultural spectrum unlike that of any other country. Negro slavery, never a gentle institution, survived in Brazil until 1888, yet the descendants of slaves are now accepted by their fellow citizens as equals without shame or rancor. The Brazilians feel that their successful experience with racial harmony may permit them to bridge some of the chasms in a world divided by race and color.

Although Brazil is an old country by Latin American standards, much that inspires Brazilian confidence in the future is new. In a sense, modern Brazil was born of social, political, and economic revolution about 1930. Its reputation as a center of the arts, architecture, and music, its thriving industries, and its population explosion are largely products of the past generation, while its inland capital and the network of highways that make surface travel rapid and easy are innovations of the past two decades. Once less populous than Mexico and less prosperous than Argentina, Brazil now outranks both its Latin American rivals in both categories. Whether it can maintain and widen its lead in the face of unprecedented population pressure and persistent economic difficulties is a question for the future to answer, but the Brazilians have faith that their current progress will continue.

Ever since the Enlightenment endowed Europeans with the concept of progress, Brazil has been known as the land of the future and its inhabitants as people of tomorrow. Even though many Brazilians are now convinced their future is imminent, or may already have arrived, these terms retain their validity, for as long as the people of Brazil believe tomorrow will or must be better than today, they will continue to strive for the "order and progress" that have been their national motto for more than three-quarters of a century. And no matter when or what that future may be, it has its roots in the present and in the past, with a pattern of alternating despair over the hesitating pace of change and unbounded optimism at each discovery of a new source of wealth. That past is the subject of this book.

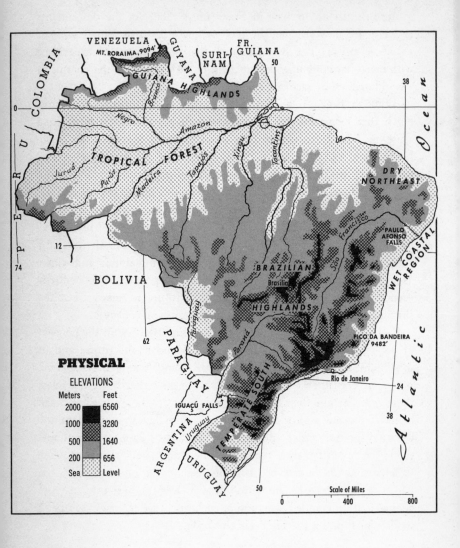

PERU

COLOMBIA

VENEZUELA

MT. RORAIMA, 9094'

GUYANA

SURI-
NAM

FR.
GUIANA

GUIANA HIGHLANDS

Negro

Branco

Amazon

Pará

50

38

Ocean

TROPICAL   FOREST

Jurú

Purus

Madeira

Tapajós

Xingu

Tocantins

DRY
NORTHEAST

PAULO
AFONSO
FALLS

São
Francisco

BOLIVIA

Paraguay

BRAZILIAN

Brasília

HIGHLANDS

Paraná

PICO DA BANDEIRA
9482'

WET COASTAL
REGION

Rio de Janeiro

PARAGUAY

TEMPERATE SOUTH

IGUAÇÚ FALLS

Uruguay

ARGENTINA

URUGUAY

Atlantic Ocean

0

12

74

62

24

38

50

PHYSICAL

ELEVATIONS

Meters	Feet
2000	6560
1000	3280
500	1640
200	656
Sea	Level

Scale of Miles

0   400   800

VENEZUELA GUYANA SURI-NAM FR. GUIANA

COLOMBIA

PERU

Boa Vista

3

Manaus

Amazon R.

50

Macapá

5

Equator

Belém

São Luís

Fortaleza

4

NORTH

2

6

Teresina

8

9

Natal

NORTHEAST

10

João Pessoa

7

11 Recife

1

Rio Branco

Pôrto Velho

17

12 Maceió

13

Aracajú

12

74

74

0

12

62

16

15

14 Salvador

CENTER-

Cuiabá

18

Brasília ★

EAST

BOLIVIA

WEST

Goiânia

19

Belo Horizonte

20 Vitória

PARAGUAY

22

21

São Paulo

Santos

23 Rio de Janeiro

24

24

38

Niterói

POLITICAL

★ National capital   ◉ State capitals

1. ACRE
2. AMAZONAS
3. RORAIMA (territory)
4. PARÁ
5. AMAPÁ (territory)
6. MARANHÃO
7. PIAUÍ
8. CEARÁ
9. RIO GRANDE DO NORTE
10. PARAÍBA
11. PERNAMBUCO
12. ALAGÔAS
13. SERGIPE
14. BAHIA

15. GOIÁS
16. MATO GROSSO
17. RONDÔNIA (territory)
18. FEDERAL DISTRICT
    (includes Brasília)
19. MINAS GERAIS
20. ESPÍRITO SANTO
21. RIO DE JANEIRO
22. SÃO PAULO
23. GUANABARA
    (city of Rio de Janeiro)
24. PARANÁ
25. SANTA CATARINA
26. RIO GRANDE DO SUL

SOUTH

Curitiba

25 Florianópolis

26

Pôrto Alegre

50

URUGUAY

ARGENTINA

Atlantic Ocean

Scale of Miles

0   400   800

Chapter 1 • The Land

Brazil is a continent." This statement is not literally true, but it is frequently used by Brazilians to describe their country, to set it apart from the rest of Latin America, and to indicate the magnitude of its problems, accomplishments, and promise. The expression is employed to evoke a vision of the vastness, complexity, and unity that distinguish Brazil from Spanish America and from the recently independent countries of tropical Africa and Asia. Brazil lends itself to such exaggeration on the part of admirers and critics alike. In sheer size, in the wealth of its natural resources, and in the make-up of its burgeoning population, Brazil can seldom be considered in the terms applied to its neighbors in Latin America or to underdeveloped nations in other parts of the world. Its negative aspects, also, are usually described in superlatives.

Brazil occupies approximately half of the continent of South America and accounts for one-third of the region known as Latin America. It covers 3,286,478 square miles, dwarfing the largest Spanish American republics. Brazil has three times as much territory as Argentina and more than four times as much as Mexico; and it is larger than the continental United States by about 185,000 square miles. Only China, the Soviet Union, and Canada surpass Brazil in contiguous land area.

Brazil's endowment of natural resources matches its "continental" dimensions. Sharing two immense river systems, the Amazon and La Plata, Brazil has one of the world's greatest potential sources of hydro-electric power. Its subsoil deposits, still not fully explored, include nearly a quarter of the proven iron ore reserves in the world and abundant quantities of most other minerals prized in an age of steel and atomic energy. The supply of essential fuels, however, is inadequate. Coal is of poor quality, while petroleum production is far below present needs. Traditionally, Brazil's principal source of wealth has been its land. The rich clay soil of the northeastern coastal strip and the red loam of the southern plateau have made Brazil a leading producer of tropical and sub-tropical plantation crops since the sixteenth century. And after more than 400 years, three-fourths of the land has yet to be turned to plow or pasture. Much of the unused area is comprised of steep, eroded slopes and of dense tropical forests, but enormous stretches of arable land in the central-western region are still awaiting settlement.

One of Brazil's most distinctive features is its population, which is an uneven blending of three major strains of the human race. While by no means all Brazilians are of mixed blood, the fusion of European, African, and Amerindian (originally from Asia) has proceeded farther in Brazil than in any other area. Perhaps even more striking than the degree of miscegenation is the success of the Brazilian experiment in racial democracy. It is unrivaled in the Western Hemisphere.

The Brazilian census ignores race but distinguishes four colors in the population: white, brown, black, and yellow. The white segment, made up of persons of predominently European ancestry and others accepted as such, comprises about 60 per cent of the total population. The browns are mostly mixed-bloods, and constitute well over one-fourth of all Brazilians. Approximately 10 per cent are identified as blacks, the descendants of Negro slaves who once represented the largest ethnic element of Brazilian society. The yellow category is comprised almost entirely of Japanese immigrants and their descendants; it accounts for less than 1 per cent of the total. Gilberto Freyre, a leading authority on miscegenation in Brazil, believes that Brazil, in some areas at least, is developing a new ethnic type similar to that in Polynesia. At the same time, he and most other authorities agree that the Brazilian population is gradually becoming whiter, or more "Aryan," as it becomes more mixed. In the absence of new infusions of African blood in more than a century, the Negro population is slowly being absorbed into the mulatto segment, while the white element is growing in absolute numbers through continued, though minor, immigration from Europe and by the passing of fairer mulattos into the white category.

Despite the high degree of racial tolerance of which the Brazilians are proud, there is discrimination and lack of full equality between ethnic groups in Brazil. By and large, the whiter an individual's skin, or the more European his physical characteristics, the greater his opportunities and the higher his standing on the social scale. But "whiteness" is determined as much by a person's activities, dress, manner, and education as by his color. A man who conforms to the popular stereotype of "white" is apt to be considered white, regardless of his skin tone. Mixed-bloods and even persons of unmixed African descent who combine native talent and ambition with education are not barred from high position in society, government, business, or the church, but the percentage of the colored population which achieves such positions is still extremely small.

After more than four centuries, the overwhelming majority of the people in Brazil continue to live within a relatively short distance of the sea. In 1970, more than 20 per cent of all Brazilians resided in the band of states from Maranhão in the north to Rio Grande do Sul in the south. Only one of these states—Minas Gerais—has no seacoast; and in nearly all of the coastal states the largest cities and heaviest concentrations of rural population are well within one hundred miles of the Atlantic. The situation in Brazil today is somewhat comparable to that of the United States at the time of independence. Although isolated islands of settlement have existed far inland since late colonial days, the interior is still thinly populated. In the four southern states in recent decades there has been a fairly steady movement of the line of permanent settlement inland, as prime agricultural land closer to the coast has been pre-empted or exhausted. In the Northeast, however,

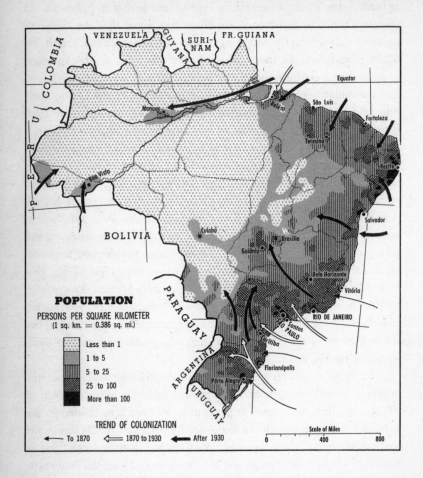

POPULATION

PERSONS PER SQUARE KILOMETER
(1 sq. km. = 0.386 sq. mi.)

- Less than 1
- 1 to 5
- 5 to 25
- 25 to 100
- More than 100

TREND OF COLONIZATION

⟵ To 1870   ⟸ 1870 to 1930   ⟵ After 1930

Scale of Miles
0   400   800

where the immediate hinterland has poor soils and an unattractive
climate, most of those with sufficient resources and ambition to migrate
usually seek the promise of a better life in or near the urban industrial
centers of the South and East. The others remain on the land where
their families have lived for generations or crowd into the mushrooming port cities on the hump of Brazil. Only since the transfer of the
national capital to the central plateau of Goiás in 1960 has there been

a deliberate, political effort to induce large numbers of people to move from the seaboard to the central-western frontier. But despite official encouragement of the "March to the West," migration from rural areas to the cities throughout Brazil continues to be much greater than from the coast to the interior.

With more than 100 million people, Brazil is emerging as one of the giants of the world community. One out of every three Latin Americans is Brazilian. There are two Brazilians for every Mexican, some four for every Argentine, and about a dozen for every Cuban. Brazil ranks eighth in population among the nations of the globe, and none of the top seven—China, India, the Soviet Union, the United States, Indonesia, Pakistan, and Japan—equals Brazil's annual growth rate of nearly three per cent. It is likely that another century or more must pass before the number of Brazilians can compare with the masses of humanity found in China and India, and for at least another two generations the population of Brazil will remain smaller than that of the Soviet Union or the United States. But at present growth rates Brazil should require only one generation to overcome the numerical gap separating it from Japan, Pakistan, and Indonesia. Brazil already has a larger population than any Western European power. This fact receives a great deal more attention in Brazil than does the nation's status in comparison with the developing countries of Asia. Brazilian spokesmen take pride in pointing out that Brazil is first among Latin nations; that it has long since surpassed tiny Portugal as leader of the Portuguese-speaking community; that it has far more people than Italy; and that it has more Roman Catholics than France and Spain combined. It seems destined, moreover, to outstrip all Latin Europe in numbers before the end of the century. By that time, even by conservative estimates, the population of Brazil should approach 200 million.

Few Brazilians are alarmed by the population explosion, for Brazil is still one of the sparsely settled regions of the globe. Its average of close to thirty persons per square mile is comparable to that of Kansas. Throughout its history, Brazil has been plagued with a shortage of manpower, while its enormous empty areas were apparently capable of absorbing almost unlimited numbers. The high rate of growth in recent years has not basically altered this situation. Under the circumstances, there is virtually no pressure for a reduction in the birth rate or for restrictions on the flow of immigration into Brazil. Rather, a continuous rapid expansion of society is regarded as inevitable and highly desirable. It is widely held that the future contribution of the increased population toward national development more than compensates for the very real immediate problems of accommodating the rising numbers of new citizens. The present generation in Brazil tends to equate a large population with national greatness.

The great majority of Brazilians are convinced that their country is destined to become a world power and that this destiny will be achieved within a short time. The foregoing glimpse of Brazil's resources suggests the basis for such optimism. Clearly, the raw ingredients necessary for great power status are to be found in more generous quantities in Brazil than in any other country of Latin America. But mere possession of the ingredients of power does not guarantee that Brazil must inevitably soon emerge as a leader of the international community. Generalizations about Brazil's actual and potential assets in almost every category must be rigidly qualified. National totals and per capita averages mask enormous discrepancies in the disposition of physical and human resources within this vast nation. Over the short term at least, the difficulties in overcoming these discrepancies appear nearly as monumental as the resources themselves. The very size of the country and the population boom that encourage Brazilian aspirations compound the difficulties inherent in the effort to transform Brazil into one of the powerful nations of the world.

Brazil has long been known as a land of extreme contrasts and contradictions. Pessimists have called it a land of unlimited impossibilities. Certainly a great deal in Brazilian experience appears to justify their contention that each progressive step in one sector tends to increase the weight of inertia in another. The South on the whole is modern and the North remains traditional. Much of the potential wealth of the nation is in the interior, while the great bulk of the population is crowded into the coastal states. Rail and water transport are woefully deficient even for present needs. Crop surpluses and critical food shortages may occur simultaneously in neighboring states. Trucks have been used to carry iron ore worth less than the gasoline burned in transporting it. But the enormous distances involved raise the cost of an adequate national transportation system to prohibitive levels. Brazil has the most extensive industrial complex and the largest urban labor force in Latin America. It also has a rural populace larger than the total population of most other Latin American republics, and it remains the area's leading producer of a long list of plantation products. Coffee alone continues to be by far the largest single source of foreign exchange earnings. For decades rural Brazilians have been pouring into the cities in a rising flood. At the same time the number of those extracting a bare subsistence from the soil increases every year. Between 1960 and 1970, for example, the urban sector expanded by about 20 million persons, from 45 to 56 per cent of the total population. During these same years the rural population increased numerically by 2.6 million.

Education in Brazil reflects an almost identical paradox. Because of the phenomenal rate of population growth, a gradual decline in the percentage of illiterates is accompanied by a staggering increase in the absolute number of persons who can neither read nor write. Industry and modern agriculture require a literate populace. Yet, a larger number of Brazilians than ever before—about half of the adult population —is completely illiterate, and nearly a third of the children between seven and fourteen years of age have no school to attend. The bulk of those who are formally literate, moreover, has received less than three years of elementary training. The existence of this untrained mass poses a continuing problem for the nation's leaders and accounts for much of the current gap between reality and aspiration in Brazil.

The distribution of the population by age group is characteristic of the pattern found in most underdeveloped countries in the postwar period. Brazilian society is composed largely of young persons, for the high rate of population growth is due almost entirely to improvements in health and sanitation which have drastically reduced the incidence of infant mortality in the more densely settled areas of the country. The average life expectancy is still below fifty years of age. In 1950 less than 10 per cent of all Brazilians were over age fifty. At the same time, nearly 42 per cent of them were under age fifteen, while slightly over half the total was under twenty years of age. The preponderance of youth is now even greater than in 1950. This situation places a tremendous burden on the relatively small, economically productive, adult population, which must support the large proportion of children. It also taxes beyond present capacity the ability of government to provide educational facilities for minors, and strains the economy to the breaking point. Brazil is expected to provide as many new jobs each year as does the United States. One of the consequences is widespread underemployment, while there continues to be a shortage of technically proficient labor for industry.

Closely related to this situation are two other problems which challenge Brazil's leadership and the public at large; the so-called "revolution of rising expectations" that has swept through the middle and lower classes, and the legacy of inflation—a by-product of the postwar urgency for rapid economic development. With the spread of mass communications media in Brazil after World War II, the common people discovered that their traditional way of life could be changed, while alert politicians vied with each other in promising the masses greater social welfare, improved economic status, and enhanced personal dignity. At the same time, the forced-draft industrialization in which Brazilians take pride was largely financed until 1964 by inflation of the currency. During the preceding decade there had been at least a tenfold increase in the cost of living and a comparable rise in the cost of government services. Thus, while the clamor for a better life was becoming more strident, it was increasingly difficult for the individual to satisfy his personal desire for a higher living standard and for the government to satisfy mounting popular aspirations for "social justice." This dichotomy was at the heart of the political revolution of 1964, and has remained a prime concern of the administrations in power in Brazil since that time.

The major miracle of Brazil is its existence as a single nation. There are actually many Brazils within the broad expanse of the national territory, and the implication of uniformity conveyed by their common flag and language is often deceptive. The country consists of several large geographic regions, each with its distinctive ethnic, economic, and cultural features, which, from the beginning of Portuguese settlement in America, evolved in comparative isolation. Only a remarkable series of fortuitous coincidences prevented the dismemberment of Brazil during the three centuries of colonial rule or its fragmentation at the time of separation from Portugal. This prolonged and, at times, precarious union of the various Brazils, however, ultimately endowed them with identical political institutions and, more significantly, encouraged the strengthening of important elements of their common heritage. The cultural and spiritual bonds which unite all Brazilians now appear unbreakable, despite considerable and carefully nurtured diversity. But the regions of Brazil continue to be distinguished by striking contrasts in physical environment, the barrier of distance, variations in the racial mixture of the population, and great differences in stage and rate of economic development.

Regionalism has long attracted the attention and interest of foreign students of Brazil. Since the early years of the nineteenth century, when the country was first opened to foreign visitors, most European and North American observers have been struck by the range of physical, economic, and cultural contrasts encountered among the different regions of Brazil. The German naturalist, von Martius, who traveled over much of Brazil during the last years of the colonial era, is generally credited as being the first to point out the need for serious study of regionalism as an important aspect of the history of the country. His advice has since been followed, knowingly or not, by a majority of the foreign scholars who have compiled an impressive array of Brazilian studies in the various academic disciplines.

Among Brazilians, however, conscious awareness of the regional diversity that characterizes their country is an even more recent development than is the fact of national unity. In large part, this stems from the almost complete absence, until a few decades ago, of sustained contact between the different Brazils. During the colonial period, communication was ordinarily less frequent between the scattered settlements along the Brazilian coast than among the separately governed

English colonies which were spread over a comparable distance in the Caribbean and on the Atlantic seaboard of North America. In fact, for long periods Bahia and Rio de Janeiro maintained closer relations with Portuguese Africa than with Maranhão, which then included the Amazon region and much of the north coast of Brazil. These conditions contributed to the development of the wide variety of customs and administrative practices which the crown and its representatives found expedient to tolerate within the Portuguese empire in America. Attempts to govern all of Brazil from a single colonial capital were regularly frustrated until the imperial court itself was transferred to Rio de Janeiro in 1808. This historical accident gave a sense of identity and a semblance of administrative uniformity to the many Brazils which carried through the transition to nationhood in 1822, and survived a full generation of separatist revolts involving four major regions. The failure of the revolts may be attributed largely to the lack of communication and co-ordination between the rebellious provinces.

Independence did not soon or significantly affect the traditional relationships of the provinces with the capital or with one another. The telegraph was introduced in the second half of the nineteenth century, as were railways linking coastal ports with their immediate hinterland. The railroad, however, was not used extensively to tie the outlying areas to the political and economic centers of the country. Thus, overland travel continued to be slow and laborious at best. The distant provinces maintained the minimum essential contact with the capital by sea. Otherwise, their perennial isolation was not substantially altered until the advent of the airplane, the radio and, more recently, inter-regional highways for trucks, buses, and automobiles. As long as the overwhelming majority of Brazilians were familiar with only one section of the country and remained uninformed about the others, they displayed a natural tendency to regard their own particular region and its customs as representative of the entire nation.

The reluctance of educated Brazilians to pay special heed to their regional differences was conditioned by the nature of government in Brazil and by their traditional view of the country's history. Regionalism, in part, is a state of mind which may be translated politically as federalism, provincial self-rule, or even political independence. These concepts ran directly counter to the highly centralized rule advocated, at least in theory, by the absolutist Portuguese monarchs and pursued without basic modifications by their Brazilian successors until 1889. While foreign observers were beginning to note the striking dissimilarities between the great regions of Brazil, the literate minority in the nation continued to study and to interpret the Brazilian past in terms of administrative history and political biography which largely ignored regional disparities. In the nineteenth century, Brazilian regionalism was most often equated with republicanism, which went out of style with the collapse of the separatist movements before 1850. Not until the last quarter of the century, when discontent with the monarchy became prevalent, did republicanism again become fashionable. Only then did a few Brazilian scholars begin to stress the variety of environment and experience that had gone into the making of Brazil.

The establishment of the republic in 1889 may be regarded in a real sense as a delayed victory for regionalism in Brazil and as the high point of its expression in national politics. The political union of the Brazils was by this time too strong to be dissolved, but federalism became the law of the land. The Constitution of 1891 exalted the individuality of the states, granting them greater autonomy than they had ever previously been authorized. Traditional accounts of Brazil continued to be written and to be used in public instruction during the early years of the republic, but these were gradually replaced by new studies which incorporated the official view of the nation as a complex of unique regions. In this atmosphere, a substantial body of scholars focused increasing attention on the diversity of cultures that were combined in Brazilian society, while denying that such diversity implied any political threat to Brazilian unity.

The shift in emphasis from political to cultural regionalism was completed before the revolution of 1930, which reasserted the primacy of the central government in Brazilian politics. Widespread disillusionment with the rampant federalism of the first republic did not signify a lessening of public or official interest in regional studies. The fifteen-year administration of Getulio Vargas founded institutes of folklore and ethnology, promoted regional research in geography, anthropology, and social history, and witnessed the rise of an entire new school of novelists concerned with regional questions. At the same time, it rigidly suppressed challenges to its political authority, launched public works programs designed to increase the interdependence of all sections of the country, and gave new voice to Brazilian nationalism.

The parallel development of these apparently contradictory trends has continued with the steady improvement of transportation and communications within Brazil in the postwar years. The flood of internal migration has made even larger numbers of Brazilians conscious of their common heritage and of their regional peculiarities. In addition, the radio, the national cinema, and now television have joined the printed word as both preservers and disseminators of regional traditions, with the result that awareness of regionalism is no longer confined to the literate and the traveled. The present generation is conditioned to regard the division of the country into distinctive geographic and cultural regions as a fact of national life, one that is fully compatible with national unity, and one which must be considered in the quest for solutions to such pressing national problems as public education and economic development. The proliferation of elaborate federal programs for the social and economic development of areas such as the Amazon Valley, the drought zone of the Northeast, the São Francisco Valley, and the Paraná basin, among others, is evidence of the extent to which this attitude is shared by government officials and the public at large.

The nearly universal awareness of regionalism in Brazil has not produced a consensus as to the number, size, limits, or key distinguishing features of the regions of the country. For three-quarters of a century, specialists in various fields of human knowledge have been arbitrarily dividing Brazil into a bewildering array of regions, subregions, areas, and zones according to its diverse physical features, its inhabitants, and the range of relationships over time between man and the land. The number of regions that have been identified varies from the two Brazils—one modern and the other archaic—described by French sociologist Jacques Lambert, to twelve culture areas indicated by Manuel Diégues Júnior. The earliest classification of regions by a

Brazilian scholar appears to be that of André Rebouças, who in 1889 discussed Brazil in terms of ten agricultural zones. Perhaps the most influential, because it is included in a textbook in continuous use since 1900, is the formula elaborated by historian João Ribeiro identifying the five principal administrative districts of colonial Brazil as separate regions. One of the more recent and interesting formulations is Charles Wagley's division of Brazil into six major regions on the basis of their physical, ethnic, historical, and cultural patterns.

The profusion of formulas for dividing the regions of Brazil reflects the variety of characteristics encountered in each large area of the nation and the absence of a widely accepted set of criteria for classifying them. The decision as to the number of divisions and the location of their boundaries—or the rejection of boundaries as meaningless—is largely a personal one, determined by the professional interests and prejudices of the individual attempting to describe Brazil's regional structure. There is general agreement that the Amazon and the Northeast constitute separate regions, although opinions differ with respect to the extent of these regions, and even authorities in the same profession rarely agree on the regional pattern in the rest of Brazil. For many years this lack of accord even extended to the central government itself, where the National Council of Geography and the National Council of Statistics, which jointly comprise the Brazilian Institute of Geography and Statistics, employed two different official versions of the regional organization of the country. The former divided Brazil into six great regions distinguished primarily by terrain features and natural resources, while the latter recognized only five regions whose outlines followed political boundaries.

While no grouping of the regions of Brazil is entirely satisfactory, the formula long employed by the National Council of Statistics is most widely known and is used here. It assigns Brazil's twenty-two states and four territories to geographic regions which respect most of the obvious physical contrasts of the country and correspond reasonably well to the historical patterns of settlement, administration, and economic activities. The five regions are: North, Northeast, East, South, and Center-West.

NORTH

The North is the largest region of Brazil, coinciding almost entirely with the immense Amazon basin. It consists of 1,382,697 square miles, or 42 per cent of the national territory. Politically it is comprised of the three states of Acre, Amazonas, and Pará, and the territories of Amapá, Roraima, and Rondônia. With a population in 1970 of 3.6 million, the North accounted for only 3.8 per cent of the total population of Brazil. Its average density of less than two persons per square mile makes it by far the least populous region of the nation. The average density figure is somewhat misleading, however, for many thousands of square miles of the Amazon Valley are entirely unoccupied. About 60 per cent of the population of the North is located in the comparatively developed state of Pará, while much of the remainder is found in the city of Manaus and in the few towns and villages scattered along the Amazon and its numerous tributaries. Traditionally, most of the inhabitants of the region, who are predominantly of mixed European-Amerindian blood, have led a semi-nomadic existence. Owning no land and few material possessions, they tend to move from one temporary farm plot or collecting area to another every few seasons. Efforts to induce large numbers of them to take up permanent residence in one locality have invariably failed.

Transportation within the region and to the outside world is almost exclusively by boat and by airplane. The Amazon Valley has only a few hundred miles of railways (in Pará, Amapá, and Rondônia) and perhaps 5000 miles of local feeder roads. The rivers serve as natural and economical travel routes, but they flow away from the populated, developed sections of Brazil, perpetuating the isolation of the North. The Belém-Brasília highway, a truck route from São Paulo to Rondônia, and the Cuiabá-Santarém highway, which are under construction, promise to give these northern areas their first effective overland links with the center of the country. It is likely, however, that the trans-Amazon highway, on which construction began in 1970, will have a more immediate impact on the society and economy of the region.

The economy of the Amazon Valley to date has been geared primarily to the collection and export of forest products, chiefly rubber, nuts, oils, lumber, medicinal herbs, and fibers. In recent decades some plantation products have been added to the list, with the introduction of jute in the central valley and pepper in Pará. The latter has been developed since the war and is largely in the hands of Japanese immigrants. The extraction of mineral resources has also become significant, particularly in Amapá, where a United States firm has been mining manganese on a large scale since 1957. But except during the heyday of the wild rubber boom before World War I, the economic activities of the region have seldom contributed as much as 2 per cent of the national income in Brazil. This situation may change if present plans to build a sugar industry in Amazonas and Pará should materialize, or if the Amazon Valley proves to have important deposits of petroleum. Two oil strikes have been made in the lower valley, but as yet no commercially feasible oil field has been discovered.

The Amazon Valley has been regarded as the land of the future since the arrival of the first Europeans in the sixteenth century, and it remains so today. No other area of Brazil has evoked so much subjective commentary from Brazilians and foreigners alike. The optimists have long pointed to its rich tropical verdure, its variety of exotic forest products, and its fertile flood plains as evidence that this immense region can—and eventually must—support a population comparable to that of China or India. The pessimists, with equal fervor, have denounced its oppressive heat, incessant rains, strange diseases, and myriads of poisonous insects and reptiles, and have denied that the valley is or can become a tolerable habitat for civilized man. Both exaggerate greatly, but over the years the weight of the argument has tended to support the pessimists. In practice it has been found that the climate, while monotonous, is not debilitating to the mind or body of persons accustomed to the weather of the temperate zones. By no means all of the region is covered with tropical jungle. Much of it consists of grasslands suitable for farming and pasture, and has elevations rising over 2000 feet in the territories of Roraima and Rondônia. Relatively modest investments in public health activities have demonstrated that malaria and other diseases endemic in the valley can be controlled. But the problems of a small, widely dispersed population, the absence of sufficient high-unit-value products to support a rapidly expanding society and economy, and, above all, the immense distances to be traversed continue to make the North the least desirable area of Brazil.

The central government is attempting to overcome these problems and to integrate the region more fully into the nation through an ambitious road-building and colonization program. The heart of the program is the trans-Amazon highway, being pushed from Maranhão to the border of Peru. It is intended to open vast forested areas south of the Amazon River to permanent settlement based on agriculture and grazing.

NORTHEAST

One of the oldest regions of Brazil, the Northeast is the region that has received the most publicity in Brazil and abroad in recent years. It is recognized as a distinct region by authorities in numerous fields, yet there are sharp contrasts in climate, terrain, vegetation, and the ethnic origins of its inhabitants. The Northeast includes the states of Alagôas, Ceará, Maranhão, Paraíba, Pernambuco, Piauí, and Rio Grande do Norte, all of which face on the Atlantic and occupy most of the north coast and the hump of Brazil as far as the mouth of the São Francisco River. The island territory of Fernando de Noronha is attached for administrative purposes to Pernambuco but otherwise is not associated with the region. The Northeast with its 372,839 square miles, or more than 11 per cent of the national territory, had a population of 20.1 million in 1970, which represented over 21 per cent of the national total and gave the region an average density of about fifty-four persons per square mile. The majority of its inhabitants are clustered in the cities, towns, and plantations within a short distance of the coast, however.

The contrasts in climate and vegetation found in the Northeast are determined largely by elevation, the direction of the prevailing winds, and distance from the sea. Each of these factors has a direct bearing on the rainfall pattern, which varies widely within the region. On the hump of Brazil, where the coastline follows a generally north-south or northeast-southwest axis, the coastal zone is a low strip of flat or gently rolling land with fertile soils. It is characterized by luxuriant tropical vegetation made possible by abundant winter rains borne by light prevailing winds from the Atlantic. The northern extension of the coastal rain belt that begins in southern Brazil covers nearly all of Alagôas and the eastern portion of Pernambuco, Paraíba, and Rio Grande do Norte. Originally it was densely forested, but much of the forest cover has long since been removed to make way for sugar plantings. Traditionally the coastal strip has been an area of large plantations.

The northeastern extension of the Brazilian Highlands approaches the sea in these states, giving some of them an intermediate zone known as the *agreste,* marked by higher elevations and less plentiful but still regular rainfall. The *agreste* is a zone of small farming, with emphasis on subsistence crops and foodstuffs for local markets, and on tobacco and other export crops that can be raised on family-size plots.

The interior is known throughout most of Brazil as the *sertão.* In the Northeast it is a semi-arid zone afflicted by periodic droughts and by extreme variations in time and place of rainfall. It has high temperatures, generally poor soils, and xerophitic vegetation capable of surviving long periods with little water. The sporadic rains usually occur in heavy downpours, not infrequently resulting in floods because of the absence of adequate ground cover to hold the run-off. The drought area, or drought polygon (*polígono das sêcas*) as it is officially designated, extends northward to the Atlantic coast in some sections and south into Sergipe, Bahia, and Minas Gerais. By and large the northeastern *sertão* is an area of livestock raising and subsistence agriculture, although some favored localities support fairly extensive production of cotton, sisal, and other commercial crops except during the most severe droughts, while the river valleys have large stands of palms which produce a valuable wax for export.

For more than a century successive Brazilian administrations have been directing a good deal of attention and money to programs for combatting drought conditions in the Northeast. Reservoirs, dams, and irrigation projects have been initiated, and many of them have been completed, but no permanent solution to the frequent shortage of water has yet been found. Recent programs have sought to reduce the dependence of the *sertanejos* (people of the *sertão*) on subsistence agriculture by developing transportation and power facilities which will encourage industry to enter the region. Roads and highways linking the *sertão* with the coastal capitals and with central and northern Brazil have been opened, while hydroelectric power from dams on the São Francisco River is now available throughout the northeastern states.

These facilities, plus ample raw materials, a large labor supply, and a widely publicized tax incentive program, have already led to a considerable industrial investment from other parts of Brazil, particularly from São Paulo, and from abroad.

The Northeast has long been known as the most depressed area of Brazil because of its geographic and related economic handicaps. Thus, the government's developmental program calls for broad educational and health benefits as well as improved employment opportunities. It anticipates, moreover, large-scale migration from the drought zone to Maranhão, the Amazon Valley, or other areas of Brazil. In this field, however, the program runs counter to the deeply rooted sentiments of much of the population. For generations the Northeasterners have been migrating to other areas of the country when they have been forced out by drought. But they retain a strong attachment for the community of their birth. Invariably, many of the migrants return as soon as they learn that the rains are falling again at home.

The three agricultural and climatic zones correspond roughly to ethnic zones in the Northeast. Along the coast, which has been occupied since early colonial times, there is a heavy concentration of Negroes, the descendants of slaves imported from Africa. The bulk of persons of unmixed European origin are also located in the coastal area. Mulattos and others who would be regarded as "colored" in the United States probably comprise the largest group in this zone, although census reports usually indicate that "whites" are in the majority. The *agreste* serves even more as a racial melting pot in northeastern Brazil, for Negro, European, and Amerindian blood is found in varying proportions in most of the people in this section. Those of unmixed African or European ancestry constitute a small minority. The Amerindian has virtually disappeared as a separate ethnic element throughout the Northeast, but the great majority of the inhabitants of the *sertão* are of mixed Amerindian-European descent. These ethnic distinctions between zones of the Northeast were formerly much sharper than they are at present. They are being blurred not only by continued miscegenation but also by the increased movement of population within the region following improvements in transportation.

The westernmost states of the region—Maranhão and Piauí—deserve special mention, for while they share many characteristics of the other northeastern states, they also reveal features common to the Amazon Valley. The western portion of Maranhão and, to a lesser extent, the coastal area of both states have climate and vegetation more typical of Amazonia than of the Northeast. Yet, southern Piauí is officially included in the drought polygon, and even some localities in southeastern Maranhão are occasionally subject to the drought conditions that scourge much of the Northeast. In recognition of these peculiarities, Maranhão and Piauí have been formally designated by Brazil's National Council of Geography as a transitional sub-region, *Meio-Norte* (Mid-North).

EAST

The region denominated East includes the six states of Sergipe, Bahia, Espírito Santo, Minas Gerais, Rio de Janeiro, and Guanabara. The latter, which became a state in 1960, is the former Federal District comprised almost entirely of the city of Rio de Janeiro. The geographic contrasts in the eastern region are as sharp as those found in the Northeast, while the range of economic activities is even greater. For these reasons the East is sometimes considered as a series of contiguous and overlapping sub-regions. By and large the northern and coastal areas which were occupied early in the colonial era retain many economic and social attitudes inherited from their colonial past. At the same time the urban-oriented areas of Guanabara, Rio de Janeiro, and Minas Gerais are-more highly industrialized and more in tune with twentieth-century trends in Western society. The disparity between the archaic and the modern that characterizes much of Brazil today can be seen more clearly in the East than in any other region of the country.

The East, with 486,509 square miles, accounts for about 15 per cent of the land area of Brazil. Its population of above 30 million in 1970 represented nearly 33 per cent of the national total. The average population density of the East in 1970 was sixty-three persons per square mile, a figure which obscures the startling discrepancy between Guanabara, with over 6000 persons per square mile, and part of western Bahia which remain virtually unoccupied. The same contrast is revealed in figures on the distribution of rural and urban population throughout the region. Over-all the East is much more urban than Brazil as a whole. In 1970 it contained 36 per cent of all Brazilians in cities of more than 50,000 inhabitants. But nearly four-fifths of the eastern city dwellers resided in the states of Minas Gerais, Guanabara, and Rio de Janeiro. More than one half of them were found in the two cities of Rio de Janeiro and Belo Horizonte.

Geographically the eastern region is dominated by the mineral-rich Brazilian Highlands which occupy nearly all of Minas Gerais and much of the interior of Bahia, Espírito Santo, and Rio de Janeiro. In some areas of the south and east coasts the Highlands appear as an escarpment rising abruptly from the sea to elevations ranging over 3000 feet. Elsewhere they are bordered by a narrow coastal strip, alternating between pockets of rich, tropical lowlands and long stretches of jungle-entangled marshes. The Highlands slope downward to the west, where they give way to the São Francisco Valley, which has long served as the principal north-south artery linking the sparsely settled interior of Brazil. These terrain features have seriously impeded the development of a satisfactory transportation system along the coast or between the coast and the interior. Few large rivers cut through the escarpment to provide natural communication routes from the Atlantic into the Highland area. Although mining, agriculture, and livestock raising have been important activities in Minas Gerais and the Bahian *sertão* for 250 years, Rio de Janeiro, Vitória, and Salvador are the only significant eastern ports through which these products can reach world markets. The railroad has linked Rio de Janeiro and Belo Horizonte for more than half a century, and within the past decade modern highways have been opened between these points and Salvador. But most of coastal Bahia, Espírito Santo, and much of the state of Rio de Janeiro still lack adequate transportation services.

In their economic activities the inhabitants of the East span nearly the entire range of Brazilian history. These include the traditional plantation and subsistence agriculture of the early coastal settlements, the cattle and mining industries of the colonial *sertão*, and the modern manufacturing industries that have sprung up in the past generation around the cities of Rio de Janeiro and Belo Horizonte. Agriculture continues to occupy the attentions and energies of more people than any other activity in the region, although the proportion of persons engaged in agriculture is much higher in the northern coastal states than in Rio de Janeiro or Guanabara. Only Minas Gerais maintains a relative balance between agricultural and non-agricultural enterprises. The East produces approximately 40 per cent of the tobacco, bananas, oranges, and coconuts which enter the domestic and export markets. It accounts for one-fifth of Brazil's sugar—a product that has been raised in the region since the sixteenth century—and 99 per cent of the cacao, which has become a ranking export crop in the past few decades. The staple foods of the Brazilian diet are grown in abundance in this region. Bahia is the leading producer of manioc, while Minas Gerais leads the nation in the production of beans, corn, and cheese. Livestock raising, again principally in Minas Gerais and Bahia, also figures prominently in the eastern economy. The region accounts for roughly one-third of all the cattle, horses, asses, mules, swine, and goats raised in Brazil, and is consequently a major source of meat, milk, and leather, predominantly for domestic consumption.

The East has one of the richest mining areas of the world. Its reputation dates from the discovery of gold at the end of the seventeenth century, when the name Minas Gerais (General Mines) was given to the largest state in the region. Gold is still being extracted, but it has long since been outdistanced by products of greater industrial value. The catalog of sub-soil deposits in the East runs from asbestos to zirconium and includes virtually all of the minerals essential to an industrial economy. The apparently inexhaustible reserves of high-grade iron ore in Minas Gerais provide the basis for the Brazilian steel industry as well as an important export commodity and source of foreign exchange. Bahia and Sergipe are the only significant sources of petroleum in Brazil. Among the leading mineral products of the nation, only two are mined in larger quantities in other regions—coal in the South and manganese in the North.

The modern industrial-commercial complex of the eastern region is concentrated primarily in the states of Guanabara, Minas Gerais, and Rio de Janeiro. Smokestacks have become commonplace and smog obscures the spectacular vistas of Guanabara Bay, the Paraíba Valley, and the environs of Belo Horizonte. These areas and much of the land between them comprise a separate economic zone or sub-region which has more in common with São Paulo than with the traditional eastern economy. The sub-region accounts for a third of the national textile industry, nearly all of Brazil's iron and steel production, and the manufacture of a broad range of consumer and capital goods, from plastic toys to oil tankers. Approximately one-fifth of all factories and processing plants in Brazil are presently located here, contributing well over a quarter of Brazil's domestic income from industry. The combined income from industry and commerce in the sub-region exceeds the entire income from agriculture for all of the eastern states. In Guanabara alone industry and commerce generate nearly as much revenue as is derived from all sources in the three states of Espírito Santo, Bahia, and Sergipe.

The outstanding economic position of Guanabara among the states of the East reflects the fact that Rio de Janeiro is Brazil's second city. It is surpassed only by São Paulo in size, as an industrial center, as a transportation hub, and as an entrepôt for domestic commerce. And it remains the country's second port as measured by volume and value of both imports and exports. The city of Rio de Janeiro, moreover, is the cultural capital of the nation and continues to be its de facto administrative capital as well. Nearly a third of the federal payroll is spent here, for despite the existence of Brasília a great number of the government agencies have remained in Guanabara. The combination of industrial, commercial, transportation, and administrative activities, plus the services required by a preponderantly urban society, give the inhabitants of Guanabara by far the highest per capita income in Brazil —much higher than that of the citizens of São Paulo and nearly triple the national average.

SOUTH

The South is the dynamic region of Brazil. In many ways it is more comparable to western Europe than to the rest of the nation, for it possesses in abundance those features Brazilians identify as modern and progressive. The most densely populated, most urban, and most highly industrialized of the five regions, the South also leads the nation in agricultural production. Its inhabitants are wealthier, have more schooling, and are more preponderantly European in origin than the residents of any other region. But, as in other regions, there are considerable differences among the four southern states. São Paulo outstrips Paraná, Santa Catarina, and Rio Grande do Sul by a wide margin in nearly every category.

These four states comprise the smallest region, with 318,773 square miles, or slightly less than one-tenth of the area of Brazil. Nearly 35 million people—over 36 per cent of all Brazilians—lived in the South in 1970, giving the region an average density of 108 persons per square mile. The distribution of inhabitants among the states is extremely uneven, however, with just over half of the total in São Paulo and fewer than one-tenth in Santa Catarina. The rest are divided about equally between Paraná and Rio Grande do Sul. About 63 per cent of the southern population was classified as urban in 1970, but São Paulo with over 14 million and Rio Grande do Sul with more than 3.5 million city residents accounted for the great majority of the urban population. On the other hand, well over half of the inhabitants of Santa Catarina and nearly two-thirds of those in Paraná were found in rural areas in 1970. Paraná, whose urban population nearly doubled between 1960 and 1970, also has the second highest rural population growth rate in Brazil.

The South has a greater variety of topography, climate, and vegetation than any other Brazilian region, although it lacks the extreme contrast between tropical swampland and semi-desert found in the East. Inland features include the jungle-covered valleys of the Paraná and Uruguay rivers, which mark the western boundary of the region; the low, rolling grasslands that extend into Rio Grande do Sul from Uruguay; evergreen-forested uplands that reach their highest elevation in Paraná; and the fertile plateau of the interior of São Paulo. Along the seaboard the surface changes from the long sandy peninsulas that separate the Lagoa Mirim and Lagoa dos Patos from the Atlantic, past the irregular, island-studded coast of Santa Catarina and Paraná, to the dense rain forest and crescent beaches of the narrow São Paulo littoral. The latter is backed by the towering escarpment, or Serra do Mar, which rises abruptly from sea level to more than 3000 feet. Most of the state of São Paulo and the northwestern portion of Paraná lie within the tropics, while the rest of the region is located in the south temperate zone. Yet the climate is affected nearly as much by elevation as by latitude. This situation is seen most clearly in the city of São Paulo and its port of Santos, forty-five miles distant. Santos, at sea level, has a distinctly tropical climate. São Paulo, at more than 2500 feet elevation, experiences almost as broad a range of temperate climate as does Pôrto Alegre, at the head of the Lagoa dos Patos 500 miles to the South.

Southern Brazil is reminiscent of Europe not only in its temperate climate but also in the ethnic composition of its population. In 1950 about nine-tenths of the inhabitants of the South were of European ancestry. This situation is due primarily to the fact that the major settlement and economic development of the region has occurred within the past century, largely as a result of massive immigration from Europe. Although São Paulo was occupied in the sixteenth century and Rio Grande do Sul was incorporated into Brazil 200 years later, when colonists from the Azores were settled there, the region did not develop the colonial plantation economy and large Negro slave population characteristic of Bahia and Pernambuco. In fact, Paraná, Santa Catarina, and Rio Grande do Sul remained essentially a frontier area until after 1850. Even earlier a trickle of German immigrants— followed later by Italians, Poles, and a variety of central Europeans —began settling along the coastal inlets and wooded river valleys of the three states, establishing isolated mixed-farming communities that were replicas of the villages they had known in Europe. For generations the descendants of these immigrants resisted absorption into the native population, and even now German is still the first language of many residents of the South, although since the 1930's consistent efforts have been made to eliminate cultural and other barriers between them and the rest of the Brazilian population.

The truly impressive flow of immigration, however, came after the abolition of slavery in Brazil in 1888. From that year until the outbreak of World War I more than 2.5 million immigrants, chiefly Italians and Portuguese, entered the country from Europe. The bulk of those who remained in Brazil settled in the South, primarily in São Paulo. Here they provided the labor that made possible the tremendous expansion of the coffee industry, supplied the sheer numbers and energy that transformed the capital of São Paulo from a sleepy provincial town into a thriving metropolis, and left an indelible stamp on the culture and society of the region.

The South virtually defies comparison with the rest of Brazil in terms of its contribution to the national economy. Its share, by volume and value, is greater than that of all other regions combined. It not only leads in industry, with 60 per cent of the national total in 1960, but also accounts for over half of Brazil's income from agriculture, and it is an important producer of livestock. There are sharp contrasts within the region, however. In Santa Catarina, which may be regarded as an economic sub-region, levels of production and income are comparable in most respects with those of the Northeast, while in Paraná —now the ranking coffee producer in Brazil—nearly two-thirds of the economic activities are concentrated in the agricultural sector. In all Brazil only one state—economically underdeveloped Goiás—is more dependent on agriculture. At the other extreme Rio Grande do Sul has experienced such rapid economic expansion since World War II that it now accounts for about one-tenth of the national income. São Paulo —the industrial giant of Latin America—provides a third of the total. São Paulo alone contributes more to the Brazilian economy than do the twelve states of the North, Northeast, and Center-West, and it nearly equals the contribution of the six eastern states.

The fantastic and continued growth of São Paulo is without precedent in the history of Brazil, which has witnessed a procession of "boom and bust" economic cycles over the past four and a half centuries. In contrast to previous bursts of economic activity—usually geared to the production of a single export commodity—the economic development of São Paulo has been directed largely toward production for the domestic market, and the process of economic growth itself has served to increase the size and purchasing power of that market. The industrial expansion of São Paulo began before World War I when there emerged a new and expansionist entrepreneurial spirit, encouraged by an abundance of investment capital earned in the lucrative coffee trade and by the availability of a literate immigrant mass determined to raise its living standards to European levels. It has been sustained by continuous injections of domestic and foreign venture capital and, since 1930, by a flood of migrants from other parts of Brazil, whose numbers now greatly exceed the total foreign immigration into the state since 1900. Under the circumstances the São Paulo economy has grown far beyond the hopes and expectations of the early industrialists. It has given Brazilians confidence in their ability to surmount all obstacles to national development and has strengthened their conviction that Brazil will soon become a world power. São Paulo serves as a model and inspiration for the other states of Brazil even while the economic gap between them is widening.

CENTER-WEST

The fifth region, known as the Center-West, is the active frontier area of Brazil today, complete with cowboys, Indians, prospectors, land speculators, and land-hungry migrants from the older sections of the country. It is surpassed only by the North in size and remoteness from the populous parts of Brazil, but it differs markedly from the North in its rate of growth and in the spirit of progress that permeates the region. The Center-West includes the Federal District and the states of Goiás and Mato Grosso, whose combined area of 725,657 square miles accounts for 22 per cent of the national territory. Its population in excess of 5 million in 1970—representing 5.4 per cent of the total population of Brazil—gave the region an average density of just over seven persons per square mile.

For nearly a quarter-century the Center-West has been the fastest growing region of Brazil, with a rate of population expansion more than twice that of the nation as a whole. The number of inhabitants increased by 73 per cent between 1950 and 1960, and by 72 per cent in the following decade. Significantly, Brazil's westward movement has given rise to the unusual phenomenon of an exploding agricultural frontier which has the highest percentage of urban expansion of any region in Brazil. At the outset the new residents who poured into the Center-West were attracted primarily to the land and tended to settle in rural areas, but in recent years they have been drawn increasingly to the cities. While the rural population doubled between 1950 and 1960, and had doubled again by 1970, the number of urban residents, starting from a smaller base, increased fivefold in twenty years, with the result that the population of the region is now distributed about equally between rural and urban districts. The Center-West still has no huge metropolitan centers to compare with those of the coastal states, although in 1970 the Federal District boasted two cities of more than 100,000 residents, and Goiás and Mato Grosso each had one city in that category. Moreover, Anápolis, in Goiás, and Cuiabá, the capital of Mato Grosso, which then had about 90,000 and 84,000 inhabitants, respectively, have both since passed the 100,000-mark.

Generalizations about the demographic pattern of the Center-West are distorted by the rate and nature of migration into the Federal District, which accounts for only .3 per cent of the land area and slightly over 10 per cent of the population of the region. The rest of the Center-West, with less than 42 per cent city dwellers, remains predominantly rural despite the impressive growth rates of such cities as Goiânia (159 per cent) and Campo Grande (101 per cent) between 1960 and 1970. On the other hand, the Federal District is now almost exclusively an urban area, and has by far the highest rate of urban expansion in the nation. Largely as the result of the accelerated transfer of government functions and personnel to the new capital, in the decade ending in 1970 the city of Brasília expanded at a staggering 487 per cent, to reach a population of 272,000 residents, while the Federal District as a whole increased by 286 per cent. Its population was in excess of 538,000 in 1970.

The heavy influx of new residents has modified the ethnic composition of the population of the Center-West. Traditionally the inhabitants of the region, like those of other areas of the interior of Brazil, were largely persons of mixed European-Amerindian ancestry. And evidence of Amerindian blood is probably still somewhat more common among them than among Brazilians generally, since a high proportion of the incoming migrants are drawn from other parts of the *sertão*. Nevertheless, the Center-West has attracted significant numbers of settlers from all areas of Brazil—individuals of varying degrees of European, Amerindian, Negro, and Japanese extraction. As a result, virtually all of the racial strains found in Brazilian society are now encountered in the Center-West. With continued heavy migration from the older areas, the Center-West promises to become, in ethnic terms, the most typically Brazilian region of the nation.

Geographically the Center-West is more nearly uniform than the other regions of Brazil. The principal geographic feature is the plateau which occupies most of the region, sloping upward from an average elevation of about 1000 feet in the south to 3500 feet in the Federal District. The natural vegetation of the plateau varies from dense tropical forest in the north and in the deeper river valleys to alternating stretches of sub-tropical forest, scrub brush, and open grasslands elsewhere in the region. The elevation of the plateau largely offsets the influence of latitude, giving much of the region a moderate tropical climate in summer when it receives ample rainfall and has warm days and nights. The winter months are generally dry, with hot days and cool nights. The chief exception to the regional pattern is the low, periodic flood plain (*Pantanal*) of western Mato Grosso. It is covered by mixed tropical forest, marshes, and swamp grasses suitable as pasture. The *Pantanal* has the typically hot, humid climate of the tropics.

Transportation and distance have always been the major obstacles to the development of the Center-West. The region is crossed by numerous ridges that serve as watersheds and have impeded travel and transportation from east to west since colonial times. Early travelers usually followed the major rivers that flow either north into the Amazon basin or south into the Paraná-La Plata system, avoiding the densely wooded areas (*mato grosso*) between rivers whenever possible. With the occupation of the region by miners and cattle ranchers, overland trails were gradually opened, but until the railroad was pushed across southern Mato Grosso in 1914, making Campo Grande the economic hub of that area, travel between the state and the national capital at Rio de Janeiro was ordinarily by boat, via Asunción and Buenos Aires. Brazil entered the Paraguayan War in 1864 in large part to preserve this vital communication link with its western province. Southern Goiás was connected with São Paulo by rail in 1913. Previously travel to the coastal communities had been exclusively by horse, while goods were generally moved on mule-back. The subsequent construction of a network of feeder roads in southern Goiás and southeastern Mato Grosso and the extension of highways to Brasília and the state capitals have given these sections a reasonably adequate transportation system, but at least two-thirds of the central-western region still has no direct and easy contact with the rest of Brazil except by air.

Because of these difficulties the economy of the Center-West grew very slowly. Although the rate of growth increased in the 1960's, the region still accounts for only about 3 per cent of national production. The inhabitants of the Center-West have devoted themselves traditionally to subsistence agriculture, grazing, mining, and the collection of forest products. Agriculture and grazing are still by far the most important economic activities and are directed increasingly toward production for the growing urban markets of the South and East. The chief farm commodities are the staples of the Brazilian diet—rice, corn, beans, and manioc. In addition, some wheat is raised in Goiás, and coffee is grown both in Goiás and Mato Grosso. Livestock raising constitutes an expanding element of the rural economy, with cattle predominating in the vast open sections and hogs in the more heavily settled farming areas. Mato Grosso, once the leading producer, now ranks fourth in the size of its cattle herd, which exceeds the human population of the state by more than six to one. Most of the minerals found in the Brazilian Highlands are also found on the central-western plateau. Thus, even though gold and diamond mining—once the principal sources of wealth—have long since declined, mining continues to occupy a significant place in the regional economy. Goiás is the leading producer of tin and titanium ores in Brazil, as well as a source of chromium, rock crystal, mica, and asbestos, while manganese, iron ore, and nickel are mined in Mato Grosso. Commercial forest products include natural rubber, which is gathered in the northern jungle areas of the region, and Paraguayan tea (*erva mate*), oil-bearing nuts, and quebracho wood from the south. Industry generates only about one-seventh as much income as agriculture in the Center-West, and is limited largely to simple processing of commodities provided by the rural sector of the economy—lumber, mineral ores, meat, hides, and a variety of farm products.

The new Federal District, which was carved out of the state of Goiás, merits individual attention, for it is an entirely artificial, political innovation in the Center-West. The idea of establishing Brazil's capital in the interior is a venerable one, dating from at least the eighteenth century, when the opening of the gold mines made the central plateau the economic heart of the colony. The proposal was revived temporarily at the time of independence and was formally incorporated as a long-range objective of the government in the Constitution of 1891. Successive administrations ignored the project, which had long seemed moribund, but it was resuscitated in the mid-1950's by Presidential candidate Juscelino Kubitschek as a major plank in his platform. Kubitschek, like earlier sponsors, maintained that the purpose of transferring the capital away from the seaboard was to force Brazil to look in upon itself—to develop its own resources—rather than to look abroad as it had always done. The controversial decision in 1956 to move the capital from Rio de Janeiro to Brasília was doubtless the most far-reaching act of the Kubitschek administration. Within four years the area of the Federal District was delineated, construction was begun on the new capital, and work was started on a network of highways to link it with each of the distant regions of the nation. The impact of Brasília was thus felt throughout the interior of Brazil before the incomplete futuristic city was formally inaugurated in April 1960.

The demographic and economic boom that currently characterizes the central-western region cannot be attributed solely, or even primarily, to the construction of Brasília, for the boom was well under way before 1956. Nevertheless, the formal transfer of the capital, more than any other single action, assures the continued growth and progress of the interior of Brazil. In a real sense Brasília already stands as the greatest monument yet erected to Brazilian nationalism, and as the symbol of the determination of Brazilians of all regions to develop the country, by their own efforts, into a power among the nations of the world.

Chapter 2 • Portuguese Settlement

In the Western Hemisphere, Brazil is unique in having been a colony of Portugal for more than three centuries. The language of Brazil is Portuguese, and much that is basic in the national culture still bears the stamp of the intrepid adventurers, priests, colonists, and royal officials who occupied and administered half a continent for the tiny Iberian realm. During the long colonial era the influence of Portugal on Brazil was paramount, for it was the Portuguese who determined the norms of government, law, religion, economic activities, settlement patterns, and relations between the members of Brazilian society. The more numerous Amerindians and Negro slaves eventually modified the speech, habits, and genes of the conquerors, but in their uncivilized state and subordinate social position they were unable to challenge the supremacy of the culture imposed on them from Europe. With its incorporation into the Portuguese empire, Brazil was drawn into the Luso-Iberian stream of Western civilization, where it has remained despite profound social and economic transformations and the severance of all political ties with the mother country.

In the absence of any written record or even a legendary tradition of past glories among the native inhabitants of Brazil, the roots of

Brazilian history must be sought in Portugal at the beginning of the modern age. As pioneers of modern European imperialism, the Portuguese were then engaged in their epic enterprise to conquer and control the seacoasts of Africa and the commercial centers of the ancient East. The discovery of Brazil was only an incidental episode in that epic.

Generations before the first Portuguese fleet touched on the shores of Brazil enroute to India, the small Christian kingdom on the western slopes of the Iberian peninsula had completed its war of reconquest from the Moors, had evolved a sense of national unity, and had been stifled in its repeated attempts to expand eastward at the expense of Castile. In these circumstances the Portuguese were forced to turn to the sea as an outlet for their ambitions. They had been fishermen since antiquity, but in the fourteenth and fifteenth centuries, in a sustained outpouring of national energy, they became the most daring and skillful seamen of Europe. Under a long series of royal patrons—of whom the most illustrious was Prince Henry the Navigator—maritime ventures were subsidized by the crown, and Portugal became a mecca for the finest navigators, cartographers, sea captains, and shipwrights of the day. Constant experimenting with ship designs and sailing techniques produced the first true ocean vessels, the caravel, derived from a Moorish bark, and the larger *nau,* the forerunner of the galleon. These were tall craft with numerous sails which could be handled by a small crew. They were created specifically to make long sea voyages and to return with large cargoes.

Possession of the caravel and the *nau* and the knowledge that had produced them made Portugal a strong sea power at a time when most of Europe still regarded the Atlantic as the rim of the world. Its nearest rival was Castile, which had seized the Canary Islands in the fifteenth century and maintained a hazy claim to suzerainty over parts of North Africa. But even though Castile was potentially far stronger than Portugal, it was to be preoccupied chiefly with internal affairs until the fall of the last Moorish bastion on Spanish soil in 1492.

As the Portuguese attained mastery of the sea they carried their faith and their arms to distant shores. Sea power was employed primarily to

serve the glory of God and the House of Aviz, and incidentally to enrich the coffers of the rising merchant class in Lisbon. Impelled by religious fervor, lust for empire, and desire for riches, the Portuguese
resumed the crusade against the Moors, attacking the North African
fortress-city of Ceuta, which they captured in 1415. Following this conquest they ranged farther west into the Atlantic and probed cautiously
south along the bulge of Africa, advancing a few leagues each year.
Before the death of Prince Henry in 1460, Portuguese sailing masters
were familiar with the winds and currents of the mid-Atlantic, the
cross and the flag had been planted on the Azores, Madeira, and the
Cape Verde Islands, and the African coast had been explored as far
as Guinea, where handsome profits were being realized in ivory, gold,
and the slave trade. In another twelve years the great physical and
psychological barrier, the equator with its belt of interminable calms,
had been crossed. Once it was established that man could survive prolonged journeys into southern waters, the ultimate objective of all
Portuguese voyages was to find a sea route to India and the spice
islands.

This lucrative goal—direct access to the Orient—seemed close at
hand when Bartolomeu Diaz reached the southern tip of the African
continent in 1488, four years before the Genoese navigator, Chris-
topher Columbus, discovered the Indies while sailing west under the
banners of Castile. For a short time it appeared that Castile, in its first
serious quest for possessions beyond the seas, had won the coveted
prize. But while Columbus was vainly scouring the Caribbean for
the elusive shores of Cathay, the persistence of the Portuguese was
crowned with success. Vasco da Gama, in 1498, led a fleet of three ships
around the Cape of Good Hope to Calicut and returned with enough
spices to pay for a dozen expeditions. For the next century Portugal
was to lavish its limited resources and manpower prodigally, winning
and defending a vast empire in Asia and Africa.

The success of Portugal in opening the sea lanes to India stemmed
not only from the technological advantages and superior naval power
it enjoyed as a modern nation in the fifteenth century, but also from
the application of medieval concepts that were to give it a foothold in

the Western Hemisphere. In accord with medieval practice, Portugal sought to establish monopolistic control over what have since been considered international waters, to seek papal sanction for its monopoly, and to resort to arbitration by the papacy when its monopoly could not be preserved by force. As Castile—which had merged with Leon and was united with Aragon by royal marriage—grew in military stature, it challenged Portugal's assertion of hegemony over the lands and waters of the Atlantic and the shores of Africa. After a short war between the Iberian kingdoms, an accommodation was reached whereby Portugal relinquished all claims to the Canary Islands in exchange for recognition of its exclusive right to govern the other islands of the Atlantic and to explore and conquer southward along the African coast. This agreement was expressed in the Treaty of Alcaçovas in 1479 and was endorsed by papal bull in 1481. Thus, both Castile, the only nation that might then have vied with Portugal overseas, and the papacy, the only supranational entity in Christendom, formally regarded most of the Atlantic as a Portuguese lake, giving the House of Aviz and its heirs a free hand to discover, convert, and rule over all such infidels and heathens as might be encountered there.

Portugal's monopoly in the Atlantic was broken by Columbus's famous voyage. On his storm-tossed return to Europe in 1493, he stopped first at Lisbon, where the Portuguese were dismayed to learn of his great success. Castile immediately appealed to Pope Alexander VI, a Spaniard, for papal recognition of its claim to the Indies and its sole right to seek Cathay and the spice islands by the western route. Alexander VI, in a series of papal bulls issued that same year, took cognizance of the new discoveries in terms favorable to Ferdinand and Isabella. In an attempt to minimize friction between Castile and Portugal the Pope proceeded to divide the unknown and newly discovered portions of the globe between them. His decision, reflecting scant knowledge of the geography of the known world, provided for an imaginary line to run from pole to pole one hundred leagues west of the Azores and the Cape Verde Islands. To the east of this line Portugal should continue to exercise a monopoly over all territories discovered and to be discovered, while Castile should be supreme over all territories to the west. The Portuguese, who had not yet rounded Africa, found the papal decision unacceptable. Threatening war, which was momentarily inconvenient to Castile, Portugal insisted on a relocation of the papal line. A new decision, achieved by direct negotiation and recorded in the Treaty of Tordesillas in 1494, moved the line of demarcation 270 leagues farther west, specifying the Cape Verde Islands as the point from which the distance should be measured. Ambiguities in the language of the treaty still left the precise location of the line of Tordesillas in doubt, but by even the most conservative estimates at least 1200 miles of the coastline of South America were to fall within the Portuguese zone of exploration and settlement. In this way, while seeking to preserve its advantage in the race for the Orient, Portugal obtained a clear claim to an as yet undiscovered part of the New World.

The Treaty of Tordesillas, signed six years before Brazil was formally discovered and claimed for Portugal, may thus be regarded as the earliest document of Brazilian history. The validity of the treaty was soon to become an academic question, for it was rejected or ignored by the emerging maritime powers of northern Europe. Nonetheless, under its terms the Portuguese were able to establish a measure of control in Brazil at a time when no other European nation was both able and willing to dispossess them.

There is still some mystery surrounding the identity and date of the first European voyage to Brazil. For more than a century Brazilian and other scholars have questioned whether the Portuguese had prior knowledge of the existence of Brazil when, at Tordesillas, they forced Castile to concede them a larger share of the western Atlantic. Logic suggests that one or another of the numerous Portuguese voyages into the Atlantic in the fifteen century may have passed close enough to Brazilian shores to sight land birds or debris swept out to sea by ocean currents, evidence of land not far to the west. Vasco da Gama reported such findings on his historic voyage to India, but did not interrupt his journey to investigate their origin. The French have claimed that a storm-driven Breton fisherman, Jean Cousin, inadvertently reached Brazil in 1488 and survived to recount his adventures. But to date no conclusive evidence has been found either to support this allegation or to establish that any European had yet landed on the coast of Brazil when the Treaty of Tordesillas was drawn up in 1494.

It has been clearly established, however, that Pedro Alvares Cabral, the admiral who formally claimed Brazil for Portugal, was not the first European to land on its shores. Two, and possibly three, expeditions under the flag of Castile touched along the northern coast of Brazil within a few months before Cabral's landing in April 1500. None of the earlier discoverers claimed the land for Castile or attempted to settle any part of it, apparently realizing that it lay within the Portuguese sector of the New World.

The effective discovery of Brazil occurred on April 22, 1500, when one of the largest expeditions Portugal had mounted to that date anchored off the coast of southern Bahia. The fleet of twelve *naus* and caravels, under the command of Cabral and carrying a complement of 1200 men, was en route to India to secure for Portugal the prize that Vasco da Gama had found two years before. Acting on the advice of da Gama, Cabral had sailed well to the west in order to avoid calms along the coast of Africa. One ship had already been lost in rough seas and, according to some accounts, spring storms drove the fleet much farther off the usual course than Cabral had intended. On the forty-fourth day out of Lisbon, the lead ship detected signs of land, and on the afternoon of the following day sighted a round-topped mountain rising above a low, forested coastline. As Easter was approaching, the mountain was called Monte Pascoal and the land, thought to be an island, was christened Ilha da Vera Cruz. Since the location offered scant protection for large vessels, Cabral sailed northward before the wind for ten leagues, where he came upon a sheltered harbor which was promptly named Pôrto Seguro. Here the fleet remained for nine days while water casks were replenished and minor repairs were made. A large wooden cross was erected to mark the land as Portuguese, and mass was held on shore on Sunday. During their stay the members of the expedition aroused the curiosity of the local inhabitants, who seemed peaceful, innocent pagans and who spoke none of the languages the Portuguese had encountered on previous voyages. Some simple barter was conducted with them, but no evidence of spices or precious metals was found. A complete report of the discovery, describing the people and physical resources of the region, was prepared by the scribe, Pero Vaz da Caminha. He recommended that a settlement be established to serve as a way station for ships in the India trade and that missionaries be sent to convert the native population to Christianity. A caravel left to carry the report to Lisbon, two exiles remained to learn the native language and customs, and the rest of the expedition proceeded on its way to India. Pedro Alvares Cabral, who lived to serve his king faithfully for many years, never returned to the new land he had added to Portugal's domains.

Cabral's indifference toward Brazil was shared by most of his contemporaries in Portugal. Far more fame and fortune were to be won in India than in the conquest of rude savages in the Brazilian forest. The parrots and monkeys taken to Lisbon by the ship bearing news of the discovery of Brazil might amuse the ladies of the court but they could not be compared with the untold treasure in jewels, silks, and spices to be gained in trade and tribute in the eastern empire. The new land to the west might offer a better site for colonization than the Orient, with its teeming populace and established civilizations, but this advantage held no appeal for the Portuguese, who had neither the numbers nor inclination to be colonists. Rather, they were occupiers and exploiters of the lands on which they imposed their will. From the outset Portugal's overseas empire was built on conquest and plunder, and those areas that promised the greatest immediate rewards had first claim on the attentions and resources of the crown.

In spite of overriding concern for the enterprise in the East, the crown did not entirely neglect its recent acquisition in the New World. Nor were all Portuguese disdainful of the relatively modest profits to be extracted from the forests of Brazil. Royal expeditions sent out in 1501 and 1503 to explore the new discovery confirmed Caminha's report of the absence of mineral wealth but determined that a valuable dyewood, the famous brazilwood that soon gave its name to the land, grew profusely along the coastal strip between the present states of Pernambuco and São Paulo. Even before the second of these expeditions sailed from Lisbon, a company of private merchants, headed by

Fernando de Noronha, had secured a license from the crown to engage in the brazilwood trade. Other merchant capitalists soon obtained similar concessions, and within a few years dozens of caravels were plying regularly between Portugal and trading posts across the Atlantic. At such posts, known as factories, trinkets, tools, and clothing were exchanged with the local natives for brazil logs and a variety of other commodities, including cotton, wild pepper, animal skins, parrots, and occasionally slaves. Portugal's economic stake in Brazil began with this prosaic trade, which did not initially provide enough revenue to the royal treasury to pay for the defense of the colony.

The trading factories were the first Portuguese settlements in Brazil. Scattered from Pernambuco to São Vicente, they were invariably found on the coastline, on islands, bays, or inlets opening onto the sea, for their location was determined by the availability of a protected anchorage near large stands of brazilwood. The attitude of the local inhabitants was also a determining factor, as the heavy labor of preparing logs for shipment was performed entirely by the native population. A few factories became substantial and reasonably self-contained establishments with large numbers of native allies living outside the walls. In these posts the Portuguese not only learned the cultivation of manioc and other products of the land, but also introduced plants, fowls, and domestic animals from the Atlantic islands to supply the needs of the garrison and to provision ships for the return journey to Portugal. In most instances, however, the factory was little more than a simple camp, with a stockade enclosing a few crude structures to house the factor, his staff, and the merchandise being collected for export on the next ship. Such factories were maintained only until the immediate supply of brazilwood was exhausted or until they were destroyed by natives or by the French, who long contested with the Portuguese for control of Brazil.

France never acknowledged the authority of the papacy or the Iberian monarchs to divide the New World exclusively between Portugal and Castile. French incursions into the brazilwood trade, which began as private ventures early in the century, gradually assumed a quasi-official stature and by the third decade were posing a serious threat not only to Portugal's monopoly of the trade but to its hold on Brazil itself. On four occasions between 1516 and 1530 coast guard forces were dispatched from Lisbon to sweep the French "pirates" from Brazilian waters. But not until after these tactics proved inadequate to counter the French challenge did the crown provide for the establishment of permanent settlements on the coast of Brazil.

By the 1530's the Portuguese—and the French as well—had learned a great deal about Brazil. They had found that it was part of a large continent, and they had heard rumors about a land rich in gold and silver somewhere in the distant interior. But they had not penetrated far from the coast, for they had discovered no navigable rivers, and they had found the dense forests which supplied them with brazilwood a formidable barrier infested with a savage foe. They had learned early that few of the Indians—as the aborigines came to be called—possessed the gentle, pacific nature so eloquently described by Pero Vaz da Caminha. Rather, the scores of small bands or clans lived in a perpetual state of war with each other. Many of them, moreover, were cannibals. One of the first sailors to go ashore from the expedition of 1501 was killed and eaten by savages within sight of his horrified shipmates. He was only one of many Europeans to meet that fate at the hands of Indian captors, although there were numerous fortunate exceptions. The accounts of the time are replete with examples of shipwrecked seamen and *degredados*—exiles abandoned on the coast in the hope that they might survive to serve later as interpreters—who were hospitably received and became members of the Indian community. Two of the most famous of these were Diogo Alvares, known as Caramurú, the survivor of a shipwreck at Bahia de Todos os Santos in 1509 or 1510, and João Ramalho, a castaway found by Indians of São Vicente at about the same time. Both men adapted readily to Indian ways, became chieftains, and sired a large progeny of mixed-bloods. Subsequently, they lent invaluable assistance to the early settlers at Bahia and São Paulo.

With the aid of squaw men of this kind, the Portuguese and the French established precarious footholds in Brazil and learned to exploit the strengths and weaknesses of the native peoples. It was soon discovered that a majority of the Indian bands, despite the myriad of mutually antagonistic groupings and sub-groupings among them, spoke similar dialects of the Tupí-Guaraní tongue. This situation was favorable to the newcomers from Europe, for it facilitated contact and communication with the Indians whose help was necessary to obtain brazilwood at widely separated points along the coast. The Portuguese and French also took advantage of the hostilities between the various Tupí bands in their struggle for control of Brazil by forming alliances, respectively, with perennial enemies. In time the Indians themselves came to distinguish each other as allies of the black beards from Portugal or the blonds from Normandy. The effectiveness of the alliance between Frenchmen and the ferocious Tupinambás against the Portuguese and their Tupiniquim allies contributed at least in part to the decision by Portugal to adopt a new and more vigorous colonial policy in Brazil.

The expedition sent to Brazil under the command of Martim Afonso de Souza in December 1530 is often regarded as the first indication of serious intent by Portugal to hold and develop its American colony, or, more accurately, to colonize the lands claimed by the crown in America. The crown gave Martim Afonso extensive powers to rid the coast of French interlopers, to establish factories, to explore more thoroughly than his predecessors for signs of gold or other precious metals, to grant lands to worthy applicants, to appoint officials and supervise royal justice over the entire colony, and to found a permanent settlement to serve as a base of operations against the foreign enemy. For the latter purpose his expedition included several settlers, some accompanied by their families. Although he did not bear the title, he was in effect the first viceroy of Brazil. After twelve months, during which his squadron ranged the length of the coast from Maranhão in the north to the Río de la Plata in the south, Martim Afonso selected São Vicente, near the present port of Santos, as the site of his colony. Here, in January 1532, he founded the first town in Brazil. A church was built, municipal government was inaugurated, town lots and rural lands were apportioned among the 400 members of the expedition, cattle and sugar cane were introduced, a sugar mill was erected, and, with the aid of João

Ramalho, friendly contacts were initiated with the Indians on the escarpment, where the village outpost of Santo André da Borda do Campo was established. It is probable also that Negro slaves were present in the colony before its founder was recalled to Portugal by a grateful monarch in 1533. Through these actions, Martim Afonso in little more than two years laid the foundations for the basic economic and social order that was to prevail along the Brazilian coast for the remainder of the colonial period.

Even before Martim Afonso returned to Lisbon to report the progress of his venture at São Vicente, the crown decided to dot the shores of Brazil with similar settlements. The method of colonization employed was an adaptation of the captaincy system that had been used successfully in the Atlantic islands during the preceding century. It involved the creation in Brazil of several colonies united only by their common ties with Portugal. From Maranhão to Santa Catarina the land was divided into fifteen parallel strips ranging in width from ten to one hundred leagues and extending inland from the sea to the vaguely defined line of Tordesillas. These huge tracts were granted as hereditary captaincies of one or more strips each to a dozen individuals who enjoyed the king's confidence. No captaincy had less than thirty leagues of coastline. Of the twelve grantees, or donatories (*donatários*), only four—Martim Afonso, his brother Pero Lopes de Souza, their companion Pero Góis, and Duarte Coelho, who had twice visited Brazil—had had previous experience in America. The others were lesser nobles and commoners who had served the crown well at court or in the conquest of India. By granting to twelve distinguished subjects the right to win and hold separate personal domains in Brazil, the crown sought to confirm its claims in the Western Hemisphere at little cost to the royal treasury, for each donatory agreed to colonize, develop, and defend his captaincy at his own expense.

The captaincy system combined elements of feudalism with the modern capitalism of the age. In feudal fashion the donatory received the captaincy as a fief from the monarch, to whom alone he was responsible and then only in person. In accepting the grant he assumed the obligation for himself and his heirs to preserve and rule the captaincy as an overseas province subject to the ultimate authority of the

House of Aviz. In this respect his relationship to the king was that of vassal to liege lord. At the same time the establishment of the captaincy represented a major capital investment and an opportunity for profit. In the absence, however, of accumulated riches for plunder, such as the Portuguese had found in the Orient and the Spaniards were encountering in Mexico and Peru, the base of wealth from which profits might be drawn would have to be created by the colonists themselves. In these circumstances every donatory hoped to establish a thriving agricultural colony and to be compensated by earnings from the exports of his own estates and from taxes levied on the proceeds of lands worked by colonists under his overlordship. Both the feudal and capitalistic aspects of the system were indicated in two formal documents—the *carta de doação*, or land grant, and the *foral*, or feudal contract—which together constituted the charter issued with each captaincy. These reserved to the crown the dyewood monopoly and the right to collect certain royal imposts, but otherwise conferred on the donatory virtually supreme political, economic, judicial, and military power in the captaincy. He was authorized and expected to recruit and transport colonists, to grant them land, to see to their spiritual welfare, to found towns and establish civil government, to issue and enforce laws, to pacify, Christianize, and rule the native population, to levy and collect taxes, to direct and conduct trade between the captaincy and the homeland, and to equip, command, and pay his military forces. Under the terms of the charter it was clear that the donatory was not only a vassal but also an entrepreneur.

The success of the captaincy depended primarily upon the resources and capabilities of the donatory. Only a man of wealth could bear the initial expense of founding a colony, and only one with the qualities of leadership and administrative skills to transform his colony into a profitable commercial venture could expect to sustain the rate of investment necessary to safeguard it against attack by Indians and by the European enemies of Portugal. The donatory could not turn for aid to the royal government, which provided no subvention and set up no administrative structure to advise him or to co-ordinate the development and defense of the various captaincies in Brazil.

As a political experiment the captaincy system failed almost entirely to meet the expectations of the crown. Only two captaincies prospered, five were not colonized, and the remainder were periodically imperiled by Indian uprisings. Four donatories lost their fortunes and two lost their lives as well in the vain effort to overcome the hazards of colonization on isolated, savage shores. It was no coincidence that the only successful colonies—São Vicente, which was ably governed by agents of Martim Afonso, and Pernambuco, under the dynamic personal direction of Duarte Coelho—were also the most generously financed and strongly garrisoned colonies in Brazil. But these two outposts of empire could not long hold all of Brazil for Portugal. After a decade and a half the crown was obliged to create a central colonial administration for Brazil or risk the loss of its American territories.

Despite serious political and military shortcomings, the captaincy experiment cannot be dismissed simply as a failure. Many of the developments of the captaincy period were to have enduring influence on Brazil, and even when measured in terms of its immediate objectives the experiment proved to be at least a qualified success. The primary goal of the crown in the 1530's was to promote permanent, fortified settlements at strategic points on the coast in order to drive the French from Brazil. These objectives were largely achieved along much of the coastline from São Vicente in the south to Itamaracá on the hump of the continent. In place of temporary factories with a transient European population, about fifteen towns and villages with resident Portuguese inhabitants existed in Brazil when the first governor-general, Thomé de Souza, arrived in 1549. The French threat had not been eliminated—indeed, it was to continue for another seven decades—but for fifteen crucial years the feeble captaincies had prevented a French seizure of Brazil.

The struggle between Portugal and France for control of Brazil, which led to the adoption and then to the abandonment of the captaincy experiment, appears in retrospect as transitory and relatively unimportant in the total legacy of the captaincy period. This brief span of years continues to be important to Brazilian history primarily because it encompassed the first sustained effort to transplant Portuguese civilization and culture in the New World. The impact of the captaincies on the society, economy, and even the administration of Brazil was felt long after the last French interloper had departed, and in certain sectors may still be detected today. For example, six Brazilian states—Maranhão, Ceará, Rio Grande (do Norte), Pernambuco, Bahia, and Espírito Santo—still bear the original names of the captaincies from which they have evolved. More significantly, the fragmentation of Brazil into separate colonies in the 1530's gave birth to the concept of many Brazils that persists in the deeply ingrained sense of regionalism in the nation. These long-range consequences were only incidental and entirely unforeseen. Likewise, some of the immediate consequences of Portuguese settlement were unanticipated, and many of the experiences of the early colonists seemed so obvious and prosaic as to escape special mention by observers of the time. But from the records that have survived it is clear that basic trends in thought and action, in patterns of land use and tenure, and in the formation and conduct of a new society that became characteristic of colonial Brazil were begun during the captaincy period.

When the donatories or their deputies arrived in the newly granted captaincies with their following of pioneer settlers and men at arms, they introduced a new phase into the economy and social order of Brazil. Doubtless the two most lasting innovations deliberately introduced during the captaincy period were European-style urban communities and a plantation economy. Both of these were in the Iberian tradition and were specifically indicated in the charters of the respective captaincies. The initiative of Martim Afonso in São Vicente was soon to be duplicated with varying results in eight other colonies along the Brazilian coast. The newcomers expected to live in urban surroundings —primitive though these might be—and under regulations and officials such as they had known in Portugal. Thus, the first task of the donatory was to found a town and appoint municipal officers. Almost immediately thereafter, he allotted the adjacent lands to those reputable colonists who possessed the means to make them productive. When conditions warranted, once the surrounding lands were taken, the entire process was repeated with the founding of a new town and the distribution of rural lands at some distance from the first settlement.

This was the process by which the donatories sought to expand the occupied area of their colonies, and it was the process that was followed throughout the colonial period nearly everywhere that new lands were brought under the control of the government. Initially, at least, the process was used in part because the Portuguese preferred community life to the isolated existence of the frontier, in part bcause the town offered relative security to settlers in hostile territory, and in part because the municipal authorities might exert control over the individualistic and often unruly elements among the colonists.

The towns were the administrative and commercial centers of the captaincies, but land was the source of wealth. The rich soil for agriculture was the only readily exploitable resource available to the colonists, as the crown had reserved the brazilwood monopoly and no mines had been discovered. In theory all land in the captaincy was the property of the monarch, but he had granted it to the donatory who in turn was empowered to distribute it in generous portions among the respectable Christians in the colony. In return he was to receive a fixed annual percentage, or tithe, of the produce of the land. The holdings varied greatly in size, from the vast estates retained by the donatory to comparatively small farms, or *roças,* granted to colonists of limited means. Those plots, known as *sesmarias,* awarded to members of the nobility and to affluent commoners to be developed into plantations, or *fazendas,* were usually measured in leagues of more than four miles each. They were seldom less than one league by two in dimension, and some *sesmarias* were as large as ten square leagues. The smallholders primarily raised foodstuffs, chiefly manioc, from which a coarse flour was made, although some of them also cultivated limited quantities of native cotton for export. These items were raised on some *fazendas* as well, but invariably the principal plantation crop was sugar, for which there was an apparently insatiable market at high prices in Europe. Cane cuttings for planting were imported in most instances from Madeira, which had been the leading sugar-producing area in the Western world for several decades. Since sugar, unlike brazilwood, had to be processed before it could be exported, the donatories and the wealthier landowners soon erected mills, or *engenhos,* to grind the cane from their own plantations and from those of their less affluent neighbors. Customarily the millowner received from one-fourth to one-third of his neighbor's harvest in exchange for grinding. Construction of the costly mills was done only under license from the donatory and was often financed by European backers, who expected to recover their investment within three or four years. Because of the quick and enormous profits to be earned in the sugar industry, no one gave much thought to crop diversification beyond the limited needs of the local population. Thus, from the outset the colonial economy of Brazil was based almost entirely on a single plantation product for export.

The broad outlines of the social order that prevailed throughout the colonial era in Brazil were drawn during the captaincy period. The Portuguese, as representatives of a strong power and advanced culture, determined the relative position of each group in the population. Society was stratified according to race, wealth, and occupation, with numerous subdivisions in each major category. There were frequent exceptions to the general pattern, however, for the social hierarchy was never entirely rigid nor uniform for all of Brazil. On the whole, Europeans occupied the top rungs of the social ladder. The other inhabitants of the colony—ranked by color and condition as free men or slaves—were in the lower positions, with mixed-bloods generally enjoying somewhat higher status than their Indian or Negro mothers.

Since land was the basis of wealth in Brazil, the size and productivity of landholdings quickly became the measure of social and economic standing among the European-born colonists. The broadest distinction was drawn between those who were large landholders and the majority who possessed little or no rural property. The donatory stood clearly at the head of society in the captaincy, not only because of the powers he had received from the crown, but because he was by far the largest landowner. According to the charter, non-contiguous tracts of land equal in area to a strip ten leagues wide and the length of the captaincy were reserved as his private estate. Next in importance to the donatory were members of the lesser nobility who went to Brazil as colonists and were granted large *sesmarias*. Immediately below and scarcely distinguishable from the few families of noble rank were the well-to-do commoners who had received substantial land grants. Among the large landholders a further distinction was soon made between those who owned sugar mills and those who did not. Millowners (*senhores de engenho*) enjoyed much greater social prestige than did the other planters whose cane they ground.

The fourth category within the landowning group was comprised of smallholders, many of whom had been peasants in Portugal. The small farmer occupied a social position somewhat above the common herd by virtue of his ownership of a parcel of land. Ordinarily he did not till the soil with his own hands but delegated such demeaning tasks to Indian slaves or to free natives contracted by barter. Nevertheless, a wide gap separated him from the social level of the plantation owners because of his humble origins, the restricted size of his farm, and the fact that he participated only marginally if at all in the export economy.

Among the more fortunate European-born inhabitants of the captaincies there appears to have been a considerable overlapping of occupations and social positions. In many, if not most instances the municipal officials and public functionaries appointed by the donatories, as well as the larger merchants in the coastal communities, appear to have received grants of land. Thus, even though their activities were chiefly urban, they ranked as plantation owners in the social hierarchy.

Most of the Portuguese in the urban settlements, however, were landless. These were the soldiers, peasants, and artisans who attended to the defense of the colony and to the material needs that could not be provided by slaves or the free native population. Initially they were found almost exclusively in the towns and villages, but as the plantations were cleared and the mills erected some of them became employees or tenants of the leading sugar planters. In Portuguese law and custom, as reflected in the captaincy charters, such persons were plebeians, or lower-class commoners, who enjoyed virtually no individual or class privileges in the social order.

The European population in the captaincies also included a relatively large number of individuals who had been exiled from Portugal for infractions of the stringent legal code. These were the *degredados,* a term which indicated a reduction in rank or status, and in the eyes of the law they held the lowest position among the free subjects of the crown. Their offenses ranged from murder to indiscreet expressions of disrespect toward the king or the Church, crimes then punishable by long imprisonment or death. Their presence in Brazil suggested close ties of blood or friendship with families of sufficient influence at court to have their sentences commuted to banishment, although in many cases it is likely that the donatories had rescued them from prison in order to obtain colonists. Some were of gentle birth, while others were university students or graduates, but sons of peasant and working-class families were probably found among them as well. Regardless of their social origin, the *degredados* shared one trait in common. They were nonconformists, restive under the restraints of authority. In Brazil, where they were immune from punishment for crimes committed in Portugal, they often had the opportunity to assume the place in the social hierarchy to which their accomplishments and family background entitled them. A few received grants of land and became prominent members of the community. Some were managers of mills and plantations, or were given lesser posts in the municipal administration. A substantial group, however, appears to have remained near the bottom of the social scale, comprising an unruly element which was the subject of frequent complaints by colonial officials.

The lowest social category recognized in the captaincy charters was comprised of slaves, drawn predominantly from the native peoples of Brazil. It is likely that some Negro slaves, perhaps household servants of the donatories and the wealthier colonists, were taken from Portugal to Brazil when the first settlements were founded, and that small shipments of slaves were imported into São Vicente from the Guinea coast during the 1530's. Negroes, however, were not numerically significant in colonial society until late in the sixteenth century, after the Indian population in the settled areas had been decimated by war and disease. Slavery was a well-established custom among the aborigines, who usually kept a few war prisoners in bondage. Slaves such as these had long figured among the products shipped to Portugal under royal license by dyewood traders. The donatories were also granted the right to export a specified number of Indians each year, but most of the slaves acquired from Indian allies or captured by the Portuguese themselves were employed in Brazil. The number of Indians enslaved in the colony is not known, but it represented only a small portion of the total Indian population during the captaincy period.

The confrontation of Portuguese, Indians, and Negroes in Brazil introduced previously unknown varieties of the human species into the society of the captaincies. The mingling of racial strains—in which twentieth-century Brazilians take pride—began almost from the first contact between Europeans and the native inhabitants of the colony, for circumstances and the customs of both peoples encouraged the union of Portuguese males and Indian women. In the absence of women of their own race, the early explorers commonly took Indian women as wives, concubines, and casual sex partners, a practice that was readily adopted by the colonists who arrived later. The offspring of such unions, known as *mamelucos,* probably numbered in the hundreds in São Vicente, Bahia, and Pernambuco before the first captaincies were established. Mulattos and *cafusos* (of mixed Indian and Negro blood) appeared subsequently with the introduction of African slaves. The place of the mixed-bloods in the social hierarchy apparently did not cause serious problems, even though initially there was no special provision for them in the law. Those *mamelucos* recognized by their fathers were given Portuguese names and accepted as subjects of the crown, while those raised by their mothers in Indian villages were regarded as part of the Indian population. In the case of mulattos, recognition by the father usually brought release from bondage. Otherwise the mulatto, like the *cafuso,* retained his mother's status. Ordinarily the *mameluco* occupied a somewhat more favorable position than the mulatto in colonial society.

The native peoples, who vastly outnumbered the Portuguese, constituted a separate and distinct category among the inhabitants of the captaincies. Opinions as to their proper place in the scheme of things varied sharply according to the interests and responsibilities of Portuguese officials and colonists. The Indians were indispensable as allies, indefatigable as enemies. They were pagans of a different and therefore inferior race. At best they were looked upon not as lords or owners of the land, but as child-like wards of the crown, which had assumed responsibility for converting them from their heathen state to Christianity. Indeed, one of the principal justifications for the establishment of the captaincies had been to enable the crown to fulfill its Christian duty to save these pagan souls from eternal perdition. Such consideration for the spiritual welfare of the Indians, however, was confined largely to the crown and the few clerics in Brazil. The colonists were primarily concerned with the material assistance the native savages were expected to lend them. It was obvious from the beginning that the captaincies would not succeed without the co-operation of the Indians, for the Portuguese were too pitifully few in number to hope to transform the vast reaches of the colony into fruitful plantations by their own efforts alone. Moreover, those who became landowners, and many who did not, felt manual labor was beneath the dignity of their rank and station. With this attitude the colonists took it for granted that the native population existed to serve them and that it would do so in exchange for the articles of barter that had become common currency in the brazilwood trade. When barter proved inadequate to attract enough Indian workers for the expanding plantations, the planters clamored for slaves. But whether as free men or as slaves, the Indians represented the only available work force and were relied upon to supply the settlers with the necessities of life and to perform most of the heavy labor in the colonies.

In these circumstances, relations with the Indians were a continuing vital concern to the colonial authorities charged with reconciling the incompatible claims of the crown and the planters on the souls and bodies of the native population. The goal of peaceful, voluntary co-operation between the two races was never fully achieved in the sugar plantation areas despite the best efforts of the donatories and the royal governors who succeeded them. The Indians did not adapt easily to the exhausting routine of field and mill, and usually attempted to avoid it once their immediate desires for hardware and articles of clothing or adornment were satisfied. The planters, in turn, soon came to regard the aborigines as a lazy, shiftless lot and sought to enslave them. Both parties, thus, were dissatisfied and became mutually antagonistic. The Tupinambás, sometimes urged by the French, were easily stirred to revolt, and even the normally friendly Tupiniquins eventually rebelled under provocation. By the mid-1540's hostilities between Indians and colonists were threatening the survival of most of the Portuguese settlements in Brazil. The inability of the donatories to resolve the Indian problem contributed directly to the reassertion of royal control over Brazil in 1549.

The objectives of the crown in Brazil were the same in that year as they had been in the 1530's, to turn Brazil into a thriving plantation colony which would bring added glory and wealth to the House of Aviz. But a new approach was adopted to attain this objective. And, while there was no intent to disrupt basic social and economic trends in the colony, important new elements were added to the pattern of colonial life that had begun to evolve during the captaincy period.

The appointment of a governor-general to rule Brazil brought far-reaching political and military changes which affected the relationship between the colonists and the crown. Bahia, strategically situated between the prosperous settlements at Pernambuco and São Vicente, was selected as the capital of Portuguese America. Here the crown purchased the hereditary rights it had granted to the original donatory, while in most of the other captaincies the autonomous powers of the donatories were revoked or were considerably reduced.* Royal justice and fiscal regulations were now more nearly uniform throughout Brazil, although royal authority was seldom enforceable outside the major settlements. With these changes the governor-general and other royal officials replaced the donatories as the principal intermediaries between the king and his subjects in Brazil.

The transfer of authority from the donatories to the governor-general was accompanied by a substantial and continuing crown investment in the development of the colony. Within a few years thousands of set-

* Pernambuco, which remained under the control of Duarte Coelho and his heirs for several decades, was the major exception, although the last of the hereditary rights and privileges granted to the original donatories in the 1530's were not recovered by the crown until after 1750.

tlers and many new plants, seeds, and animals were sent to Brazil. Initially, most of these went to Bahia, where the local aborigines were subdued and additional lands were apportioned for conversion into sugar plantations. The colonial capital was soon a bustling community in which the sugar mill was the chief symbol of affluence and social status. But it was not enough merely to introduce new food crops and to increase the Portuguese population in a few enclaves along the Brazilian coast. The desired expansion of the colonial economy was still hindered by the lack of an adequate labor force and by continuing threat from the French and hostile Indians.

In its efforts to correct these closely related difficulties, the royal government assigned to three institutions which had been relatively insignificant in the early captaincies—the Church, irregular military forces, and Negro slavery—important roles in dealing with the Indian problem, long the fundamental issue facing colonial authorities. The men responsible for Brazil's destiny reasoned that if sufficient Indians could be persuaded or obliged to serve the Portuguese as allies and laborers the French threat would be reduced, the Portuguese settlements would be secured against attack, and manpower would be available for the plantations. The crown decided to try persuasion and called upon a new and zealous religious order, the Society of Jesus. It was to be the willing, if at times unwitting, agent for Indian affairs, whose task was to pacify, Christianize, and concentrate the free Indians near the Portuguese towns, where they might be used alternatively as laborers or as a striking force against the French and their Tupinambá allies. To supplement the limited regular forces supplied by the crown for the defense of the colony, all large landowners were required to maintain private military establishments to protect their own properties and to provide armed contingents when needed for the common defense. And to ameliorate the critical shortage of plantation workers, the royal government authorized the importation of Negro slaves directly from Africa.

In this way, with the encouragement of the crown and its officers in Brazil, the African slave traffic, the private army, and the Church became prominent features on the Brazilian scene. They were to be integral parts of society and the economic life of Brazil for three centuries or more. Ultimately, the influence of Negro slavery was all-pervasive. The regular slave trade between Portuguese Africa and Brazil, which was begun as a temporary expedient in the 1550's, persisted for 300 years, while slavery continued for a generation longer. During this period slavery was confirmed as the mainstay of the economy, and Negroes and their descendants became the most numerous sector of the population. Private armies, led by and loyal to individual landowners, were a permanent and often disruptive element in rural Brazil until recent decades, permitting the more powerful planters and ranchers to flout the law at will. And the Church, as an organization, was a major instrument of the state and ubiquitous symbol of royal authority from the arrival of the first governor-general until late in the nineteenth century.

The increased importance of the Church in Brazil after 1549 reflected the higher priority now accorded Brazil by the crown. Church policy in the colony was directed by the king of Portugal in his capacity as Grand Master of the Order of Christ, a position which enabled him to exercise patronage of the Church in all possessions of the House of Aviz. Prior to the establishment of the royal government the Church had been poorly represented in Brazil, even though clergymen were associated with every official venture in the colony from the time of discovery. Franciscan friars had accompanied Cabral and later explorers, and members of at least one missionary order apparently visited the trading factories and worked among the Indians before 1530. After that date the donatories took a few secular priests to Brazil to attend to the spiritual needs of the colonists. They were probably the first priests to reside permanently in Brazil, although the colony had been included since 1514 in the vast overseas diocese under the jurisdiction of the bishop of Funchal in Madeira. The bishop, however, appears to have exercised little supervision over the clergy in Brazil, for reports sent to Lisbon and Rome after the arrival of the royal governor regularly lamented the immoral, materialistic conduct of the priests and the generally irreligious life of the colonists. It was to correct this situation that the colony was made a separate diocese in 1551. The following year the first bishop of Brazil reached Bahia and began the task of eliminating indifference toward religion and violations of the laws of the Church among clergy and communicants alike. But neither he nor his successors were able to eradicate all of the pagan influences brought by Indians and Negroes to religious practice among Catholics in colonial Brazil.

A stronger impact was made by the Jesuits, who as missionaries and educators consistently exerted influence out of all proportion to their numbers in Brazil. In the sixteenth century there were never as many as 200 Jesuits in the entire colony, and during most of that time the number was much smaller. The first contingent of six men arrived with Thomé de Souza in 1549, while a second group of seven followed four years later. This small band of dedicated and capable missionaries, led by Manoel da Nóbrega and José de Anchieta, initiated the practices that for two centuries were to arouse the hostility of the planters and bring fame to the Jesuits as defenders of the Indian population. Although other religious orders were also represented in Brazil, the Jesuits remained the most prominent and the most controversial until their expulsion from the colony in 1759.

The early Jesuits were essentially teachers who relied heavily upon education in their efforts to convert the pagan Indians to Christianity. One of their first objectives was to learn the Tupí-Guaraní tongue and reduce it to written form so that they might communicate readily with their primitive charges and instruct them in the articles of the Christian faith. Such instruction, coupled with training in agriculture and handicrafts, was most often provided at missions built to house the converts. Somewhat more advanced training was supplied at schools (*colégios*) where selected Indian boys were given the rudiments of formal education. The missions were occupied only by Christian Indians, but the *colégios* were also attended by orphan wards of the crown and by sons of Portuguese colonists in Brazil. The early missions were established at the edge of the settled areas, with the largest concentration near the colonial capital. Gradually, however, these were abandoned and new missions were constructed farther inland, often well in advance of effective settlement by Portuguese and Brazilian colonists. The *colégios,* on the other hand, were usually located in the larger towns, although São Paulo, the most famous of the original Jesuit schools, was founded in 1554 on the frontier a few miles inland from the Portuguese community at São Vicente.

The missions were designed primarily to segregate the Christian Indians in order to protect them against the deleterious influence of both pagan savages and the lay Portuguese. The missionaries soon discovered that converts who had accepted baptism eagerly and by the thousands were prone to lapse into heathen practices when not closely supervised. The Jesuits long fulminated against the twin abominations of cannibalism and polygamy, but with only partial success outside the missions, for cannibalism was deeply rooted in Indian culture, while both native customs and the example of the colonists made it indeed difficult for priests to persuade converts of the advantages of monogamy. The missions were also economic enterprises, often veritable plantations, on which the Indians labored without material compensation other than food, clothing, and shelter which they provided for themselves. In these circumstances the colonists, who had only limited access to mission Indian labor, tended to dismiss as hypocrisy Jesuit expressions of concern for the souls of the converts. The sugar planters, in particular, felt they had a prior and overriding right to Indian labor and argued that priests seeking to save souls could work as easily among slaves as among free Indians. This contest, usually verbal but at times violent, continued until there were few Indians left to exploit or defend in the settled portions of Brazil.

War was employed as an important instrument of colonial policy by a long succession of royal governors. Armed force both supplemented the missionaries' campaign to pacify the natives by persuasion and preserved the colony against repeated French efforts to seize permanent possession of much of the coast. The planters regularly advocated war against the aborigines as a direct means of obtaining additional labor for the plantations, and even the Jesuits occasionally concurred in order to subdue Indians who persisted in pagan beliefs and practices. The major French bid to carve out an American empire at the expense of Portugal came in 1555, when Admiral Nicholas Durand de Villegagnon founded the colony of Antarctic France on Guanabara Bay. A twelve-year campaign—involving two expeditions from Bahia and strenuous efforts by the Jesuits to enlist Indian support —was required to expel the French colonists and to exterminate their local allies, the Tamoios. The French continued to probe sporadically at various isolated points south of Bahia for another quarter-century before transferring their attentions to the unoccupied north coast in the 1590's. Again their designs were opposed by the colonial government. The French were gradually pushed westward from Paraíba to the Amazon, and were driven from their last Brazilian stronghold, São Luiz do Maranhão, in the second decade of the seventeenth century.

In the course of the prolonged contest with the French, the Portuguese perforce explored most of the coastline from São Vicente to the Amazon, conquered or expelled many of the hostile Indians from the coastal area, and established numerous new settlements to hold the land against foreign encroachment. The capital cities of the present states of Paraíba, Rio Grande do Norte, Ceará, Maranhão, and Pará owe their origins to Luso-French rivalry for empire. The earliest and by far the most important of the new Portuguese towns, however, was São Sebastião do Rio de Janeiro. It was founded as a military encampment near the entrance to Guanabara Bay in 1565 by members of the expedition that defeated the French and Tamoios two years later. With the pacification of the region a Jesuit mission was erected at Rio de Janeiro and colonists were attracted from other parts of Brazil and from Portugal. Because of its excellent harbor and strategic location, Rio de Janeiro quickly became the leading port and administrative center for the southern part of the colony, serving briefly as co-capital of Brazil on several occasions after 1572. Its rise accompanied and contributed to the gradual decline of São Vicente, which long marked the southernmost limit of Portuguese colonization in America.

The basic characteristics of the plantation economy and society that survived with little change for three centuries were firmly fixed in the Portuguese communities along the coast before the last of the French were driven from Brazilian soil. The production of sugar for export to Europe dominated the economic life of the colony from São Vicente

to Pernambuco, and plantation agriculture was being introduced on
the north coast as new settlements were established. The widely separated clusters of settlement remained largely isolated from each other
except by sea, although by the end of the sixteenth century overland
routes for riders and pack animals had been opened between the towns
and plantations from Bahia to Paraíba in the north, while in the south
São Paulo was connected by precipitous trails with the ports of Santos
and Rio de Janeiro. Except at São Paulo, however, the Portuguese continued to cling to the seaboard, for they were still tied spiritually, cul-
turally, and economically to the mother country and had not yet
discovered the mineral wealth that would later lure many of them
permanently into the trackless interior.

Thus, a century after the discovery of Brazil the Portuguese had
occupied only a small portion of the territory allotted to them by the
Treaty of Tordesillas. Within the occupied area, however, they were
masters of the land and the predominant element in a society that had
stratified along the lines set during the captaincy period. Contemporary
estimates of the size of the population in the settled areas are uncertain
and contradictory, but they reveal that the relative proportions of the
three ethnic groups in Brazilian society had changed considerably
since the mid-century. There is no question that the number of Portuguese and their descendants increased remarkably between 1550 and
1600. The 1000 men who accompanied Thomé de Souza in 1549 comprised the largest single contingent of immigrants to Brazil to that date,
raising the total European population in the colony to perhaps as many
as 3500. Immigration of both men and women from Portugal and the
Atlantic islands continued at a rising rate as more of the coastline was
pacified, and by the end of the century the Portuguese population of
Brazil had expanded tenfold. At the same time the ranks of "civilized"
Indians were drastically reduced. In 1562 the Jesuit missions in Bahia
alone had claimed a population of 34,000, with tens of thousands more
in the villages and missions in other captaincies. Twenty-three years
later José de Anchieta could account for only 18,000 such Indians in
the entire colony, and by 1600 the figure was undoubtedly much
lower. The decline of the Indian population was largely offset by the

importation of Negro slaves from Africa, particularly to the older plantation regions of the northeast. Observers in the 1580's noted the presence of about 3000 Guinea slaves in Bahia and from 4000 to 5000 in Pernambuco, with possibly 14,000 in all of Brazil. By 1600 it is probable that Negroes accounted for a quarter of the total population of the Portuguese communities, which was then approaching 100,000 persons. Significantly, at this time chroniclers of the Brazilian scene did not place *mamelucos* and mulattos in a separate category for census purposes, even though other records of the period imply that mixed-bloods were one of the fastest growing sectors of the population, more numerous than Indians in many communities and probably outnumbering Negroes in the colony as a whole. Nor did the inhabitants of Brazil yet regard themselves as "Brazilians," a term then applied in a derogatory sense to the more barbarous peoples of the interior. But, in retrospect, it is apparent that the process of acculturation and racial mixture that was eventually to give rise to a distinctive Brazilian society had begun well before the turn of the seventeenth century.

Chapter 3 • Trail Blazer, Cowboy, and Prospector

Exploration of the interior, or *sertão*, of Brazil continued throughout the entire colonial period.* From the arrival of the first Europeans on the shores of Brazil, sporadic probes were made through the barriers of forest and mountain in search of fabled Indian treasures like those the Spaniards encountered in Mexico and Peru. With the establishment of the coastal towns, missionaries concerned for the souls of the aborigines, and slavers interested only in their bodies, penetrated the *sertão* with increasing regularity. The latter wrought havoc for a time among the native population but left no lasting traces of their presence in the wilderness. Nor, except at São Paulo and at a few points along the Amazon and Uruguay, did the early missions survive to become town sites. It was the cowboy, following his herds to greener pastures, and the prospector, seeking signs of mineral wealth in the streambeds of the great plateau of Brazil, who founded the first permanent inland communities. With rare exceptions, the oldest interior towns of Brazil

* The word *sertão* was employed in the colonial period to designate all unexplored and unsettled inland areas in Portuguese America. In modern Brazilian usage it refers generally to empty, uncultivated, and underdeveloped regions of the interior, and specifically to the semi-arid backlands of the Northeast.

trace their origins to cattle ranches and mining camps of the seventeenth and eighteenth centuries.

Effective occupation of the hinterland east of the line of Tordesillas and the phenomenal expansion of Brazil to the west of that line, thus, began during the seventeenth century. Although few settlements were established in the *sertão* until after 1700, men from the coastal provinces had long since come to regard vast reaches of the continent as their own. As a practical matter, by 1700 the borders of the Portuguese empire in America had been pushed toward the headwaters of the Amazon in the north, to the estuary of the Río de la Plata in the south, and to the shadows of the Andes in the west. This epic of territorial aggrandizement was brought about by a series of shifting international, dynastic, and local circumstances which encouraged the colonials—and sometimes the crown as well—to disregard the limits established in the Treaty of 1494.

Uncertainty as to the precise location of the line of Tordesillas and persistent misconceptions about the width of the continent contributed to the expansionist movement. It was long assumed by royal officials in Lisbon and Brazil that the mouth of the Amazon and that of the Río de la Plata lay well within the area originally allotted to Portugal. Thus, the expulsion of French, English, and Dutch interlopers from the Amazon delta during the first half of the century, and the erection of a Portuguese fortress on the north bank of the Río de la Plata in 1680, could be justified not only as precautionary measures to secure the flanks of the colony against foreign attack, but also as belated occupation of lands pertaining to the crown of Portugal. Similarly, in the absence of accurate knowledge of South American geography, the Portuguese could easily persuade themselves that the Spanish colony at Asunción, and perhaps even the fabulous silver mines at Potosí, should have been included among the dominions of the House of Aviz.

From 1580 to 1640, however, this was largely an academic consideration, for during the six decades of the so-called "Babylonian Captivity," Portugal was ruled by the reigning monarchs of Spain. While the overseas colonies of the two kingdoms retained their respective laws and language, restrictions against travel and trade between them were not

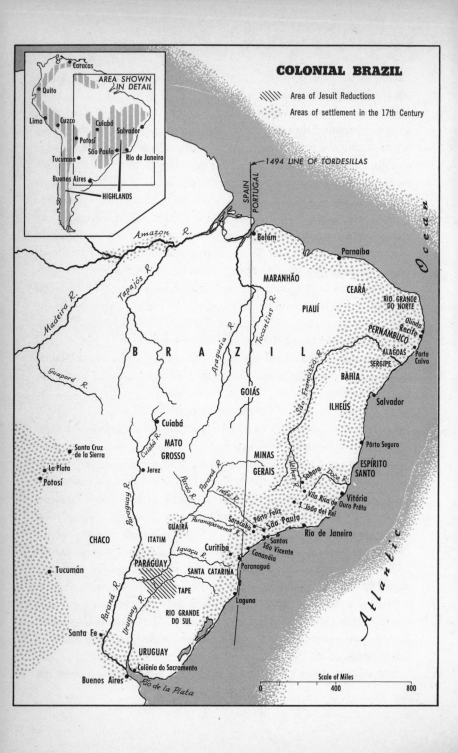

COLONIAL BRAZIL

||||||| Area of Jesuit Reductions

Areas of settlement in the 17th Century

1494 LINE OF TORDESILLAS

AREA SHOWN IN DETAIL

Caracas
Quito
Lima   Cuzco
Cuiabá
Potosí   Salvador
São Paulo
Tucuman   Rio de Janeiro
Buenos Aires

HIGHLANDS

SPAIN
PORTUGAL

Ocean

Amazon R.

Madeira R.

Tapajós R.

Guaporé R.

B R A Z I L

Araguaia R.

Tocantins R.

Belém

Parnaíba

MARANHÃO

CEARÁ

PIAUÍ

RIO GRANDE
DO NORTE

Olinda
Recife
PERNAMBUCO

ALAGOAS

SERGIPE

Porto
Calvo

GOIÁS

São Francisco R.

BAHIA

ILHÉUS

Salvador

Cuiabá

Santa Cruz
de la Sierra

MATO
GROSSO

Cuiabá R.

Pôrto Seguro

La Plata

Jerez

MINAS
GERAIS

Velhas R.

Sabará
Vila Rica de Ouro Prêto
S. João del Rei

Doce R.

ESPÍRITO
SANTO

Vitória

Potosí

Pardo R.

Paraná R.

Tietê R.

Sorocaba

Pôrto Feliz
São Paulo

Rio de Janeiro

GUAIRÁ

Paranapanema R.

Santos
São Vicente
Cananéia

CHACO

ITATIM

Iguaçu R.

Curitiba

Paranaguá

Tucumán

PARAGUAY

SANTA CATARINA

Paraguay R.

TAPE

Laguna

Uruguay R.

RIO GRANDE
DO SUL

Paraná R.

Santa Fe

URUGUAY

Buenos Aires

Colônia do Sacramento

Rio de la Plata

Atlantic

Scale of Miles

0   400   800

rigidly and consistently enforced. In this period a thriving commerce developed between Brazil and Buenos Aires, overland routes to Asunción, Potosí, and Lima were well frequented, and the Portuguese penetrated the upper stretches of the Amazon and its principal tributaries. The reassertion of Portugal's independence under the new Bragança dynasty brought war with Spain and the adoption of policies to check the advance of Spanish outposts eastward from Peru and Paraguay and northward from Buenos Aires.

Within Brazil the proliferation of sugar plantations along the coastal strip from Bahia to Paraíba during the "Babylonian Captivity," and the prolonged contest with the Dutch for possession of the Northeast (1624-54), forced the cattle industry inland to find new grazing lands and, incidentally, to begin the conquest and occupation of the São Francisco Valley and the plains of Piauí. Cattlemen from Bahia and Pernambuco did not migrate beyond the line of Tordesillas during the colonial era, but the uncounted herds of wild cattle on the pampas of Rio Grande do Sul and Uruguay to the west of that line provided an economic basis for the colonists sent from Brazil and the Atlantic islands to hold these disputed lands for Portugal.

Throughout much of the seventeenth century the demand for Indian slaves, which reached its peak during the interruptions in the regular African traffic before 1648, supplied the strongest incentive for probes into the *sertão*. Men from all of the coastal areas carried out slave raids on the native population, but none were as successful as the intrepid Indian hunters from São Paulo, who preyed on the docile Guaraní in the Jesuit reductions east of Asunción and on the savage bands along the upper São Francisco River. In the second half of the century the quest for slaves was pushed to the heart of the continent and was increasingly subordinated to the search for silver and precious stones. These far-ranging activities which greatly enhanced knowledge of the *sertão* on both sides of the line of Tordesillas in no sense represented colonizing ventures. Primarily they were forays by men operating from settlements on or near the Atlantic, who left the interior less populated than they found it.

Not until the discovery of gold in Minas Gerais at the end of the seventeenth century and in Mato Grosso and Goiás in the first quarter of the eighteenth would a substantial and sustained influx of people from the seaboard and from beyond the seas begin to settle the interior of Brazil. The existence of widely scattered but permanent settlements of Portuguese and Brazilians from Rio Grande do Sul to the banks of the Guaporé and in the Amazon basin enabled Portugal to uphold the claims to half of South America which were confirmed in treaties with Spain in 1750 and 1777.

The exploration and conquest of the interior of Portuguese America was directed from four principal centers. The vast Amazon Valley—which was separated administratively from the rest of Brazil in 1626—was subdued largely by expeditions dispatched, usually under official auspices, from the town of Belém at the river's mouth. On the southern fringe of the colony, the establishment of fortified outposts on the Río de la Plata and in Santa Catarina and Rio Grande do Sul were primarily military enterprises, supervised at times by the governor-general at Bahia and more often by the crown in Lisbon. In both the North and South, the cross and the flag preceded or accompanied the first settlers. But in the hinterland of the plantation colonies in the Northeast the occupation of the backlands of Bahia and Pernambuco was initially a spontaneous movement by mixed-blood renegades and cowboys, and by the predominantly European owners of cattle herds escaping from the comparatively overcrowded and closely regulated coastal communities. Colonial officials usually made no serious effort to impose the laws of God or king in the northeastern *sertão* until the region had been penetrated and partially pacified by such unwitting agents of empire. Only in this area of Brazil did the opening up of the frontier approximate the process on the great plains of the United States three centuries later.

The remainder of the Brazilian wilderness was first traversed by the *bandeirantes* from São Paulo, who were the most spectacular trail blazers and Indian fighters to emerge in South America. The *bandeirantes* were so called for the *bandeiras,* or quasi-military expeditions that they mounted into the interior for a century and a half after

1600.* The men from São Paulo were also the only group to take part in the exploration and subjugation of every major region included within the boundaries of modern Brazil.

In many respects the Paulistas were unique among the inhabitants of colonial Brazil. Their community, which grew out of the merger of Santo André da Borda do Campo and the Jesuit mission village of São Paulo de Piratininga in 1562, was a remote, relatively impoverished, and largely self-sufficient frontier settlement. It was located atop the escarpment on the plateau, where the land sloped to the west and the rivers formed part of the watershed of the Río de la Plata. Although less than fifty miles from the Atlantic, São Paulo was separated from the coast by some of the most hazardous terrain in all Brazil. The Paulistas engaged in subsistence farming and livestock raising, producing but few goods that could profitably be transported over the steep, forest-covered inclines of the Serra do Mar to Santos, the chief port of the captaincy after 1545. They raised some sugar for local consumption as food and brandy, but were unable to compete for overseas markets with the wealthier, favorably situated seaboard plantation areas. Thus, the Paulistas had no chance to develop either the stratified plantation society or the strong commercial ties with Europe that characterized the coastal communities of Brazil. Nor were they closely integrated into the colonial administration, although they regarded São Paulo indisputably as part of Brazil and themselves as loyal subjects of the crown. In view of the difficulties of communication with the colonial capital, and the absence of ready sources of wealth to attract royal attention, they were left largely to their own devices for extended periods of time. These circumstances encouraged the residents of São

* The origin of the term bandeira (literally, flag), as it came to be used in São Paulo, is obscure. At the beginning of the seventeenth century it appears to have been used interchangeably with companhia (company). Both were medieval Portuguese terms for relatively small, mobile, military assault forces. The name may have derived from the fact that expeditions from São Paulo customarily carried a flag or similar insignia. The expression bandeirante appears to have come into use in the eighteenth century.

Paulo to look to the *sertão* rather than to the sea for their future and their fortunes.

The frontier society of São Paulo was more open and egalitarian than that on the coast, for it lacked dramatic contrasts in wealth and living standards, but it was by no means democratic. The social structure was predominantly rural and patriarchal. The head of the family exercised almost complete authority over his numerous progeny, dependent kinsmen, servants, and Indian slaves. The slave element also came to include a small proportion of Negroes, but these were never numerically important in the populace. The top positions in society were occupied by persons of European or largely European descent. For the most part they were of Portuguese ancestry, although Spaniards and other subjects of the Spanish crown entered São Paulo in comparatively large numbers before 1640. Some sons of aristocratic families may have been included among them, but most were of modest, if not humble, social origins and achieved prominence only after establishing themselves at São Paulo. Social status and prestige rested not only on family connections and on the number of slaves and retainers, which in turn determined the effective size of landholdings and herds, but also on such personal qualities as courage, leadership, and mastery of the lore of the *sertão*. An individual who excelled as a *bandeirante*, capturing enough slaves to enlarge his fields and herds, could rise in the social scale to become one of the good men (*homens bons*) of the colony, despite inauspicious family background. To the extent that São Paulo enjoyed self-government, it was local administration by, and largely for, the minority of *homens bons*, who were the Christian heads of families of substance and standing in the community. Candidates for election to the town council (*câmara*), whose jurisdiction included both the town and its enormous hinterland, were nearly always drawn from this group, as were most of the electors. By preference, when not on *bandeira*, the Paulista lived on his rural estate, but political and social leaders usually maintained a house in the town, where they resided during meetings of the *câmara* and the periodic religious festivities that broke the routine of frontier existence.

The frontier mentality and way of life of the Paulistas also revealed a strong ethnic influence. By weight of numbers Indians—of whom a majority were free men—predominated in the society of São Paulo in the sixteenth century and probably through most of the seventeenth, while *mamelucos,* both legitimate and illegitimate, comprised a substantial and growing segment of the population. The latter outnumbered persons of European descent at least until late in the colonial era. The leading families, moreover, generally bore some Indian blood in their veins, and those who could claim descent from the Tupí consorts of João Ramalho or similar sixteenth century squaw men took pride in their native ancestry. These families provided most of the leaders of *bandeiras*—although there were notable exceptions, such as Antônio Rapôso Tavares, who was European-born. But regardless of place of birth or racial strain, the successful *bandeirantes* were those who adopted Indian practices that permitted them to find their way and to survive in the wilderness to the north, west, and south of São Paulo. They seem to have inherited from Indian forebears or acquired by exposure to their Tupí companions a wandering streak that was often merely the sheer excitement and adventure of discovering new lands.

The *bandeirantes* exhibited many other Indian traits. Out of convenience and necessity, they adopted a modified form of Indian dress. They generally wore short trousers and an over-shirt of cotton, perhaps covered by a leather jerkin or vest, and a fur cap or broad-brimmed hat for protection against sun and rain. On treks into the interior they usually traveled barefoot. A pair of fine boots, to be worn on formal occasions, might be passed from father to son for several generations. In combat the *bandeirantes* wore the quilted cotton armor devised by the aborigines as defense against arrows. By and large they also used the weapons of their Indian allies and enemies—the bow and arrow or spear. The *bandeirantes* prized firearms, especially the shotgun and a long-barreled musket, but possessed relatively few of these expensive arms. Their basic foods and many utensils likewise were Indian. Maize, beans, and to a lesser extent manioc, were staples in the Paulista diet. They slept on hammocks or on leather cots. Imported household items were extremely rare. Richard Morse reports that only one decent European-style bed existed in the town of São Paulo as late as 1620. Indian influence extended even to the speech of the Paulistas. Portuguese was always the official language, in which formal records were kept, but few Paulistas were trained in Portuguese grammar or other areas of academic study. The documents of the *bandeirante* era suggest that at times even the scribes were barely literate. The common speech of São Paulo was the *lingua geral,* a variant of the Tupí-Guaraní tongue, which served as a lingua franca throughout the interior of Brazil and in Paraguay. The European and *mameluco* males in São Paulo, as elsewhere in Brazil, readily adopted the attitude of the Tupí toward native women. Casual alliances with the compliant squaws were customary, and some *bandeirantes* were renowned for the number of concubines who accompanied them on their ramblings through the *sertão.*

The *bandeiras* that departed from São Paulo for the *sertão* appear to have shared basic features imposed by environment and experience. They were tightly organized, armed expeditions designed to operate for an indefinite period in hostile territory. Although some *bandeiras* might spend only a few months on the march—and the majority probably returned to São Paulo within two years—journeys of several years' duration were not uncommon. At least one *bandeira* in the seventeenth century was reported to have remained in the interior for eighteen years. These expeditions varied greatly in size according to their purpose, from a few dozen men to as many as 3000. A *bandeira* to the Guairá region in 1629, for example, was composed of 69 Paulistas, 900 *mamelucos,* and 2000 Indian auxiliaries. The latter included both Tupiniquim allies as fighting men and slaves employed as porters. The *bandeirantes* traveled light and on foot, with no equipment that could not be carried on the backs or heads of men. Although they raised horses and mules in São Paulo, they did not use these animals for transportation or as beasts of burden in the *sertão* until after the opening of the mines in the eighteenth century. With rare exceptions they traveled overland, sometimes covering twenty miles in a day, following Indian trails along mountain ridges and river valleys. Although their principal routes to the west and south were along navigable waterways, canoes were not used regularly by *bandeirantes* until the 1720's, and then only on the long route between São Paulo and the gold fields of Cuiabá. The *bandeirantes* expected to live off the land. Usually they carried only salt and a coarse flour from which they made a sort of hardtack as supplemental rations, although experience proved that this was often not adequate. Many men died in the *sertão* for lack of food. Those anticipating a prolonged stay in the wilderness might take cattle or hogs, to assure some meat in their diet, and seeds to be planted en route. Sometimes they halted long enough to harvest the crop. At other times it was left to be consumed on the return trip.

In organization the *bandeiras* combined military, communal, and patriarchal characteristics. The leaders were frequently members of a single large family or clan. The number of officers depended upon the size of the expedition, but each one was commanded by a field master with full authority over his followers. According to the circumstances, he might be a crown official or a private individual acknowledged by his companions for skills and experience gained on successive ventures into the *sertão*. On the march each member of the expedition, even those who had contributed most heavily to its outfitting, was expected to submit to his discipline. Unless financed outright by colonial authorities, the *bandeira* was ordinarily sponsored by its members, each according to his means, in anticipation of a proportionate share of the profits. Not until after the discovery of gold did the practice of sharing the expenses and rewards of the expedition disappear.

Documents of the period reveal both the esteem in which the Paulistas were held for their prowess as pathfinders and fighting men, and the disdain with which their Indian blood and customs were viewed by Portuguese contemporaries in other parts of Brazil. The *bandeirantes* were berated with particular vehemence by the clergy for their cavalier disregard of many rules of Christian conduct and their insatiable lust for Indian slaves. Twice during the seventeenth century the Paulistas—defying the wishes of the crown—expelled the Jesuit Order from São Paulo because the priests protested against their slave raids. Nonetheless, the men of São Paulo were frequently called upon by crown officers to assist in the conquest of distant regions, where local

Brazilian and Portuguese forces were inadequate or ineffective. One such *bandeirante*, typical of his kind, was Domingos Jorge Velho, who in 1694 helped to destroy the so-called "Negro republic of Palmares" —an armed community of runaway slaves that had existed for half a century in Alagôas. In a scathing report on this Paulista, the bishop of Pernambuco reflected the bias of the clergy and the sense of superiority of the Portuguese. He expressed grave doubts about the mental state and religious orthodoxy of Domingos Jorge Velho, whom he described as one of the worst savages he had ever met, no different than the most barbaric Tapuia. It is difficult to ascertain whether the bishop was repelled more by the fact that the Paulista, a recently married man, was attended by seven Indian concubines, or that he employed an interpreter when conversing with Portuguese officials.

Such accounts exaggerate unduly in portraying the *bandeirantes* as uncultured barbarians, but leave no doubt that the colonial Paulistas were men of action who lived primarily for the moment. Their lack of interest in scholarly pursuits and their unconcern for the judgment of history is seen in the fact that they produced neither contemporary poets to immortalize their deeds nor faithful chroniclers to record the numbers, dates, and destinations of the scores of *bandeiras* that departed from São Paulo in the course of nearly two centuries. The paucity of detailed information about the activities of the Paulistas also reflects the spontaneous nature—and frequently the unlawful objectives—of many *bandeiras*.

The *bandeiras* of São Paulo may be divided into numerous, although often overlapping, categories according to the auspices under which they were formed, their chief objectives, and the regions they traversed. The earlier ones—beginning in the 1560's—were usually called *entradas*, and were indistinguishable from expeditions known by the same name which set out for the interior from captaincies farther north along the Brazilian coast. They were official ventures, organized in response to directives by the monarch or his representatives in America. Official *entradas* or *bandeiras*, financed by the crown, continued to be organized in São Paulo through the seventeenth century. After the first decade of that century, however, *bandeiras* sponsored and led by private individuals, who were often municipal officers in São Paulo, became more numerous. It is probable that the private expeditions into the *sertão* outnumbered official ones during the so-called "cycle of *bandeiras*," which is usually considered to have lasted from about 1600 to about 1750.

A strong profit motive may be detected in nearly all of the *bandeiras* originating in São Paulo, but it is not always clear which of several forms of wealth was sought by a particular expedition. In the beginning, and again after 1650, they mainly were searching for mineral riches or precious stones. Even before the creation of the first captaincies, Europeans on the coast of South America had been fascinated by tales of green stones—which they assumed to be emeralds, by legends of a shining mountain of jewels or silver—"Itaberabuçú," which the Portuguese corrupted to "Sabarabuçú"—and by rumors of a distant land of gold and silver somewhere to the west. In the 1520's a Portuguese castaway, Aleixo Garcia, was killed while leading a band of Guaraní from Brazil in search of a fabled silver mountain ruled over by a white king. A decade later Martim Afonso sent eighty men with a survivor of that expedition on the same quest. The early ventures failed completely, but the tales lost nothing in the re-telling over the years. In fact, they were reinforced by the opening of the silver mines of Potosí by Spaniards in far Peru in 1545, and by discoveries of small deposits of alluvial gold and green stones—probably tourmalines—a few leagues inland from Santos in 1560 or 1561, and in the Mantiqueira mountains near Jaraguá in the 1590's. After the latter find, Governor-General Francisco de Souza dispatched a series of prospecting *bandeiras* north from São Paulo until his death in 1611. It was to be another eight decades, however, before *bandeirantes* prospecting in that same area would discover Sabarabuçú and the famous black gold of Minas Gerais.

A hundred years before the great gold strike in Minas Gerais, the Paulistas had gained notoriety as hunters of men. From the days of João Ramalho and the early Jesuits, the colonists on the plateau of Piratininga had been forced to become Indian fighters in order to survive. In the 1560's the Tamoios and Carijós allied with the French

posed a direct threat to the existence of São Paulo. With the defeat
and expulsion of French forces from Guanabara Bay, the Paulistas took
the offensive, gradually eliminating enemy bands from the valleys of
the Paraíba do Sul and Tietê. Captives were invariably enslaved to
labor on the farms of their captors or to be sold to coastal planters.
During the last quarter of the sixteenth century, after the security of
São Paulo had been assured—and despite a series of royal edicts and
decrees guaranteeing the freedom of the king's Indian vassals—the
Paulistas continued to wage war on the aborigines for the purpose of
taking slaves. The wild bands were sometimes induced to attack the
colonists in order that a "just war" might be launched against them,
since prisoners taken in such a war might legally be enslaved. Frequently, however, the Paulistas dispensed with even this transparent
subterfuge. With the active co-operation of Tupiniquim kinsmen and
allies, they pursued their human prey simultaneously northward to
the headwaters of the São Francisco and southwest along the Paraná
and the Uruguay. *Bandeirantes* from São Paulo appear to have ranged
from the area of Minas Gerais in the north to Rio Grande do Sul in
the south, and as far west as Paraguay, before the close of the sixteenth
century. Regardless of their ostensive purpose—whether to raid Indian
villages, to search for minerals, or occasionally, to trade with the Spaniards at Asunción—they usually returned with Indian captives. By 1600
the slave-seeking *bandeira* had thus become an established, if still marginal, institution in the economy of São Paulo, as well as a regular
outlet for the surplus energies of the male population. But the great
era of Indian slaving was yet to come.

Slave raiding became the principal economic activity and way of
life of two generations of Brazilian *bandeirantes* as the result of a novel
experiment begun early in the seventeenth century in Paraguay. In an
attempt to end long-standing conflicts between the Guaraní Indians
and the Spanish colonists at Asunción, the crown in 1607 awarded
the Jesuit Order exclusive jurisdiction over the native population in
the ecclesiastical Province of Paraguay—a vaguely delimited jungle
domain extending from what is now southern Bolivia to northwestern
Uruguay and including most of the area of modern Paraguay, the

Misiones region of Argentina, and portions of the present Brazilian states of Mato Grosso, Paraná, Santa Catarina, and Rio Grande do Sul. Missionaries were sent into the forests to establish centers, known as reductions, where the Guaraní should be congregated, pacified, Christianized, and segregated from all contact with the colonists.* The Jesuits were highly successful in the first three objectives, but the latter was seldom fully realized, for the presence of large numbers of Indians in the reductions proved an irresistible attraction to the *bandeirantes* from São Paulo.

By 1610 missions had been opened in the region known as Guairá, along the Paraná between the Paranapanema and Iguaçú Rivers. Within a decade assaults on the reductions in this area were begun by *bandeirantes* led by Manuel Prêto, who had raided Indian villages in Guairá early in the century. The destruction of the Guairá missions occurred during the five-year period from 1628 to 1632, when wave after wave of *bandeirantes,* in collusion with lay officials at Asunción, fell upon the reductions burning the buildings, expelling or killing the priests, and carrying off tens of thousands of domesticated and defenseless Indians. A single *bandeira* in which Antônio Rapôso Tavares participated in 1629 is reported to have taken more than 4000 Indians from one Guairá reduction, in addition to an unspecified number of savages captured in the vicinity.

During the second quarter of the century every able-bodied Paulista must have taken part in the raids on Jesuit missions in Guairá, in Rio Grande do Sul, and in Mato Grosso. By 1641 most of the reductions east of the Uruguay River and those in Mato Grosso had been decimated by slave hunters from São Paulo, and the Jesuits had been forced to withdraw into the area now known as Misiones. Here, however, the priests and their Guaraní proselytes offered effective resistance. After repeated petitions to the crown the missionaries were permit-

* The word "reduction" is derived from the Latin for the expression "to lead back." Because of surface similarities between Guaraní and Christian religious symbols and practices, the early churchmen in South America were convinced the Guaraní had once known the true faith but had been led astray by Satan. For this reason, the missions in which the Guaraní were to be "led back" or "reduced" to Christianity were called "reductions."

ted to arm and train their charges, who defeated the *bandeirantes* in a major engagement near the Mbororé River in 1641. The size and frequency of *bandeiras* assaulting the Paraguayan reductions declined sharply after that date, although sporadic raids continued until the reopening of the Negro slave traffic from Angola in 1648 greatly reduced the demand for Indian labor on the coastal plantations of Brazil. Other factors also contributed to this end. The long distance from São Paulo to Misiones, the availability of wild Indians in the prospecting regions of Mato Grosso and Goías, and the separation of the crowns of Spain and Portugal in 1640 all combined to discourage attacks by the Paulistas on the mission Indians. After the mid-century the large *bandeira* organized exclusively for slave raiding became a rarity in São Paulo.

By 1650 the depredations of the *bandeirantes* had halted the expansion of missionary activities eastward and northward from Paraguay, laying the basis for future Portuguese claims to lands beyond the line of Tordesillas. At the same time, the surviving Jesuit missions prevented the further movement of Paulistas to the southwest into territories claimed for the flag of Spain.

Bandeiras of still another type co-existed with the prospecting and slaving expeditions from São Paulo during the seventeenth century. These were chiefly military expeditions formed in response to official requests for assistance against foreign enemies, hostile natives, or rebellious slaves in other regions of Portuguese America. While a few were essentially colonizing ventures, the majority had slave hunting as their ultimate goal, for the Paulistas were ordinarily attracted by the prospect of retaining the slaves they conquered by force of arms. In 1639, while slave raids on the Paraguayan reductions were still under way, Antônio Rapôso Tavares led a contingent of 150 Paulistas against the Dutch in northeastern Brazil, and in the next few years other groups of *bandeirantes* were called upon to aid in that war. After 1669 several *bandeiras* entered the São Francisco Valley to assist men from Bahia in a "just war" against Indians who had risen in revolt in that area. Before the end of the Indian wars at the turn of the eighteenth century, some former *bandeirantes* had settled as lords of the land as far north as the *sertão* of Maranhão. One of these was Domingos Jorge Velho, who had previously carved out a private domain in the São Francisco Valley before leading his *bandeira* against the Negroes at Palmares in the 1690's. To the south, Paulistas were included among the garrison and settlers at Colônia do Sacramento, established in 1680 on the Río de la Plata opposite the Spanish colony of Buenos Aires. Four years later an expedition from São Paulo led by Domingos de Brito Peixoto founded Laguna in Santa Catarina. Descendants of these Paulistas would later migrate farther south, contributing to the occupation of Rio Grande do Sul by subjects of the Portuguese crown. Paulistas who settled on the frontiers of Brazil as farmers or ranchers ceased to be *bandeirantes*.

The *bandeira* of Antônio Rapôso Tavares, which journeyed some 8000 miles from São Paulo, across Mato Grosso to the Bolivian Andes, through the upper reaches of the Amazon Valley, and down the great river to the sea between 1648 and 1651, does not fit neatly into any of the established categories. It shared some characteristics with the slaving and prospecting *bandeiras* and was apparently organized as a military expedition as well, for it was comprised initially of 200 Paulistas and 1000 armed Indians. They are believed to have searched for mines of silver and gold and are known to have delivered the final blow to Jesuit missionary aspirations in Mato Grosso. There are grounds for speculation, however, that the *bandeira's* purpose was geo-political—to extend the limits of Portuguese America. Jaime Cortesão, one of the leading modern historians of the *bandeirante* era, believes that Antônio Rapôso Tavares was attempting to determine the boundaries between the two great empires in South America. The vast distances traversed, the route taken, and the fact that the exploit occurred during a period of revived Portuguese nationalism suggest this possibility, while the paucity of detailed information about its itinerary and exact objectives have lent this *bandeira* an air of mystery that still surrounds it. But whether its original goal was imperial expansion or something more prosaic, it did in fact link the hinterland of São Paulo with Amazonia, and served to reinforce Portuguese claims to the Amazon basin at a moment when agents of the Spanish crown were beginning to move eastward from the viceroyalty of Peru. For these reasons, and because it ranks with the most audacious journeys of exploration in the Western Hemisphere, it has been described as the greatest *bandeira* of them all.

The element of drama inherent in the life of the *bandeirante* was epitomized in the last years of Fernão Dias Pais, the emerald hunter, whom Jaime Cortesão has compared to a terrifying biblical patriarch who died within sight of his Promised Land. In 1674, when he was about sixty-six years of age, Fernão Dias Pais set out from São Paulo with a *bandeira* whose exploits have since been obscured and distorted by legend. He bore a commission from the governor-general to seek out the wealth of emeralds believed to abound in the mountains to the north. The quest became an obsession, prevailing over all considerations for personal safety and the welfare of his followers. For eight years, defying every hardship, his expedition of some thirty Paulistas and a large number of Indians explored the rugged terrain along the upper Rio Doce and the tributaries of the São Francisco. At one point, according to the traditional account, the aging *bandeirante* put down a mutiny among his men, executing all of the rebel leaders, including his own son. He refused to go home empty-handed. Legend has it that his efforts were finally rewarded when a few "emeralds" were discovered on the shores of a fetid lake, which vanished when the *bandeirantes* departed, never to be found again. Fernão Dias Pais poured out his remaining energies in a futile search for the elusive lake. Exhausted and disappointed, he died on the Rio das Velhas in 1681. The survivors of his party now returned home, there to learn that the old man's emeralds were in fact tourmalines. He had been seeking a treasure that did not exist, while tramping back and forth across the very region where gold and diamonds were to be discovered in abundance a few years after his death. But even though his mission had been in vain, the *bandeira* of Fernão Dias Pais merits a prominent place among the prospecting expeditions of the seventeenth century. It gave the Paulistas intimate knowledge of the zone soon to be known as Minas Gerais. Its members later blazed the best routes to Rio de Janeiro and to the cattle ranches of Bahia. And the *bandeira* provided at least one of the men who would shortly reveal the true mineral wealth of the Brazilian *sertão*. In a real sense the quest of Fernão Dias Pais marks the transition from the cycle of the *bandeiras* to the age of gold in Brazil.

In the twentieth century the *bandeirantes* of colonial São Paulo have been elevated to the stature of Brazilian folk heroes. Such distinction, however, has not been accorded to their contemporaries, the *vaqueiros* of the northeastern *sertão,* whose exploits as frontiersmen and Indian fighters rival those of the cowboys of the western United States two centuries later. Unlike the *bandeirante,* who extended the boundaries of empire but left the face of the land unchanged, the cowboy of the Northeast transformed the area he conquered. Wherever he penetrated with his herds, from the São Francisco Valley to Maranhão, the Indians, outlaws, and runaway slaves were killed, expelled, or drawn into a pastoral society ruled over by cattlemen who owed allegiance to the House of Bragança. The effective incorporation into Portugal's American empire of these formerly untamed lands and peoples east of the line of Tordesillas was primarily the work of the *vaqueiro.*

The extension of Portuguese rule inland from the coast of Pernambuco, Bahia, and other northeastern captaincies was a gradual process, reflecting the growth of the sugar plantation economy and the exclusion of livestock herds from the humid zone bordering the sea. The cattle industry began as an adjunct to sugar production, for oxen were used in large numbers as draft animals in the mills and canefields. Many sugar mills were powered by oxen, and even water-powered mills required a minimum of one hundred oxen per season to haul firewood for the boilers and cane for grinding. As long as ample grazing lands were at hand the sugar planters and mill-owners raised their own herds. By the second half of the sixteenth century, however, much of the pasture land in the older captaincies was being converted into canefields. Sugar producers found it more profitable to buy oxen when needed for the harvest than to maintain large herds throughout the year. Under these circumstances, cattle raising became a separate occupation, and ranchers competed at a disadvantage with planters for space on the narrow coastal strip. It was the migration of cattle ranches

north from Bahia and south from Pernambuco that led to the settlement of Sergipe and Alagôas before 1600. For a time these areas supplied the traditional plantation zones with livestock, but here, too, sugar was soon introduced, and the contest between grazers and cultivators continued. By 1627, cattle growers were obliged by law to fence their pastures in order to protect the canefields. Such a law, although honored largely in the breach for many years, marked the beginning of the end for the coastal cattle industry. Three-quarters of a century later, in 1701, all grazing was prohibited by royal decree within ten leagues—approximately forty miles—of the Atlantic. In the meantime the northeastern *sertão* had been transformed into a vast cattle-raising area.

As early as the 1620's a few hardy cattlemen pushed beyond the

Paulo Afonso Falls of the São Francisco River, establishing corrals as much as 200 miles inland from the coast. This movement into the interior was interrupted for several years, however, following the Dutch capture of Recife in 1630. The Dutch invasion of the Northeast (1630-39) wrought havoc among both the sugar and cattle industries. Plantations and mills were abandoned, herds were scattered, and thousands of head of cattle were slaughtered to prevent their use by the enemy. In the Sergipe campaign alone Brazilians destroyed 5000 head and carried off 8000, while the Dutch killed 3000 and captured a much greater number. It was largely to secure a dependable supply of cattle as draft animals and food that the Dutch extended their conquest to Rio Grande do Norte and Ceará. In these areas and in Alagôas the cattle industry was revived and expanded during the period of relative calm under Maurice of Nassau, governor of Dutch Brazil from 1637 to 1644, thus providing a surplus for later expansion into the *sertão*. The resumption of full-scale warfare after 1644 also helped to pave the way for the subsequent occupation of the interior by herdsmen from the coast. In the course of hostilities large numbers of Brazilians operated behind Dutch lines in the *sertão,* where for the first time they became familiar with the terrain and aware of the potential value of the region as grazing land.

Even before the Dutch threat to Brazil was eliminated in 1654, there was a significant migration of *vaqueiros* moving inland along every river and stream bed from northern Bahia to Ceará. The major thrust, into the São Francisco Valley from Bahia and Pernambuco, was slowed but not halted by Indian attacks in the 1650's and again after 1669, when a "just war" was declared. *Bandeirantes* from São Paulo, whose slave raids had already reached the upper São Francisco, responded enthusiastically to repeated calls for assistance in pacifying the region. The principal *bandeiras* operating in the middle São Francisco Valley and the interior of Pernambuco and Ceará were those of Estevão Bayão in the 1670's, Domingos de Carvalho in the 1680's and Mathias Cardoso in 1690. The latter, with the help of *vaqueiros* from all the northeastern captaincies, finally broke the resistance of the Indians. The victors were rewarded with slaves and grants of land in the territory they had conquered. The middle valley and *sertão* as far west as Piauí were settled chiefly by men from Bahia, Pernambuco, and Ceará, while most of the *bandeirantes* were awarded landholdings in the upper valley and along the Rio das Velhas in what is now the state of Minas Gerais. There, with slaves and livestock from the Northeast, more than a hundred Paulista veterans of the Indian wars were established as ranchers before 1700.

The occupation of the northeastern *sertão*—disorderly and hazardous in execution—appears in retrospect to have followed a reasonably consistent pattern. In the vanguard were missionaries seeking to gather the Indians into villages, to Christianize them, and to defend them against those who would come later. But always the number of priests was small and their successes were few in this part of Brazil. After the missionaries, criminals or slaves fleeing from the plantation areas usually led the move to settle permanently in the backlands. Some became subsistence farmers, a few renegades adopted Indian ways, and others grouped together as bandits preying on frontier settlements and ranches. From time to time independent *vaqueiros,* traveling at their own risk and without the knowledge or approval of colonial authorities, followed small droves of cattle in search of inland pastures, hoping eventually to expand their herds, build a ranch, and rise on the social scale. Some were successful. Ordinarily, however, when it was learned that a section of the *sertão* was infested with bandits or that an appreciable number of squatters had settled there, the area in question was awarded in a huge tract, or *sesmaria,* as a veritable feudal domain to a powerful cattleman. In exchange, he was expected to impose order in the region. In this fashion the Avila family came into possession of more than 200 leagues of land on the left bank of the São Francisco River in Pernambuco and extensive holdings in Piauí; the Munizes family received large tracts along the Jacuipe River in Bahia; and the de Brito family gained control of 160 leagues on the upper São Francisco and the Rio das Velhas. In addition, hundreds of smaller *sesmarias,* of from four to ten square leagues, were awarded to pioneer cattlemen and Indian fighters. Most of the land grants to *bandeirantes* were this large. But whether the grant was large or small, the owners followed essentially the same process in taming it. The grantee, or more often his deputy, with a body of armed *vaqueiros*, drove in a herd of cattle from properties nearer the coast. A fortified ranch was established, together with a string of villages for those who wished to live in peace as retainers of the landholder. Peace was enforced by the *vaqueiros*, who defended the new communities against attack by marauding Indians and outlaws, and in some instances by ex-bandits, who were authorized to use any means to suppress their former colleagues. Captured Indians and outlaws were given the choice of death or life as a *vaqueiro* in the service of the landowner. While the surrounding territory was still being pacified, cowboys were dispatched with small lots of cattle to establish corrals a day's ride or more from the main ranch. Corrals were started with as few as ten cows and a bull, with one or two *vaqueiros* to tend them. When this nucleus had expanded sufficiently, a new ranch was built and the process was repeated. By the beginning of the eighteenth century the São Francisco Valley was so heavily dotted with ranches that a traveler could ride more than 1500 miles to the minefields without spending a night out of doors. João Antônio Andreoni, in 1711, reported 500,000 head of cattle along the right bank in the captaincy of Bahia and 800,000 across the river in Pernambuco.

The human inhabitants of the northeastern *sertão*, known as *sertanejos*, were woefully few as compared with the numbers of cattle they raised for sale in the sugar zone and the mining camps. They were, however, a hardy, self-reliant lot, inured to the hardships and isolation of life on the frontier. Except on the most heavily traveled routes, ranches and villages were seldom less than a day's journey apart, and in much of the *sertão* they were even more widely dispersed. Contact with the settled regions was limited to the annual trail drives that had begun to link the interior with the coast while the Indian wars were still in progress. Under these circumstances, each cluster of population was obliged to be almost entirely self-sufficient, producing its own food, drink, equipment (largely of leather), and clothing, also of leather or a coarse cotton cloth of local manufacture. Metal goods, firearms, and in some sections salt were the only indispensable imports.

Few women from coastal communities entered the *sertão* during the first half-century. The ranks of the *vaqueiros,* the most numerous segment of the population, were made up overwhelmingly of mixed-bloods and Indians. An occasional Negro or mulatto could be found among them, but runaway slaves usually congregated in remote redoubts, or *quilombos,* such as Palmares, and did not figure prominently in the society or economy of the backlands. The original *vaqueiros* were predominantly *mamelucos,* with some impoverished Portuguese, who saw no opportunity to improve their position in the stratified social structure prevailing in the established seaboard settlements. On the frontier they consorted with Indian women, thus diminishing the proportion of European blood in the veins of their offspring. The Indian males, once subdued, also tended to become *vaqueiros,* for they found the nomadic, outdoor existence of the cowboy infinitely preferable to hard labor in coastal sugar mills or canefields. Not until the eighteenth century, after the pacification of the cattle region, did the influx of women of European ancestry begin to check, and eventually to reverse, the progressive Indianization of the pastoral society in the northeastern *sertão.*

The advance of the Portuguese into the Amazon Valley surpassed even the daring probes of the *bandeirantes* from São Paulo, and far outstripped the leisurely pace of the cattle drovers moving inland from the coast of Bahia and Pernambuco. Nowhere were the boundaries of Portuguese America pushed so far to the west, nor was so much territory incorporated into the empire during the seventeenth century.

In the Amazon the motives for Portuguese expansion were even more varied than in the hinterland to the south. Unlike the spontaneous extension of São Paulo beyond the line of Tordesillas, the conquest of Amazonia at the expense of four European rivals was a deliberate process of imperial aggrandizement, designed to enhance the grandeur of Portugal. For nearly a century, from the capture of São Luiz and the founding of Belém in 1616 until the final explusion of Spanish priests from the Solimões in 1710, the Portuguese waged intermittent warfare against subjects of France, England, Holland, and Spain, and their Indian allies, for possession of the vast Amazon region. Then, as now, the valley was a land of legend, said to hold untold riches for those hardy and enterprising enough to overcome the perils of life in the "wet land." Unfulfilled visions of mines and treasure were slow to fade, and from the beginning men risked their lives and fortunes to gather the "drugs of the *sertão*"—pepper, nuts, cloves, cinnamon, indigo, and vanilla—and the exotic birds and animals thriving in the tropical forest. But for the colonists who had received lavish land grants from the king or his representatives, and for the clerics concerned for the salvation of pagan souls, the Indian was the most important product of the land. As in São Paulo, slave raiding over ever-greater distances was a vital and continuing occupation of settlers, whose well-being depended upon a ready supply of servile labor. The planters, striving to clear and maintain tobacco and cotton plantations, protested virulently and at times violently against the efforts of crown and Church to limit the use of slaves and mission Indians as field hands and household servants. In the race to gain control over the native peoples, missionaries of several orders—chiefly Jesuits, Franciscans, and Carmelites—became intrepid explorers and advance agents of empire along the Amazon and its principal tributaries. And here, perhaps more than anywhere else in Portugal's world empire, the region itself exerted an irresistible attraction. The sheer immensity of the river-sea and its endless jungles worked a spell on the men from Belém and São Luiz, drawing them repeatedly into the trackless environs that they claimed for the House of Bragança.

In order to achieve their overlapping, if often contradictory objectives, the civil and military authorities, traders, missionaries, and slave hunters mounted a steady flow of expeditions, or *tropas*, upstream to the west, north, and south from the delta area. In the beginning the expeditions set forth occasionally from São Luiz and more frequently from Belém, although Gurupá, on the Amazon midway between the Xingú and the Tocantins, later became a favorite point of departure for ventures into the great valley. The Amazonian *tropas* were similar in organization and composition to the *bandeiras* of São Paulo. There were few land trails, however, so that nearly all incursions were water-borne. Thus, canoes and boats powered by Indian oarsmen were the explorers' chief means of travel into the heartland of tropical South America. Some *tropas* were veritable flotillas, with dozens of barks and more than a thousand men.*

Penetration of the lower Amazon Valley began in the 1620's with slave raids against Indian villages, which did not go beyond the Tapajós, for the Portuguese at Belém were then engaged in a protracted campaign to drive English and Dutch interlopers from the delta region. Yet, in 1637, before the last of these foreign rivals were expelled, the Portuguese flag was to be carried in one surge more than 2000 miles to the west. At this time two Franciscan friars from Quito, who had begun to establish missions among the Encabelado Indians in the upper valley, arrived at Belém. The governor of Pará, regarding the activities of the Spanish Franciscans as an encroachment on his domain, immediately dispatched a large expedition to claim the area formally for Portugal, and to make this fact known to the Spanish authorities in Quito. The expedition could not have enjoyed royal sanction, for the king of Spain still ruled over all Iberian colonies in the New World, and in any case virtually the entire Amazon Valley lay beyond the line of Tordesillas. The governor's actions have been explained as a manifestation of resurgent Portuguese nationalism, anticipating the separation of Portugal from Spain three years later. In October 1637 the expedition of more than 2000 men, including some 70 Portuguese and 1200 Indian bowmen under the command of the notorious Indian fighter, Pedro Teixeira, set out for Quito. It returned to Belém twenty-six months later, after accomplishing its mission and completing one of the longest treks in the annals of Portuguese imperialism. In August 1639 at the confluence of the Napo and Aguarico Rivers—which marks the easternmost point of modern Ecuador—Teixeira founded the settlement of Franciscana to mark the boundary between the dominions of Spain and Portugal in the Amazon basin.

* The terms "expedition" and *"tropa"* (literally, troop) appear to have been used indiscriminately to describe many organized ventures into the Amazon Valley. Purely military expeditions against rebellious Indians, however, were known as *tropas de guerra,* while slave raids came to be called *tropas de resgate* (rescue missions), a euphemism derived from the fact that Indians captured by enemy tribes and subsequently "rescued" by the Portuguese might be legally enslaved. To circumvent laws against Indian slavery, the slave hunters claimed all of their captives fell into this category.

Portugal was to prove unable to uphold its right to all of the region claimed by Pedro Teixeira in 1639, but before the end of the seventeenth century, by their presence and force of arms, the Portuguese were to confirm possession of most of the Amazon Valley now included in Brazil. With Teixeira's return and the successful completion of the campaign against the English and Dutch in the delta area, the Portuguese and Brazilians at Belém were free for successive advances into the interior. In the years that followed, forts, missions, trading posts, and fishing villages were established along the Amazon, Tocantins, Araguaia, Xingú, Tapajós, Madeira, Negro, and Branco Rivers and on the Atlantic coast of Amapá north of the delta. Perhaps as early as 1669 a fort was built near the junction of the Negro and the Amazon, the present site of Manaus, which was then the westernmost point of permanent occupation by subjects of Portugal. Explorers and slave raiders pushed even farther. Some discovered the route to the Orinoco Valley by way of the Cassiquiare canal, while others went up the Madeira, the Mamoré, the Solimões (as the Amazon is known above Manaus), and the Purús to the Spanish outposts of eastern Bolivia and Maynas. In 1687 a German Jesuit, Samuel Fritz, reached Belém after establishing missions along the Solimões under the flag of Spain. Twice in the following decade officials from Belém were sent to advise the Jesuits to withdraw, but they were not finally expelled until force was employed in 1710. In 1697 the French, moving south from their colony at Cayenne, seized Amapá, but were promptly forced to withdraw. By the end of the century the governor of Pará had repeated formal acts of possession, incorporating into the Portuguese empire all of the lands along the Amazon and Solimões and their major tributaries, as well as the north coast as far as the Oyapoque, which marks the boundary between Brazil and French Guiana.

For a century and a half, from the 1620's until the 1770's, Maranhão and the Amazon Valley in the north and Brazil in the south constituted separate "states" within the Portuguese empire. The basic administrative unit continued to be the captaincy-general, of which there were two in the *Estado do Maranhão e Grão Pará* and eventually seven in the *Estado do Brasil*. This division between north and south, adopted as an administrative convenience by the crown, was a reasonable practice as long as contact between the Portuguese settlements in America was entirely by sea, for the voyage from Belém or São Luiz to Salvador or Rio de Janeiro was longer and more hazardous than the voyage to Lisbon. The artificial distinction between the two colonies proved difficult to preserve, however, as men from São Paulo and Gurupá roamed farther into the interior without regard for arbitrary boundaries drawn by authorities in Europe. For a hundred years after the exploits of Antônio Rapôso Tavares, *bandeirantes* pushed into the Amazon watershed in search of slaves, and in the eighteenth century men from the north joined in the rush to the gold fields in the *sertão* of Brazil. Miners in remote camps along the upper stretches of the Tocantins, Araguaia, and Guaporé found it easier to drift downstream to Belém than to journey overland to Minas Gerais, Rio de Janeiro, or Bahia. Thus, despite the administrative barriers raised by the court, the two Portuguese colonies in South America drew closer together as the interior was explored and occupied.

The belated discovery of gold in unprecedented quantities brought about a more profound change in the economy and settlement pattern of Brazil than any development since the experiment with the captaincy system over a century and a half earlier. Within a decade Portugal's huge agricultural colony—which had been suffering a gradual economic decline following the expulsion of the Dutch—emerged as the world's leading source of gold and the brightest star in the Bragança crown. For the first time a large, heavily European population was fixed permanently in the interior, enabling a Brazilian variant of European culture to prevail over indigenous influences. And the sudden appearance of a new, apparently inexhaustible source of wealth in the mountains of Minas Gerais worked a price revolution throughout the colony. The raw mining camps that sprang up overnight along every rivulet and stream flowing out of the Serra do Espinhaço were insatiable markets for all varieties of domestic and imported commodities. Gold overcame all obstacles of distance and terrain. Foodstuffs, cattle, horses, mules, slaves, tools, weapons, and the fineries that miners bestowed on their women of the moment were funneled into the gold fields from north, south, east, and beyond. From the hump of Brazil to Rio Grande do Sul trails were opened and trading patterns were established that tied the isolated self-contained regions of Brazil together more effectively than any royal decrees prompted by visions of empire in America.

The exact date and location of the first gold strike in Minas Gerais is still a matter for conjecture. According to tradition, the discoverer was the son-in-law and former companion of Fernão Dias Pais, the *bandeirante* Manuel de Borba Gato. In 1682 he was implicated in the murder of a crown official searching for precious metals along the Rio das Mortes. Choosing to remain in the wilderness rather than face the charges against him, Borba Gato spent nearly two decades in self-imposed exile. During this period, probably after 1690, he is said to have found alluvial gold in the shallow waters of the Rio das Velhas—where the city of Sabará was later erected—but to have revealed his find only after several years in exchange for a full pardon. Meanwhile, numerous prospecting expeditions from São Paulo probed the future mining zone. At least two of these, led by Antônio Rodrigues de Arzão and Bartolomeu Bueno de Siqueira, found important placer deposits. C. R. Boxer, who has scrutinized the surviving records of the mining era, concludes that there were several strikes on the Rio das Mortes, Rio das Velhas, and Rio Doce between 1693 and 1695. By 1696, if not earlier, news of the discovery had reached the coast and was reported to Lisbon. In another year Brazil was subjected to the first great gold rush of modern times.

Gold fever, like a devastating plague, swept across Brazil in the last years of the century, carrying off much of the population and disrupting the established way of life of the survivors. People of every condition and class flocked to the mine fields, many in such haste and with so few provisions that they died of starvation en route. But the tragic fate of the hapless failed to discourage the hordes that followed. Fields were left untended as planters went in quest of greater wealth, or sold their slaves at exorbitant prices to would-be miners. Merchants left their shops or transferred operations to the more lucrative mining camps, and those who remained behind had barely time to train new clerks before these, too, abandoned employment for the chance to become rich in the distant El Dorado. So many skilled artisans and manual tradesmen departed for the mines that essential services were available only at highly inflated prices in the coastal towns and in São Paulo. The lure of gold also attracted a large contingent of the unruly and the lawless—adventurers, gamblers, prostitutes, and ruffians-for-hire—who went to prey on the fortunate or to sell their services to the highest bidder. Sailors abandoned their ships in the harbors, and soldiers deserted their posts in such numbers that coastal defenses were seriously undermanned, as the French assault on Rio de Janeiro was to demonstrate in 1710. Each of these elements was a source of concern to harried colonial authorities, but, in the eyes of scandalized officials and chroniclers of the time, the most disreputable lot of all were the priests and friars who deserted their spiritual calling for base material pursuits, in defiance of the laws of God and king.

The craze for gold could not be confined to the colony. Before the turn of the century the contagion had spread to Portugal, the Atlantic islands, and the rest of western Europe, infecting the high born and the low. Never before had Brazil appeared so attractive to so many. The exodus from the single province of Minho e Douro reached such proportions—perhaps 5000 per year—that in 1705 the crown adopted stringent measures to reduce the flow of able-bodied young men to Brazil. Despite legal impediments, however, thousands of emigrants, mostly Portuguese, sailed in each annual fleet from Lisbon. Those who had the means went directly to the gold fields, and most of the others followed as soon as they had accumulated a grub stake on the coast. By 1711 Andreoni could estimate conservatively that 30,000 persons resided in the region of the mines. And the flood was to continue for another generation.

The throngs of confident, enthusiastic gold seekers pouring into Minas Gerais were accompanied by a somewhat smaller wave of involuntary immigrants. These were Negro slaves transported from the coastal plantations and from Africa. The South Atlantic slave traffic, which had been dwindling with the decline of the plantation economy, recuperated and expanded rapidly in response to the suddenly increased demand for servile labor in Brazil. The sporadic efforts of the crown to limit the number of Negroes entering the mine fields were generally frustrated, for the actual labor of mining was performed largely by African slaves. Indians proved less suitable than Negroes in the mines, and in any case were in short supply as the Paulistas turned from slave raiding to mining. Affluent Brazilians and Europeans took Negroes with them to the mining area, and the other mine owners ordinarily refused to work their gold washings or diggings personally after collecting enough nuggets to buy or hire slaves. Negro men from the Guinea coast, for the most part experienced miners, were in great demand, and the women fetched fabulous prices as mistresses because of their reputed uncanny powers to detect gold deposits. Thus, after the opening of the mines a substantial Negro population was settled in the highlands of Brazil, and miscegenation inevitably produced a considerable mulatto element. Only the continued, larger influx of Europeans prevented Negroes and mulattos from becoming a majority in the mining region, as they were in the settled areas along the coast.

The gold rush was resented by the men from São Paulo, who claimed a prior and exclusive right to exploit the mineral wealth of Minas Gerais. They had discovered the region, had conquered its original inhabitants, and were working its gold-bearing streams before the arrival of the first outsiders from the coast and from Europe. They looked upon the mining area as a legitimate part of their domain, just as they regarded other distant reaches of the *sertão* that *bandeirantes* had brought under the undisputed, if vague and intermittent, jurisdiction of São Paulo. But in the region of the mines the Paulista pioneers were unable to uphold their preclusive claim to the land against the hordes of strangers who soon outnumbered them by five or ten to one. From the outset friction was more common than co-operation between the two groups. Each felt superior to the other. The newcomers, taking pride in their authentically Portuguese, and therefore more refined, culture, looked down on the Tupí-speaking *mamelucos* from São Paulo as uncouth barbarians as brutal and insensitive as the beasts of the forest. The Paulistas, for their part, regarded the European Portuguese as haughty, grasping greenhorns, and gave them the derisive epithet of *Emboabas.** For over a decade an uneasy truce prevailed, since the numerical superiority of the outsiders was offset by the well-earned reputation of the Paulistas as fighting men. Finally, in 1709, the growing animosities erupted in civil war, known as the War of the *Emboabas,* which raged erratically for two years before it was put down with the defeat of the Paulistas. The civil war in the mining camps provided an opportunity for the crown to assert its authority, although the victorious *Emboabas* also proved difficult to control until their leaders, in turn, were suppressed by force following a revolt at Vila Rica de Ouro Preto in 1720.

An unanticipated consequence of the War of the *Emboabas* was the proliferation of important gold strikes throughout much of the Brazilian *sertão.* For a time all Paulistas were excluded from the mines, and, even though some of them were able eventually to return to their properties in Minas Gerais, others quit the region in disgust. These men reverted to their former way of life, hunting for Indian slaves and prospecting for new treasures in the far interior out of reach of all authority. Some of the Portuguese, as well as prospectors from other provinces of Brazil, also preferred to seek their fortunes in less troubled and less crowded areas. In this way Europeans and Brazilians found a new El Dorado in the table lands of central Bahia, and in 1718 men from São Paulo and Sorocaba discovered the gold fields of Cuiabá, 800 miles northwest of Ouro Preto. This strike was described as so rich that a man could gather more gold than he could carry simply by picking it off the ground, and hunters in the district were said to use nuggets of pure gold instead of lead pellets in their muskets. Such tales, while grossly exaggerated, were less preposterous than they appear, for most of the gold here was found within two feet of the surface. When these shallow mines were beginning to play out, a similar pocket of

---

* The meaning of the term *"emboaba"* (*ambuaba, emboava, imboaba*) as applied to newcomers to the mining zone is not certain, but the implication is clear. In the lingua franca spoken by the Paulistas *emboaba* appears to have meant a bird with feathered legs. Many of the Europeans wore leggings as protection against the brush, in contrast to the Paulistas who wore short trousers tied just below the knee. Thus, *emboaba* may first have conveyed the idea of a tenderfoot, but the expression, used in a derogatory sense, came to refer to strangers intruding where they were not welcome.

gold was discovered by slave raiders in the even more distant Mato Grosso field on the banks of the Guaporé. Meanwhile, in 1725 Bartolomeu Bueno da Silva, an elderly *bandeirante* better known as *Anhangüera (the Old Devil)*, had struck gold in the land of the Goiases, roughly midway between Ouro Preto and Mato Grosso. News of these discoveries and dozens of lesser ones was immediately followed by a rush of prospectors, slaves, and the usual riff-raff from the older mining camps. Most of the new communities that materialized overnight disappeared just as quickly, but a few survived to become towns. Among these were Rio de Contas and Jacobina in Bahia, Cuiabá, and Vila Bela in Mato Grosso, and Vila Boa in Goiás.

The imperial government was ill-prepared for the sudden emergence of Brazil as the major gold-producing area of the world. Even though the crown after 1650 had directed increasing attention toward the search for mineral wealth, no one had anticipated the magnitude of the discoveries in Minas Gerais or the host of problems that followed in their wake. The mining code was a century out of date, and was virtually unknown to the individuals most concerned. No special provisions had been taken to regulate or restrict access to the mining area, to govern the allocation of mining claims, to record the output of the mines, to guarantee safe delivery of raw gold to smelters or mints, or to ensure full payment of royal taxes. It was generally understood that a fifth of all gold extracted was due the crown, but most of the miners ignored this obligation. In any case the nearest collection point was the smelter at Taubaté, a difficult and often hazardous journey from the camps along the Serra do Espinhaço. The only mint in Brazil in the 1690's was a portable affair used to turn out coins of low intrinsic value for circulation within the colony. For a decade after the first rich strike on the Rio das Velhas, miners seeking to convert raw gold into specie were obliged to send it to the royal mint at Lisbon.

As the eighteenth century opened the Portuguese crown was beginning to recognize the importance of its American colony as a source of gold, the purest and most desirable form of wealth according to prevailing mercantilist theories. Thereafter, the government was primarily and continually concerned with the royal revenue from the gold fields. The belated measures taken to regulate the mining industry invariably were intended to assure the crown a steady and rising income from the mines. To achieve its overriding objective, the court and its representatives in Brazil sought by directive and decree to maintain and increase gold production, to improve the system of tax collection, and to guarantee that Brazil remained securely within the confines of the empire.

In the quarter-century after 1700 the Overseas Council in Lisbon and crown officials in Brazil issued an imposing body of laws and regulations designed to make the presence of the royal government felt throughout the mining areas. Much of the new legislation was in force for the remainder of the colonial period. The new laws, bewildering and often contradictory in detail, affected every aspect of the mining industry. In general, they were intended—and wherever possible were interpreted—to reward the discoverers of new gold fields, to discipline or to exclude unreliable and unruly subjects, and to favor with wealth and power those persons whose social station or actions indicated respect for royal authority. In the beginning the crown was obliged to rely almost exclusively upon Paulistas as fiscal and police agents in the mining districts, but after the War of the *Emboabas* such functions were usually entrusted to individuals born in Portugal. The court was determined not to permit the residents of Minas Gerais to develop the habits of independent action long characteristic of the Paulistas. Foreigners were soon barred entirely from the mines, and strict censorship was imposed on all publications that might reveal to potential enemies the great wealth and scant defenses of Portugal's American colony. Under this policy the finest contemporary account of the early mining era—Andreoni's *Cultura e Opulência do Brasil*—was banned immediately after its publication in Lisbon in 1711.

Frequently, measures adopted in Lisbon proved unenforceable or impractical in the colony. The court, moreover, was subject to continuing pressure from miners and coastal planters, whose views of the crown's best interests were often diametrically opposed. Both of these factors were apparent in the decision, taken in 1701 and countermanded the following year, to close the São Francisco Valley route to Minas Gerais.

The original order was issued in response to protests by sugar planters whose supply of slaves and livestock was being diverted to the mines. It also reflected the intention of the court to regulate access to the gold region by obliging all travelers to and from Minas Gerais to use the Rio de Janeiro route. The crown seems to have assumed that travel in the Brazilian *sertão* was confined to "highways," as in Europe, and that it would be possible to seal off the remote mining zone by posting guards along the principal thoroughfares. In practice, the closure of the northern route succeeded only in curbing the movement of herds to the gold camps. The outcry from the miners, who depended for their very existence on the cattle and other provisions imported from the São Francisco Valley, brought the surprisingly prompt reversal of the instruction of 1701, but the court long persisted in its refusal to authorize the opening of new and shorter routes to the mines despite abundant evidence that those who wished to avoid detection traveled at will in the roadless, uninhabited interior.

Under these circumstances the influx of undesirable persons and traffic in prohibited articles was never fully controlled, nor were royal officers in Brazil ever able to halt the illegal export of gold. The collection of taxes on gold did rise significantly with the expansion of mining operations and with the opening of royal mints at Rio de Janeiro, Salvador, and Ouro Preto by 1725. Nevertheless, much of the gold mined in Brazil—estimates vary from 20 per cent to more than half—entered the contraband market. Over the years the crown resorted to a variety of expedients to correct this situation. The *quinto*, or royal fifth (which was seldom a full 20 per cent), was reduced to 12.5 per cent, later to be replaced by a fixed annual levy regardless of the quantity of gold actually produced. This system, in turn, was abandoned in favor of a capitation tax applied at first to all residents of the mining districts and later only to slaves. Finally, at the request of the miners, the crown reverted to an annual levy, although the amount to be paid now fluctuated somewhat from year to year. In addition, there were occasional special levies to meet unusual demands on the royal treasury, such as the rebuilding of Lisbon after the earthquake of 1755. None of these systems was particularly efficient or equitable. Widespread grumbling and tax evasion were tolerated, however, as long as the royal revenue from the mines continued to rise.

The tolerance displayed by the crown toward gold miners was entirely lacking in its treatment of the diamond industry. Diamonds, previously known to exist in quantity only in India and Borneo, were discovered in Minas Gerais in the 1720's. The exact date is not known, for several years passed before the brilliant stones were recognized as diamonds. According to traditional accounts, one of the first persons to appreciate their true value was the governor at Rio de Janeiro, who amassed a fortune in the gems before reporting the discovery to Lisbon in 1729. In that same year an important strike was made in the Serro do Frio region, where gold mines had been operating for a quarter-century. The provisions of the mining code, however, were not to be applied to the diamond field. Within a decade diamonds were declared a crown monopoly under the supervision of an intendant, who was given exclusive power to control the mining and sale of the stones. The area of the strike was closed by troops to all unauthorized persons, existing gold mining rights in the proscribed zone were canceled, and all free Negroes and mulattos were expelled. Nowhere else in Brazil was the authority of the crown so rigidly and consistently enforced. Diamond deposits later found in other areas could not be legally worked, and contraband traffic in diamonds was punishable by banishment to Angola. The restricted zone at Serro do Frio, where the settlement of Tijuco arose, became the world center of diamond production, supplying more than one and a half million carats in a span of thirty years.

During the first half of the eighteenth century a dozen towns and five new captaincies were created in the interior of Brazil as the crown sought to maintain authority over the constantly expanding population of the scattered mining districts. Initially, the region of the mines was included within the captaincy of São Vicente—still nominally a possession of the heirs of Martim Afonso—and the sprawling camps of the Serra do Espinhaço were subject to the jurisdiction of the town council of São Paulo. In 1709, however, the crown purchased the remaining rights of the donatory and created the royal captaincy of São Paulo e

Minas de Ouro. The governor sent out from Lisbon the following year resided in the mining zone. The disturbances of the War of the *Emboabas,* and the French attacks on Rio de Janeiro in 1710 and 1711—which commanded the attention of the governor—convinced the court of the necessity for permanent administrative organs in the mining camps. In an attempt to meet this need, the crown in 1711 raised three of the larger camps to the status of towns (*vilas*) with elective municipal councils. These were Vila Rica de Ouro Preto, Ribeirão do Carmo, and Vila Real de Sabará. At the same time, in partial compensation for its loss of jurisdiction over the new *vilas,* São Paulo was made a city (*cidade*). In the next seven years five additional mining camps in Minas Gerais were given the rank of *vila*: Vila Nova da Rainha, Pitanguí, São João d'El Rei, São José d'El Rei, and Vila do Príncipe. In 1720 Minas Gerais was detached from São Paulo and created as a separate captaincy, with a governor appointed by the crown. Thereafter municipal government was introduced into other mining regions soon after rich strikes were reported or a sizable population had gathered. Jacobina and Rio de Contas in the captaincy of Bahia became *vilas* in 1722. Four years later the governor of São Paulo made the hazardous journey to Cuiabá, where he installed the council of the newly created *vila* on January 1, 1727. The largest gold camp in Goiás became a town, with the designation of Vila Boa, in 1736. Ribeirão do Carmo, henceforth known as Mariana, was elevated in 1745 to the rank of *cidade* and seat of the first bishopric in the mining area. The captaincy of São Paulo, which had lost the southern regions of Santa Catarina and Rio Grande do Sul in 1738, was completely dismembered a decade later, when Goiás and Mato Grosso became separate captaincies, and the rest of its territory was placed under the authority of the governor at Rio de Janeiro. São Paulo did not reappear as a captaincy for fifteen years. The last town to be created as a result of the mining boom was Vila Bela, established on the Guaporé River in 1752. Nine years later it replaced Cuiabá as the capital of Mato Grosso.

The most compelling evidence of the impact of mining on the colonial administration occurred in 1763, when the capital of Brazil was transferred to Rio de Janeiro. Military requirements arising from the protracted Luso-Spanish rivalry along the Río de la Plata also weighed in the decision, but the overriding consideration was the importance of the mining zone and its chief port as sources of revenue. Ironically, the administrative change took place just as the production of the mines began to decline, although the over-all growth of the economy during the second half of the eighteenth century fully justified the transfer of the capital.

In striking contrast to the generosity with which civic honors and administrative responsibilities were bestowed on rude gold mining camps, the crown consistently denied *vila* status and a measure of local self-government to the large and wealthy community of Tijuco. The diamond zone remained an autocratically-ruled enclave within the captaincy of Minas Gerais until after Brazil separated from Portugal.

The long mining boom brought about the introduction of new methods of transportation and the opening of regular communications between the distant regions of Brazil. The monsoon (*monção*), or river-borne expedition, which linked São Paulo and Mato Grosso annually after 1720, was perhaps the most novel depature from traditional modes of travel in the *sertão*. The Paulistas, who had formerly looked upon rivers at best as trail markers and more often as obstacles to overland travel, soon recognized the advantages of the canoe for transporting the bulky foodstuffs and other supplies they required as miners in Mato Grosso. Some of the canoes were small, bark-covered craft, but others—hollowed from a single log—could carry up to thirty men and over five tons of cargo. The name monsoon appears to have been applied to the canoe fleet by veterans of Portuguese India, probably because it departed at the onset of the rainy season and, like the India fleet from Goa to Lisbon, required at least five months to reach its destination. In the beginning there was no fixed pattern to the voyages. Alternate routes were used, with canoes traveling singly or in small groups throughout the year. After some experience, however, the voyagers learned to wait until the rivers began to rise, and to travel in a large convoy for greater protection. The monsoons usually followed the Tietê-Paraná-Pardo route from Pôrto Feliz to the narrowest point on the watershed separating the Paraná and Paraguay basins, where the way station of Camapuã was established. Here various tributaries led to the Paraguay, which was ascended to the São Lourenço, which in turn opened onto the Cuiabá, from which the principal mining camp took its name. For decades virtually all of the food, equipment, slaves, and even livestock purchased by the miners in Mato Grosso was transported over this route. The yearly fleets sometimes included as many as 400 vessels.

In many respects the monsoon was an extension of the *bandeira*. It was a large armed expedition, comprised chiefly of Paulistas, traversing a hostile region in quest of gold. Yet, the very nature of the *bandeira* changed when the *bandeirantes* took to the water. The canoe fleet, even when transporting crown officials and treasure, was essentially a convoy of prospectors and merchants, each traveling on his own account and responsible for all profits or losses of his individual venture. The pilots and oarsmen were professionals who served for hire. Only the risks of travel were shared. These, however, were great. In addition to the hazards posed by more than a hundred rapids, which took an annual toll of canoes, cargoes, and men, there was always the likelihood of ambush by the most deadly foe ever faced by the Portuguese in Brazil. The Paiaguá, who attacked on the water, and the Guaicurú, the wide-ranging horsemen of the plains who assaulted voyagers portaging around shallows and rapids, annihilated several entire fleets, and were said to have killed 4000 travelers along the river route during the eighteenth century. The monsoons survived all such adversities, but became less and less frequent after the first decade of the nineteenth century with the depletion of the gold deposits of Cuiabá and Vila Bela. The cycle of the monsoons ended, more than a century after it had begun, when a smallpox epidemic along the Tietê in 1838 took the lives of most of the remaining pilots.

In most of the mining districts of Brazil—unlike Mato Grosso—the rivers were not suitable as arteries of trade and travel. Even the São Francisco, which flowed north from Minas Gerais into Bahia, could be used for only part of the journey between Salvador and the mining camps, and there were no navigable streams linking the gold fields with Rio de Janeiro. With the rush of humanity to the mines, there was thus an immediate and imperative need for a reliable system of overland transportation, since everything required to sustain the mining communities had to be imported. The royal roads to the mines were never adequate for wagons or coaches, and slaves were too valuable in the gold diggings to be employed as burden bearers over long distances. In these circumstances, the need for transportation was met by the pack train, comprised chiefly of mules, which could pick their way over the steep mountain trails.

Within a few years after the opening of the mines, overland travel and transportation settled into the patterns that were to persist throughout the interior of Brazil for two centuries. Long strings of heavily laden mules soon became a common sight in the mining districts and along the routes leading to the coast, for every commodity exchanged between the seaports and the hinterland—except slaves and cattle, which walked to market—was carried on the backs of mules. Each animal bore a double pack weighing 250 pounds or more. Every seven mules was attended by a muleteer, usually a mulatto or *mameluco,* who strode along beside them. Large caravans included ten or more such men and their charges, under the direction of a mounted *tropeiro,* equipped with whip, boots, poncho, and broad-brimmed hat. Travelers might arrange passage with a pack train, or accompany it on their own mounts, for convenience and safety. In addition, the special trains which transported gold or diamonds were accompanied by an armed escort. An average day's journey ranged from six to twelve miles, according to the terrain, weather, and condition of the road.

The mule, little used in Brazil before the discovery of gold, was now a highly prized animal. To meet the demand for such pack animals, ranchers and subsistence farmers in the southern regions became mule breeders on a large scale. In 1733 the land route from Rio Grande do Sul to São Paulo was blazed by ranchers driving livestock to the new market. Regularly thereafter until the end of the colonial period herds from the southern pampas were driven north to Sorocaba, which became the site of the largest livestock fair in Brazil in the eighteenth century. As many as 30,000 mules were sent to Sorocaba in a single year for sale to dealers from the mining zone. Eventually, as gold mining declined and an increasing number of the miners turned

to the land for their livelihood, Minas Gerais came to rival Rio Grande
do Sul and Sorocaba as a source of mules. The pack train, however,
continued as the predominant means of commercial transportation in
the interior until the introduction of the railroad, and was not entirely displaced as a major carrier until the use of motor trucks became widespread after 1930. The mule train—a by-product of the
gold rush—was the indispensable link between the regions of Brazil
during the late colonial era and for at least a century afterward.

The expansion of Brazil southward to the Río de la Plata was
primarily a crown enterprise, determined more by the changing fortunes of empire and by the course of events in Europe than by the
interests or desires of the residents of Brazil. Spanish claims to the region were refuted by the court in Lisbon, which held that the discovery of the Río de la Plata by Amerigo Vespucci in 1501, and the
formal act of possession by Pero Lopes de Souza three decades later
gave Portugal the right to occupy the lands on both sides of the river.
Nonetheless, preoccupied with its eastern realms, Portugal did not in-
terfere when Spaniards established Asunción in 1537 and revived the
settlement at Buenos Aires in 1580. The union of the crowns of Portugal and Spain in the latter year, and the thriving trade—both legal and
contraband—between Brazil and Buenos Aires during the so-called
"Babylonian Captivity," brought Portugal many of the advantages of
control over the "gateway to Potosí" without the expense of conquest.
These advantages were lost when Portugal asserted its independence
in 1640, but four decades elapsed before the new Bragança dynasty
was able and willing to risk war with Spain for command of the Río
de la Plata. In 1680 Portugal erected a military outpost, Colônia do
Sacramento, on the unoccupied north shore of the river across from
Buenos Aires and well over a thousand miles by sea from the southernmost settlement in Brazil. This act initiated an armed contest for
possession of Uruguay that was to rage—with occasional intervals of
truce—for a century and a half, and would not be concluded until after
both Portugal and Spain had been forced to withdraw from the South
American continent.

Because of its isolated position and exposure to recurrent hostilities by Spanish colonial forces from Buenos Aires and the Jesuit missions on the Uruguay, Colônia do Sacramento never became a true colony. Even though at times—as a result of enforced colonization from the homeland and Brazil—it was actually larger than some coastal communities to the north, it remained essentially a military garrison and entrepôt for contraband trade with the Spanish colonies until 1777, when it passed for the fourth and last time under the flag of Spain. During this long interval, however, the presence of the Portuguese stronghold on the Río de la Plata delayed effective occupation of Uruguay by Spain while allowing time for Brazilians and Portuguese to settle the empty lands between Uruguay and São Paulo.

Colonists from Brazil had only recently begun to migrate southward into Paraná and Santa Catarina when Colônia do Sacramento was founded. Four small settlements—Paranaguá, São Francisco do Sul, Curitiba, and Desterro (now Florianópolis)—had been formed during the preceding three decades, and in 1684 a party of settlers from São Vicente and São Paulo established themselves at Laguna. Here, however, the wave of spontaneous migration halted for forty years before continuing into Rio Grande do Sul. Meanwhile, Spanish Jesuits—who had been driven across the Uruguay River by *bandeirantes* in 1638—returned to the Tape zone of western Rio Grande do Sul. Between 1682 and 1706 they founded the missions of the Seven Peoples, the *Sete Povos* that flourished and long threatened Portuguese territorial ambitions in the region. To counter that threat a small expedition was sent down the coast from Laguna in 1725 to settle the "fields of Viamão" at the upper end of the Lagoa dos Patos.

Thereafter, the settlement of eastern Rio Grande do Sul proceeded rapidly. The present site of Pôrto Alegre was occupied, and large cattle ranches (*estancias*) dotted the entire western shore of the lake within a decade, as immigration from Laguna was supplemented by colonists arriving over the new inland route from Curitiba and São Paulo. In 1737 a fort was built on the narrow channel linking the Lagoa dos Patos and Lagoa Mirim with the sea, and the village of Rio Grande was founded by colonists sent by the crown from Rio de Janeiro, Bahia, and São Paulo. About a decade later they were joined by the first contingent of immigrants from the Azores and Madeira. As early as 1746 the crown began to encourage peasant families and married couples (*casais*) to migrate from the Atlantic islands to southern Brazil, where they were expected to provide a loyal, agricultural element among the ranchers in the east and the mission Indians in the west. When the Jesuits refused to abandon the Tape zone—which Spain conceded to Portugal by the Treaty of Madrid—the islanders were settled near the Lagoa dos Patos. So many of them congregated on the Guaíba estuary that their community took the name Pôrto dos Casais, later changed to Pôrto Alegre. By 1760, when the southern frontier colony was detached from Santa Catarina, the population had begun to spread onto the pampas and to push up the valleys of the Jacuí and Taquari toward the mission region.

The crown's interests in peopling the southern pampas were primarily geo-political—to strengthen and expand the outpost of empire on the Río de la Plata—but it was livestock, chiefly cattle, that attracted men to the area and provided the economic basis for settlement. The Jesuits, who appear to have been the first to introduce cattle east of the Uruguay River, left 5000 head to fend for themselves when the Tape missions were abandoned in 1638. Before the arrival of the Portuguese at Colônia do Sacramento, this nucleus had increased a hundredfold or more, and hunters from Buenos Aires had begun to prey on the wild cattle for their hides. From the beginning the hide trade was a mainstay of the economy of Colônia do Sacramento and of the settlements in Rio Grande do Sul. The Portuguese in Uruguay also exported some tallow and prepared jerked beef (*charque*) for sale to the ships that called at the port, but for a century the cattle continued to be exploited mainly for their hides. The value of the southern herds was increased by the opening of the overland route to Sorocaba in 1733 by a cattle dealer at Colônia do Sacramento. This event, occurring just as Rio Grande do Sul was being settled, converted some ranchers from hunters of cattle into producers of livestock for export. In addition to the mules sold as pack animals in the north, thousands of head of beef cattle and smaller numbers of horses were driven to Sorocaba each year, giving the remote ranching area a direct economic link with São Paulo and the mining zone. Only a small percentage of the potential beef supply could be sent to market in this fashion, however. The bulk of it was wasted until 1780, when the ranchers of Rio Grande do Sul began to export jerked beef to the major slaveholding regions of Brazil. The *charqueada,* where the meat was salted and sun-dried, soon became a vital part of every ranch near the Lagoa dos Patos and a market for beef cattle from the interior. Within twenty years some 10,000 tons of dried beef were shipped annually from Rio Grande do Sul, chiefly to Pernambuco, Bahia, and Rio de Janeiro. With this development the grazing industry of the south was integrated into the larger Brazilian economy before the end of the colonial period.

While the shoreline of Rio Grande do Sul and Uruguay was slowly being occupied by subjects of Spain and Portugal the hinterland—called the "continent" of Rio Grande by Brazilians—long remained a no man's land. It was the domain of nomadic Indians, outlaws, adventurers, runaway slaves, and deserters from both Spanish and Portuguese garrisons. The fusion of these unruly human elements produced the *gaúcho,* or southern cowboy, who differed in important respects from his counterpart in the northeastern *sertão.* Like the *vaqueiro,* he was an expert horseman, skilled in the lore of the frontier, and inured to a harsh and often brutal existence. But the *gaúcho* was also a product of the clash of empire and cultures on the Río de la Plata. His speech was a blend of Spanish and Portuguese, with an admixture of various Indian tongues. His dress was the loose, baggy costume of the Argentine cowboy. His diet consisted almost entirely of beef and Paraguayan tea, and his tools were the bola and the rawhide rope borrowed from the pampas Indians. Accustomed to the violence of the border warfare, he was indifferent to human life, yet fiercely independent. Acknowledging neither God nor king, the *gaúcho* respected authority only in those who excelled in horsemanship, fighting ability, courage, and physical endurance. As ranchers from the Spanish colonies and Brazil encroached on the pampas, those who displayed such qualities attracted *gaúchos* to their service as cowboys and warriors. Men of this breed comprised the irregular forces that fought most of the battles for Spain and for Portugal during the colonial era. Their descendants fought in the same fashion over the same terrain against these countries during the first quarter of the nineteenth century, and against each other after independence was won.

The long military contest between Portugal and Spain on the Río de la Plata ended in 1777, when Portugal withdrew from Uruguay in exchange for possession of Rio Grande do Sul. This agreement, reached by diplomats in Europe, could not alter the ingrained habits of the *gaúchos* on both sides of the border or extinguish Portuguese territorial ambitions in the region. Relations between the residents of Uruguay and southern Brazil continued to be characterized by contraband and violence during the remaining years of the Spanish colonial era and after Spanish power had been broken. Raids into Rio Grande do Sul by Uruguayan revolutionaries in 1816 were used to justify Portuguese military occupation of the country, which was annexed to Brazil as the Cisplatine Province in 1821. Thus, 141 years after the founding of Colônia do Sacramento, Portugal's long-sought objective was attained. The victory, however, was short-lived, for Brazil separated from Portugal in 1822, and six years later the Uruguayans in turn gained independence from Brazil. The precise location of the boundary was to remain in dispute for several decades, but the southward expansion of Portuguese America was checked in Rio Grande do Sul.

Portugal's great victory in the contest for empire in South America was the elimination of the line of Tordesillas, achieved at the conference table in 1750. By the Treaty of Madrid in that year Portugal and Spain agreed to observe the then-novel principle of *uti possidetis* (as you possess) in determining the boundaries between their respective colonies. The decision was not fully implemented until 1777 in the Treaty of San Ildefonso, and the principle of *uti possidetis* was not scrupulously followed in the division of Uruguay and Rio Grande do Sul, but elsewhere on the continent Spain relinquished claim to all lands actually occupied or controlled by subjects of the Portuguese crown. In this fashion Portuguese sovereignty was confirmed over the

Amazon basin, the mining zones of Mato Grosso, much of São Paulo, Paraná, and Santa Catarina, and all of Rio Grande do Sul, which lay to the west of the imaginary line drawn at Tordesillas in 1494. Brazil, thus, had reached substantially its modern limits before the end of the eighteenth century.

The diplomats at Madrid and San Ildefonso merely ratified the accomplishments of trail blazers, cowboys, prospectors, and others since about 1600 in expanding the frontiers of Portuguese America. The gold rush in the eighteenth century reinforced Portugal's claims to vast areas traversed earlier by *bandeirantes*. The mines spawned settlements where none had existed before. In Minas Gerais the new communities were clustered together, but in Bahia, Goiás, and Mato Grosso they were widely separated. As the mines were exhausted, the ebb tide of the gold rush left isolated villages and towns scattered across the *sertão*. Elsewhere the paucity of settlers condemned frontier outposts to stagnation. There were simply not enough people in the colonies to occupy the land. The population of Portuguese America, which probably tripled during the seventeenth century, and increased again by roughly ten times before 1800, still averaged only about one person per square mile at the end of the colonial era. Nor was there a frontier line, in the usual sense, between settled and unoccupied areas. Although the great majority of the inhabitants were concentrated in Minas Gerais and in a few ports and plantation areas along the coast, the map of Portuguese America was dotted with islands of urban settlement. From the Oyapoque to the Lagoa Mirim, and from the Serra do Mar to the Guaporé, these hollow frontiers were surounded by empty lands, perhaps thinly held in large cattle ranches, but more often left entirely to the aborigines. The Tape Indians in Rio Grande do Sul were not subdued until 1801, Botocudos still dominated from the Province of Rio de Janeiro to Pôrto Seguro after the mid-nineteenth century, and much of Santa Catarina remained Indian country until the twentieth century. The Indians have since been absorbed or expelled from all but the most remote regions of the country, but the hollow frontier evident in the eighteenth century is still characteristic of Brazil.

Chapter 4 • Boom and Bust

Brazil has never been economically independent. Moreover, it is only in the past few decades that Brazilians have come to regard economic independence as an attainable goal. For more than four centuries, as colony, kingdom, independent empire, and republic, Brazil maintained an essentially colonial economy, supplying Europe —and later the United States as well—with foodstuffs and raw materials in exchange for manufactures. Until recently the export-import trade was vastly more important, by volume and as a source of revenue, than the exchange of goods within the country. During the colonial period it was taken for granted, in Portugal and Brazil alike, that the colony existed to supplement the economy of the motherland. After political independence was achieved, economic policies in Brazil continued to be determined by men who equated economic growth with overseas commerce and believed that the nation's prosperity derived inevitably from its natural advantages as a producer of tropical commodities for sale to northern markets. The persistence of these attitudes and the circumstances that seemed to justify them account in large part for the remarkably consistent pattern in the evolution of the Brazilian economy from 1500 to about 1930.

The economic history of Brazil may be viewed as a series of cycles, or alternating periods of "boom and bust," which in retrospect appear to have followed a clear, predictable, and almost inexorable course. During each cycle a single commodity—or at most two—for a time dominated the export trade and commanded a monopoly or highly privileged position in international markets. Since 1500 Brazil has been the sole or leading source of numerous plantation, mine, and forest products, only to lose its position of primacy when easily accessible reserves were depleted or, more often, when aggressive competitors entered the field. Thus, in turn, brazilwood, sugar, gold, diamonds, cotton, and rubber have declined in relative importance or have disappeared entirely from Brazilian export lists. The coffee cycle, which began in the nineteenth century, reached its apogee before World War I, although Brazil remains the world's leading producer of coffee and continues to derive about one-third of its foreign exchange from the sale of that product.

The cyclical pattern of Brazilian economic growth, with its emphasis on the few favored items that successively dominated the export lists, served to obscure several significant aspects of the export economy. Despite the overriding importance of the major exports, at no time was Brazil's overseas trade restricted to just one or two articles. Even the merchant adventurers who exploited the coastal forests for brazilwood early in the sixteenth century, also shipped parrots, monkeys, pepper, tree cotton, medicinal herbs, and animal skins on the return voyage to Europe. As the colony was settled the list of secondary items was extended to include scores of additional commodities that figured consistently among Brazilian exports during the colonial period and the century that followed. Outstanding among these were cacao, corn, hides and leather, spices, timber, tobacco, and a variety of palm nuts, oils and waxes. Some were the chief source of revenue for substantial segments of the population, while others gave rise to regional economic cycles. Over the span of Brazilian history, moreover, there was an enormous expansion in the total volume of exports, with the result that the aggregate value of such perennial, secondary commodities as tobacco, hides, and cacao surpassed that of brazilwood, diamonds, and rubber—exports which remained in the primary category for less than a century.

The first article of value discovered by the Portuguese in America was the brazilwood for which the colony was named. The new land, christened Vera Cruz by Cabral and long designated officially as Santa Cruz, was soon known popularly as the brazil coast, and then simply as Brazil—in the same manner that the ivory and gold coasts of Africa and the spice islands of Asia were known by the name of their principal exports. Brazilwood, a variety of the dyewood *Caesalpinia* that had previously been obtained only from the East, was highly valued by the textile industry of Europe as the source of a red dye, the color of live coals, or *brasas*.

The brazilwood trade, which persisted for more than three centuries, dominated Brazilian commerce for the first several decades. It is probable that the caravel returning to Lisbon in 1500 with news of the discovery of Brazil also carried a sample cargo of dyewood. In any case, the expedition that explored the shores of Brazil in 1501-02 confirmed the existence of large stands of brazilwood along the coast from Pernambuco to Cabo Frio. Here was an economic basis for exploitation of the new colony. While the profits from brazilwood could not compare with those to be earned from trade in the silks and spices of Portuguese India at the opening of the sixteenth century, they were sufficient to arouse the interest of small merchants and new Christians, who were barred from the India traffic because of limited financial resources or Jewish heritage. As early as 1502 the crown granted trading rights in Brazil to a consortium headed by the Jewish merchant Fernão de Loronha or Fernando de Noronha. The contract provided that the consortium 1) should enjoy a monopoly for three years, 2) should send ships to Brazil annually to explore and fortify 300 leagues of the coastline, 3) should import 20,000 quintals (approximately 1200 tons) of brazilwood each year during the contract period, and 4) might sell brazilwood to Spain and Italy at about five times its cost in Brazil. For its part, the crown agreed to prohibit the importation of dyewood from the Orient, and to forgo any payment from the consortium during the first year of the concession. The crown was to receive one-sixth of the value of all imports from Brazil in the second year, and one-fourth of the total value in the third year.

The surviving documents of the period do not reveal whether the Noronha consortium met its commitments to import an average of 1200 tons of dyewood annually. Probably it did not, for the first large shipment of brazilwood reached Lisbon only in 1504. It is known, moreover, that the consortium was unable to develop and hold any substantial section of the Brazilian coast. Nonetheless, the venture was a commercial success. By 1505 the Noronha group was realizing a handsome profit. Its concession was renewed, perhaps more than once, but without the monopoly provision. After 1505 several Portuguese firms were licensed to import brazilwood on payment of an annual royalty, and by 1510 at least one French and one German merchant had received licenses as well.

A significant contraband trade also developed by the 1520's, if not earlier, as Norman and Breton interlopers ignored Portugal's claims of sovereignty over Brazil to barter with the Indians for dyewood and other forest products. Their unauthorized and frequently violent competition increased the hazards of the trade and must have reduced both the profit margin and the volume of shipments to Portugal. On both sides trading posts were attacked and cargoes captured or destroyed. In his classic study of the colonial economy, Roberto Simonsen estimates that because of the great irregularity of the trade, an average of only 300 tons of brazilwood was sent to Portugal annually between 1500 and 1532.

The competition for brazilwood, which evolved into a major struggle for empire between France and Portugal, led to the adoption of the captaincy experiment in the 1530's. In each captaincy the crown delegated much of the substance of its sovereignty to the donatary, but insisted upon retaining exclusive authority to regulate and license the dyewood trade, even when its actions hampered the work of the colonists. Duarte Coelho, the donatary of Pernambuco, where the finest stands of brazilwood were located, protested vociferously but to no avail that concessionaries exporting dyewood from his captaincy enjoyed an undue advantage in competing with settlers for native labor. Nor was he successful in obtaining permission to clear the dyewood in certain areas where his colonists wished to build sugar mills. Although the crown occasionally acceded to such requests, on the whole it was adamant in upholding the royal monopoly, since brazilwood was then the only important source of revenue from the colony.

It is likely that a decline in the volume of shipments of brazilwood, as a result of the conflicts between settlers and Indians, contributed to the decision of the court to establish the colonial administration at Bahia in 1549. At the same time royal control over the brazilwood monopoly was tightened. Thereafter, despite the Indian wars and French incursions along part of the seaboard, the dyewood trade increased. As many logs were shipped between 1560 and 1570 as during the entire period before 1532. The trade, which offered a profit of 15 per cent on a fairly large investment, appears to have remained largely in the hands of Portuguese merchants, for the colonists generally were unable to meet the financial requirements for a concession, while the wealthy ones preferred to invest in the more lucrative sugar industry.

For a short period about the turn of the seventeenth century the crown monopoly was abolished, and trade in brazilwood was thrown open to all subjects without limit on the number of logs that might be cut. In place of the annual royalty payment, a fixed tax was levied on every quintal of logs exported from Brazil. This experiment in free enterprise, designed to enhance revenues, proved unsatisfactory, and was soon replaced by the old system of concessions under license from the crown. The royal monopoly remained in effect for the rest of the colonial period and was continued under the Brazilian monarchy after 1822.

The peak of the brazilwood cycle appears to have been reached about 1570, after sugar had become the leading export by volume but before it surpassed dyewood as a source of revenue for the crown. The expansion of the trade to that date had depended upon the availability of brazilwood trees and a ready labor supply near the coast, for Indians performed the heavy tasks of preparing the logs and transporting them to the trading posts. By the last quarter of the century, however, the destruction of much of the coastal forest and the decimation of the native population caused a sharp drop in the level of exports. As early as 1555 the French had begun to venture inland fifty miles or more in search of dyewood, and before 1600 such activity had become common. In the first quarter of the seventeenth century Portuguese concessionaires were employing Negro slaves to cut the logs and were using pack animals to carry them long distances to the coast. This pattern persisted throughout the colonial period, with production averaging about one hundred tons annually in the seventeenth century and probably less in the eighteenth. No effort was made to replant the logged areas or to cultivate brazilwood as a regular crop in the plantation zones. In 1799 the crown established a dyewood conservatory at Bahia, but it seems to have had no discernible impact on the industry. Henry Koster, a keen observer who lived near Itamaracá for several years at the beginning of the nineteenth century, reported that he had never seen a brazilwood tree, even though Itamaracá had formerly been one of the principal centers of the dyewood trade.

A steady rise in the value of brazilwood in European markets, however, more than offset the declining volume of exports caused by the destructive practices of the concessionaires. Simonsen estimates the total value of brazilwood exports during the colonial period at £15 million—more than $150 million in terms of modern purchasing power.

The brazilwood trade came to an end in the nineteenth century when its European market disappeared. This resulted in part from competition from other natural dyestuffs produced in the tropical colonies of France, Holland, and England, but chiefly because of the development of aniline dyes made from coal. The synthetic dyes were superior in quality and less costly to produce. Under the circumstances the court in Rio de Janeiro was willing to relax its monopoly, which now yielded little income to the treasury. In the 1840's, for example, an English firm seeking to introduce steam navigation on the Rio Doce received a franchise to export free of duty all brazilwood found along its route. Similar efforts were made in other areas, but without result even when the crown monopoly was abandoned altogether in

1859. The steady downward trend of the industry was reflected in sporadic exports to Great Britain between the 1820's and 1850's. In
1827 a shipment of about ten tons of brazilwood sold for the equivalent of $435,000 in modern value; nine years later English buyers
paid about $259,000 for less than five tons; and, in 1856 approximately
two tons of brazilwood brought about $90,000. The last shipment of
any significance was made in 1875, although modest amounts of
brazilwood were included among exports from Bahia and Alagôas as
late as 1889. The brazilwood cycle, which launched the colonial economy and reached its peak before 1600, had run its full course before
the founding of the republic.

Sugar looms larger than any other commodity in the history of
Brazil. The sugar cycle, beginning with the first settlement of the colony
and continuing for the rest of the colonial period, molded the traditional
plantation society and economy that persisted into the twentieth century. During the long colonial era sugar accounted for perhaps half the
value of all exports and yielded a greater income to Portugal than any
other product, including gold. Simonsen estimates the value of sugar exports from Brazil between 1500 and 1820 at £300 million, or twenty
times the value of dyewood exported.

At the time of the discovery of Brazil, sugar was the only crop
raised in the West that rivaled eastern spices in value and profit in the
markets of Europe. The Portuguese were the leading producers, supplying about 2000 tons of sugar annually from the island of Madeira.
But despite their experience in the cultivation, processing, and distribution of sugar, they were not the first to introduce it into the New
World. Spanish colonists, who had learned sugar culture in the
Canary Islands, established plantations in Santo Domingo as early as
1506. By the 1550's there were forty sugar mills on the island, and
sugar was being produced for export from Mexico as well. The industry, however, was allowed to languish in order not to compete with
sugar production in the Canaries and with the quest for precious
metals in the Spanish colonies. Under these circumstances Brazil was
to become the first great agricultural colony in America.

Sugar was probably planted in Brazil before 1520, chiefly as an experiment by men stationed at the temporary brazilwood factories. Even under these conditions production expanded sufficiently to support one mill by 1526, when a small amount of sugar was exported to Lisbon from Pernambuco and Itamaracá. The results of these early efforts demonstrated conclusively that the soil and climate of much of the coastal strip were ideal for the cultivation of sugar cane. One of the first concerns of Martim Afonso de Souza at São Vicente in 1532 was to apportion lands for sugar plantations and to begin construction of a sugar mill. Cane and cattle from the Atlantic islands, and probably Negro slaves from Africa, were present in São Vicente by 1534, even though it was another eight years before the plantations were in full operation. Meanwhile, sugar was being introduced into each of the captaincies where colonization was attempted. The most striking success was achieved in Pernambuco, where Duarte Coelho imported skilled laborers from Madeira to lay out the plantations. Before 1550 there were sugar mills, or *engenhos,* in São Vicente, Espírito Santo, Pôrto Seguro, Ilhéus, Bahia, Pernambuco, and Paraíba. Some of these were later destroyed in the Indian wars, but the over-all production of sugar in Brazil appears to have risen steadily through the middle years of the century. With the introduction of the colonial administration in 1549, the crown began a policy of subsidizing the construction of mills and in 1573 added a three-year tax exemption as a further incentive to the sugar industry. By the latter date Brazil was supplying over 2500 tons of sugar annually to Europe, much of it directly to refineries in Holland.

During the last quarter of the sixteenth century there was at least a tenfold increase in sugar production in Brazil, principally in the Northeast. In 1576 Pernambuco alone had twenty-three mills, and eighteen were operating in Bahia. Seven years later these numbers had risen to sixty-six and forty-six, respectively. By 1600 Brazil had far surpassed the Atlantic islands—where production had been expanded to about 8000 tons—to become the largest producer of sugar in the world. In that year, by a conservative estimate, there were 120 mills in Brazil producing about 30,000 tons of sugar worth approximately $2 million in present value. Annual production continued to average

over 30,000 tons until 1630, when the Dutch began the conquest of Pernambuco and the captaincies to the north.

The structure and operation of the sugar plantation—with its big house, slave quarters, mill, distillery, canefields, woodlots, and pastures —were fixed during the seventeenth century. In the best sugar areas nearly all suitable land on the plantation was cleared and planted to cane. Little, if any, was left for food crops, despite frequent royal directives to that end. Power for the mill was provided by a stream or by oxen, while the boilers were fired by wood. Not until the second quarter of the nineteenth century was bagasse regularly used as fuel. To preserve fuel supplies the crown, in 1682, prohibited the erection of mills within half a league of each other, a ban that was not lifted until 1827. On plantations with water-driven mills, the number of oxen used to haul cane and firewood to the mill and processed sugar to the port was roughly equal to the number of slaves; elsewhere, cattle probably outnumbered slaves by two or three to one, since several span of oxen were needed to turn the grinding stones. The traditional *engenho* produced two grades for export, crystalline white and an unrefined brown variety known as *mascavado*. Both types were usually shipped in wooden chests containing about 1100 pounds each. A sort of rum made from the juice of the cane was produced in large quantities for local consumption and for export to Africa, where it was an important commodity in the slave trade.

A few skilled artisans and overseers—usually Portuguese—directed operations and maintenance of the sugar mills, while heavy, routine tasks were performed by Negro slaves, who comprised the primary labor force in the sugar zones after 1600. Negroes proved much more effective as workers and commanded a far higher price than the Indian slaves sold by the *bandeirantes*. Some Indians, however, continued to be employed in the sugar fields during interruptions in the African slave traffic, and by less affluent planters throughout the century. The wealth of the millowner and the number of his retainers was determined chiefly by the size of his mill. Small *engenhos* with a capacity of about 50 tons of sugar per year required five or six Portuguese and twenty Negro slaves; those with a capacity of 65 to 80 tons annually required eight to ten Portuguese and fifty Negroes on the average; and, large ones that processed 100 to 130 tons required fifteen to twenty Portuguese and one hundred Negroes. By the middle of the seventeenth century there were a few mills employing two hundred men, and at least one in Pernambuco with three hundred and seventy slaves.

The Dutch conquest of northeastern Brazil caused the first great crisis in the Brazilian sugar industry. North of the São Francisco River production was drastically reduced for several years, as mills and plantations were destroyed or abandoned, and slaves and livestock were scattered into the *sertão*. After 1637, when Maurice of Nassau became governor of Dutch Bazil, a truce was arranged and many plantations resumed operation, but sugar output in the Dutch zone did not reach pre-invasion levels. Between 1638 and 1645 exports from areas under Portuguese control averaged about 20,000 tons. The resumption of open warfare in the 1640's again disrupted the industry in the Northeast, although the loss of production was largely compensated by a considerable expansion of sugar culture in the captaincy of Rio de Janeiro and by a substantial rise in sugar prices in Europe. The trend toward higher prices continued for about a decade after the final expulsion of the Dutch in 1654, while exports of sugar from Brazil surpassed prewar records.

This period of prosperity was short-lived. By the mid-1660's the sugar industry had entered a prolonged decline from which it did not fully recover until the end of the colonial era. Paradoxically, as Brazilian exports were falling, the consumption of sugar in Europe was rising due to the increased use of tea, chocolate, and coffee. The source of the paradox was competition from the Dutch, French, and English, who established thriving sugar colonies in the West Indies after 1650. Following their expulsion from Pernambuco, the Dutch, who had long controlled the marketing of sugar in much of northern Europe, transferred the production techniques they had learned in Brazil to the Caribbean, where French and English planters soon emulated them. By the last quarter of the seventeenth century, Britain, France, and Holland were importing sugar almost exclusively from their own overseas dominions and in the process causing great financial loss to the Portuguese and Brazilians. As early as 1670 Brazilian sugar planters were finding it difficult to dispose of their products. In that year Lisbon merchants accepted only half of the 65,000 tons of sugar available for export from Brazil. As a result prices plummeted, the usual sources of credit were closed, and many sugar growers faced ruin. The extent of the crisis may be seen in the royal decree of 1673, which stated that neither the lands, mills, nor slaves of sugar planters could be seized for debt, a ruling that was reiterated on various occasions from more than a century. By 1700 sugar exports had fallen to 26,000 tons. The figure seldom rose above that level before 1820.

The depression in the sugar industry, which adversely affected the entire colonial economy, gave rise to the doleful lamentations of Padre Antônio Vieira—the leading orator of the day—who predicted in 1689 that Brazil was doomed to return to savagery. In a more positive vein the court responded to the loss of revenue from sugar exports by pressing the search for precious metals within Brazil, and by establishing its outpost on the Río de la Plata, chiefly to gain access to Spanish silver from Potosí. Ironically, the massive rush into the interior following the discovery of gold in the 1690's temporarily caused a further reduction in sugar output, as money and manpower were diverted from the plantations to the mines.

Although Brazil never again dominated the European sugar market, it has remained over the centuries one of the major sugar-producing areas of the world. Throughout the eighteenth century—the so-called "Golden Age of Brazil"—sugar continued to head the export lists, except during the peak years of the gold-mining boom. For a short period at the beginning of the nineteenth century the dislocations in foreign commerce caused by the Napoleonic Wars reduced Brazilian exports to the lowest point in more than 200 years, but with the resumption of normal trade after 1815 sugar sales reached new heights. In 1817, nearly 11,000 tons were shipped from the port of Rio de Janeiro alone, and by 1822, the last year of the colonial era, the figure for all of Brazil had risen to 76,000 tons. After 1830 coffee was the leading export by value, but sugar production and exports continued to expand in absolute terms. For the remainder of the century sugar ranked second to coffee except for the decade 1865-74, when it was surpassed by cotton, and after 1890, when rubber became a primary export commodity. Yet, even while sugar occupied the third rank among Brazilian exports, annual sales by volume were consistently higher than the average for the colonial period.

The traditional sugar industry of Brazil, which had changed little in 250 years, was profoundly affected by technological innovations introduced during the nineteenth century. The earliest of these was the development of the beet-sugar industry, begun in France during the Napoleonic Wars and continued in several European countries in succeeding decades. By the 1890's more than half the sugar consumed in Europe was locally produced. Only the continued high rate of population growth in Europe enabled Brazil to retain a substantial overseas market for its sugar. But while science was discovering a new source of sugar, it also contributed to a remarkable expansion in the production of cane sugar in Brazil. In 1815 the steam engine was used for the first time to power sugar mills, greatly increasing productive capacity and freeing mill-owners from dependence on water wheels and oxen to turn the grinders. Dependence on animal power was further reduced after 1850 by the introduction of the railroad, which permitted cane to be hauled in larger quantities over longer distances to the mills, and permitted mills to process sugar for export profitably at previously unknown distances from the ports. As a result of the railroad the coastal sugar zones were expanded to their maximum extent, and some areas of the interior, particularly in São Paulo and Minas Gerais, gradually developed as significant centers of sugar production. The abolition of slavery in 1888 caused a temporary, but severe, dislocation of the labor force on the plantations, and many sugar planters were ruined before landowners and laborers adjusted to the new situation.

The plight of the planters and the widespread use of railways in the plantation areas combined to favor the establishment of huge new mills, known as *usinas,* which could grind as much cane as fifty mills of the traditional type. The *usinas* were literally factories in the field, usually devoted exclusively to the processing of sugar cane obtained under contract from renters, share croppers, and independent growers. *Usinas* made their first appearance just as slavery was abolished, and by 1910 there were 40 in Pernambuco alone. The largest of these could grind over 300 tons of cane in twenty-four hours. By 1924 there were 215 *usinas* in Brazil, with capacities ranging from 20 to more than 300 tons in only twelve hours. The number and size of *usinas* continued to rise. In 1930 the 302 *usinas* had a potential capacity greater than the entire harvest for that year. Although some 15,000 old-fashioned *engenhos* were still scattered throughout Brazil, mainly in the interior, their numbers were declining rapidly. Under the impact of the *usina* the self-contained *engenho,* which had survived since the sixteenth century, largely disappeared from the coastal sugar zones within a generation. Sugar production passed from a family enterprise to a corporate operation, and a traditional way of life soon ended.

Perhaps the most striking change in the sugar industry after about 1890 was its transformation from an export industry to one geared chiefly to domestic consumption. Throughout the colonial era and the years of the empire sugar production and exports had tended to rise in response to the growth of population in Europe. After 1890 the steady expansion of population in Brazil created a large home market for this traditional export crop. In the four decades ending in 1930 sugar production fluctuated greatly but followed a generally rising trend, averaging over 300,000 tons per year. During this period exports never exceeded 26 per cent, and seldom accounted for more than 10 per cent of the total. The balance was consumed within the country as food, liquor, and fuel. In 1930, when 84,000 tons were exported, the national yield surpassed 1 million tons—nearly as much as was produced during the entire first century of the Brazilian sugar cycle.

Tobacco was an important export commodity during much of the colonial period and the nineteenth century. Indigenous to Brazil, it was found in nearly every region of the colony, but thrived best in the *agreste* zone between the coastal rain forest and the semi-arid *sertão* of Bahia and the Northeast. Within this zone the area around Cachoeira in Bahia became the leading center of tobacco culture, although by the end of the colonial era substantial amounts of tobacco were grown in Minas Gerais and São Paulo, and before 1900 the industry had spread as far south as Rio Grande do Sul. Since tobacco could be raised in small plots on lands unsuited for sugar cane, it came to be the principal cash crop of independent farmers, share croppers, and squatters, who were excluded from the colonial plantation economy by lack of financial resources. Unlike sugar, tobacco required neither extensive plantings nor costly processing equipment. The members of a single family could perform all the tasks involved in preparing the product for market. The dried tobacco was twisted into rope-like cords, coiled into

tight rolls, and wrapped in coarse leaves for shipment. The added pre-
caution of encasing each roll of tobacco in leather—a practice that persisted into the nineteenth century—was introduced by the Dutch in
the 1630's. In Bahia and Pernambuco, where tobacco was transported
almost exclusively by water, the rolls usually averaged about 250
pounds each, although before 1800 rolls of more than 600 pounds were
common. In the south the weight per roll seldom exceeded 160 pounds,
and those shipped in the Africa trade were even smaller.

It is not known when tobacco was first exported from Brazil. In all
likelihood Portuguese and French dyewood traders took small quantities of tobacco to Europe during the early decades of the sixteenth century, and it is probable that the herb itself had been planted in Portugal by 1548. According to the traditional account, the tobacco plant
was introduced into France from Portugal in 1560 by Jean Nicot, the
French ambassador for whom nicotine is named. Tobacco, however,
did not figure significantly among exports from Brazil until late in the
century, after its alleged health-preserving qualities had been well
publicized.

Without exception the early chroniclers of Brazil reported the Indians' custom of smoking loosely rolled leaves of tobacco, and noted
the marvelous medicinal properties ascribed to the "holy herb." Father
Manoel da Nóbrega, leader of the first Jesuits in Brazil, described it as
an aid to digestion and as a purge for phlegm of the stomach. Nóbrega's contemporary, Jean de Léry, in his widely read commentaries
on the natives of Brazil, stated flatly that Tupinambá warriors smoked
tobacco to assuage hunger on the march and carried a small pouch of
the leaves to distill superfluous humours of the brain. Gabriel Soares
de Souza, author of the celebrated *Tratado descriptivo do Brasil em
1587,* insisted he was recounting facts well known in Brazil when he
asserted that the juice of the tobacco plant cured sores and wounds,
killed worms in the flesh of man and beast, and was effective against
the plague, while smoking not only suppressed hunger and thirst, but
alleviated asthma and counteracted the intoxicating effects of wine.
Accounts such as these undoubtedly contributed to the growing use of
tobacco, which became fashionable in European court circles before

1600. By 1610 some 10,000 rolls—about 1250 tons—of tobacco were shipped annually from Brazil to Portugal for distribution within the kingdom and elsewhere in western Europe.

At the same time that enthusiasts were describing tobacco as a God-given panacea for the physical ills of man, ecclesiastical leaders in Portugal regarded it as the work of Satan and called upon the monarch to discourage its use. Under pressure from the Church, the crown imposed a prohibitive tax, popularly known as a "sin" tax, of one *cruzado* (equal to about $13.75 in present value) on each roll of tobacco imported into Lisbon. The unanticipated result of this action was to enhance the attraction of tobacco as a luxury and a vice. With the increase in price there was a substantial rise in consumption, even among clergymen. Control of the growing tobacco market was one of the incidental objectives of the Dutch in their conquest of northeastern Brazil in 1630.

For 250 years after the arrival of the Dutch in Pernambuco, tobacco was a vital export and source of revenue from Brazil. Although the Dutch planted tobacco on a large scale in the areas they conquered, production could not keep pace with the expansion of overseas markets. Not only did the demand for tobacco continue to rise in Europe, but an even more lucrative market was opened in Africa, where agents of the Dutch West India Company introduced the drug as an article of barter in the slave trade. Even before the expulsion of the Dutch from Brazil the crown acknowledged the economic importance of tobacco by eliminating the restrictions against its cultivation and by making it a royal monopoly product. Some of the restrictions were later reimposed, for tobacco culture spread so rapidly that production of basic foodstuffs was neglected, but the monopoly—farmed out each year to the highest bidder—remained in force for the rest of the colonial period. Royal income from the tobacco monopoly increased more than sixfold between 1640 and 1659, and was equal in the latter year to half the yield of the tithe in Brazil. Receipts continued to climb during the last quarter of the century. In 1710 the export of 27,500 rolls—about 3500 tons—produced twice as much revenue as the royal fifth on gold. Throughout the eighteenth century, despite strong competition from English,

French, and Dutch colonies in America and Asia, Brazil exported between 3500 and 4000 tons of tobacco annually, with as much as three-
fourths of the total destined for Africa. In 1761, in an effort to divert
more tobacco to Lisbon and to discourage a thriving contraband trade,
the crown limited each slave ship to approximately 150 tons of tobacco
per year. Nonetheless, the pattern of the tobacco trade remained
substantially unchanged until the opening of the nineteenth century,
when the Napoleonic Wars disrupted normal commercial channels.
With the restoration of peace in Europe, however, Brazilian tobacco
exports quickly returned to prewar levels, even though the prohibition
of the slave traffic north of the equator in 1815 caused a drop in shipments from Bahia. The decline in the Bahian industry, which had
been tied closely to the slave trade on the Guinea coast, was largely
compensated by the expansion of exports from the south. In 1817 about
1500 tons of tobacco were shipped from Rio de Janeiro alone, and the
volume rose sharply in succeeding years. Simonsen estimates the total
value of tobacco exported from Brazil in the colonial period at £12
million.

The significance of tobacco in the commerce and culture of Brazil
was illustrated by the selection of a sprig of tobacco, with one of coffee,
as the symbol emblazoned on the seal and flag of the independent empire of Brazil in 1822. The choice was an appropriate one, for during
the imperial era there was a ninefold increase, by value, in Brazilian
tobacco shipments. At the same time the home market continued to
absorb a larger share of the annual crop than the entire export trade.
Even the loss of the African market, with the complete abolition of the
slave trade after 1850, did not interrupt the expansion of the industry
to meet rising domestic needs and to satisfy the spectacular, sustained
growth in the demand for tobacco in Europe. Germany became Brazil's
major foreign market in the second half of the century. Between 1822
and 1889 the value of tobacco sales abroad was at least £19 million.
The peak period was reached in the 1880's, when exports regularly exceeded £500,000 per year. Paradoxically, because of the unprecedented
expansion of the export economy under the empire, tobacco declined
to sixth rank among commodities in Brazil's foreign commerce.

The abolition of slavery in 1888 and the politico-financial disturbances accompanying the establishment of the republic in 1889 plunged the tobacco industry into a prolonged period of crisis in which exports first declined and then fluctuated wildly in an erratic upward course. By the end of the second decade of the republic, however, foreign sales attained relative stability at new heights. Between 1909 and 1929 exports ranged from about 26,000 tons to almost 38,000 tons annually. During these years the domestic market expanded until it consumed nearly three-fourths of the total crop. Thus, even though Brazil remained one of the world's leading producers of tobacco and was shipping larger quantities abroad than ever before, by 1930 tobacco accounted for only a minor portion of the nation's export trade.

The eighteenth century was the age of gold and diamonds in Brazil. The economic importance of these prestigious articles can easily be exaggerated, as it was by the crown, by most royal officials in the colony, and by the tens of thousands who flocked to the mining camps. The romantic aura that surrounded the discovery of apparently endless quantities of the precious metal and gems obscured the fact that more prosaic commodities continued to provide the bulk of the income of crown and colonists alike even at the peak of the mining boom. Nonetheless, gold and diamonds deserve a prominent place in the economic history of Brazil, both as sources of wealth in themselves and for their great contribution to the development of other areas of the colonial economy. The general price rise that followed the gold rush brought a substantial increase in royal revenues from the tithe, monopolies, and taxes on all commercial transactions. The wealth generated by the mines was vital in attracting population and investments to previously unoccupied regions and in spurring demand for foodstuffs and locally produced consumer goods. For the first time, with the opening of the mines, there was a significant domestic market for many Brazilian products. When mining production eventually declined, the fortunes earned from gold and diamonds were diverted into the slave trade, livestock raising, and agriculture, with the result that at the end of the colonial period the principal mining zone, Minas Gerais, was not

only the most populous captaincy, but also an important supplier of
cattle, hides, cotton, tobacco, and coffee.

It is difficult to determine the full amount of gold extracted from
Brazil in colonial times, for once the crown appreciated the magnitude
of the Brazilian strike it attempted to seal off the mining districts and
prohibited the dissemination of information that might arouse the envy
of powerful foreign nations. Under the policy of secrecy, for more
than a century after the banning of Andreoni's *Cultura e Opulência do
Brasil* in 1711 no comparable work escaped the censor. The official
records of the mining era give partial data on output and ample evidence that tax evasion and contraband were widespread. At least 20

per cent, and perhaps a much higher proportion, of all Brazilian gold entered the contraband trade. In these circumstances estimates of the volume and value of gold production vary widely, but even by the most conservative computations gold ranked second only to sugar in value in the economy of colonial Brazil. Early in the nineteenth century Alexander von Humboldt calculated the value of Brazilian gold shipments to 1803 at £194 million, of which £39 million were contraband. Baron Eschwege, in 1833, placed total production between 1600 and 1820 at slightly over 951 tons, worth £130 million. Roberto Simonsen struck a balance between these two figures, estimating gold production for the colonial period at £160 million—equivalent to about 1160 tons by volume. Simonsen asserts that Brazil yielded as much gold between 1700 and 1770 as the rest of America produced from 1492 to 1850, and nearly half as much as the entire Eastern Hemisphere in the sixteenth, seventeenth, and eighteenth centuries. João Pandiá Calógeras, an authority on the financial history of Brazil, estimated Brazilian production from 1700 to 1930 at 1400 tons, of which 983 tons were mined before 1801. Approximately half of the gold output of Brazil after that date was from a few deep mines operated by foreign companies.

The diamond industry never rivaled gold mining in economic value, although it was an important and jealously guarded source of royal revenue until after the close of the colonial era. Simonsen estimates the total value of the colonial diamond industry at about £10 million, earned almost exclusively from the export of gem stones. The earliest authorized study of diamond mining in Brazil was published in 1812, when production under the royal monopoly was declining. By 1832, when the monopoly was abolished, some 615 kilograms—more than 3 million carats—of diamonds had been produced. Between 1832 and 1936 more than five times as many stones were mined in Brazil, but the industry was less significant than it had been in the eighteenth century, for the opening of the rich South African fields after 1870 caused a permanent drop in the level of world prices. Only the allegedly superior quality of Brazilian gems prevented the ruin of the industry in the waning years of the empire. Since 1900 industrial diamonds have accounted for the bulk of Brazilian production.

Leather is one of the few consistently important Brazilian exports for which there has been a large domestic market since colonial times. The long colonial period has been called the age of leather. In Europe as in America hides and skins were then the best available material for the fabrication of impermeable clothing and a vast array of utilitarian and luxury items now made of textiles, metal, or plastics. Cattle have supplied the overwhelming percentage of the leather produced in Brazil, although from the earliest days of Portuguese exploration the skins of wild animals were included on the export lists, and since the nineteenth century goat and sheep skins have been exported in quantity.

For more than a hundred years after colonization began in Brazil the production of leather was incidental to the production of cattle as draft animals and for meat. Nearly all of the hides appear to have been used locally. Substantial amounts of leather were exported from the Northeast during the period of the Dutch occupation, but the royal decree of 1680—prohibiting the use of hides processed outside the empire—suggests that supply did not yet equal demand for leather in all parts of the colony. By the second quarter of the eighteenth century, however, the herds in Bahia and Pernambuco were so numerous that many cattle could be slaughtered just for their hides. In 1711 Andreoni had observed that a good cured hide sold for about half the price of the animal that produced it. Two decades later the hide alone was worth one-third more than the live animal. After 1725, when the Portuguese occupied Rio Grande do Sul and began serious exploitation of the herds of wild cattle on the southern pampas, the hide trade, both legal and contraband, expanded prodigiously. By 1777, when nearly 290,000 hides were shipped to Portugal, the trade was second in value to sugar. Simonsen states that the legal trade in hides exported from Brazil averaged about £100,000 annually in the eighteenth century, and reached £15 million for the colonial period.

In addition to those hides sold as leather, and registered as such in the customs records of the Portuguese empire, many more were used as wrappings or containers for other commodities that were exported in vast quantities. Throughout the colonial period and well into the nineteenth century most of the tobacco and cotton and at least a portion of the other products exported from Brazil were shipped in cowhides. On the average it required half a hide to wrap one roll of tobacco and one or two whole hides to cover a bale of cotton. Until the opening of the railroads the sugar, coffee, and other products carried from the interior to the ports on pack animals were invariably transported in leather bags or in boxes covered with leather. Often they were sent abroad in the same containers. Some grades of sugar, for example, were frequently exported in large leather sacks, as was all coffee until fiber bags were introduced after 1820. There is no accurate estimate of the number or value of hides consumed in this manner, but the totals probably approximated those of the legitimate hide trade for the colonial period.

Two distinct trends may be discerned in the pattern of Brazilian leather exports from the latter years of the colonial era to about 1930. One was the generally uninterrupted rise in the quantity of hides and skins shipped abroad. The second, reflecting the varying fortunes of other export items, was the slow decline and then recuperation in the relative standing of leather in Brazil's foreign trade. Neither trend appears to have been directly affected by the political changes from colony to kingdom in 1815, from kingdom to independent empire in 1822, or from monarchy to republic in 1889. Leather ranked third on Brazil's export lists in 1808, when it was estimated that over 700,000 hides were exported annually from Rio de Janeiro and Bahia. A decade later, when more than half a million hides were shipped from the capital alone, leather ranked fourth. In the next seventy years the value of leather shipments increased by tenfold, while leather dropped to sixth place behind coffee, sugar, cotton, rubber, and tobacco. By 1902 Paraguayan tea and cacao had also surpassed leather among Brazilian exports, depressing it to eighth rank. At this point, however, the downward trend was checked. Coffee and rubber continued to dominate

Brazilian trade by a wide margin in the years before World War I, but sales of the other five commodities either declined absolutely or failed to keep pace with the expansion of the leather industry. By 1910 the nation's cattle herds had grown to at least 15 million head, Rio Grande do Sul alone was exporting about a million hides a year, and total exports of hides and skins exceeded 35,000 tons. Leather was again in third place on the export lists. In 1918, after the collapse of the rubber market, leather advanced to a weak second position behind coffee. During the 1920's, as the cattle population was rising to 40 million head, an average of over 50,000 tons of hides and 4000 tons of skins were exported annually. This volume accounted for less than 5 per cent of total exports, but was sufficient to maintain leather as Brazil's second export commodity by value, until after 1930.

Cotton, indigenous to Brazil, was among the first items exported from the colony, but it did not become a leading article of trade until late in the colonial period. Although cotton grew readily in all parts of Brazil—and thrived in the North and Northeast, where almost ideal conditions of climate and soil prevailed—for 200 years the colonists raised little more than the amount required to clothe the slaves and lower classes. There was limited demand for cotton in Portugal in the sixteenth and seventeenth centuries, and even this was reduced by the Methuen Treaty of 1703 that gave England a virtual monopoly to supply the textile needs of both Portugal and Brazil. It was the Industrial Revolution, reflected in the tremendous expansion of the textile industry in England after 1750, that created an unprecedented demand for raw cotton. In Portuguese America the boom was felt first in Maranhão, where by 1771 cotton shipments were valued at £50,000. Seven years later they had risen to £120,000, and the market was still rising. Exports from Maranhão reached £200,000 by the turn of the century and nearly £800,000 in 1818. Meanwhile cotton plantations had been established in every province from Pará to Rio de Janeiro. Cotton accounted for one-fifth of Brazil's exports by value in 1796, and 28 per cent at the highest point in 1805. At that time it ranked ahead of sugar among exports from Pernambuco, where provincial revenues had doubled in only fifteen years. By 1817 Pará was exporting more than 3000 tons of cotton and Rio de Janeiro well over 4500 tons. In 1820 Rio de Janeiro alone shipped 6700 tons, much of it from Minas Gerais. According to Simonsen, the total value of cotton exports during the colonial period was £12 million. The great bulk of this sum was earned in the half-century before 1820.

The end of the first cotton cycle coincided closely with the founding of the Brazilian empire in 1822. The two events, however, were unrelated except in time, for the creation of the empire was a deliberate act taken in response to political changes in Brazil and Portugal, while the crisis in the cotton trade arose from a sharp break in world prices over which Brazil had no control. The basic factor here was competition from the United States, which had surpassed Brazil in volume of exports as early as 1800 and had gone on to become the leading cotton producer in the world by the 1820's. With virgin lands, better transportation facilities, and modern techniques of cultivation and processing, planters in the United States could produce cleaner cotton at lower prices than their Brazilian rivals. This situation, as well as competition from Egypt and India, coupled with political unrest and revolutions at home, severely affected the Brazilian cotton industry in the early decades of the empire. Although cotton continued to rank third or fourth among commodities in Brazil's foreign trade, the level of exports decreased steadily through the 1840's, when only 111,000 tons were sold abroad in the entire decade. By 1845 the world price was barely adequate to pay production costs and shipping charges on cotton from northern Brazil. In the 1850's, with political stability in Brazil and a rising demand for cotton in Europe, shipments rose by about a third, but retained their modest position on the export lists, producing slightly less income than hides and only one-eighth as much as coffee.

The second cotton cycle began after 1860, when civil war effectively eliminated the United States as a source of raw cotton for the English market. British firms looked to Brazil as an alternate source of supply and took direct action to increase production by providing improved seeds and credit to planters. They were particularly active along the new railroads in São Paulo province, which became a major center of cotton culture in Brazil. The cotton boom lasted for about fifteen years. In the 1860's exports more than doubled and income quadrupled over the levels of the preceding years. About 289,000 tons of cotton were shipped abroad during the decade, the largest quantity for any comparable period before 1930. The peak years came between 1864 and 1874, when cotton ranked second among Brazilian exports, producing 40 per cent as much income as coffee in the same span and about half of all income earned from cotton shipments during the entire imperial era.

There was near panic among Brazilian cotton planters as the Civil War in the United States drew to a close. Between January and April 1865 the price of cotton in Brazil dropped by more than one-third, largely in anticipation that the United States would quickly regain a commanding position in the European market. To protect themselves against the crash, which they viewed as imminent and inevitable, many planters in São Paulo began to shift to coffee production. While they did not abandon cotton entirely or at once, there was a noticeable decline in output in the province as early as 1867, and a substantial drop after 1870. Elsewhere production remained high, but was less remunerative as rising exports from North America again depressed the world price structure. By about 1875 the value of cotton shipments from Brazil was only one-third the average for the previous decade, and cotton had fallen to fourth rank behind coffee, sugar, and rubber.

The crisis in the cotton industry, however, was not as drastic as it had been half a century earlier. The pattern of shipments was erratic after 1875, and cotton usually ranked no more than fifth or sixth in Brazil's export trade, but the volume of foreign sales was consistently well above the pre-1860 level. Total production, moreover, actually increased to meet the demands of the growing domestic textile industry, which largely offset the loss of revenue from exports. In 1865 there had been only eleven small cotton mills in all of Brazil. Twenty years later there were forty-nine mills, and by 1905 the number had risen to one hundred, of which two-thirds were concentrated in Minas

Gerais, São Paulo, Bahia, and Rio de Janeiro. In the thirty years ending in 1903 the consumption of Brazilian cotton textiles trebled, while the output of raw cotton increased by 61 per cent.

After 1900 Brazil remained one of the leading cotton-producing areas of the world, yet cotton seldom placed higher than sixth among exports before 1930. In the years prior to World War I the overseas market was strong, but with the outbreak of hostilities in Europe exports from Brazil dropped to insignificant levels, from which they did not recuperate until 1920. During the decade beginning in 1921 cotton was Brazil's eighth export product by value, even though 228,000 tons were sold abroad—the largest ten-year total since the 1880's. In 1930, when over 125,000 tons of cotton were produced in Brazil, approximately 30,000 tons were exported. Domestic consumption accounted for the balance of the crop.

Since 1930 cotton has again become one of Brazil's leading exports, consistently holding second rank after coffee. In the depression decade the abrupt drop in world commodity prices and the dwindling market for such traditional export items as tobacco, sugar, and hides coincided with a sharp rise in the demand for cotton. Germany, Italy, and Japan were the major consumers of Brazilian cotton in the years before World War II. Between 1931 and 1940 cotton accounted for 14 per cent of Brazil's foreign exchange earnings as production soared to previously unknown levels and exports increased sevenfold to more than 1.5 million tons. In the 1940's cotton provided only 11 per cent of the nation's exports by value, even though shipments continued to expand to a record high of nearly 2 million tons to meet the wartime needs of the Allies and the postwar requirements of Europe and Japan. After 1950 cotton exports declined erratically to total about 1.2 million tons for the decade. During the same period, however, production continued to rise. In the 1960's production approached 2 million tons annually, of which about 30 per cent was shipped abroad.

Rubber provides the most striking example of the "boom and bust" phenomenon in the Brazilian economy since the end of the colonial period. The rise and fall of the rubber industry is the classic case

cited by Brazilians as evidence of the prodigality and lack of foresight
that has caused them time and again to lose a natural monopoly of a
valuable product and to be displaced in the world market by efficient
foreign competitors. One critical authority, Caio Prado Júnior, states
that the story of rubber in Brazil is a more fitting subject for historical
novels than for economic history.

Natural rubber is derived from latex, a liquid substance found in the
bark of various trees and shrubs native to the tropical rain forests of

the Western Hemisphere. The most important of these is the *Hevea brasiliensis*, which grows throughout the Amazon basin. From time immemorial the Indians of this vast region used rubber as a waterproofing material for patching canoes, and by the end of the colonial period the Portuguese in the valley had learned to use it for making boots, but elsewhere, until the nineteenth century, rubber was regarded as an exotic novelty of scant commercial value. The chance discovery in 1823 of the method for impregnating textiles with rubber to make them impermeable created a small market for this commodity in Europe. It was not until the vulcanization process was discovered in 1842, however, that rubber became a prime industrial raw material and an important article in international trade. Thereafter, the rapid rise in the demand for rubber in Europe and North America was reflected in the mounting volume of exports from Brazil, which was virtually the only source of rubber in the world before 1900. From an initial shipment of 31 tons in 1827, Brazil's exports of rubber rose to nearly 1500 tons in 1850, 3000 tons in 1867, and about 7000 tons in 1880. In the latter year rubber ranked a weak third behind coffee and sugar among commodities in Brazilian commerce. Almost all of the rubber shipped from Brazil originated in the provinces of Amazonas and Pará, where the population at least doubled, exports expanded fivefold, and provincial revenues increased by fifteen times in the last two decades of the empire. On a per capita basis the value of exports from these two jungle provinces in 1888 was higher than that of Argentina and more than twice that of the United States. And the rubber boom was just getting under way as the empire drew to a close.

The boom days of the rubber cycle in Brazil lasted for nearly three decades, from the 1880's to 1910. This period witnessed the invention of the pneumatic tire, which made possible the bicycle craze and the introduction of the automobile in the industrialized countries of the world, causing a sustained and unprecedented demand for rubber far in excess of available supplies. What had been a profitable industry now became a highly lucrative one. During the early years of the republic the fortunes of the rubber "barons" of the Amazon rivaled those of the coffee "kings" of São Paulo, and for a time Manaus, nearly a thousand miles from the sea, was the richest and most modern city in Brazil, with electric lighting, tramways, a fabulous opera house, and the latest Paris fashions. By 1890 annual exports were running about 17,000 tons and rising, to average well above 20,000 tons per year in the next decade. Between 1901 and 1910 a total of 345,079 tons of raw rubber, valued at more than £13 million, was shipped from Brazil. Rubber was easily the republic's second export by value, producing 28 per cent of foreign exchange earnings from 1905 through 1909. The following year, when prices reached an all-time high, Brazil accounted for 88 per cent of the world supply, and rubber represented nearly 40 per cent of Brazil's exports, yielding almost as much income as coffee.

Rubber gathering in Brazil was an extractive industry in which output depended more upon the availability of labor than upon the customary rules of supply and demand for the new raw material itself. The spurt in production in the 1880's resulted largely from the influx of tens of thousands of refugees from the prolonged drought that scourged Ceará after 1877. In the ensuing years, as the boom continued and employers recruited actively in other parts of Brazil and abroad for rubber workers, additional thousands from the Northeast and adventurers from all areas of the world were drawn to the Amazon to supplement the thinning ranks of *caboclos* and native Indians in the valley. Large profits were made by the individuals and corporations wealthy enough to acquire promising tracts of forest lands and to advance passage, tools, weapons, food, and liquor to the rubber gatherers. Few of the latter, however, survived the system of debt peonage and the hazards of life in the jungle to win the fortunes they sought. Invariably the rubber worker—known as a *seringueiro*—was in debt before he reached the isolated stretch of river bank where he lived alone for up to six months at a time. Each man tended two strings of erratically spaced Hevea trees, which were tapped on alternate days. The trees were seldom less than ten minutes apart in the dense forest. The *seringueiro* also prepared his own crude shelter, hunted for much of his food, and gathered oily nuts and wood for the smoky fire over which the day's collection of latex was cured and formed into large balls. These he was obliged to sell to the company agent at the end of the season, a transaction that was nearly always a simple bookkeeping operation, for the harvest was rarely sufficient to cancel his debt. The *seringueiro* had little hope of escape. He might flee to another part of the valley, there to begin the process anew with a different employer, but if he tried to leave the Amazon he was subject to arrest by authorities downstream. As a general rule the rubber gatherer remained, growing deeper in debt each year until he met death by accident or disease. Under this inequitable and inefficient system, Brazil was never able to realize the full potential of its immense forest resources or to satisfy the world demand for natural rubber. Nonetheless, as long as rubber prices continued to rise, the lure of wealth in the Amazon attracted enough new workers each year to replace the casualties and to permit a steady expansion in output.

Rubber gave great economic significance to the Amazon basin for the first time, and brought the threat of war to the nations and colonies with conflicting territorial claims in that vast region. Since the Treaty of San Ildefonso in 1777 it had been generally recognized that most of the Amazon Valley was part of Brazil, but neither Brazil nor its neighbors had felt an urgent need to determine the precise location of their boundaries. Before the rubber boom the region was sparcely settled at best, and the border zones were practically uninhabited. Initially, the rubber exported from the Amazon had come from indisputably Brazilian territory in the lower valley, but before 1900 scores of thousands of Brazilian *seringueiros* had pushed to the outer reaches of the Amazon watershed to occupy territory also claimed by Bolivia, Peru, Ecuador, Colombia, Venezuela, and British Guiana. It is no coincidence that long-standing boundary questions with all of Brazil's neighbors in the Amazon basin were resolved—most often by diplomatic means and usually to Brazil's advantage—during the heyday of the rubber cycle in the first decade of the twentieth century.

The richest of the contested areas was Acre, a region of some 73,000 square miles, nominally part of Bolivia but separated from the inhabited portions of that republic by almost impenetrable jungles. At the turn of the century Brazilian rubber gatherers comprised nearly the entire population of about 60,000 persons. In 1899 and again in 1902 they rebelled, declared Acre independent, and petitioned for annexation to Brazil. The government of Brazil officially ignored the first incident, but when troops were dispatched from La Paz in 1903 to put down the second rebellion, the Brazilian army occupied and administered the territory while diplomats of the two nations negotiated a peaceful settlement. By the Treaty of Petropolis in 1903 Bolivia ceded Acre to Brazil in exchange for lands bordering on the Madeira River, a Brazilian commitment to construct the Madeira-Mamoré railroad—thus providing an outlet for rubber from the Bolivian forests—and an indemnity of $10 million. Revenues from Acre, which produced more rubber than either Amazonas or Pará, amply compensated the Brazilian government for the costs of acquiring the disputed territory.

The end of the Brazilian rubber boom was in sight even while prices and exports were rising to the peaks they would reach, respectively, in 1910 and 1912. The cause was competition from British rubber plantations in Asia, which entered production in 1900. Ironically, the source of plantation rubber was the *Hevea brasiliensis* developed from seedlings smuggled out of Brazil in 1875 and after. With efficient management and abundant, cheap labor, the plantations quickly outstripped Brazil in total output, although the quality of the Brazilian wild rubber was long regarded as the highest in the world. From a yield of only four tons in 1900, plantation production rose to 145 tons in 1905, 8000 tons in 1910, and 28,000 tons in 1912. In 1913 the volume of exports from Asia surpassed those from Brazil for the first time, and thereafter soared to previously unknown heights. Because of the unusual demand for rubber during the war years, Brazilian exports dropped only moderately from the high of 43,000 tons in 1912 to average over 31,000 tons per year from 1913 to 1920. Through the next decade exports ran about 20,000 tons annually, but by 1930 Brazil was shipping less than 15,000 tons to account for under 1 per cent of the world supply. The decline in exports, while serious, was far less drastic than the fall in prices, which plummeted from an average of $4.42 per kilogram in 1910 to $1.40 in 1913, and $0.30 in 1921. In the 1920's world prices fluctuated somewhat, but tended to remain near the lower figure. Well before 1930 rubber had fallen to an insignificant position on Brazil's export lists, and the Amazon Valley had ceased to play an important role in the national economy.

When rubber prices broke, the exporters called upon the government to save them from an untenable position. In 1912 an attempt was made to shore up the price structure through a government-sponsored valorization scheme similar to that used to protect coffee producers. But it was already too late, and each year Brazil exerted less influence on the world price for rubber. Out of inertia, most producers continued to use the traditional, inefficient methods of rubber collection. A few turned to the *mangabeira* shrub—another source of latex—and established plantations in Piauí and Ceará, but these never accounted for more than 5 per cent of the national output. Henry Ford, in 1927, was the first to try to establish a large scale plantation rubber industry in the Amazon Valley using the *Hevea brasiliensis*. Employing the latest techniques in agriculture, medicine, and management, Ford demonstrated that the environmental problems could be conquered, but he was unable to overcome the perennial labor shortage and the nomadic proclivities of the local populace. After nearly twenty years the experiment was finally abandoned, for it had proved impossible—even at the artificially high prices paid for rubber during World War II—to attract and hold enough laborers to make the plantations economically feasible. The Brazilian rubber cycle came to a definite close in the 1950's when Brazil became a net importer of natural rubber.

Of the regional products that have figured prominently in Brazil's export trade, cacao ranks second only to rubber. There are numerous parallels between the two commodity cycles and their impact on the economy and society of the nation. Both cacao and rubber are tropical forest products indigenous to the Amazon Valley. Both were known during colonial times, but neither became a major export item until after the founding of the republic. Each cycle brought economic prosperity and social injustice to a depressed area of Brazil, and has since inspired stirring literature of social protest. And, in both instances, during the first quarter of the twentieth-century European colonies in the Eastern Hemisphere far surpassed Brazil in production for the world market.

The similarities, however, are perhaps less significant than the differences between the cacao and rubber cycles. In Brazil rubber remained primarily a forest commodity, collected from the same area and by the same methods employed in the colonial era. Originally, cacao was harvested in a similar fashion in the Amazon basin, but plantation culture was introduced at an early date in Pará, Maranhão, and Bahia. The latter state has long since become the center of production, for there the cacao tree encountered an ideal environment and yielded much more than in its native habitat. Even though cacao was not an outstanding article of colonial commerce, it appeared consistently among the exports of Brazil from the mid-seventeenth century, and produced more income than rubber until after 1850. In contrast to its position in the rubber market, Brazil was never the sole or leading producer of cacao, being surpassed by Ecuador and São Thomé until the second decade of this century and thereafter by the Gold Coast of West Africa. Within Brazil, moreover, cacao has not placed higher than third among major exports for any decade in the nation's history. More significantly, the world market for cacao has continued to expand somewhat faster than production. Consequently, while prices have fluctuated, there has been no sharp or prolonged decline to mark the end of the Brazilian cacao cycle.

Cacao, from which chocolate is made, was first introduced into Europe from Mexico in the 1520's, and for more than a century Spain's American colonies held a monopoly of the world supply. A small export trade from Portuguese America began after the 1650's when missionaries and slave hunters found wild cacao trees in the Amazon Valley. The volume of shipments rose gradually as permanent settlements and a few plantations were established, but despite frequent royal directives to increase output, cacao production in the colonial period remained limited. The missions, with relatively large numbers of Indians to collect the wild fruit, appear to have provided most of the cacao exported from the colony. Cacao was classed—along with vanilla, cloves, pepper, cinnamon, indigo, and various medicinal herbs —as one of the "drugs of the *sertão*." According to Simonsen, the combined export value of all commodities in this category did not exceed £3.5 million in the colonial period.

In the century after Brazil became independent the volume of cacao exports expanded nearly sixtyfold, from an annual average of about 1100 tons in the 1820's to more than 63,000 tons in the 1920's lifting cacao to third rank in the nation's foreign commerce. During the same period the huge states of Amazonas and Pará were displaced as the principal source of cacao by the coastal area of southern Bahia—a region, once included in the captaincies of Ilhéus and Pôrto Seguro, that had remained virtually unexplored through most of the colonial era. Cacao had been planted there late in the eighteenth century, and figured inconspicuously among exports to Portugal as early as 1806. By 1825, when a modest 26 tons were shipped to Great Britain, Bahian planters were supplying 2 per cent of the cacao exported from Brazil. In 1890 Bahia produced more than Amazonas and Pará together, and by 1926 provided 98 per cent of Brazil's cacao exports. The movement of the cacao frontier inland from the coast was steady but not spectacular during the years of the empire, for planters in Bahia faced the same labor shortage problems that plagued the Amazon rubber industry. The long drought in the northeastern *sertão* beginning in 1877, and the abolition of slavery in 1888, however, stimulated cacao production by making impoverished, migrant laborers available in large numbers. The bonanza period of unrestricted expansion of the cacao zone—so graphically portrayed in the novels of Jorge Amado—began in the 1890's and continued for a generation. While cacao exports from Brazil as a whole quadrupled in thirty years, those from Bahia increased by fifteen times, rising from 3500 tons in 1890 to 13,000 tons in 1900, 25,000 tons in 1910, and 53,000 tons in 1920. In the latter year Brazil was easily the second largest producer in the world. For a time it seemed that cacao might become as important as coffee in Brazil's foreign trade, and that Bahia might rank with São Paulo in wealth and political prominence. But this dream was not to be realized. In the face of competition from the Gold Coast, where production soared from 13 tons in 1895 to more than 220,000 tons in 1925, Brazil barely retained its share of the international market. During the 1920's when exports from Ilhéus and Salvador ranged between 42,000 and 75,000 tons per year, Brazil accounted for slightly over 13 per cent of the cacao moving in international trade, just as it had done in the years preceding World War I.

The Brazilian cacao boom was over before 1930, but the cycle persisted with output and sales continuing to rise in response to growing world demand. Exports surpassed 100,000 tons for the first time in 1935. In the decade ending in 1970 cacao was being shipped in larger quantities than ever before but accounted for a steadily dwindling portion of Brazil's expanding export trade.

The history of coffee in Brazil is invariably written in superlatives, for coffee dwarfs all other commodities, past and present, in the export economy. The value of coffee shipments from Brazil during the sixty-seven-year span of the empire alone was at least equal to that of all exports for the entire colonial period. Rubber is the only product that has briefly challenged the preponderant position of coffee in the nation's foreign trade, and even at the peak of the rubber boom coffee was the leading export, as it has been each year since the 1830's. Coffee has earned more than half of Brazil's foreign exchange income in every decade but one since 1870. Brazil, moreover, has long been by far the ranking coffee-producing country on the globe. Between 1850 and 1950 it regularly contributed from about half to more than three-quarters of the world supply. Thus, inevitably, changes in world coffee prices have had a direct and often dramatic impact on the national economy.

Coffee, native to Ethiopia, appears to have been introduced into the Western Hemisphere by the French, who established plantations in their Caribbean colonies before 1700. Haiti was the chief source of coffee from America until its plantation economy was destroyed by revolution and slave revolt in the 1790's. According to the traditional account, the Brazilian coffee industry began in Pará with a few seeds that Francisco de Mello Palheta brought from Cayenne in the 1720's. The first exports were in 1750, when twelve tons were sent to Portugal. Coffee subsequently spread to Amazonas, Ceará, Pernambuco, and Bahia, where it developed as a minor export commodity before the end of the colonial period. Bahia, for example, exported some eighty tons of coffee in 1806. But the Amazon basin and the Northeast were not to become important coffee-producing regions, for better conditions of soil and climate were found farther south. Coffee seedlings were planted in Rio de Janeiro in 1770, and within a few years the new crop was being raised on scattered plantations, or *fazendas,* on the coastal lowlands, the steep hillsides of the Paraíba Valley, and the rolling slopes of southern Minas Gerais. By 1809 the coffee frontier extended to Campinas on the São Paulo plateau. The rapid expansion of coffee culture in the Rio de Janeiro hinterland was comparable only to the explosive growth of the cotton industry then taking place in Maranhão and northeastern Brazil. In 1796 about 127 tons of coffee were exported from the colonial capital. A decade later over 1200 tons were shipped, and new levels were reached nearly every year. Brazilian coffee producers profited directly from the troubles in Haiti during this period. Not only did Haiti disappear as a serious competitor for the European market, but the quality of the coffee from Rio de Janeiro was markedly improved by the adoption of processing techniques introduced by a refugee planter from the French colony. Johann von Spix, the Bavarian naturalist who visited Brazil in the last years of Portuguese rule, observed that coffee ranked third after cotton and sugar among exports from Rio de Janeiro in 1817, when over 4300 tons were sold. In the remaining five years of the colonial period nearly 35,000 tons of coffee passed through the same port. Simonsen estimates that £4 million worth of coffee was shipped from colonial Brazil, and that 80 per cent of the total was exported after 1812. Thus, in the final decade of the colonial era coffee produced nearly as much income as all the cacao and other "drugs of the *sertão*" extracted from Brazil in the preceding three centuries.

The expansion of the coffee industry continued at an accelerated rate after the empire was established. The rising market for coffee, and the simultaneous depression of world prices for cotton and sugar, led to a veritable "coffee rush" into the mountain valleys near Rio de Janeiro, where land values soared and the demand for slaves increased each year. Despite adverse political factors—sporadic revolts at home and the government's treaty commitment to outlaw the African slave

traffic—the forested slopes of the proven coffee zone were denuded and planted to the new crop, while tens of thousands of slaves were imported as plantation workers. Under this impetus the empire rapidly outstripped all other areas in coffee production. In 1826 Brazil provided one-fifth of the world's coffee. By 1830 it had become the leading producer, supplying about 40 per cent of the total, and before 1850 Brazil was exporting half of the coffee that entered the world market. Annual shipments increased some eightfold in four decades, rising from an average of 19,000 tons in the 1820's to 58,000 tons in the

1830's, over 100,000 tons in the 1840's, and 158,000 tons in the 1850's. Coffee, which accounted for 18 per cent of Brazil's exports by value in 1822, comprised 49 per cent in the 1850's. In the course of the coffee boom the Paraíba Valley became the richest agricultural area in Brazil, and its new class of wealthy landowners—whose activities accounted for much of the national income—began to challenge the traditional predominance of sugar planters in the economy, society, and political life of the empire. Increasingly, members of this group were elevated to the ranks of the imperial aristocracy.

During the second half of the imperial era the coffee industry had to adjust to basic changes in the conditions of labor in Brazil. The *fazendas* were manned almost exclusively by slaves before 1850. Thus, the abolition of the slave traffic in that year—universally recognized as the first step in the eradication of slavery in Brazil—obliged coffee producers to develop a new source and system of plantation labor. The transition was difficult and costly, but by 1888, when slavery was finally abolished, Negro bondsmen had already been largely replaced on coffee *fazendas* by free contract workers from southern Europe. In 1888 over 90,000 European immigrants entered the province of São Paulo, which was becoming the center of a greatly enlarged coffee zone.

The expansion of the area under cultivation was first and foremost a response to the sustained world demand for coffee, but several additional factors also coincided to encourage the westward movement of the coffee frontier in the last years of the empire. These were the growth cycle of the coffee tree, the destructive system of cultivation employed by coffee growers, the availability of prime coffee lands in the interior of São Paulo, and the introduction of the railroad, giving frontier plantations ready access to the seaports. In Brazil the coffee tree grows easily from seed. With a minimum of care it begins to bear at five years, matures in twelve, and continues to produce for another twenty to forty years, or even longer, according to the quality of the soil. The best coffee land proved to be the purplish-red soil (*terra roxa*) that stretched across much of the province of São Paulo. Given the abundance of such land, and the nearly universal desire of coffee growers to extract maximum profits from their investment, *fazendas* were usually operated only as long as yields remained high. In the third quarter of the nineteenth century the older coffee orchards of the Paraíba Valley, which were beginning to suffer the effects of erosion and soil exhaustion, were gradually abandoned, and new ones planted farther inland. While the movement of the coffee frontier did not acquire the characteristics of a rush until the 1890's, it was discernible by 1867, when Santos and São Paulo were joined by rail, and gained momentum as the Paulista Railway pushed its tracks to Campinas and beyond in the remaining years of the empire. By 1886 Santos was the fastest growing port in the nation, although Rio de Janeiro still continued to handle the great majority of all coffee shipments from Brazil.

Until the end of the empire the increase in coffee production in Brazil tended to keep pace with the expansion of the world market. Substantially all of the annual crop was exported every year. Since the founding of the republic, however, output in Brazil and elsewhere has risen faster than consumption, with the result that coffee has experienced the difficulties of overproduction, foreign competition, and drastic world price fluctuations that have long plagued other Brazilian export commodities. The magnitude of the problem may be seen in the fact that in the seven decades from 1891 to 1960 Brazil exported 45,-667,000 tons of coffee, as compared with exports of 10,448,000 tons between 1821 and 1890. The principal innovation in the coffee industry in the twentieth century has been the series of measures taken by the Brazilian government, unilaterally and in co-operation with other nations, to regulate production, exports, and world prices for coffee.

This innovation grew out of the great coffee boom of the 1890's that began when disease destroyed many of the plantations in Asia. The price of coffee doubled between 1887 and 1892, and remained well above previous levels for another several years, setting off an unprecedented increase in new plantings in the state of São Paulo. Output and exports shot upward as the new orchards came into production late in the decade. Brazil's share of the world coffee market was 73 per cent in 1897, and reached its peak at 81 per cent in 1901, when exports exceeded 14 million bags of sixty kilograms each. By 1907 production was running over 20 million bags, of which only 15 million could be sold at the lowest prices in more than two decades. The situation had already called for a radical solution. Representatives of the leading coffee states—São Paulo, Minas Gerais, and Rio de Janeiro—met at Taubaté, São Paulo, in 1906 to agree upon a coffee valorization plan. This was a price-raising scheme, whereby the state governments undertook to purchase a large part of the harvest and withhold it from the market until a compensatory price level was reached. Meanwhile, the establishment of new coffee *fazendas* was prohibited, although no limit was placed on the expansion of existing orchards. The so-called "Taubaté Convention" was extended until 1912, and a similar state-sponsored program was adopted for a short time after World War I. In 1924 the federal government assumed responsibility for maintaining coffee export prices.

The valorization programs were highly successful in the short run but were overwhelmed by a rash of bumper crops in the late 1920's and the world economic depression in 1929. Between 1906 and 1929 coffee continued to average from half to two-thirds of Brazil's exports —ranging from 31 per cent in 1918 to 76 per cent in 1924; Brazil continued to supply from two-thirds to three-fourths of the world's coffee; and Brazilian coffee shipments produced an income of nearly £1 billion. Over a long term, however, coffee valorization could not satisfy the demands placed upon it. The program applied only to Brazil, and even there it failed to provide adequate safeguards against overproduction. By 1925 São Paulo alone was producing more than enough coffee each year to meet the entire world demand of some 21 million bags. Faced with falling prices, a stockpile of about 9 million bags, and a harvest of over 29 million bags, the price support program collapsed in 1930. This situation contributed to the revolutionary climate in which Getulio Vargas seized power in October of that year.

Each administration in Brazil since 1930 has continued to obtain much of its revenue from coffee sales while seeking to reduce the country's great dependence upon its leading product. The Vargas regime concentrated first on the coffee surplus problem. It promoted exports, uprooted old orchards, banned new plantings, destroyed accumulated

stocks, and encouraged diversification of the economy. Between 1931
and 1940, as world prices tumbled to one-third the pre-depression
level, exports increased well over 8 million tons. At the same time approximately half that amount, purchased by the government at a fixed
minimum price, was burned or dumped into the sea. A new step was
taken in 1941, when Brazil joined with other coffee-producing nations
of Latin America to form the Inter-American Coffee Board, which established wartime export quotas. The results of these efforts were seen
in the 1940's. The volume of exports declined for the first time, and
coffee's share of Brazilian foreign trade was reduced to 43 per cent.
After the war, as world prices rose and the new democratic government
in Brazil lifted restrictions on production, there was uncontrolled expansion in the coffee zone. The coffee frontier expanded steadily across
northern Paraná, into Mato Grosso, and even into Paraguay. Simultaneously, coffee production was increasing rapidly in Africa, with the
result that in spite of two severe frost years in Brazil in the 1950's,
world output again surpassed demand, provoking a sharp downturn in
prices late in the decade. Although Brazilian coffee shipments between
1951 and 1960 reached a new high in excess of 9 million tons, to earn
60 per cent of the nation's foreign exchange income, the government
still faced the problem of financing large unsaleable coffee surpluses.
To cope with this situation successive administrations after 1950
worked actively to increase sales to traditional markets, to open new
ones in eastern Europe and the Soviet Union, and to create and
strengthen the new international body of coffee producers and consumers that determines annual export quotas and an acceptable coffee
price. While Brazil remains the leading coffee producer, it now accounts for only about 30 per cent of the total and no longer seeks to
achieve its objectives unilaterally. In participating in international
coffee organizations the chief objective of the Brazilian government
has been to eliminate the violent fluctuations in export earnings that
disrupt the rhythm of economic growth and perpetuate coffee's hold
on the economy.

The recurrent cycles in the traditional export economy reflected
attitudes and material factors deeply ingrained in Brazilian culture and

experience. The "boom and bust" pattern was both cause and consequence of the one-crop or one-product mentality long prevalent among government and business leaders. The government—whether Portuguese or Brazilian, monarchical or republican—regularly derived the bulk of its income from taxes on commerce, and therefore encouraged production of commodities that yielded the largest revenues to the treasury. It established economic priorities by granting or withholding favors to private entrepreneurs. The latter, who early in the twentieth century still perpetuated many concepts and practices of merchant capitalists of sixteenth-century Portugal, were primarily exploiters of natural resources, concerned above all for maximum short-term profits. Quantity was more important than quality. These factors contributed to the tendency to concentrate on one or two new commodities, or old ones for which a new and lucrative market had suddenly opened abroad. As long as Brazil enjoyed a monopoly or decided advantage in the market, it seemed unnecessary to depart from established methods of production, no matter how outmoded and wasteful these might be. If a stand of brazilwood was destroyed, a patch of cotton or gold diggings depleted, or a hillside plantation ruined by erosion, the entrepreneur could always move to a new site. The land appeared endless and its resources inexhaustible. When the Brazilian monopoly or advantage was lost, producers invariably looked to the government to protect them against competition, or to assist them in the costly shift to modern and more efficient techniques. Not until the twentieth century, in the coffee valorization scheme, however, were such appeals effective. A demoralizing by-product of this situation was a feeling of inferiority and frustration amounting to a conviction that Portuguese and Brazilians could not compete on equal terms with foreigners. It was long accepted as a self-evident truth—by Brazilians and foreigners alike—that the Brazilian product must be of lower quality and higher cost than the same commodity produced by the British, Dutch, French, or North Americans. This sense of inferiority was perhaps most apparent in the cotton cycle, when Brazilian producers withdrew voluntarily from the market, convinced beforehand that they would be unable to meet competition from the United States. In these circumstances, once

Brazil had been supplanted as the principal supplier, there was an irresistible tendency to seek a new export article, and to begin a new cycle.

The so-called "colonial mentality," which was a common attitude of Brazilian entrepreneurs until very recently, was shaped in large part by practical considerations that greatly restricted their freedom of action. The demand and price for Brazilian commodities were always determined chiefly in foreign markets over which Brazil was seldom able to exert more than marginal and temporary influence. During the colonial period Portugal served primarily as an intermediary between its American colony and the British and Dutch who commanded commercial outlets throughout northern Europe. After Brazil gained its independence, this role was assumed by Great Britain, and later in part by the United States. Brazil remained a supplier of raw materials, dependent for prosperity on the fluctuating world prices of its major exports. The apparent remedies for this situation—to concentrate on the domestic market, to export a broad range of items, or to lower production costs of the principal commodity—were beyond the reach of Brazilian entrepreneurs during most of the period under review. The internal market was insignificant because most of the sparse population was outside the money economy. The perennial shortage of labor simply did not permit the simultaneous, large-scale production of numerous export items. And the lack of credit and technical services stifled the efforts of the few entrepreneurs who sought to introduce modern, labor-intensive production techniques. Trained agronomists, geologists, foresters, engineers, and other technicians are still in extremely short supply in Brazil. During the colonial period and most of the nineteenth century there were almost none, for these professions were not highly regarded by the educated elite, and were unattainable for the illiterate majority. As a practical matter, the entrepreneur faced with declining output as a result of soil depletion or the exhaustion of easily accessible ores or timber usually had no viable alternatives other than to move and begin the process anew, or to turn to another product. Only in recent decades, with the spectacular growth of population, has Brazil been in a position to attempt conservation practices, crop diversification, and the development of an important domestic market.

The traditional export economy played a dual role in the history of Brazil. On the one hand, it preserved Brazil as an economic dependency of Europe long after political ties with Portugal were severed. On the other, it contributed directly and indirectly at every stage to the exploration, occupation, and development of the country. The dyewood trade first drew Europeans to the coast of Brazil. Sugar, the real treasure of the colony, created the first permanent settlements, built the fortunes of the plantation aristocracy, and financed the importation of millions of African slaves. The sugar industry, moreover, promoted territorial expansion by providing a market for cattle from the northeastern *sertão* and for Indian captives taken by *bandeirantes* throughout the interior of the continent. The gold rush attracted the first large wave of European immigration, and fixed a substantial population in the hinterland. The hide trade, both legal and contraband, supplied an economic basis for expansion southward toward the Río de la Plata, while the European market for exotic forest products added a profit motive to the exploration and settlement of the Amazon. Cotton created a new group of plantation owners from Maranhão to São Paulo, while cacao did the same in the much smaller region of southern Bahia. Coffee filled in much of the empty land from Espírito Santo to Paraná, served as the basis for the development of São Paulo, and provided employment for the millions of Europeans who swarmed into Brazil in the nineteenth and early twentieth centuries. Rubber brought a brief period of prosperity to the Amazon and added Acre to the national territory. Exports regularly financed the government and, after the mid-nineteenth century, paid for the improvements in transportation, communications, and the urban services that made the cities of Brazil fit places in which to live. And it was the investment of profits from the sale of agricultural products, chiefly coffee, that initiated the Brazilian manufacturing industry, which now promises to free the nation from the "boom and bust" cycles that have marked its history.

Chapter 5 • The Immigrant

Brazil, like the United States, is a nation of immigrants. Its society, economy, and political institutions—although modified in the American environment—are almost exclusively of foreign origin. In the past 450 years perhaps as many as 10 million voluntary and involuntary immigrants became permanent residents of Brazil, eventually overwhelming the native peoples by sheer weight of numbers. During the same period the aboriginal population, which did not exceed 1.5 million at the beginning of the sixteenth century, was reduced by conquest, disease, and civilization to a few tens of thousands. While the Indian of Brazil made a much greater impact on colonial society and culture than did his counterpart in British America, his contribution today is expressed chiefly through the Brazilian language, which retains many words and expressions of Tupí derivation, and through his numerous mixed-blood descendants, who preserve primitive folklore and agricultural practices throughout the interior of the country. But these exotic reminders of the former importance of the native inhabitants serve merely as a spice to flavor the dominant European and African strains in the ethno-cultural potpourri that is modern Brazil. Over 99 per cent of the people of Brazil can trace their ancestry wholly or in part to immigrants from Europe, Africa, or the Levant. Even the Japanese, who in 1960 still accounted for less than 1 per cent of the total, are far more numerous and more effective as participants in the national life than are the surviving Amerindians, who exist in remote jungle areas as charges of the Indian Service, a challenge to visiting anthropologists and a curiosity to energetic tourists.

It is impossible to determine the full number of immigrants who have entered Brazil since 1500. During the colonial era no systematic records of entries and departures were kept, and censuses were sporadic and incomplete. Moreover, as yet there has been no serious effort by modern scholars to collect and analyze the statistical data on the colonial period that has survived in the archives of Portugal and Brazil. Information on the slave trade is also fragmentary, in part because much official documentation on the importation of slaves from Africa was destroyed by the Brazilian government after the abolition of slavery in 1888. Nonetheless, the general pattern and the order of magnitude of immigration into Brazil before 1850 is known, and the massive influx of Europeans after that date has been reasonably well documented.

Immigration started with the arrival of the first Portuguese on the coasts of South America. Cabral began the practice of depositing exiles on shore to learn the language and habits of the natives. In the ensuing three decades several scores or more of European men—*degredados* from Portugal and castaways from Portuguese, Spanish, and French ships wrecked in Brazilian waters—inadvertently became residents of the new land. Those who escaped death by starvation or at the hands of the Indians tended to become squaw men. Some, such as Diogo Alvares and João Ramalho, later opted to remain in Brazil rather than to return permanently to their homeland. The first true settlers, including the first European women, migrated to Brazil in the 1530's when the captaincies were founded, while the first substantial groups of Portuguese and the first regular contingents of African slaves arrived after the establishment of the captaincy general in 1549. During the remainder of the sixteenth century a fairly steady flow of emigrants from Portugal and slaves from Africa must have continued to enter

Brazil, for it is estimated that in 1600 the population of the colony, excluding pagan Indians, amounted to about 100,000 persons, of whom some 30,000 were of European descent and 20,000-25,000 were Negro slaves.

During the seventeenth century the population of Brazil roughly tripled to about 300,000 with the number of those regarded as white remaining at about one-third of the total. This suggests that immigration was limited primarily to Negroes, who did not reproduce at the normal rate in Brazil because of the heavy preponderance of males and the short life expectancy among slaves. The expansion of the white population reflected little more than natural growth. There was probably a small net increase as a result of the Dutch effort to colonize the Northeast and of the short-lived Portuguese program to settle families from the Azores in Maranhão. The crown, however, discouraged the entry of foreigners, while few Portuguese were attracted to the colony now that the entrenched sugar aristocracy blocked most avenues of social and economic advancement.

This situation, and the level of immigration, changed drastically with the gold rush at the beginning of the eighteenth century. There are no reliable records of the number of persons drawn from Europe to the gold fields, but students of the period agree that the discovery of the mines in Brazil led to the largest sustained trans-Atlantic migration the world had yet seen. And after the waves of gold seekers had been absorbed, the influx of immigrants continued at a lower but significant level, as peasant families from Portugal and the Atlantic islands were settled in Rio Grande do Sul and larger numbers were lured by rising prosperity to the older coastal towns and agricultural zones of the colony. It is probable that nearly half a million Europeans, preponderantly but not exclusively from the dominions of Portugal, migrated to Brazil between 1700 and 1800, contributing, together with natural growth, to approximately a tenfold increase in the number of white residents of Brazil. The slave population—comprised only of Negroes and mulattos after the abolition of Indian slavery in 1755— expanded even more rapidly during the eighteenth century to meet the needs for service in the mines, on the plantations, and as artisans and domestic servants. According to an official calculation of 1798 there were then 1,500,000 slaves in Brazil. It is likely that two-thirds or more of these were Negroes and that at least half were recent arrivals from Africa, for the average life span of the adult slave was only seven to eight years in most of the activities in which they were employed.

The nineteenth century witnessed the great surge of immigration, both voluntary and involuntary, into Brazil. The tremendous economic expansion during the last years of colonial rule and under the empire could not have occurred without a comparable expansion of the labor force. Until 1850 this requirement was met by rising imports of new slaves from the coast of Africa. Even earlier, in the 1820's the crown had initiated a program to attract non-Portuguese Europeans —chiefly Swiss and Germans—as colonists. The program gained momentum after the slave traffic was abolished in 1850, and took on unprecedented dimensions following the abolition of slavery in 1888. German-speaking immigrants continued to enter the country throughout the century and after, but Mediterranean Europe supplied the bulk of the newcomers, who were directed largely to the burgeoning coffee plantations of São Paulo. The heavy flow started in the 1870's, and in the last decade alone about 1.2 million Europeans, chiefly from Italy, Spain, and Portugal, migrated to Brazil. In 1900 the total population was almost 18 million, or more than five times as large as it had been a century earlier.

The wave of immigration from Europe continued during the years preceding World War I, rising to a peak in the three years from 1911 through 1913, when more than 500,000 entered. It dwindled during the war years but revived again in the 1920's, to average slightly over 100,000 annually in the last four years of that decade. In all, at least 3 million persons migrated to Brazil in the first six decades of the century, three-fourth of them before 1930. The net increase in population, however, was substantially lower than these figures would suggest, for even in the peak years there was a considerable return flow of those who had become disappointed with their adopted homeland. In the 1930's and for a time after World War II the exodus was nearly equal to the number of arrivals. A new development in this century has been the inclusion of Japanese as a major component in the stream of immigration to Brazil. The immigrants and their descendants now comprise the largest Japanese community in Latin America.

Until the beginning of the present century immigration was the major factor in the expansion of the population in Brazil. The information available on living conditions in the colonial and imperial eras indicates that between 1500 and 1900 there was little change in birth and mortality rates or in the life expectancy of the free population. If anything, the frequency of epidemic diseases increased after the mid-nineteenth century. The lack of sanitation probably killed half of the babies within the first year, and smallpox, yellow fever, plague, or other epidemics carried off at least half of the survivors before they reached adulthood. Under the circumstances, without immigration, the population would increase by about threefold every hundred years. After 1900, however, sustained efforts by the government to introduce public water and sewer systems into the larger cities and to eradicate smallpox, yellow fever, and malaria substantially reduced the infant mortality rate, and since World War II the widespread use of antibiotics has not only further lowered the death rate among children but has begun to raise the life expectancy of adults as well. Among the manifold consequences of these developments is the current population explosion, approximately 3 per cent per year. Since 1930 the flow of immigrants into the country has been lower than the average for the eighteenth century, when the population rose from about 300,000 to over 3 million. Yet, since 1900 the population has increased more than fivefold and promises to double again before the end of the century without additional immigration.

The account of immigration in Brazil is inseparable from the history of Negro slavery and the African slave traffic. For more than three centuries these institutions were integral parts of the social and economic structure of the colony, kingdom, and empire. Without exception the present Negro citizens of Brazil and the much larger number of Brazilians who carry some Negro blood in their veins are descended from slaves brought into the country forcefully to comprise the labor force in the plantations, mines, shops, and households of the proper-tied class. Negroes were never listed among voluntary immigrants to Brazil.

It is not known for certain when the first Africans were taken to Brazil. In all probability the earliest to reside there permanently ar-rived from Portugal in the 1530's, for the letters and instructions of the donatories in that decade contain numerous references to the transportation of slaves by colonists traveling to the captaincies. At least two donatories, Duarte Coelho, in 1539 and again in 1542, and Pero de Góis, in 1545, requested Guinea slaves from Lisbon. By the latter year occasional small lots of slaves may have been imported di-rectly from Africa, but the crown did not authorize such transactions until 1559. The first substantial shipment of Negroes to Bahia in 1550 —which marked the beginning of the regular slave traffic to Brazil— was sent by way of Portugal. After 1559, however, slave ships built, manned, and financed by Brazilians plied the south Atlantic annually, carrying human chattel directly from the west coast of Africa to the principal ports of the colony. Since the supply of Negroes was virtu-ally unlimited, the volume of the traffic was governed primarily by the demand in Brazil, although occasional restrictions were posed by the crown and, in wartime, by the fleets of enemy powers.

Until near the end of the colonial period it was taken for granted in Brazil that Negro slavery and the African traffic were indispensable to the prosperity of the colony. From time to time outspoken critics de-nounced the mistreatment of Negroes by brutal masters and overseers, much as they might condemn needless injury to other of God's lesser creatures, but they did not object to the enslavement of Negroes. The few persons who concerned themselves with the philosophical and ethical aspects of Negro slavery defended the institution on two grounds: First, in their view, God had created the African as a "natural slave," and, second, the removal of the Negro from barbarism and his exposure to Christianity more than compensated for his lack of free-dom in Brazil. This attitude persisted in Brazil long after the Indus-trial Revolution and the Enlightenment in Europe had begun to per-suade the political and intellectual leaders of the Western World that

slavery was neither economical nor a morally defensible institution.
When Joaquim José da Silva Xavier—better known as Tiradentes—the
precursor of Brazilian independence, first called for the abolition of
slavery in the 1780's he was regarded as a crank. His political ideas,
including advocacy of a republic, later led to his trial and execution
as a dangerous radical, but few Brazilians were moved by his arguments against slavery.

By the 1820's the views of the educated minority had changed some-what, and numerous sons of the Enlightenment had come to the fore in Brazilian politics. The most distinguished of these was José Boni-fácio de Andrada e Silva, the first prime minister of the empire, who attacked slavery on moral grounds, but recognized that abrupt and total abolition of the institution would bring economic chaos. He rec-ommended prohibition of the African traffic in order to provide time for planters and other users of slaves to develop an alternate labor supply before the inevitable extinction of slavery itself. It is a matter for conjecture when or whether José Bonifácio's advice might have been followed had Brazil been allowed to work out the slavery prob-lem in isolation. But the question was not to be decided by the Brazil-ians alone.

During the first half of the nineteenth century abolition of the slave traffic, and eventually of slavery as well, became the great moral issue of the civilized nations of Europe, and the most serious and exacerbat-ing issue in Brazil's relations with Great Britain. The crusade to rid the world of slavery and the traffic was headed by England, then the leading industrial and imperial power. Impelled by strong humani-tarian and economic motives, England banned the two institutions throughout its vast dominions in the three decades ending in 1837, and exerted continuing pressure on other nations to do the same. By the 1840's nearly all of the European states and most of the young republics in the Western Hemisphere had complied, but Brazil, the United States, and the Spanish colonies of Cuba and Puerto Rico were still recalcitrant. As a practical matter, these countries had already outlawed the African traffic by legislation or treaty, but were unwilling or unable to enforce the ban.

In a series of treaties with Great Britain the Portuguese crown had agreed to end the traffic north of the equator in 1815 and to work toward the total elimination of the slave trade. The new Brazilian mon-archy accepted these commitments in the treaty of November 23, 1826, which called for complete suppression of the African traffic to Brazil within three years. The treaty was to run for fifteen years or until its objective had been attained. The exchange of ratifications was concluded on March 13, 1827, thus making March 13, 1830, the presumed date for termination of the legal slave trade to Brazil. The contracting powers assumed, correctly, that without an uninterrupted flow of replacements from Africa it would be only a matter of time until slavery disappeared from Brazil. In the short run, however, the results were not as expected. In fact, the contraband trade to Bahia from the Guinea coast, north of the Line, was nearly as large as and apparently more lucrative than the earlier legal traffic had been, while the influx of Negroes from Angola into Rio de Janeiro increased so rapidly as the date for extinction of the traffic approached that the market was temporarily glutted. Furthermore, the Angola trade, now illegal and increasingly in the hands of foreigners, revived in the 1830's, notwithstanding the law of November 7, 1831, which declared that all slaves thereafter entering Brazil from abroad were automatically freed. Imports reached new heights after 1845, when the Brazilian government announced the expiration of the treaty and Great Britain set out unilaterally to sweep all slavers from the south Atlantic.

Despite the efforts of the British fleet and repeated directives by Brazilian authorities against the illegal slave trade, the treaty agreements with Great Britain were neither enforced nor enforceable in Brazil before 1850. Various economic, political, and emotional factors coincided to bring about this situation. It was an open secret that some persons in high places had a financial stake in the traffic, although the influence of such men on the policies of the empire was probably less than was commonly believed at the time. More significantly, nearly all officials and bureaucrats had financial or family ties with the plantation owners, who remained sincerely convinced that without Negro slaves Brazil's agricultural economy would collapse. It was accepted as fact that Caucasians were not suited to heavy labor in the tropics. The planter class, seeking to postpone the day when the African source would be shut off, provided the chief market for the illegal trade. Under the circumstances, the regime itself, always hard-pressed for income, may have found it expedient not to force the issue, for the high taxes on the sale and transportation of slaves within Brazil supplied much of its revenue. The basic problem, however, arose from the fact that until mid-century the central government was simply too weak to impose prohibition of the traffic against the will of the large planters, whose support was vital for preservation of the empire. For more than two decades the land forces of the monarchy were fully occupied in suppressing separatist revolts in the provinces, and its naval forces were never adequate to patrol the extensive coastline or to prevent British seizure of Brazilian vessels suspected as slavers. The latter practice, although authorized by treaty, was resented as an affront to national sovereignty, causing rising anti-British feeling during the 1840's and, paradoxically, lending the slave trade a degree of respectability it had not enjoyed as a legitimate branch of commerce. In Brazil, as in the United States at that time, many officials and private citizens who opposed the traffic on moral grounds bitterly protested England's assertion of the right to search and seize slave ships flying the national flag.

British action was the catalyst that brought the issue to a head in 1850. In April of that year the British squadron was authorized to pursue suspected slavers into Brazilian ports, there to be sunk or captured. The immediate outburst of indignation by Brazilian officials, intellectuals, and men of property reflected frustration over the nation's military impotence and humiliation that Brazil had been forced into the position of appearing to condone traffic in human flesh, long since condemned as an abomination by European civilization. The situation was intolerable. Procrastination was no longer possible, and war with England was out of the question. In these circumstances the government of Brazil moved to end the slave trade on its shores once and for all. Although the law of 1831, banning the traffic and providing heavy penalties for its violation, was still technically in force, a new law to this effect—named for its sponsor, Euzébio de Queiroz—was passed by the congress on September 4, and promulgated by the emperor on November 14, 1850. In contrast to the situation two decades earlier, public opinion and the police power now supported the government's actions. Imports of slaves dropped abruptly from 23,000 in 1850 to 3287 in 1851, to 700 in 1852, and to 512 between 1853 and 1856. Thereafter the African traffic ceased altogether.

The effectiveness of the Queiroz Law of 1850 demonstrated both the enhanced authority of the central government and the remarkable change in public opinion since 1830. Several factors contributed to the shift in attitudes toward the slave trade. Perhaps the most important of these was the presence in public offices throughout the empire of a new generation of intellectuals, largely trained in Europe, who objected to the traffic on humanitarian grounds. The members of this elite group were also acutely sensitive to the threat posed to the security, culture, and society of the empire by the continued heavy importation of Negroes from Africa. They expressed their alarm in the press, in public gatherings, and in formal speeches before the national and provincial legislatures. In their view the sharp rise in the number of slaves raised the specter of Negro rebellions, such as those that had broken out repeatedly in Bahia before 1840; the steady increase in the Negro sector of the population was undermining the basically European culture of Brazil; and, the expansion of the slave labor force was the chief deterrant to massive immigration from Europe, which they presented as the panacea to resolve the nation's chronic labor shortage and to check the progressive Africanization of Brazil. They noted further that while Brazil received the full onus of the unsavory traffic, most of the profits were being reaped by foreigners, principally Portuguese, Spaniards, and North Americans. Opponents of the slave trade maintained that even though England's motives in seeking to suppress the illegal traffic were not entirely altruistic, continued defiance of the British ban was not in the best interests of the empire. Once these views were generally accepted by the Brazilian people, it was possible to enforce the laws against the African trade. In the final analysis, it was the enforcement of the law in Brazilian territory rather than the efforts of the British coastal patrols that ended the slave trade across the south Atlantic.

One of the least certain and more controversial subjects in the social history of Brazil concerns the number of Negroes imported during the three centuries from 1550 to 1850. Estimates of the total vary from slightly over 3 million to about 16 million. Recent scholars prefer the lower range, but whether high or low, the estimates for the colonial period are little more than guesses, based on fragmentary and often contradictory indications of the number of slaves, the nature and condition of their employment, and the life span of the Negro in captivity in Brazil. The scattered references of chroniclers, crown officials, ecclesiastics, and foreign observers suggest that the Negro slave was a fairly expensive property, that his life expectancy varied greatly from one occupation or master to another, and that without continued imports the slave population tended to decrease steadily. After the first generation there were many Negroes born into bondage in Brazil—despite the relative scarcity of Negro women and obstacles to marriage or normal family relations between slaves—but such increments were more than offset by heavy losses among adults. The major cause of the losses was death from overwork and disease, although voluntary manumission and the practice of allowing bondsmen to purchase their freedom also led to some reduction in the number of slaves. On occasion an adult Negro might survive for thirty years after reaching Brazil, but a far larger proportion died within the first five years. While the records of the colonial era are replete with the clamors of planters and officials for additional slaves, the colonists seem always to have thought it more economical or less bother to buy new ones than to prolong the effective life of those on hand by better treatment. The average life span of the adult male Negro in Brazil appears to have been mercifully brief during the sixteenth century and to have lengthened only gradually to more than a decade by the end of the colonial period. Differences of opinion on this point—and thus on the number of replacements necessary to sustain a rising slave population—by authorities on slavery in Brazil, largely account for the great disparity between the estimates of the number of involuntary African immigrants to the colony and empire.

While it is not possible to state categorically how many Negroes were taken to Brazil, the existing evidence permits a reasonable approximation of the trend and volume of the traffic to 1850. It is generally accepted that the Negro population was on the order of 14,000 in the 1580's and had not yet doubled by 1600, even though 70,000 to 80,000 new slaves were shipped from Angola for Brazil between 1575 and 1591. Less than half of them reached Brazil, for at least 20 per cent died on the Atlantic passage and many more were taken illegally to Spanish America, but Angola was then neither the only nor most important source of slaves for Brazil. In all probability several tens of thousands of Negroes were shipped to Brazil from various embarkation points in Africa before 1590, and the rate of imports must have risen considerably to account for the striking increase in sugar production in the following decade. Imports could scarcely have been less than 80,000 from 1550 to 1600, and may well have exceeded 100,000. Brazilian slaveholdings expanded slowly in the first half of the seventeenth century, apparently because the traffic was hampered by the conflict with the Dutch in Africa and Brazil from 1621 to 1654. The most generous estimate for the mid-century placed the slave population at about 50,000, of whom two-thirds were Africans. Even under wartime conditions, however, the slave trade continued. It is known that the Dutch brought some 23,000 slaves to Pernambuco in the decade after 1636. Presumably, imports into Portuguese America were on a similar scale at that time, and they must have risen significantly thereafter, for there were 100,000 or more Negroes in bondage in Brazil in 1700. In the absence of any notable improvements in the birth rate or living conditions of slaves in Brazil, there must have been imports of 400,000 to 600,000 during the century to account for this figure, which represented at least a third of the total population of the colony.

While in preceding centuries the trade in Negroes to Brazil had been enormous, in the eighteenth century the number brought to Brazil as labor for the gold and diamond mines and the revived plantation economy exceeded all previous records. The new wealth produced an insatiable market for slaves, as not only the upper class, but virtually all whites, many mulattos, and even some Negro freedmen became slaveholders. Rio de Janeiro, the gateway to the mines, became a major port of entry for slavers, while the traditional plantation zones from Bahia to Maranhão continued to import significant numbers of slaves, with the volume rising after 1760. Angola alone is reported to have supplied over 640,000 Negroes between 1759 and 1803, and it is likely that as many more were brought in from other parts of Africa during those years. In any case, the evidence is clear that the Negro slave population expanded about twelvefold between 1700 and 1798. Thus, it would appear that a minimum of 2,000,000—and probably more than 2,500,000—Negroes entered Brazil in the course of the eighteenth century.

The first ostensibly complete census of the colony, in 1798, revealed 1,010,000 whites, 250,000 civilized Indians, 406,000 freedmen, 221,000 mulatto slaves, and 1,361,000 Negro slaves, for a total of 3,248,000. The accuracy of the figures may be questioned, but contemporary observers agreed that the preponderance of Negro slaves was both large and increasing. This trend persisted through the remaining years of Portuguese rule. Some 38,000 Negroes were said to have entered in the year 1806, when immigration from Europe was negligible. According to the official census ordered by Dom João VI, in 1817-18 there were 3,817,900 inhabitants over ten years of age in the kingdom, as follows: 1,043,000 whites, 259,400 civilized Indians, 585,500 free mulattos and Negroes, and 1,930,000 slaves. The Marquês de Queluz, a member of the royal council, estimated the number of whites at 1 million and the slave population at more than 2 million in 1821. There appears to have been a rapid increase in all categories of the population in the next three decades. Estimates during the last years of the African traffic varied widely, but recent scholarship suggests that there were some 3 million Negro slaves in a total population of about 7 million in 1850.

The influx of foreign visitors to Brazil and the mounting concern of the Brazilian and British governments over the slave trade gave rise after 1810 to a plethora of estimates of yearly imports of Negroes from Africa. Such estimates, often reflecting the reporter's bias against the traffic or against British efforts to suppress it, invariably were drawn from incomplete data and ranged over a broad spectrum. Nonetheless, they confirm that the number of Negroes sold into slavery in Brazil in the first half of the nineteenth century was far greater than the total for any previous fifty-year period. Partial gleanings indicate the rising trend by decades. Between 1810 and 1819, for example, Pernambuco received 22,359 slaves from Angola in a six-year period; Bahia imported over 40,000 Negroes from the Costa da Mina in equatorial Africa in a five-year span; and Rio de Janeiro obtained at least 85,657, chiefly from Angola and Benguela, in seven years. Ostensibly complete figures on imports into the capital are available for each year during the 1820's, when not less than 298,106 Negroes passed through the port of Rio de Janeiro in annual lots that ranged from 18,957 in 1820 to 44,205 in 1829. During the last four years of the decade 38,979 slaves also arrived at Bahia. There are few estimates for the 1830's because of the illegality of the traffic. It is known, however, that Bahia received 8425 slaves in 1830 and that at least 66,903 were landed at or near Rio de Janeiro in 1837-38. By 1840 the volume of the illegal slave trade had reached such proportions that the governments of Brazil and Great Britain, as well as various European anti-slavery societies, again issued periodic reports on the entry of Negroes. The official Brazilian statistics indicated a total of 368,738 in the eleven years from 1840 through 1850. The British figures were somewhat higher. The peak year was 1848, when 60,000 Negroes arrived.

These partial data, together with the estimate of 38,000 for 1806 and the 4499 known to have been imported between 1851 and 1856, account for more than 971,666 slaves taken to Brazil in the last half century of the traffic. The full number for the nineteenth century may have been nearly twice as high, and could not have been less than 1,300,000. Therefore, in the three centuries from the 1550's to the 1850's Brazil must have received a minimum of 3,750,000 Negroes from various parts of Africa. The total probably approached 5,000,000 or roughly comparable to the number of European immigrants absorbed in more than 450 years.

Negro slavery—the major factor discouraging large-scale immigration from Europe—persisted as a legal institution in Brazil for a long generation after the issue of the African traffic had been resolved by the law of September 4, 1850. For a decade and a half no action was taken to relieve those still in bondage. The men who had protested vehemently against the immorality and inhumanity of the slave trade—which had seen losses of 60 per cent and even higher in the 1830's and 1840's—felt no compulsion to emancipate the Negroes who had survived the frightful passage. The capital released by abolition of the slave traffic was now invested heavily in agriculture, contributing directly to the boom in the plantation economy, which was still based overwhelmingly on servile labor. In fact, a new domestic slave trade developed after 1850, as tens of thousands of Negroes were imported from the traditional plantation areas of the North and Northeast to work the thriving coffee *fazendas* in the provinces of Rio de Janeiro and São Paulo. While it was tacitly accepted that slavery must eventually disappear, the question was not regarded as one of great urgency.

This complacent attitude was shaken by the impact of the emancipation proclamation of President Lincoln in 1863 and the Union victory in the Civil War two years later. Except for Spain, which still permitted slavery in its Caribbean colonies, Brazil was now the only Western nation in which slavery was tolerated. The empire was the primary propaganda target of abolition societies in Europe and North America. In these circumstances many Brazilians came increasingly to look upon Negro servitude as contrary to the laws of God and Nature. The rate of voluntary manumissions rose sharply. In view of Brazil's involvement in the bloody Paraguayan War (1864-70), the leaders of both political parties declared a moratorium on proposals to alter the laws affecting slaves. Their action was generally acknowledged as a necessary wartime measure, but did not quiet the mounting protests against slavery as a legal institution. Unexpectedly, the war itself, which strained the manpower resources of the empire, contributed to the emancipation process. Slaves who agreed to serve as soldiers in the conflict were granted freedom in exchange. Some 20,000 Negroes, including the wives of soldiers, were emancipated in this fashion. The crown also helped to keep the slavery issue alive. As early as 1864, on the occasion of the wedding of the princess royal, Pedro II freed the slaves who would normally have been included in her dowry. In 1866, in response to a plea by internationally renowned French abolitionists, the emperor replied that the emancipation of the slaves was only a question of form and the appropriate moment, to be decided at the conclusion of the war. The following year, in his annual address to congress, Pedro II pointedly called attention to the need for the legislators to consider the problem of the "servile element" at an opportune time. The trend was not lost on the political leaders of the nation. In 1869 the Liberal party formally announced that it would seek the abolition of slavery after peace was restored. Meanwhile, on September 15th of that year one of the most offensive aspects of slavery—the public slave auction—was prohibited by law.

With the conclusion of the Paraguayan War in 1870, abolition became the principal political issue of the day. The chief concern of both parties was to devise a formula to promote the gradual emancipation of slaves without violating the property rights of slave owners or seriously disrupting the agricultural economy. The moral and ethical aspects of the problem were subordinated to economic considerations. The result, approved by the congress on September 28, 1871, was the Law of Free Birth (*Lei do Ventre Livre*), also known as the Rio Branco Law for its sponsor, Prime Minister José Maria da Silva Paranhos, the Visconde do Rio Branco. Under this law all children henceforth born of slave mothers were free, although with important limitations on their liberty. Until the age of eight they were to remain in the care of the mothers' master, who could then elect either to employ them in his service without remuneration until they reached age twenty-one, or to emancipate them forthwith in exchange for compensation equivalent to about $300 per child. The slave had no voice in this matter. Compensation was to be paid from a national emancipation fund established by the Law of Free Birth. The law also provided for the immediate emancipation of all slaves of the national government, and further stipulated that slaveholders were obliged to free any bondsman who could earn or borrow his market price. With the passage of this legislation, which seemed to guarantee the extinction of slavery in two generations, public interest in abolition again waned.

The attempt to legislate the gradual extinction of slavery proved unworkable in the Brazilian environment of the 1870's. The abolitionists, who had placed their faith in the efficacy of the Law of Free Birth to destroy an odious but long-established national institution, were placated for several years, but the planters—who owned five-sixths of all slaves in Brazil—remained adamantly opposed to change. They defied the letter and spirit of the legislation by selling young slaves illegally or registering them incorrectly, if at all. Northern sugar and cotton growers, faced with declining markets and prices, felt the law was designed to deprive them of their remaining source of wealth—the slaves they sold in increasing numbers to southern coffee planters. The latter, by and large, refused to consider the shift to wage labor as long as slaves were available. In this situation the imperial government, responsive to the interests and dependent upon the co-operation of the large landowners, was unable to insist upon full observance of the law. In practice, death remained the only escape from bondage for the great majority of slaves in Brazil. This distressing fact was evident in the official figures published by various ministries of the empire. According to the census of 1872 there were then 1,510,806 slaves in Brazil. Twelve years later the slave population was still estimated at about 1,200,000, even though during those twelve years approximately 500,-000 had died and some 90,000 had been manumitted by their masters. Fewer than 20,000 had gained freedom under the provisions of the Law of Free Birth.

Confronted with mounting evidence of this nature, a handful of abolitionists in congress revived the emancipation campaign in 1879, and did not permit it to subside until victory had been won. The leading exponent of abolition was Joaquim Nabuco, a fiery young deputy from Pernambuco, who jeopardized a promising career to pursue the politically hazardous crusade. Among his ablest supporters demanding immediate and unqualified emancipation of all slaves were the Negro, José do Patrocínio, a man of slave parentage described as the most eloquent orator and persuasive writer of the day; Luiz Gama, a self-made mulatto lawyer, the son of a Negro bondswoman, who had been sold into slavery as a child by his Portuguese father; and André Rebouças, a mulatto engineer, one of the prominent intellectuals of the empire. They were later joined by Ruy Barbosa, a journalist and congressman from Bahia, perhaps the most flamboyant statesman-politician Brazil has yet produced. For a decade, under Nabuco's direction, the abolitionists waged an intensely emotional propaganda campaign. In contrast to their predecessors in 1871, they dealt with the question of emancipation above all as a moral issue. Ignoring the economic interests and property rights of slaveholders, they condemned slavery as a moral wrong and a stain on the national honor that must be expunged at all costs.

The movement quickly attracted popular support, particularly among the literate urban population conscious that Brazil was the only Christian nation tolerating slavery. Anti-slavery newspapers were founded and abolitionist societies sprang up in the major cities. By 1883 these were merged in a national confederation capable of exerting pressure on the political parties. The next year the Liberal party endorsed the abolitionist cause. Even earlier, on May 24, 1883, an important breakthrough had occurred when slavery was abolished in the northern province of Ceará. Two years later the provincial government in Amazonas took identical action. The slaveholders finally realized that abolition was imminent. In an effort to stem the rising tide, the Conservative majority in congress, on September 28, 1885, approved a bill it had previously rejected, granting freedom after another three years of service to their masters to all slaves over age sixty.

But it was too late for half measures. The clamor for total abolition continued unabated. With public opinion against them, slave owners began releasing their human chattels by the scores of thousands, until the ranks of free Negroes were nearly double the number of slaves still in bondage. At the same time a flood of runaway slaves deserted the *fazendas,* and the authorities seemed powerless to retrieve them. The end of slavery was clearly in sight by 1887, when army officers refused to lead troops in pursuit of escaped slaves and insisted it was beneath the dignity of officers and gentlemen to employ the national armed forces for such an ignoble purpose. Thus, it was a foregone conclusion that slavery would be abolished entirely when congress met the following year. The famous Golden Law (*Lei Aurea*), extending immediate and unrestricted liberty to all slaves in Brazil, was passed by the Senate and signed by the princess regent on May 13, 1888. By the stroke of a pen over 700,000 slaves, almost exclusively Negroes, were transformed into free subjects of the empire. The former slaveholders re-

ceived no compensation for the loss of human property valued at about
$250 million.

The elimination of slavery contributed indirectly to the political
transition of Brazil from monarchy to republic in 1889, but it provoked
no grave social or economic upheaval. Unlike the situation in other
countries of the hemisphere when slavery was abolished, emancipation
in Brazil was accomplished without bloodshed. There was no division
of region against region, class against class, or race against race. The
ex-slaves, moreover, were accepted by their former owners as members
of a free society without lasting rancor. In these respects it is highly
significant that the abolition campaign was almost entirely a verbal
contest, fought out within the ruling circles of Brazil. The only Negroes and mulattos to play a prominent role in the process were free
men of exceptional talents who had already won a conspicuous place
in society. Although some abolitionists had presumed to take the law
into their own hands, aiding and abetting slaves to escape from their
masters, neither they nor the more responsible leaders of the emancipation movement could be regarded as social revolutionaries. The Brazilian abolitionists considered emancipation as a right that should be
granted to the slave population. Freedom was decidedly not a goal that
slaves should seek to achieve for themselves. Liberty, obtained through
the laborious parliamentary process, was just and sufficient compensation for their long captivity. The Emancipation Law made no provision
for formal education or other training to prepare ex-slaves to meet their
new obligations as self-supporting citizens. Emancipation was to bring
justice to an oppressed people, and incidentally to ease the conscience
of the emancipators, all of whom had been slaveholders at one time.
It was not intended to bring about a substantial change in the Negro's
role in the political, economic, or social life of the nation. Nor was the
ex-slave led to expect any miraculous improvement in his lot.

In these circumstances it is not surprising that both the former slaves
and the former slave owners adapted to the new situation with a minimum of hardship. In the coffee zone, where many freedmen succumbed
to the lure of the cities, European immigrants were soon available to
fill the labor gap. In the older slaveholding areas of the Northeast

there was a temporary dislocation of part of the rural labor force, as liberated slaves, intoxicated by the heady wine of freedom, refused to perform their usual tasks. By and large, however, the freedmen remained on the land or in the households of their former masters, bound as effectively by the familiar ties of dependency, friendship, and godparenthood as they had once been by the legal chains of bondage. For the great majority, life continued in its accustomed routine.

The change in the legal status of the slave, nonetheless, was the most important and far-reaching result of the abolition of slavery, because the Golden Law removed the last formal barrier segregating the slave from the rest of society. Slaves in Brazil had always been relegated to the bottom of the social hierarchy, the victims of discrimination and prejudice, but their plight stemmed from their condition of servitude rather than from race or color. After 1888 there was no longer in Brazilian law or custom any insuperable obstacle to the advancement of ex-slaves as far as opportunity and ability might take them. As a practical matter, opportunity was still rare, for it was extremely difficult to attain the levels of education, wealth, and culture required for acceptance into the middle and upper classes, but these were difficulties faced by all free men regardless of ethnic origin. Had abolition occurred a century earlier, when first proposed, the liberated slaves in Brazil would surely have met much the same social resistance encountered by those in the United States after 1865. In the intervening century, however, colonial restrictions against the social and economic rise of free colored persons—never rigidly enforced in Brazil—had gradually fallen into disuse, and after the abolition of the slave trade the social distance between races had been notably reduced. Commenting on this phenomenon in the 1860's, Agostinho Marques Perdigão Malheiro, the leading authority on slavery in Brazil, observed that persons of color, even slaves, were seen side by side with whites in church and on public conveyances. He added:

> This did not happen in the United States. But there the question was not only one of slavery, it was also one of race; a question that in Brazil is not taken into consideration by the laws or by customs. To be colored, even to be descended from an African Negro, is no reason not

to be someone in our country, to be admitted into societies, into families, on public vehicles, to certain places in the churches, in employment, etc.; far from this, in the Empire the man of color enjoys as much consideration as any other who is his equal; some have occupied and occupy the highest positions in government, in the bureaucracy, in the Council of State, in the Senate, in the Chamber of Deputies, in the Diplomatic Corps, in short, in all positions; others have been and are distinguished physicians, lawyers, illustrious professors of the most advanced sciences; in short, among us the whole field of the application of human activity is entirely free and open to them.*

The trends described by Perdigão Malheiro were still sufficiently novel to merit special comment during his generation. A quarter-century later they had become commonplace. Thus, with the elimination of the legal stigma of servitude in 1888, the ex-slaves could disappear almost unnoticed into the established community of free Negroes and mulattos—which was itself being absorbed through miscegenation into the larger Brazilian population—and the Brazilian people as a whole were able, when social and economic conditions were propitious in the twentieth century, to move without effort or misgiving toward the racial democracy for which they are noted.

Dramatic political changes between 1807 and 1822—sparked by events in Europe and culminating in Brazilian independence from Portugal—could not fail to affect the tone, if not the broad trends, of social and economic development in Brazil. In the course of the Napoleonic Wars, in which Portugal was aligned with England against France, the crown revived an eighteenth-century plan to transfer the seat of the imperial government to its American colony, where it would remain until it was safe to return it to Portugal. The plan was put into effect when a French army under Marshal Junot invaded Portugal in November 1807. As the French approached Lisbon, the fleet bearing the royal family sailed under British escort for Brazil. In March 1808, after a stormy passage and an unscheduled stop in Bahia, the court reached its new capital at Rio de Janeiro. More than thirteen years

* Agostinho Marques Perdigão Malheiro, *A escravidão no Brasil; ensaio histórico-jurídico-social,* 2d ed. (São Paulo, 1944), II, pp. 123-4.

would pass before the crown returned to Lisbon. In this long interval the customary positions of the colony and the mother country were reversed. Brazil was the de facto center of the Portuguese empire and, for all practical purposes, an independent kingdom. Each of the seventeen captaincies of Brazil, as well as the outlying colonies in Africa and Asia, were now governed from Rio de Janeiro, while Portugal, after the explusion of the French late in 1808, was ruled by a regency. With the establishment of direct trade between Brazil and other nations the mother country ceased to serve as an intermediary in Brazilian foreign commerce, and the people of Brazil discovered that Portugal was not essential for their prosperity or well-being. Imperial taxes formerly sent to Lisbon were now sent to Rio de Janeiro, which began to reflect a new affluence, as prosperous landowners established residence in the city in order to be near the court. Brazilians found it much easier than ever before to make their views and needs known to the crown. Despite some discomfiture over the closer supervision caused by the royal presence in Brazil, the Brazilians generally were pleased by the transfer of the court, while the Portuguese were increasingly distressed by the subordinate position to which the metropolis had been reduced. In December 1815, after the final defeat of Napoleon at Waterloo, the prince regent (who was soon to become King João VI) decreed the creation of the United Kingdom of Portugal and Brazil, thereby giving Brazil equal status with Portugal.

This belated recognition of Brazil's position within the empire was extended primarily to make João's sojourn in America less unpalatable to his Portuguese subjects and British allies, who could not understand his reluctance to return to Lisbon. But the Portuguese were not placated, and continued to clamor for the restoration of Lisbon as capital of the empire. Meanwhile, separatist and republican feeling was developing among a vociferous minority in Brazil. It was particularly strong in Pernambuco, where stern measures were required to suppress an armed revolt in 1817. Although Recife was long to remain a regional center of republicanism, Brazilian independence owed far more to the Liberal Revolution of 1820 in Portugal than to the radicals of the Northeast. This movement, which demanded the return of the king and the imposition of constitutional restraints on his authority, initially attracted considerable support throughout Brazil, where sentiment in favor of a constitutional monarchy was on the rise. Unable to stem the tide, João VI embarked for Portugal in April 1821, leaving his heir, Prince Pedro, as regent in Brazil. Shortly before his departure the king advised Pedro to seize the leadership of the independence movement if necessary to preserve Brazil for the House of Bragança.

In retrospect it is evident that during the period from April 1821 to September 1822 Brazil was moving steadily toward political independence. At least four major factors coincided to give the confused and uncertain progression of events the appearance of an inevitable, irreversible trend. The first of these was the general political climate of the day, in which nationalism and self-government were exalted while colonial rule and royal absolutism were being challenged in much of the Western world. Secondly, the ineptness of the Portuguese Liberals, who refused to acknowledge the changes that had occurred in Brazil since 1808, contributed directly to the spread of the independence movement. Brazilian delegates to the constituent assembly in Lisbon were soon convinced that their Portuguese colleagues were determined to restore rigid colonial controls over Brazil. Many Brazilians who would have been content to remain within the empire were alienated by the attempts of the Liberal majority in the Cortes to turn back the clock and erase the gains achieved in Brazil under João VI. For them, the fact that a member of the royal family was head of the government in Brazil, defending the rights of the kingdom against the reactionary pressures of the Cortes, lent the movement for independence an air of respectability it would not otherwise have had. After all, the break with Portugal, if it came, should be only temporary, for Prince Pedro was expected to succeed to the throne upon the death of the elderly João VI. Such considerations doubtless influenced Pedro's decision to lead the forces for independence. He was increasingly convinced that Brazil would break away, with or without him. His role was also determined in large part by the counsel of his prime minister, José Bonifácio de Andrada e Silva, since known as the "Patriarch of Brazilian Independence."

José Bonifácio was an unlikely rebel. A Paulista, at the age of twenty he had gone to Portugal, where he remained for thirty-five years as student, professor, minister of mines, and trusted agent of the crown to various European courts. He was one of the savants of an age that included von Humboldt, Linnaeus, and others whom he numbered among his friends and correspondents. Choosing to remain in Portugal throughout the Napoleonic Wars, José Bonifácio did not return to Brazil until 1819 at the age of fifty-six. There he launched a new career, employing his great prestige and talents in the political movement for independence. Appalled by the violence and bloodletting in the neighboring Spanish American republics, he was convinced that Brazil should remain a monarchy under the House of Bragança. As master of the largest of the Masonic Lodges in Brazil and, after January 1822, head of Pedro's cabinet, he was in a commanding position to influence public opinion and the views of the prince regent. It was on his advice that Pedro defied the Cortes, summoned a constituent assembly for Brazil, and on September 7, 1822, proclaimed Brazilian independence in the *Grito de Ipiranga*.

The prince regent became Pedro I, emperor of Brazil. He was publicly acclaimed on October 12, while the formal coronation took place on December 1, 1822. His stormy reign lasted less than nine years. It was marked by the expulsion of the remaining Portuguese forces in 1823, the promulgation of a constitution issued by the crown in 1824, recognition of Brazil's independence by Portugal in 1825, and the loss of Uruguay in 1828. Pedro's popularity, which began to wane when he forcibly dissolved the constituent assembly in 1823, declined steadily thereafter. By 1831 he had lost the confidence of his subjects, who accused him of being more interested in the affairs of Portugal than in Brazil. In April of that year, a decade after the departure of João VI, Pedro abdicated in favor of his five-year-old son and sailed for Europe. After a series of regents during the 1830's, the young prince ascended the throne in 1840. As Pedro II he was to rule until 1889.

Immigration from Europe to Brazil began with the transfer of the court from Lisbon to Rio de Janeiro during the Napoleonic wars. Even before reaching his new capital, while still at Bahia, the Prince Regent signed the royal decree of January 28, 1808, opening the ports of Brazil to direct trade with foreign countries. With this act, and the treaties of commerce and navigation subsequently signed with friendly powers, Portugal opened the doors of Brazil to foreigners. For the first time the subjects or citizens of other countries were welcome to enter in substantial numbers, to become permanent residents and property owners in Brazil.

Although the change in policy led, by 1822, to the largest influx of foreigners since the Dutch invasion in the seventeenth century, the main stream of newcomers continued to flow from Portugal. In fact, some 15,000 civil and military officials, functionaries, servants, and assorted hangers-on at court accompanied the royal family in its flight from Junot's army in November 1807. And in the next thirteen years, while Rio de Janeiro was the capital of the Portuguese empire, nearly 10,000 more migrated from the mother country to Brazil. Yet, except for the circumstances of their departure from Europe and the high proportion of the noble and well-born among them they differed little from the hundreds of thousands of Portuguese who, since 1500, had gone to Brazil to make their fortunes. They merely reinforced the cultural, religious, and ethnic currents already dominant in the upper rungs of colonial society. The Portuguese, of course, were not regarded as foreigners, and few, if any, considered themselves immigrants. Like their predecessors, they seem to have anticipated only a brief sojourn in the colony—a self-imposed exile which, for the great majority, eventually became permanent.

Much the same situation prevailed among the non-Portuguese who made the uncomfortable voyage from Europe to Brazil. Relatively few of them severed all ties with the Old World before journeying to the New. The opening of this long-secluded land drew the ambitious and the adventurous from all parts of Europe: merchants in search of profits; scholars of the various sciences eager to explore and catalog its flora, fauna, and mineral resources; artists to paint its vistas and leading personalities; and masters of all the crafts and professions needed to satisfy the European tastes of the court and its entourage for food,

dress, adornment, and entertainment. In the end, many of the foreigners remained to add their names to the list of distinguished families of Brazil, but originally their goals were wealth, knowledge, or
renown and a quick return to the comforts of home and civilization.
The English, who enjoyed an early advantage, were the first to arrive
in force. For the most part they were representatives of British commercial firms, who established branches engaged largely in wholesale
trade. English textiles and metal wares, previously scarce because of
additional taxes and the cost of shipment via Portugal, now flooded the
market to affect the buying habits of the public and discourage local
manufactures. Letters and fashions were influenced by the French, who
comprised the largest foreign element in the capital after 1815. Hundreds of retail merchants, tailors, modistes, hairdressers and the like
arrived from France to introduce something of Parisian style to the
well-to-do residents of Rio de Janeiro. The Reverend Mr. Walsh,
writing in 1829, noted that the French—more than twice as numerous
as the English—then formed a community of about 1400 persons, and
that their shops added "elegance and gaiety" to some of the principal
streets. The most outstanding of the French were the members of the
artistic mission invited by João VI in 1816 to record the wonders of
Brazil with pen and brush and to form the nucleus of an academy of
fine arts. Occasional German-speaking scholars had been present in
Brazil since the turn of the century, but the greatest impact was made
by the delegation that accompanied Archduchess Leopoldina, the future empress of Brazil, from Vienna to Rio de Janeiro in 1817. It was
comprised of Austrian, Lombard, Czech, German, and Bavarian scientists, of whom the Bavarian naturalists Spix and Martius are best re-
membered today. While these men did not long remain in Brazil, they
traveled extensively in the country and recorded their observations in
great detail. Their writings helped to make the land familiar to
German-speaking peoples throughout Europe, thus contributing to
future immigration. The other nationalities represented among the several thousand foreign visitors and immigrants to Brazil in the waning
days of Portuguese rule included Swiss, Italians, Russians, Dutch,
Scandinavians, and a handful of North Americans.

The Chinese comprised an exotic foreign element introduced shortly after the transfer of the court to Brazil. A few families of Chinese workers were imported by the crown in 1810 to conduct experimental plantings of oriental tea in the new botanical gardens on the outskirts of Rio de Janeiro. The plants thrived, but the experiment lapsed for want of royal interest after João VI returned to Portugal in 1821. The Chinese, left to their own devices, disappeared from public view within a few years. Later efforts to import Chinese laborers, as a substitute for Negro slaves in the 1850's and 1860's, proved unfeasible because of opposition by the imperial government of China and Brazilian fears of the alien race. These failures, and the overriding problem of distance, prevented significant immigration from China or other parts of Asia during the nineteenth century. After the establishment of the republic immigration from Asia—and Africa as well—was permitted only with special authorization by the congress.

One of the principal objectives of the immigration policy adopted by Dom João and followed by Pedro I after Brazil's independence was to attract European farmers to the land. An indication of this desire was revealed in the decree of November 25, 1808, which permitted the granting of rural lands (sesmarias) to foreigners on the same conditions as to vassals of the crown. The old practice of settling peasants from Portugal and the Atlantic islands in agricultural colonies in Brazil continued, but only on a small scale. The crown preferred colonists from northern Europe because they were believed to be more industrious and to employ more advanced agricultural techniques than immigrants from the Latin countries. It was expected, moreover, that they would improve the quality of the population and help to reverse the progressive Africanization of Brazil. The preference for German-speaking colonists was pronounced after the marriage of the crown prince to a daughter of the ruling house of Austria in 1817. The first substantial colony of foreigners was created two years later under royal subvention. This was Nova Friburgo, a settlement of 1700 Swiss Catholics on the Serra do Mar in the province of Rio de Janeiro. The colony prospered, but its unexpectedly high cost to the royal treasury discouraged further such ventures by João VI. In 1824 Pedro I granted land in Rio Grande do

Sul to German mercenaries who had been engaged for the war in Uruguay. The new colony, known as São Leopoldo, began with 126 settlers and eventually grew to become one of the most successful ever established in Brazil. At about the same time, however, an attempt to settle Irish mercenaries in Bahia proved a complete fiasco. Thereafter, for many years the crown restricted new European colonies to the temperate southern provinces and to the mountains near the capital. At least half a dozen new farming communities of Swiss and Germans were founded in Rio Grande do Sul, Santa Catarina, and Paraná before 1830.

By and large the early European agricultural colonies failed to meet the expectations of their sponsors, either as benevolent influences on the native population or as meccas to attract large-scale immigration into the hinterland. Most of the foreigners and the recently arrived Portuguese settled in the coastal towns. Rio de Janeiro alone had received over 4000 foreigners by 1822, and the influx continued. The quiet colonial capital, which had only about 50,000 inhabitants in 1800, expanded to about 100,000 in 1822, and to perhaps 150,000 in 1830. By the latter year less than 7000 Germans and probably even fewer Swiss had entered Brazil. By no means all of these settled in rural areas.

For decades the agricultural colonies remained small, self-contained, subsistence-level communities which had no direct or frequent contact with the political and economic centers of the province or the empire. Fewer than 12,000 colonists immigrated between 1820 and 1840; the fourteen settlements existing in 1850 had a combined population of under 20,000; and, as late as 1867 there were only about 40,000 European farmers in sixty-eight different colonies scattered across Brazil from Maranhão to Rio Grande do Sul. In most instances these were located in remote, empty regions where there was little or no local citizenry to be affected by their example of industry and culture. The European colonies thus developed as isolated replicas of the villages from which the immigrants had come. The transplanted Swiss or German farmers retained their own language, customs, and values. Later, when colonies of Italians were founded in Rio Grande do Sul and Espírito Santo, a similar situation developed. The colonists tended to call relatives and friends from their home villages when new immigrants were requested, and to look to Europe rather than Brazil for the doctors, teachers, artisans, and priests or pastors they could not provide for themselves. As the isolated colonies expanded, they imposed upon the Brazilian minority in the surrounding area the language and cultural patterns of the European settlers. In Santa Catarina even the Negroes spoke German. After the isolation of the frontier was broken and regular contact with Brazilian communities was established, the Italians intermarried freely with the native population. The Germans, however, tended to resist assimilation. Throughout the nineteenth century, and in some instances well into the twentieth, the German settlements remained as alien to the rest of Brazil as the *quilombos* of runaway slaves had been in the colonial period.

The persistent foreign character of the rural colonies did not come to be regarded as a liability by the government until 1917, when Brazil and Germany were at war, and even then Brazilian critics continued to praise the contributions of German and other immigrants to the development of the nation. Perhaps the primary contribution was the settling and civilizing of lands that had remained untamed for over 300 years after the discovery of Brazil. In the southern provinces and in parts of Bahia and Espírito Santo these lands were still Indian territory when the first colonists arrived in the nineteenth century. By hard labor and perserverance the immigrants transformed large stretches of wilderness into productive farming areas, thereby hastening the disappearance of the aboriginal population. They introduced new crops and industries, such as grapes and wine making in Rio Grande do Sul, lumbering in the pine forest of Paraná, and breweries wherever the Germans congregated. They brought in new strains of sheep, hogs, and dairy cattle, and established mixed farming as a rural way of life in a country where landowners had traditionally concentrated on plantation crops. The European colonists, moreover, maintained standards of health and sanitation unknown elsewhere in rural Brazil and probably unmatched even by the urban upper class before 1900. Consequently, the rate of natural growth in the isolated colonies was much higher than that of the native Brazilian population, for while the wives of the European settlers bore as many children as other women in Brazil, they raised more of them to adulthood. In the southern provinces the steady expansion of the population—much faster than the trickle of new immigrants would indicate—gave rise to a phenomenon not previously known in Brazil. This was the contiguous, inland-moving line of settlement, similar to the western frontier in the United States until 1890. When there was no longer enough unoccupied land in the original colonies to be divided into family-size plots among the sons of immigrants, new settlements were founded a few miles inland, and the colonizing process was repeated. In their conquest of the frontier the successive generations of rural colonists not only brought about impressive material change, but bequeathed a spirit of progress and self-reliance that continues to distinguish southern Brazil from the rest of the country.

The agricultural colonies, despite their ultimate success, never attracted more than a small percentage of the immigrants entering Brazil. This was due in part to the hardships and isolation everywhere inherent in frontier existence, in part to the difficulties in becoming a small landowner in Brazil, and in part to changes in the objectives of Brazil's immigration policies. Brazil never enacted legislation comparable to the Homestead Act in the United States. The practice, begun by João VI, of granting lands outright to rural immigrants was not continued after 1822. Although crown lands might be allotted to a colony, the settlers or the colonizing company were expected to reimburse the government for the plots they received. And after passage of the law of September 18, 1850, public lands could be obtained only by purchase. While this legislation was designed to protect buyers against squatters who might already have occupied the property, it raised in practice a serious financial obstacle to rural immigration. Even when the immigrant bought supposedly public land, he could not be certain of retaining it, for there were no accurate surveys and the courts tended to favor native-born landholders who might contest his title. There were enough instances of injustice in this area to discourage any massive influx of European peasants to the Brazilian frontier. But more important than such discouragements were the attitudes of the large landowners, whose views usually prevailed in the congress. While they might give tacit consent to the government's proposals to establish occasional settlements of independent small farmers on crown lands in outlying regions of the country, they resisted pressures to create such colonies where much of the land was already held in enormous tracts by families predominantly of Portuguese descent. After the suppression of the African traffic, moreover, they insisted that the government should promote immigration of plantation labor as a substitute for the dwindling supply of Negro slaves. As long as slavery persisted, these arguments were only partially effective, but in the long run the need for manpower to sustain rising production of plantation exports overcame the regime's initial preference for immigrants who would become independent freeholders. More than half of all European immigrants entering Brazil between 1870 and 1920 were directed to the coffee *fazendas* of São Paulo.

Even before the slave trade was prohibited, a few far-sighted coffee planters began to look to immigration as the solution to their labor problems. The first of these men was a senator from São Paulo, Nicolau Pereira dos Campos Vergueiro, who in 1840 established several dozen Portuguese peasant families on one of his *fazendas* under a form of sharecropping. In 1847 the experiment was extended to include immigrants from some of the German states. The system, known as *parceria,* was originally a privately financed contract arrangement between the landowner and the immigrant laborers, whereby the former advanced passage and costs until the first crop was harvested. If a new orchard were being planted, the contract might run five years or longer. The immigrant and his family were provided with housing, tools, and credit. They were assigned a specified number of trees to tend, and were usually allowed to raise their own food crops and a few cattle or other livestock. Net profits from the sale of the harvest were shared equally between the immigrant family and the planter.

The introduction of the contract labor method required considerable adjustment on both sides, and was not accomplished without friction. The landowners, accustomed to dealing with slaves in a paternalistic society, frequently adopted a cavalier attitude toward their obligations to the immigrant workers, while the latter's depressed economic and social condition gave them little recourse against inequities. In practice the planter was both employer and arbiter of any disputes arising out of the contract. Not until 1858 did the Brazilian government send agents into the coffee zone to investigate charges of unfair treatment to immigrants. On the basis of such charges by German immigrants, Prussia banned all emigration of its nationals to Brazil in 1859, and several other German states enacted similar measures in ensuing years. The ban was partially lifted in 1896 to permit emigration to Paraná, Santa Catarina, and Rio Grande do Sul. By that date Italy had proscribed emigration to Espírito Santo, and in 1902 prohibited recruitment of immigrants by agents from São Paulo as a result of alleged injustices suffered by Italian plantation workers in those states.

With all its imperfections, the *parceria* system functioned as a device to provide immigrant labor for Brazilian plantations. It was adopted with minor variations by planters throughout the coffee zone as they shifted from slave to free labor. A major modification was made in 1881, when the provincial government of São Paulo began to subsidize the recruitment and passage of immigrants. Later the normal length of the contract was reduced to one year, renewable by mutual consent, and provision was made for an additional wage payment to workers during the harvest season.

Developments in Europe after the mid-nineteenth century helped provide both the motivations and the means for a massive transfer of population to the Americas. For a time the political unrest preceding national unification in Italy and Germany served as a spur to emigration. Later many able-bodied men emigrated to escape compulsory military service. The fundamental factor, however, was the rapid industrialization of western Europe, which gave rise to unprecedented population growth, urbanization, overcrowding on the land, and serious economic hardships among the peasantry and the urban working class. At the same time the growth of industry created a constantly expanding market for food and raw materials from overseas, stimulating, in turn, the development of fast, inexpensive ocean transportation.

Within a few years dozens, and then hundreds, of steamships were plying the Atlantic, heavily laden eastbound with products of American fields and mines. On the return voyage they offered cabin, deck, and steerage space for passengers. Never before had the Western Hemisphere been so accessible to so many.

Consistently, the great bulk of the emigrants from Europe went to the United States, and a considerable flow was directed to Argentina. Brazil remained relatively unattractive to potential immigrants as long as slavery existed. In fact, there was an unmistakable correlation between the decline of slavery and immigration to Brazil. With each forward step toward the elimination of Negro bondage the volume of immigration increased. The number of immigrants entering the empire seldom exceeded 2000 per year before 1850. Following the suppression of the African traffic in that year, the level of immigration rose sharply to surpass 19,000 in 1859. It fell off badly during the Paraguayan War, but still remained high enough to average about 10,000 annually for the two decades ending in 1871. The census of 1872 noted the presence of 243,481 foreign-born, as opposed to 1,510,806 slaves, in a total population of 9,930,478. The enactment of the Law of Free Birth in 1871 brought another substantial increase in the number of immigrants entering the country, raising the average to more than 20,000 per year. The upward trend continued with the revival of the abolition campaign in 1879 and the emancipation of Negro sexagenarians in 1885. In the latter year over 35,000 immigrants arrived. Nearly 56,000 came in 1887, and a peak of 133,253 was reached in 1888 when slavery was abolished. By conservative estimate at least 750,000 European immigrants had entered the empire to that date. Thereafter, the immigrant stream became a flood, far surpassing the gold rush of the eighteenth century or the heyday of the slave trade before 1850 in the number of newcomers who poured into Brazil.

The great wave of immigration came in the quarter-century following the establishment of the republic in 1889. According to the figures published by the National Council of Statistics, Brazil received 5,063,-946 immigrants from 1884 to 1970. About half of these, nearly all Europeans, arrived between 1889 and 1913—over 1,000,000 in the decade preceding World War I. In the next half-century two major wars, the world economic depression, and the imposition of immigration quotas by the government of Brazil in 1934 held the total to about 2,300,000, of whom nearly 250,000 were Japanese. The proportion of immigrants who stayed to become permanent residents of Brazil varied greatly from one national group to another. The Italians and Spaniards, for example, were prone to return home or migrate to another country if they were disappointed in Brazil. At the other extreme, virtually all of the Japanese remained. Over-all, the return rate appears to have been under 30 per cent. Thus, net immigration for the eighty-seven years ending in 1970 probably exceeded 3,500,000.

Although Brazil has accepted immigrants from more than fifty nations of Europe, America, the Levant, North Africa, and the Orient, the great majority have come from half a dozen countries. Portugal, Italy, and Spain have contributed three-fourths of all immigrants to Brazil since 1884, while Japan and Germany have provided about one-tenth. Russia, which supplied substantial contingents before World War I, ranks sixth with slightly over 2 per cent. Among other nations that have been relatively important sources of immigrants for brief periods are the Ottoman empire and the United States.

Of the three leading nationalities among immigrants to Brazil, the Portuguese hold the top place by a slim margin. They have been favored by the close ties between Portugal and its former colony, by the near identity of language and cultures in the two countries, and by the absence of a limit on the number that may be admitted per year. Because of these advantages they have regularly constituted the largest or second largest immigrant group in each decade since 1822. More than two-thirds of the Italians migrating to Brazil after 1884 arrived before 1902, when the government of Italy discouraged emigration to São Paulo. During those two decades six of every ten immigrants to Brazil were Italians. Since 1902 Italians have continued to rank among the larger immigrant groups, but have never comprised as much as 20 per cent of the total in a single decade. Spain ranks a strong third among the nations that have regularly contributed to immigration in Brazil. The number of Spaniards entering the country fell to only a few hundred a year during the decade of war in Spain and Europe from the mid-1930's to the mid-1940's, but rose sharply again after 1945.

Well behind the Spaniards, in fourth position are the Japanese, who first appeared in the stream of immigrants in 1908. Japanese immigration is unique in being entirely a phenomenon of the twentieth century and in long representing the only sizable flow of population to Brazil from the Far East. In the beginning all immigration from Japan was subsidized. The immigrants were chiefly peasants from the main islands and Okinawa, recruited for work on the coffee plantations of São Paulo by Japanese emigration companies operating under contract with the Brazilian government. There was little spontaneous movement of Japanese into Brazil until after World War II. The rate of immigration, moreover, fluctuated greatly, rising to more than 100,000 between 1924 and 1933, ceasing altogether for several years after Pearl Harbor, climbing again to over 50,000 in the decade ending in 1963, and falling off sharply after that date. By 1970 a total of 248,420 Japanese had entered Brazil—more than twice as many as all Russians entering, and perhaps as many as all German immigrants since 1822.

The figures on German and Russian immigration to Brazil are somewhat misleading, for they include significant blocs of foreign minorities who emigrated from the pre-World War I German and Russian empires. According to official tabulations, 78,103 Germans settled in Brazil before 1884, and an additional 200,483 entered the country in the next eighty-seven years, totaling 278,586 by 1970. But this figure should be substantially reduced by subtracting the large number of Poles and the smaller contingent of Alsatians who traveled to Brazil on German passports before 1918. Even if the Volga Germans who migrated to Brazil from imperial Russia were included in the total, the full number of German immigrants to Brazil since independence would probably not reach 250,000. Of the 110,175 immigrants from Russia between 1884 and 1970, it is likely that considerably less than half were in fact Russians. The largest bloc appears to have been made up of Poles, while each of the other Baltic peoples and some Germans then ruled by the czar were also represented as "Russians" among the immigrants

IMMIGRATION INTO BRAZIL BY NATIONALITY, 1884-1970

Years	Portuguese	Italians	Spaniards	Japanese	Germans	Russians	Others	Total
1884-93	170 621	510 533	103 116		22 778	40 589	36 031	883 668
1894-1905	157 542	537 784	93 770		6 698	2 886	63 430	862 110
1904-13	384 672	196 521	224 672	11 868	33 859	48 100	106 925	1 006 617
1914-23	201 252	86 320	94 779	20 398	29 339	8 196	63 697	503 981
1924-33	233 649	70 177	52 405	110 191	61 728	7 953	201 120	737 223
1934-43	75 634	11 432	5 184	46 158	17 862	275	40 693	197 238
1944-53	146 647	61 692	46 141	2 340	15 440	1 801	74 382	348 443
1954-63	181 095	53 362	75 036	51 889	9 382	91	88 430	459 285
1964-70	21 680	4 080	4 064	5 576	3 397	284	26 300	65 381
Total	1 572 792	1 531 901	699 167	248 420	200 483	110 175	701 008	5 063 946

Sources: *Anuário Estatístico do Brasil*, 1959, p. 38; 1961, p. 52; 1962, p. 40; 1963, p. 38; 1964, p. 50; 1969, p. 111; 1971, p. 115.

reaching Brazil. It is only as a result of the massive exodus of such minorities before World War I that Russia remains among the six major sources of immigration to Brazil. The Soviet Union has supplied fewer than 20,000 immigrants in half a century. During the same period Brazil received over 50,000 from Poland. Were it possible to enumerate the Poles separately from the pre-1918 German and Russian contingents, they would surely rank well ahead of Russians among the foreigners arriving in Brazil since 1884.

The number of immigrants from lands once included within the Ottoman empire is undoubtedly larger than the total for Poles or Russians. Before 1918 they were usually, but not consistently, identified simply as "Turcos" by Brazilian immigration officials, and were commonly known by that name throughout Brazil. These peoples include Arabs from Palestine, Armenians, Egyptians, Jordanians, Lebanese, and Syrians as well as Turks. Since 1918 immigrants of these nationalities have been recorded separately, but cumulative totals have been published only for those from Turkey, Syria, and Lebanon. Such data indicate that about 120,000 immigrated to Brazil between 1884 and 1960. In all probability, true Turks comprised a small minority of the total.

The presence of Turcos—almost certainly Syrians and Lebanese—has been noted in Brazil for more than a century, although they did not arrive in force until after the establishment of the republic. Because of their propensity for trade, and the extraordinary financial success achieved by some immigrants from the eastern Mediterranean, a "rags-to-riches" legend soon grew up about Turcos in Brazil. According to the legend, the typical immigrant from the Levant was an impoverished young man, who began his career as an itinerant peddler. After a few years he saved enough money to open a small shop, which enabled him to send home for relatives and a wife. With their aid he then enlarged his business, entered the wholesale trade, and eventually became a millionaire. As a wealthy man, he ceased being a Turco and was known by his proper nationality. Obviously, not all immigrants who traveled on Turkish passports became rich, but the legend does reveal several valid characteristics of the Turcos in Brazil. They have been oriented predominantly toward urban, commercial pursuits, and have participated actively in the economic life of the nation. At the same time, largely by preference they have tended to retain their identity as an ethnic minority. And some of the largest family corporations in Brazil are controlled by the descendants of Lebanese and Syrian immigrants.

Surprisingly, the United States occasionally has supplied a significant number of immigrants to Brazil. Since the 1860's Brazil has received about 40,000 immigrants from the United States. The first substantial group was made up of disgruntled Southerners who preferred to try to rebuild their old life in a new country rather than remain in the United States after their defeat in the Civil War. By 1872 some 4000 had migrated to São Paulo, Espírito Santo, and the Amazon, where they sought to establish themselves in rural colonies. A few of these survived, such as Vila Americana in São Paulo, but most soon failed and the disheartened settlers returned home. Immigration from the United States virtually ceased for the next fifteen years. After the founding of the republic a few North Americans again entered each year, but only a small percentage of them became citizens. Mainly they were businessmen for whom immigrant status was a convenience. This pattern still prevails among Americans residing in Brazil. The number of immigrants from the United States was usually well under 1000 a year until the 1950's. In the decade 1954-63 the 12,434 immigrants from the United States comprised the fifth largest contingent of foreigners entering Brazil. Over the next seven years the number fell to only 6580 persons, but the United States rose to second rank, after Portugal, as a source of immigrants. In the same period more than 15,000 Brazilian-born immigrants entered the United States.

The massive influx of immigrants could not fail to have dramatic repercussions throughout Brazilian society. The major impact had been felt by the end of World War I. In the half-century ending in 1920 the arrival of some 3.5 million foreigners altered the size, distribution, ethnic composition, activities, and outlook of the population. During those years the population of Brazil tripled, from nearly 10 million to more than 30 million. The immigrants, and their children and grand-children, were responsible for a great deal of the increase. This fact is made clear in the census returns, which reveal a much higher sus-tained rate of growth in the six areas of recent immigration than in the provinces heavily settled during the colonial period. The combined population of Espírito Santo, the national capital, São Paulo, and the three southern provinces increased by fivefold between 1872 and 1920, from 1,916,000, or 19 per cent of the total for Brazil, to about 9,750,-000, which represented nearly one-third of all Brazilians. In the same period Minas Gerais, Bahia, and Pernambuco expanded by less than three times, from 4,261,000 to 11,377,000, while declining in relative strength from 42 per cent to 37 per cent of the national population. It is significant that the percentage increase in the mixed-farming zones of Rio Grande do Sul, Santa Catarina, and Paraná, which received only a small minority of the newcomers after 1870, was nearly identi-cal to that in São Paulo, with over 2,400,000 immigrants in fifty years. Because of the larger numbers, the impact of immigration was more evident in São Paulo, which contained one of every seven residents of Brazil in 1920, and one in every six by 1940. Foreign immigration continued to add to the population of São Paulo, but the sustained population explosion in the state since 1920 has been due far more to natural growth and the migration of Brazilians from other parts of the country than to the arrival of immigrants from abroad.

Immigration has also contributed heavily to the spectacular rate of urbanization in Brazil since the last quarter of the nineteenth century. Although this phenomenon occurred in all regions of the country, it was most pronounced in the areas that received the largest contingents of immigrants, for while Brazil looked to immigration as a source of agricultural laborers, many of the foreigners preferred life in the cities. Whenever possible, the Portuguese and Spaniards tended to settle in the cities from the outset, and the Italians abandoned the *fazendas* in droves with every drop in the price of coffee. Again the impact was strongest in São Paulo. The capital of the province was a sleepy coun-try town of 31,000 inhabitants in 1872. Even then 8 per cent of its population was foreign-born. By 1890 it had grown to 65,000 residents, of whom 22 per cent were immigrants. In the next decade São Paulo nearly quadrupled in size to 240,000 and was known as a city of Italians. By 1920 it contained half as many people as Rio de Janeiro and more than twice as many as the total for Salvador and Recife, the third and fourth cities of Brazil. Of its 579,000 residents, 35 per cent were foreign-born. This was the high point. While the number of immigrants remained large, they comprised a steadily decreasing proportion of the city's population, falling off to 27 per cent in 1940, and to 14 per cent in 1950. Rio de Janeiro, as the major port and national capital, had attracted a disproportionately large immigrant population since 1808. By 1872 it was a city of about 275,000, of whom 84,000 —or 30 per cent—were foreigners. Thereafter, however, the influx of immigrants failed to keep pace with the growth of the city. Since 1890 Rio de Janeiro has had a smaller proportion, but a larger number of foreign-born residents than São Paulo. The population of the capital surpassed half a million in 1890, of whom one-fourth were immigrants, while in 1920 barely one-fifth of the 1,158,000 persons in Rio de Janeiro were foreign-born. The immigrant share of the city population dropped to 12 per cent in 1940, and to 9 per cent in 1950. Santos, Campinas, Curitiba, Pôrto Alegre, and other cities in southern Brazil followed a similar pattern during the period under review.

Except for the immigrants from Japan and a statistically insignificant number from other countries of the Orient, all new arrivals to Brazil after the 1850's may be regarded as white. Their impact on the ethnic composition of the population was immediate and obvious. The gradual dilution of Indian and Negro blood among the inhabitants of Brazil had been going on since the beginning of the colonial period, as a result of the ready access of white and near white Brazilian males to women of color. Given the continuation of this trend, and the cessation of the African traffic, the population of Brazil would inevitably have become whiter without immigration. Yet, there is no question that the addition of well over 5 million immigrants from Europe and the Levant in little more than a century tremendously accelerated the whitening, or "bleaching," process. The following table provides a breakdown of the population by color for selected years between 1835 and 1940 and shows clearly that the proportion of whites increased most rapidly after the years of heaviest immigration from Europe:

POPULATION OF BRAZIL BY COLOR, 1835-1940
(population in thousands)

Color	1835		1872		1890		1940	
White	845	24.2%	3787	38.1%	6302	43.9%	26,172	63.4%
Brown	648	18.6%	4188	42.1%	5934	41.4%	8744	21.2%
Black	1987	57.0%	1959	19.6%	2097	14.6%	6036	14.6%
Yellow							243	0.5%

Sources: F. J. Oliveira Vianna, *Evolução do povo brasileiro,* 2d ed. (1933), p. 172; José Honório Rodrigues, *Brazil and Africa,* p. 73; *Anuário Estatístico do Brasil, 1958,* p. 24.

These data should be regarded as impressionistic approximations, for the classification of individuals by color—which appears to have been based primarily on social and cultural criteria—varied from region to region and from one census to another. Indians, moreover, were omitted from the 1835 estimate, but were lumped together with all manner of mixed-bloods in the brown category in the census returns for later years. No doubt some dark mulattos were listed with Negroes in the black sector, while many of lighter pigmentation were included among the whites. Despite such limitations, however, the statistical data are indicative of the broad trends occurring within the Brazilian population during a century that witnessed the suppression of the slave trade, the abolition of slavery, and the great surge of European immigration into Brazil. The censuses of 1900 and 1920 did not tabulate the population by color or race, but the continuing influence of immigration was evident in the returns for 1940, which showed that whites constituted upwards of two-thirds of the total. The declining importance of immigration, and the persistence of miscegenation were reflected in the 1950 census, in which the relative standings were: white, 61.6%; brown, 26.5%; black, 10.9%; and yellow, 0.6%.

The conseqences of large-scale immigration between the 1870's and the 1920's are still being felt throughout the economic, political, and cultural life of Brazil. The contribution of immigrants to the modernization of the nation will be dealt with in the following chapter, but it is appropriate to note here that even while hundreds of thousands of European workingmen were making possible the great agricultural boom of the last years of the empire and the early years of the republic, others were building the railroads, widening and paving city streets, digging sewers, installing electric lights, erecting new buildings, and contributing as laborers, managers, and entrepreneurs to the introduction of new processing and manufacturing industries. They also introduced new ideas about labor organizations and political parties, made European football a national sport, and modified long-established patterns of dress, food, and speech. By the early 1920's non-Portuguese names were appearing among the leading artists and writers of the country, and by 1930 the sons and grandsons of immigrants had entered national politics to stay. It was obvious that the distinctions between immigrant and native-born were becoming blurred before restrictions were placed on the entry of newcomers in 1934. In the 1970's the descendants of immigrants of all nationalities were prominent in every occupation and profession in Brazil. The country's debt to the voluntary immigrants of the nineteenth and twentieth centuries is at least as great as its debt to the Negroes imported as slaves during the long colonial era.

Chapter 6 • Order and Progress

During the half-century from 1870 to 1920 Brazil was caught up in a frenzy of uneven growth and modernization that affected every aspect of national life. These five decades witnessed an expansion of agriculture and industry unparalleled in the nation's history—as dramatic in its impact on the economy, and more far-reaching in its consequences for the social and political order than the opening of the gold fields in the eighteenth century. Change, equated with progress, was the order of the day. Old methods, institutions, and ideas that had served for generations were discarded because they were out of fashion. Immigration replaced slavery, and so contributed to a tripling of the population and the emergence of an urban proletariat. The monarchy gave way to a republic, bringing Brazil into conformity with the other independent countries of the hemisphere. The territory of the nation was enlarged by conquest, purchase, and arbitration at the expense of Brazil's neighbors. A new constitution exalted regionalism and the authority of the states at the expense of the central government, leaving the armed forces as the custodians of national values. The locus of political power shifted permanently to the South, where São Paulo became the economic heart of the country, and a new class of wealthy industrialists, drawn from immigrants and the landholding elite, competed with plantation owners for prestige and political influence. Foreign capital was borrowed in unprecedented amounts to pay for the technological innovations of the age—steam-driven rail and water transport, the overland telegraph, the trans-Atlantic cable, electric light and power, and the latest techniques of medical science and hygiene. These knit the country more closely together than ever before, pushed the area of effective settlement far beyond the line of Tordesillas, and permitted Rio de Janeiro, São Paulo, and even Manaus to rank among the most modern, healthful cities of the world. At the same time the seaboard society and economy were drawn more fully into the cultural and commercial orbit of western Europe. A new generation of leaders emulated French modes and manners, and shared the general European confidence in the steady, irreversible advance of Western civilization.

Confidence in the future was elevated to an article of faith by the briefly influential minority of Brazilians who adopted Auguste Comte's philosophy of positivism, with its formula for a regimented social order and unlimited material progress. Although positivism did not prevail, its motto, Order and Progress, was emblazoned on the flag of the republic in 1889, symbolizing the determination of the new leadership to transform Brazil into a modern nation.

The modernization of Brazil—already well under way when the republic was founded—took place in successive waves or phases, receiving new stimulus and direction in each period. The first of these, from the close of the Paraguayan War to May 1888, coincided with the campaign for the abolition of slavery. Inspired by the new spirit born of military victory and the rising wealth from agricultural exports, the imperial government underwrote a major program to improve transportation and communications in the larger cities and the coastal provinces. The considerable progress registered in these fields represented primarily a continuation of trends established earlier. The railroad and the telegraph, first introduced in the 1850's, and the steam engine, known in Brazil since the reign of João VI, now became the symbols of progress. There was a modest expansion of the small industrial sector, but few new enterprises were launched without subsidies or special concessions. By and large the changes introduced between 1870 and 1888 were intended to support the burgeoning plantation economy or to enhance the efficiency and power of the central government.

The second phase opened with the emancipation of the slaves on May 13, 1888, and continued through the first decade of the republic. These years embraced the period of wildest financial speculation and inflation Brazil had yet seen. During the final eighteen months of the monarchy the relaxation of credit restrictions and the increase in state-sponsored immigration—authorized to ease the transition to wage labor by rural planters—contributed unexpectedly to a surge of urban business growth. In that short span the volume of new business investments, principally in banking, textile manufacturing, and food processing, was nearly equal to the total for all the preceding years of the imperial era.

With the establishment of the republic, all restraints on economic expansion were removed. In their uninhibited enthusiasm the spokesmen for the new regime insisted that Brazil had finally thrown off the shackles of the past and was prepared to enter the modern age. As a practical matter the traditional plantation and forest products, and the railroads and river navigation needed to transport them, continued to receive sympathetic and generous treatment, but particular attention was focused on manufacturing. In the euphoria of the moment all manner of business enterprises seemed to offer a glowing future. Raw materials existed in abundance, immigrants were expected to provide both an expanding market and an endless supply of labor skilled in all the crafts and trades of the Old World, and credit was available for the asking. Banking flourished. When more money was needed, more was printed. In this climate literally hundreds of corporations were created by Brazilian and foreign entrepreneurs, many with sound programs, but many more purely for speculation. The bubble burst late in 1891, sweeping away much of the nominal growth of the preceding two years. In the depression that followed the exchange value of Brazilian currency plummeted, thus reducing income from exports and raising the cost of many imported items to prohibitive levels. While this situation was detrimental to agricultural producers and caused grave concern to the national and state governments, it served to shield Brazilian manufacturers against the hazards of foreign competition. Despite the lingering depression, the number of manufacturing and processing plants in Brazil nearly doubled between 1890 and 1895, and the new group of industrialists began to make its voice heard in the councils of state.

The third phase was initiated in 1898 by the incoming Campos Salles administration, which adopted stern measures to check inflation and restore the value of the currency. This policy—followed with only minor changes by the next several presidents—favored agriculture and commerce, as did the government's programs to enlarge and modernize port facilities and to extend rail lines ever farther into the interior. The most striking transformation, however, was the revitalization and beautification of the cities after the turn of the century. The improvements in the physical and financial health of the community, and the introduction of electricity as an inexpensive source of power, proved a boon to domestic industries, which still enjoyed considerable, if unequal, tariff protection. Between 1899 and 1910 more than 200 large national and foreign firms were registered to operate in Brazil. The number of small concerns founded during the same period was much higher. As early as 1907, the first industrial census of Brazil listed over 3000 establishments employing 150,000 workers, chiefly in the fields of textiles and clothing, food processing, and metallurgy. Nearly two-thirds of the plants, and an even larger percentage of the labor force, were concentrated in the Federal District and the states of São Paulo and Rio Grande do Sul. The expansion of industry during these years could also be seen in the formation of a purportedly nation-wide manufacturers' association, the *Centro Industrial do Brasil,* in 1904, the first significant strike by factory workers in São Paulo in 1907, and the creation of the Brazilian Labor Confederation in 1912. In the latter year the spokesman for the manufacturers claimed that Brazil's industrial plant was producing goods worth more in the aggregate than the combined value of coffee and rubber exports.

The outbreak of World War I in 1914 marked a new phase in the modernization of Brazil. The initial shock disrupted normal trade patterns, depressing the volume of exports and imports, reducing public revenues, and causing a sharp drop in the exchange rate. As soon as it became evident that the war would continue indefinitely, however, exports of raw materials rose to new heights. Even some manufactured goods were shipped to Europe. The annual value of Brazilian exports trebled between 1914 and 1919 despite the obstacles to trans-Atlantic commerce. With the usual flow of imports from the industrialized nations drastically curtailed, Brazilian consumers were obliged to buy local manufactures or do without. Under this stimulus there was a surge of industrial development, particularly in the city of São Paulo, which boasted some 350 factories by 1915. Two years later the sales tax on Brazilian industrial products was yielding the government slightly higher revenues than the dwindling customs receipts from imports. Food processing was now the leading industrial activity, thanks largely to the introduction of refrigerated meat packing in Rio Grande do Sul and São Paulo. Recurrent labor unrest in 1917, 1918, and 1919 called attention to the steady rise in the cost of living, but did not interrupt the continuous expansion of industry. By 1920 there were 275,000 workers employed in over 13,000 industrial establishments, almost half of which had been founded during the war years.

For the most part the national industry was still comprised of small, owner-operated concerns, unable to compete under peacetime conditions in range, price, or quality of products with the foreign manufacturers who had supplied most of Brazil's needs before 1914. The entire industrial labor force represented less than 1 per cent of the population of Brazil. By the end of the war some Brazilians could perceive that an economic revolution was taking place in their country, but few were yet prepared to accept the domestic manufacturing industry as a permanent and essential element of the national economy. None could foresee that the economic revolution had set the stage for political and social revolution as well.

The transformation of Brazil between 1870 and 1920 was similar in broad outline to that of various other countries of Latin America, Asia, and the Mediterranean during the same period. The common process of change—involving the revolution in transportation, rapid urbanization, improvements in standards of health and sanitation in the cities, the rise of new and influential groups in society, and the imposition of industry on a pre-existing agrarian economy—has since been interpreted as a logical and inevitable outgrowth of the Industrial Revolution and of the competition by European powers for economic hegemony over so-called "backward" areas of the globe. These factors were clearly present in the Brazilian case. Yet, the particular path to modernization followed in Brazil was neither entirely logical nor inevitable and was never universally acclaimed by the Brazilian people as desirable. The following review of circumstances and attitudes affecting social and economic change in Brazil indicates how it was possible for the nation to modernize as much as it did, and no more, in these five decades.

The Paraguayan War, which Pedro II described as a salutary shock to Brazilian nationalism, was the major stimulus to the modernization of the empire. The need to maintain large land and naval forces beyond the frontier pointed up glaring deficiencies in communications, transportation, and industry in Brazil. The introduction of steam navigation had shortened the time required to sail from Brazilian ports to Asunción, but overland communication with Paraguay remained as slow and difficult as in the days of the *bandeirantes*. It was necessary to import much of the materiel of war, for even though Brazilian artisans and manufacturers had the capacity to produce a large part of the weapons, uniforms, medical supplies, and other paraphernalia used by nineteenth-century armies, their small plants were widely dispersed, were geared to restricted local markets, and lacked facilities for shipping goods rapidly or economically over long distances. In short, Brazil in 1865 was poorly equipped to fight a war on foreign soil.

Measures were taken to alleviate this situation even as the war progressed. Communications received high priority. The telegraph and cable network—which had linked government offices in Rio de Janeiro with the summer capital at Petropolis in 1857, and with Cabo Frio in 1863—was hurriedly extended to the Uruguayan border. There it connected with new lines that shortly reached Buenos Aires, reducing message transmission time from weeks to hours. At the same time work continued on three of the four railways that had already begun to probe inland from Rio de Janeiro, Santos, and Recife, and concessions were granted by the imperial and provincial governments to ten new railroad companies during the war years. In all, about 200 miles of track were opened to traffic, bringing the total to about 450 miles by 1870. Each railroad, moreover, installed a telegraph line along its right-of-way, further expanding the national communications net. In the industrial sector the long-neglected national iron foundry at Ipanema, São Paulo, was reorganized and expanded, and the principal military factory—the naval arsenal at Rio de Janeiro—was enlarged, some steam-powered machinery was installed, and facilities were added for the construction of iron-clad vessels and other implements of modern naval warfare. A minor boom in private industry, chiefly in the city and province of Rio de Janeiro, was an incidental by-product of the war; it was facilitated by the increase in the supply of money and short-term securities issued by the government to meet its rising military expenses. According to the census of 1872, roughly 19,000 of the empire's 10 million inhabitants were engaged in "industrial" professions, presumably as owners and managers, while the labor force—including self-employed operators—in the metal, textile, and clothing industries exceeded 190,000.

The trends initiated or encouraged during the war were greatly accelerated after peace was restored in 1870, for it was discovered that changes introduced primarily to meet pressing military needs brought immediate and continuing benefits to the civilian population. The telegraph was quickly seized upon by businessmen as a vital aid to commerce. It proved a boon to agriculture as well by opening large areas of the country to settlement. Maintenance of the lines passing through outlying sections required the building of roads, which in turn made the new regions accessible to settlers, raised land values, and, in due course, increased agricultural production. Railroads, too, served both old and new sectors of the economy. Not only did they contribute directly to the rise in export levels by speeding the shipment of foodstuffs and raw materials to the coast, but they permitted easier movement of passengers and merchandise to interior points, and in the process expanded the market area that could be served by domestic industry.

One of the more significant results of the Paraguayan War was the emergence of the army as a consistent and influential force for change. In the wake of victory the prestige of the military was high, and its opinions on national issues received attention from the press and political circles throughout the country. Eventually, the army would be instrumental in bringing Brazil's political institutions up to date, but in the 1870's its leaders were primarily concerned with technological change. Their bitter experiences in Paraguay—where inability to keep troops supplied with food and medicine had caused thousands of deaths—had convinced them that the empire must have an efficient, rapid system of transportation and communications. The army was particularly interested in strategic lines to link the populated areas with distant frontier zones in the south and west. Where railroads and telegraph lines could be justified on economic grounds, they might be built and operated by private enterprise, but elsewhere, in the interests of national security, the cost should be borne by the state. Since these views coincided with the monarchy's desire to establish closer control over the frontier provinces, they were favorably received by the imperial government. In fact, the army was given major responsibility for the installation of telegraph facilities in remote areas of the nation. By 1889, wires had been strung from Jaguarão on the southern border to Belém in the north, placing Rio de Janeiro in telegraphic communication with the capitals of all but three provinces—Amazonas, Goiás, and Mato Grosso.

The telegraph was relatively inexpensive to erect, and operating costs were largely offset by charges for commercial use. This was not the case, however, with the strategic railroads sought by the army. Nonetheless, considerable progress was made on railways of obvious military importance. In the early 1870's several routes to the frontier were surveyed, and authorization was granted for the construction of two lines across Rio Grande do Sul. The first of these, built by the imperial government, was to connect Pôrto Alegre with Uruguaiana, over 400 miles away in the southwestern corner of the province. The second, built and operated by a British company, ran roughly parallel to the Uruguayan border from the port of Rio Grande to Bagé, a distance of 175 miles. By 1889, the latter had been completed, more than one-third of the former was open to traffic, and work had commenced on a branch line northward from Uruguaiana along the Brazilian side of the frontier with Argentina. Not until after the establishment of the republic, however, were steps taken to link Rio Grande do Sul with the capital, or to extend railroads toward the border of Paraguay.

While the monarchy was somewhat slow to meet military needs for rail transportation on the frontier, it responded promptly to civilian pressures for railroads in the settled portions of the country. Railroads became the most striking evidence of material progress during the last two decades of the empire. Over 2190 miles of railways were built between 1870 and 1880, and in the next five years nearly 2375 miles were added. There were eighty-three separate lines in 1889, with approximately 5600 miles of track in operation and about 1250 under construction. Fourteen were government lines. Two short ones—in Pará and Bahia—had been built by provincial administrations. The rest were in private hands. Of the latter, thirty companies, accounting for more than 2500 miles of rail lines, were subsidized in one fashion or another. Some received a cash subvention for each section of track completed. For others the national or provincial governments guaranteed a minimum annual profit, usually 7 per cent, on the capital invested. These arrangements were continued by the new federal and state regimes that took office in 1889. The private sector included both Brazilian and foreign firms, but regardless of nationality the railroad companies obtained their materials, rolling stock, supervisory personnel, and usually operating capital as well, in England or France. By the 1880's Baldwin locomotives manufactured in Philadelphia were replacing British engines on some steep mountain runs, and the larger Brazilian firms were beginning to build their own freight cars, but English equipment still predominated.

Despite the impressive gains registered under the empire, Brazil did not achieve a national transportation system in the usual meaning of the term. With rare exceptions the railroads were lines of penetration, running inland from the coast to tap rich agricultural or pastoral zones. The majority operated in only one province, or at most two. There were few connections between them, and even where two or more lines served the same city the rolling stock of one company frequently could not be operated on another's track because different gauges were used. Seven gauges in all were employed in Brazil, and at least one major company, the Dom Pedro II Railroad, used two within its own exclusive territory. Only in 1877 were Rio de Janeiro and São Paulo linked by rail, and not until 1888 did work start in Minas Gerais on an extension of the north-south trunk line into southern Bahia. As the railroad boom continued, new highway construction virtually ceased, and some existing roads fell into disrepair. At the same time, coastal shipping services were vastly improved, with the addition of large, fast steamers. Thus, at the end of the empire the movement of passengers and freight between north and south was more dependent upon ocean transportation than it had been a generation earlier.

The same spirit of progress that brought the railroad and telegraph to the rural areas was also at work in the cities of the empire, affecting the physical appearance of the communities and the attitudes of their leaders. Many conveniences of urban life that are now taken for granted, such as paved, lighted streets, running water, sewage disposal, and public transportation, were first introduced or notably improved in Brazilian cities in the years following the Paraguayan War. These became symbols of growth and prosperity for the communities that could afford them, and aspirations for the smaller ones that still measured "progress" in the number of public fountains or square meters of streets paved with cobblestones. The pace of modernization was uneven, for such services were costly to establish and required continuing outlays for maintenance. Yet, by the end of the empire municipal water systems had been modernized, running water had been piped into private residences, and sewerage systems were in operation or under construction in Rio de Janeiro, Salvador, Recife, and half of the smaller provincial capitals from Pôrto Alegre to Belém. Other innovations that spread rapidly after 1870 included gas lighting and tramways. As with railroads, a start had been made earlier in Rio de Janeiro, where a few gas street lights and horse-drawn streetcars had appeared in the central district in the 1850's. By 1880 they were becoming commonplace. Gas lighting had been installed for public and private use in more than a dozen cities and towns, and at least twenty had either trams or street railways linking the city center with sprawling suburbs or adjacent towns. The telephone, which reached Brazil while it was still a novelty in the United States and Europe, was perhaps the only completely new municipal utility introduced in the latter years of the empire. The first instruments were ordered by Dom Pedro II in Philadelphia in 1876 for use in government offices. Public telephone service was available in Salvador, São Paulo, and Campinas by 1884, and in Rio de Janeiro five years later.

For the most part the new gas, traction, and telephone services were privately operated, usually by foreign companies, whose contracts with the provincial governments assured a fixed minimum return on their investment. On occasion a single firm might enjoy a monopoly in the city, but more often separate concessions were granted for different districts. There were two traction companies in Recife, for example, and twelve in Rio de Janeiro. In the beginning nearly all of the equipment was imported. In Rio de Janeiro water and sewer pipes, lampposts, wire, rails, and tramcars could be locally made, but elsewhere even these were purchased abroad, as were all engines, telephones, switchboards, globes, gas fixtures, and the coal from which the gas was generated. For many years the gas companies were predominantly British, while the telephone services and public transportation were divided between British, American, and Brazilian firms.

Contemporary observers were impressed by the changes in the urban way of life in Brazil brought about in part by the introduction of the new municipal services. Gas street-lighting, for example, while inadequate by today's standards, made the cities pleasanter and safer by night, and perhaps indirectly helped to raise the cultural level of the inhabitants by encouraging larger, more frequent attendance at the theater, opera, and similar functions, not only in the national capital but in the leading provincial centers as well. This trend was also encouraged by the existence of tramways and street railways, which provided dependable, inexpensive transportation into the downtown area. By the same token, tramways contributed to the spread of the suburbs by enabling a much larger segment of the population than ever before to travel relatively long distances between residence and place of employment. It was a new streetcar line, authorized in the 1870's "to facilitate sea-bathing for the population," that eventually made Copacabana beach part of the city of Rio de Janeiro and added a new dimension to the life of the Carioca. A similar change occurred in other coastal cities as public transportation services were extended to formerly isolated beaches, converting them into popular recreation sites. While the beaches did not become fashionable residential areas until after 1920, entire new suburbs were developed and old districts were refurbished by those who shared in the rising level of prosperity after 1870. The increasing comforts and attractions of life in town, plus the ease of rail transportation from the interior, drew many wealthy planters and their families to the cities for at least part of the year. There they built fine town houses that added to the architectural beauty and air of modernity of imperial Brazil's growing urban centers.

At the same time, new working-class neighborhoods sprang up around the factories and workshops that were erected on the edge of town, for the growth of industry, which accompanied the expansion of the railroads and the modernization of the cities, was also an urban phenomenon. By the late 1870's, according to official reports, the empire was approaching self-sufficiency in some industrial products and was manufacturing a variety of articles that competed with imports from Europe. In addition to such items as sugar, rum, tobacco products, soap and candles, lumber, and cotton textiles, which had long been produced in the country, there were plants turning out shoes, hats of felt, silk, and straw, matches, glass and optical instruments, coarse wrapping paper, furniture, ironware, some chemicals, stationary steam engines, beer, and even a domestic gin. The official lists did not include household industries or the innumerable blacksmiths, coopers, carpenters, potters, leather workers, and others in the interior, who met the needs of a simple agrarian society for tools and utensils of everyday use. Roughly 200 enterprises were large enough to be included in the category of "industries" and to enjoy some tax benefits or tariff protection. The leading and most widely disseminated industrial activity was textile manufacturing, with twenty-nine cotton mills and one woolen mill employing about 2000 workers in all in 1876. Foundries, machine shops, hat factories, and breweries—of which there were eighteen in Rio de Janeiro alone—ranked next in order of importance at that time. The pace of industrial growth appears to have continued without major interruption for the next dozen years, and then spurted sharply in the waning months of the empire. In 1889 there were over 600 factories in operation. Textile mills comprised the largest category. Food preparation, chemicals, wordworking, clothing, and metallurgy—including Brazil's first small steel mill—accounted for the rest. At the end of the imperial era Rio de Janeiro was still by far the leading industrial center in the country, and the naval arsenal, with over 3000 workers, was the largest single employer of industrial labor. Salvador and Recife were beginning to decline in relative standing, and São Paulo was just starting on the path that would make it the industrial capital of the nation two generations later.

It is one of the paradoxes of Brazilian history that the first sustained surge of industrial growth should occur during the final decades of the empire, when the nation had a highly centralized government whose economic policies were determined by a conservative, rural-oriented elite. In fact, much of the impressive financial and industrial development following the Paraguayan War was an unintentional by-product of the drive to modernize the agricultural economy. It was only a coincidence that occasional fiscal measures approved by the congress—such as the levying of high import duties on selected manufactures, and the expansion of credit in the late 1860's and again in 1888—stimulated the industrial sector, for this was not the objective of the legislation. The views and values of the dominant rural aristocracy were seldom attuned to the needs of infant industry.

Not that the members of the ruling group, who regarded themselves as progressive and realistic, were unalterably opposed to industry per se. They recognized that some sugar, tobacco, and cotton mills were needed to provide a local market for crops that encountered stiff competition abroad. There was room for a certain amount of manufacturing in other lines as well, in order to preserve foreign exchange for debt servicing and the purchase of essential imports. But this did not mean that industry should be encouraged at the expense of agriculture. They held it self-evident that Brazil was destined to remain an agricultural country, that the real wealth of the empire lay in its plantations and export crops, and, thus, that free trade and a sound currency were indispensable for national prosperity. The planters could appreciate the value of the railroads, steamships, telegraphs, and cables that brought the *fazendas* of Brazil closer to foreign markets, and they could take pride in the new systems of light, water, and transport that were modernizing the cities, for these were clearly marks of "progress." The actions of their representatives in congress, however, left little doubt that such "progress" should be brought about mainly by their friends and in the interests of their own class. Thus, when a group of landowners formed a company to build a railroad, or joined with a foreign firm to install a tramway, gas works, or commercial bank, the imperial and provincial governments were inclined to act favorably in granting concessions, contracts, or other considerations. Business ventures organized by outsiders were less apt to receive sympathetic treatment. Since new businesses were not likely to thrive without the assistance or acquiescence of the political authorities, the attitudes of the ruling group were a vital factor limiting possibilities for economic development under the empire.

This situation did not entirely preclude the rise to prominence of industrialists and business leaders from other social levels, but it did effectively discourage the emergence of free-wheeling tycoons of the type common in the United States and western Europe in the last third of the nineteenth century. Only one such individual arose in imperial Brazil, and even he was not powerful enough to survive without timely support from the royal government. This was Irineu Evangelista de Sousa, the Viscount Mauá, a self-made man of humble origins, who was ennobled for his contributions to the nation. His accomplishments included construction of the first stretch of railroad in Brazil in 1854, installation of the first gas lighting in Rio de Janeiro that same year, and completion of the first trans-Atlantic cable between Brazil and Europe two decades later. For a quarter-century he rode roughshod over all opposition to become the leading industrialist and banker in the empire, with interests in England, Uruguay, and Argentina as well. Mauá weathered successive economic crises in large part because he had access to British venture capital and because he enjoyed the confidence of the Brazilian crown. At the same time he accumulated an impressive array of political enemies among the landholding elite. His downfall came during the sharp economic depression of 1875, when he was forced to appeal to the imperial regime for a loan to avoid bankruptcy. The loan was refused, and his overextended financial organization was allowed to collapse.

While Mauá's successes were unique, his failure was typical of the fate of many would-be industrial giants in imperial Brazil. The reluctance of the government to come to the aid of such men reflected the fears and prejudices of the rural aristocracy and revealed the narrow limits of change acceptable to the conservative ruling group. In the prevailing view, the government should not encourage industries that competed with the traditional export economy for subsidies and manpower. The planters could not welcome the emergence of an urban, industrial labor force as long as there were not enough hands on the coffee *fazendas*. They looked with suspicion on the growing middle class of shopkeepers, artisans, white collar workers, managers, and professionals in the cities. They could not trust this vocal, educated, urban-centered element which lacked roots in the land. And they could approve neither the manners nor ambitions of parvenu industrialists and bankers whose fortunes stemmed from manufacturing or money lending. In the final analysis, no matter how often and sincerely the leaders of the empire might applaud the material progress of Brazil, they were not prepared to accept meaningful change in the social or political order.

The social order remained substantially intact, but the political system Brazil had known since 1822 was changed abruptly with the establishment of the republic in 1889. Many factors contributed to the collapse of the imperial government, which toppled like a house of cards at the first assault. Among these were the personality of the prematurely aged emperor, Pedro II, who took no measures to protect the throne and permitted full freedom of expression to its critics; the lingering disaffection of the clergy following a bitter dispute with the crown in the mid-1870's; the lack of public enthusiasm for the heir apparent, Princess Isabel, and her French consort, the Conde d'Eu; and the appearance of an organized Republican party, which called attention to the anachronism of the monarchy in a hemisphere of republics. Running through this tapestry of discontent was the sharp increase in political tensions accompanying, and stemming from, the long campaign for the abolition of slavery after 1871. But none of these issues, nor all of them together, was sufficient to destroy the empire, which rested upon the support of the large landholders and the armed forces. By 1889, however, these two bulwarks of imperial authority had been undermined. The plantation owners, who felt betrayed by the uncompensated emancipation of the slave labor force, were indifferent to the fate of the crown, while key army commanders and a majority of the junior officers were actively opposed to its survival. Under these circumstances, when the army garrison in Rio de Janeiro deposed the emperor and proclaimed the republic on November 15, 1889, no one in Brazil rose to his defense.

The army deserves special mention in this context, both because it had previously been apolitical and because, after 1889, it was to remain a decisive element in the formulation of national policies. The new role of the military in Brazilian politics began after the end of the Paraguayan War in 1870. The brunt of the sacrifice in that long and costly conflict had been borne by the army. The returning officers, hailed as heroes by the public, resented the alleged indifference of the emperor to the needs and aspirations of the service. A few of the more disgruntled began to compete for public office in order to bring their grievances to the attention of the political parties and the parliament. Until after the death in 1880 of the Duke of Caxias, Brazil's outstanding military figure and strong supporter of Pedro II, military protests—largely limited to complaints about low pay and inadequate army appropriations—had limited political impact. Subsequently, however, the growing ranks of politicized officers took an active part in the abolition campaign and were increasingly sensitive to what were presumed to be affronts to military honor by civilian politicians. Some became dedicated republicans despite their oath of allegiance to the crown. The radicalization of the officer corps owed much to the influence of Benjamin Constant Botelho de Magalhães, head of the small positivist movement in Brazil and instructor of mathematics at the military academy. Under his inspired guidance the postwar generation of cadets became convinced of the need for drastic political changes to bring "order and progress" to Brazil. As officers, the disciples of Benjamin Constant were prepared to follow any military leader who would put his teachings into practice. That leadership was provided by Marshal Deodoro da Fonseca, a highly esteemed veteran of the Paraguayan War and ardent defender of the interests of the military class.

Once the foundations of the monarchy had crumbled, it took only an incident to bring the empire to a quiet, non-violent end. That incident, not immediately related to the pressing issues of the day, was sparked by unfounded rumor circulated in the republican press that Marshal Deodoro was to be imprisoned and his followers dispersed among distant garrisons in the interior. Some agitators also maintained that the army itself was to be dissolved and replaced by an imperial guard made up of ex-slaves. Accepting such rumors as truth, military units in Rio de Janeiro seized control of the government. A provisional regime under Marshal Deodoro was installed, the imperial family was sent into exile, and the republic, born of a military coup d'état, was accepted passively by the Brazilian people.

The great institutional changes of 1888-89 demonstrated that the fears and suspicions of the rural aristocracy were well founded. In a real sense the abolition of slavery and the overthrow of the empire may be seen as a successful urban protest against the perennial predominance of landholders in the economy, society, and politics of Brazil. Ironically, the modernization process, which had been intended to strengthen the plantation export economy, and thereby to reinforce the position of the planter class, nourished the very forces that now jeopardized the traditional order. The sudden creation of the republic in November 1889 brought to power military and civilian leaders with fresh approaches to the nation and its needs. For a time the rural aristocracy—and its views on economic development—were overshadowed by men who felt the pace of "progress" had been too slow.

A curious assortment of groups, with varying backgrounds and attitudes, was represented in the leadership of the new republic. The most conspicuous was the military, which had never before assumed political responsibility in Brazil. The officers were drawn largely from established rural families, but for the most part during their professional careers had served alternately in remote frontier garrisons and in the larger coastal cities. They tended to believe that this experience gave them a uniquely "national" perspective on national problems. A substantial minority of the army officers and some civilian leaders of the Republican party were also positivists and adherents to Auguste Comte's religion of humanity. They advocated the establishment of a voluntary republican dictatorship to lead the nation on an orderly path to material progress and prosperity. This alien ideology, however, was unable to compete against the secular liberalism of the age, which exalted the freedom of the individual, and against federalism, with its appeal to the strong regional sentiments of the Brazilian people. The small Republican party itself was a heterogeneous organization of individuals from different social and economic levels. It included planters and exporters, industrialists and bankers, and former monarchists such as Ruy Barbosa, who had broken with the old regime over the slavery issue. The rank and file of the party, and the staunchest defenders of the new government, appear to have been members of the emerging middle class and the literate segment of the working class in the cities —persons with predominantly urban incomes and inclinations whose influence had been negligible under the empire.

In these circumstances it is not surprising that the incoming regime lacked a coherent set of economic policies and that it failed to devise a balanced program for economic development. Not only was the concept of state planning alien to the economic liberalism of the nineteenth century, but the new rulers of Brazil were subject to conflicting pressures of ideology and practical politics which prevented easy agreement on specific fiscal and economic measures. Among the ideological factors restricting the range of government action was the belief, widely held in republican circles, that the states rather than the federal administration should have primary authority to tax or otherwise regulate economic enterprises. Equally strong was the conviction that if the impediments to economic growth were removed and private initiative were given free rein, a surge of economic development would follow automatically. According to this theory the entire economic base of the nation would be modernized and enlarged. The traditional plantation economy would increase in absolute terms, but would decline in relative importance with the growth of the manufacturing sector. This view was not fully accepted by the proponents of industrialization, who were often doctrinaire federalists as well. They maintained that manufacturing in Brazil could not thrive without protection against foreign competition.

The potential contradiction between the advocacy of states' rights on the one hand and the use of government power to shelter infant industries on the other was seemingly resolved in the Constitution of February 1891, which granted to the individual states exclusive authority to levy and collect taxes on exports and on industries, while leaving to the national government control over the tariff and the income from import duties. This quixotic arrangement—which persisted until 1930—was apparently intended in part to encourage official support for industry at the state and federal levels, but in practice it proved a deterrent to industrialization. The prosperity of the states was now tied directly to the volume of exports, and the federal administration could not erect an effective tariff wall against foreign manufactures without risking a sharp reduction in its revenues. Thus, under the republic as under the empire, government assistance to industry was often the incidental or secondary result of measures designed to attain other objectives.

During the first years of the republic these objectives were primarily political. The overriding problem was to complete the transition from constitutional monarchy to democratic republic without major violence or serious interruption in the economic life of the nation. In order to secure diplomatic recognition and access to foreign loans, the new administration promptly acknowledged the contractual obligations of the empire to foreign bankers and bondholders, but its ability to honor these commitments depended ultimately on the continued productivity of Brazil's plantations. Even though the republic drew much of its support from the cities, it could permit no weakening of the traditional plantation economy, which directly and indirectly supplied the bulk of the government revenues and the foreign exchange required for debt servicing. Aside from its immediate preoccupation with finances, the government was vitally concerned with the political attitudes of the rural landowners, whose support or tolerance was essential to the survival of the republic. The planters had been disgruntled by the monarchy's alleged neglect of their needs for manpower and credit, which had increased with the abolition of slavery and the conversion of the former bondsmen into wage earners. Many planters were now in an untenable financial position. They had not fought to defend the old regime, but neither were they enthusiastic about the republic. Unless placated, they might yet hurl the nation into the chaos of civil war. This crucial consideration weighed heavily in the government's early decisions to expand the money supply and to intensify the recruitment of agricultural labor in Europe.

At the same time the republican administration could not fail to be influenced by the attitudes and demands of its urban constituents, who were suspicious of the rural aristocracy and determined that it should not be permitted to regain its former dominance of the economy and the political process. They exposed their own economic interests, social aspirations, and political motivations in asserting that the planter class had been responsible for the backwardness of the empire, and that an urban, industrial society was the firmest base on which to construct a progressive, democratic republic. Indeed, industry should be promoted in order to create such a society. No less a spokesman for the new order than Finance Minister Ruy Barbosa echoed these views in defending his proposal for a frankly protective tariff. He left no doubt that the traditional, patriarchal plantation system, with its roots in slavery, was ill-suited to train citizens for a democratic country. The nation must have industry. The factory was the crucible in which an "intelligent and independent democracy" would be formed in Brazil. Such open calls for the use of economic means to achieve political and social goals—regarded as improper conduct by government officials under the empire—were to become common practice under the republic, in which the influence of the small, urban middle class was increasingly evident.

The financial situation of the country—which has been described by a later finance minister as deplorable—reflected the often irreconcilable pressures on the young republic, as well as the idealism, enthusiasm, inexperience, and political expediency of its leaders. To satisfy the demands of industry and agriculture for credit, many private banks were granted extensive power to issue currency backed by little more than faith in the future prosperity of Brazil. The consequences of this policy were soon felt. Within two years the volume of paper money in circulation more than doubled, and the foreign exchange value of the *milréis* dropped from 27 to 15 English pence. At the same time the easy money policies of the republic ushered in a period of unrestrained financial speculation in which even normally staid bankers and businessmen succumbed to get-rich-quick schemes to plunder the stock market.* By the end of 1891 the nominal value of capital invested in corporation stocks was five times greater than it had been at the end of the empire. Much of this investment evaporated in the panic which began before the second anniversary of the republic and continued for over a year, ruining some established firms as well as a plethora of paper organizations. The government did little to ease the situation, in part because it was felt the economy should be allowed to right itself, and more importantly because the violence the regime had feared broke out in 1892 and raged as a full-scale civil war in Rio Grande do Sul from 1893 to 1895. In order to pay the costs of the military campaign, the federal administration continued to run the printing presses and

* This period came to be known in the argot of Rio de Janeiro as the *encilhamento*—literally, the place where horses are groomed before a race—because the frenzied buying and selling of stocks on hunches resembled the behavior of gamblers far more than the studied actions of serious investors.

so contributed to the further decline in the value of the currency both at home and abroad.

The economic and social consequences of Republican policies were not, however, uniformly negative. Monetary inflation, by reducing the purchasing power of the currency, had the effect of lowering the price of Brazilian commodities in foreign markets, while raising the local price paid to the producers. In these circumstances there was a sharp rise in the sale of coffee and rubber and a general increase in the level of exports of other traditional products—with the notable exception of sugar. The expansion of exports, nonetheless, was not sufficient to prevent a reduction in foreign exchange earnings, with the result that imports were curtailed. This situation helped Brazilian manufacturers, but made it more difficult for the national government to meet its financial obligations abroad. To offset the loss of revenues from import duties, the republican regime required that a portion of the import tax be paid in gold, thus in effect imposing an additional tariff which further aided local industry. The soft money policies also meant that planters, exporters, and manufacturers could and did find it easy to borrow money to pay rising wage bills and other costs. Urban bankers were eager to advance substantial sums against mortgages on real property or future harvests. By and large the industrialists, coffee planters, and rubber merchants had little difficulty in repaying such loans with debased currency.

In the traditional sugar zone of the Northeast, however, where depression conditions persisted through the 1890's, many marginal producers lost their lands. Here the financial disorders of the early republican period combined with changing fashions in exports to accelerate a process that had begun before the fall of the empire—the consolidation of already large sugar *fazendas* into vast landholdings under absentee, corporate ownership. The transition destroyed a segment of the traditional aristocracy, weakened the familial ties that had softened man-master relationships in a patriarchal society, and hastened the introduction of the *usina,* which converted the sugar workers into a rural proletariat. In a sense, the regional society was being modernized, but at the same time the transfer of rural properties to urban corporations tied the northeastern cities more closely to the agricultural economy and heightened their dependence upon one major commodity. Investments that might have gone into other crops or into industry were now channeled increasingly into sugar production.

A different change in landholding patterns was initiated in the former coffee zone between Rio de Janeiro and São Paulo during the early years of the republic. In this area some of the exhausted coffee *fazendas* were sub-divided and sold on credit as family farms or truck gardens. Most of the purchasers appear to have been recent immigrants to Brazil. At that time the process was not carried far enough to alter the basic agricultural, social, or political structure of the region, for the new owners generally lacked the capital and technological skills required to restore the fertility of the eroding hillsides, but the nucleus of a class of independent smallholders was formed. An area that had once produced a single crop for export was gradually occupied by families who looked to nearby cities as the market for their products.

Armed opposition to the regime also served as a gauge of the effectiveness and limitations of the policies followed by the young republic. The civil war of 1893-95, while serious, was confined to the southern part of the country, and was directed primarily against the alleged political excesses of state and national administrations. In the long run the revolt could not succeed without the support of São Paulo and Minas Gerais. Here, however, the planters, who had benefitted from the influx of immigrants and the financial measures of the state and federal governments, refused to become involved in the conflict. The protracted revolt in Rio Grande do Sul—and the costly, poorly comprehended rebellion in the backlands of Bahia in 1896-97, which was soon to be immortalized in Euclides da Cunha's epic *Os Sertões*—re-emphasized the politico-military need for strategic rail lines within Brazil. In both campaigns the victory of government troops was delayed by the lack of rapid means of transportation. Despite the cost, construction of the so-called "São Paulo-Rio Grande" rail link was pushed during the period of hostilities in the south, and was continued until 1897, when the precarious state of the nation's finances forced an indefinite postponement.

By the mid-1890's disillusionment with the republic was widespread and growing, even among many who had welcomed the new regime enthusiastically in 1889. While few Brazilians seriously advocated a return to monarchy, it was impossible to avoid the invidious comparison of the political violence and economic disorder prevailing since the fall of the empire with the long period of internal peace and order under Pedro II. No matter where they placed the blame for the nation's difficulties, Brazilians were shamed by the signs of political and financial irresponsibility that, in their eyes, pulled Brazil down to the level of its unruly Spanish American neighbors. Those who attributed the republic's shortcomings to its military leadership were cheered for a time by the election of the first civilian president, Prudente de Morais of São Paulo, in 1894. But his administration, too, was disappointing, for he was obliged to use force to stay in office, and he seemed powerless to check the tide of inflation inherited from his military predecessor. When his term ended, on the ninth anniversary of the republic, the revolts in the South and Northeast had been suppressed, but the economic situation was approaching chaos. There was nearly twice as much paper money in circulation as at the height of the *encilhamento,* coffee prices in local currency were at their lowest point in many years, the exchange value of the *milréis* had plunged to 5 pence, federally-sponsored public works had been halted, and the budget forecast bankruptcy of the national treasury. This final calamity was averted only by a last-minute funding loan of £10 million negotiated by President-elect Manoel Ferraz de Campos Salles with the House of Rothschild in London. The first decade of the republic had made a shambles of national finances, and the outlook for the economy was not bright.

The situation called for heroic measures, which were undertaken and vigorously enforced by Campos Salles and his finance minister, Joaquim Murtinho. These men, trained in the liberal economic theories of the day, demanded a return to the "sound" fiscal policies that had brought financial and political stability to the empire. The Campos Salles administration looked upon the economic problem simply as a financial problem. Once the government's revenues were brought into line with its obligations, the value of the currency would be restored and the economic difficulties that plagued the country would resolve themselves. Therefore, all "unnecessary" government spending was eliminated, deficit-producing federal railroads were leased to private companies, and taxes were raised. Much of the paper money acquired by the national government was publicly burned to remove it from circulation. The results of these austerity measures were felt before Campos Salles left office in 1902. The inflationary spiral was checked, the cost of living was stabilized, the foreign exchange value of the currency rose steadily, and Brazil's credit in the money markets of the world was restored. Perhaps even more important was the restoration of confidence, in Brazil and abroad, in the future prosperity of the nation.

The Campos Salles administration marked a turning point in official attitudes toward economic development and the role of the state in the economy. The president and his advisers held no brief for the thesis that urban industry was indispensable for national prosperity or for the growth of republican institutions. They took it for granted that export agriculture was the basis of the nation's wealth and that the producers of such wealth were best equipped to interpret national interests. Thus, the former ruling group of planters and exporters, who had been castigated by early republican zealots, were brought fully back into politics, not as opponents but as bulwarks of the regime. They were to remain so until 1930.

The leaders of the national government were not opposed to industry as such, but they believed firmly in Darwin's inexorable law of the survival of the fittest. Firms that processed "national" products, such as sugar, cotton, minerals, timber, and the like might be tolerated, or even encouraged as long as they could compete with foreign manufacturers. Federal resources, however, should not be used to shelter inefficient industries. Those who shared this view found much to criticize in the domestic manufacturing sector. There seemed little logic in raising the tariff on European matches, for example, when not only the chemicals, but even the boxes, labels, and sticks for "Brazilian" matches were imported from Europe. Critics were quick to point out the incongruity of importing butter from France while maintaining a high-cost domestic perfume industry which imported all its raw materials from France.

The local product, moreover, was said to be inferior to French perfume.

In these circumstances it is somewhat ironic that the administration's fiscal policies contributed, on the whole, to industrial expansion in Brazil. Since the federal government could not increase revenues by taxing exports, it relied heavily upon customs for additional income, enacting a highly protective tariff and raising the portion of import duties to be paid in gold from 10 per cent to 15 per cent. These actions, justified as revenue measures, created a substantial barrier behind which Brazilian manufacturers were able to expand their share of the domestic market at the expense of foreign competitors. Brazilians in the money economy were still dependent on foreign sources for most of the manufactured articles they purchased, but local industry was neither weakened nor destroyed by the planter-oriented Campos Salles regime which professed to adhere to current economic theories of free trade and the international division of labor.

This situation reflected the presence and influence of industrialists in the national congress. Even though agricultural producers and exporters dominated that body and again held key decision-making positions within the administration, the cities were better represented than they had been under the empire. Congressmen with urban industrial constituencies might be outvoted, but they could not be excluded or entirely ignored. The advocates of local industry in and out of congress, moreover, became more adept at couching the demands and objectives of manufacturers in terms acceptable to the administration. They no longer stressed the exaggerated political and social benefits to derive from industrialization, but emphasized the immediate economic advantages to the government and the nation. A high tariff on manufactures, for example, would increase revenues to the federal treasury at the same time that it reduced the drain on foreign exchange for unnecessary imports, thereby permitting the government to balance the budget, to import those essential articles that could not be produced locally, and to meet the schedule of payments to foreign creditors. With rare exceptions this line of argument was used effectively in defense of Brazilian industry from the late 1890's until after the outbreak of World War I in Europe.

The restoration of financial stability under Campos Salles paved the way for a new and more impressive burst of modernization and industrial growth under his successors. Material progress again became the order of the day, as Brazil experienced a resurgence of the optimism and drive that had characterized the first years of the republic. There was much to be done to overcome a decade of depression and retrenchment. The "modern" water, light, and tramway services installed in the major cities before the end of the empire were now inadequate to meet the needs of a burgeoning population. The inland movement of the coffee frontier in São Paulo and the expansion of the mixed-farming zone in the south of the country had lagged since the suspension of railway building in 1897. Nonetheless, agricultural production was on the rise, and the heavy flow of exports was straining the facilities of Brazil's antiquated, fever-ridden ports. All of these problems were attacked simultaneously, for foreign loans and private foreign investments equal to the task were once more available to Brazil, and abundant immigrant labor was at hand. Beginning in 1903, contracts were let to British, French, and North American companies for the rebuilding and operation of each of the country's principal ports. Railway construction was resumed, again for the most part by private firms. The long-sought rail link between São Paulo and Rio Grande do Sul was completed in 1910, opening the interior of Paraná and Santa Catarina to settlement by immigrants from Europe. By 1914, the coffee zone stretched westward along the rail lines halfway across the state of São Paulo, and an extension of the railroad had reached Campo Grande in Mato Grosso. Public attention, however, was focused on the changes taking place in the larger coastal cities, where an all-out campaign was under way to eliminate the endemic and epidemic diseases that had become more devastating as the population increased.

The campaign was initiated in Rio de Janeiro in 1903, concurrently with major public works projects to improve municipal utilities and the appearance of the nation's capital. The sanitation program was placed under the direction of Dr. Osvaldo Cruz, who was given full authority to enforce all necessary health measures. Over the strident protests of the great majority, the populace was vaccinated en masse against smallpox. The mosquito-borne scourges—malaria, known since colonial times, and yellow fever, which had become endemic in the city since the first outbreak in 1849—virtually disappeared as swamps were filled in and adequate water and sewerage systems were installed. Broad avenues were cut through crowded, unsanitary districts to improve the circulation of air and traffic. Within three years the national capital was transformed into one of the most healthful and beautiful cities in the tropics. The successful experiment in Rio de Janeiro served as a model for United States canal builders in Panama, and inspired similar programs in other cities of Brazil. The latter were usually sponsored by state governments and carried out, under concession, by private foreign companies.

Foreign firms came to be conspicuous, if not dominant, in large areas of the Brazilian economy after 1900. Great Britain, as the financial center of the world, supplied the bulk of the capital invested in Brazil, but German, French, Italian, Belgian, and North American companies competed with British corporations for a share in the economic development of the young republic. Foreigners owned or controlled 160 of the 201 new corporations authorized to operate in Brazil between 1899 and 1910. In part this situation reflected the fact that Brazilian businessmen continued to prefer family-owned concerns or partnerships—in which personal relations were all-important—over corporations ruled by distant, anonymous shareholders. It also indicated that the large accumulations of capital required to finance major business enterprises were only available in the wealthier, industrial countries. For the most part the foreign companies confined their activities to banking, public works and utilities, transportation, mining and the production and shipping of Brazil's traditional exports. The largest firms were the British-owned São Paulo Railway Company, dating from 1867, and the Rio and São Paulo Tramway, Light and Power consortium, organized in Toronto in 1901, of mixed Canadian, United States, and British capital. Prior to 1920 manufacturing remained almost entirely in the hands of native-born Brazilians and immigrants who had made their home permanently in Brazil.

Although foreign companies generally did not engage in manufacturing, their activities contributed directly to the notable expansion of the industrial sector during the early years of this century. Foreign banks supplied credits, foreign-operated railroads transported the raw materials and finished products of Brazilian industry, and foreign firms employing foreign technicians and imported machinery provided electricity for Brazilian cities and factories. Hailed initially as a source of light, electricity was soon recognized as a new form of energy for transportation and industry. As it became available, electric trolleys replaced horse-drawn trams, some railways were electrified, and factories were converted to electricity for both light and power. The first electric generator in Brazil—a 52-kilowatt unit—was installed in Minas Gerais in June 1883. Manaus, in 1896, became the first large Brazilian city to introduce electric street lights, a full decade before Rio de Janeiro. Nonetheless, by 1900 there were thirteen electric power plants in Brazil, with a capacity of more than 10,000 kilowatts. Most of these were concentrated near the national capital and São Paulo, enhancing their attractiveness as sites for new mills and factories of all kinds. Much of the rapid industrial growth of São Paulo and Rio de Janeiro was due to the abundance of water power along the Serra do Mar, where imaginative engineers dammed westward-flowing streams to reverse their direction and tapped the current as it spilled over the escarpment into the Atlantic. Elsewhere, the generating plants were usually thermal units, fired with imported coal or oil. Despite this limiting factor, which increased costs somewhat, the availability and consumption of electric power soared in Brazil after 1900. The number of generators rose to 88 in 1910 and quadrupled to 356 a decade later, while the use of electric power by industry jumped more than twenty-five times between 1907 and 1920, from some 5500 horsepower to 146,000 horsepower. In 1920 electricity accounted for nearly half of all the energy consumed by industry in Brazil.

The expansion of industry during these years, particularly in cities served by electric power, was highly impressive. The census of 1907 listed 3258 "industrial" establishments. Textile mills and food-processing plants accounted for approximately half of these. The great bulk of all industrial production in Brazil was concentrated in four states and the Federal District. The metropolitan area of Rio de Janeiro, including the national capital and nearby towns in the state of Rio de Janeiro, clearly dominated the field with 40 per cent of the total, while São Paulo and Rio Grande do Sul, with 16 per cent and 15 per cent, respectively, were important manufacturing centers. Minas Gerais supplied just under 5 per cent of Brazil's industrial output by value. The economic recession of 1907, combined with the defeat in congress that year of a proposal to raise tariff barriers, contributed to a temporary slackening in the rate of industrial growth. Only 166 new firms appeared in the next three years. By 1915, however, the number of industrial plants had doubled, and, under the impact of the war in Europe, nearly doubled again in the five years ending in 1920. By the latter year the number of establishments had risen to 13,569, while the value of production was four times greater than in 1907. Food processing now accounted for 40 per cent of all industrial activity in Brazil, with textiles contributing about a quarter of the total. The other significant industries in order of importance were clothing, chemicals and pharmaceuticals, lumber and wood products, metallurgy, tobacco processing, glass and ceramics, and leather goods. As in 1907, three-quarters of the industrial plants were concentrated in the center and south of the country, but their distribution within that favored region had been substantially altered during these thirteen years. São Paulo was now the industrial center of the nation, with 31 per cent of the production. Greater Rio de Janeiro had dropped to second rank with 28 per cent. Rio Grande do Sul accounted for only 11 per cent of the industrial product, or just double the output of Minas Gerais in 1920.

Many reasons have been put forth to explain the rise of São Paulo as the leading industrial area of Brazil and South America. The Paulistas frequently attribute their progress to the invigorating climate of the plateau and to the enterprising spirit of the people. These qualities no doubt contributed, but they had been present throughout the long colonial period when the captaincy was one of the poorest in Portuguese America, and in any case were not unique to São Paulo. Obviously, some new factors had been added to the equation during the empire and the early years of the republic. Coffee accounted directly and indirectly for most of the transformation of São Paulo. Before the end of the empire coffee had given São Paulo the finest network of railroads in Brazil, a rail system that linked the province with the populous areas of Rio de Janeiro and Minas Gerais. By the first decade of the twentieth century São Paulo alone was supplying about half the coffee in the world market, and the state export tax on coffee made São Paulo by far the wealthiest unit in the federal republic. In addition, for a generation São Paulo received a large influx of immigrants from Europe. In the quarter-century ending in 1914 over half of all immigrants to Brazil went to São Paulo. Drawn initially as laborers for the coffee *fazendas,* tens of thousands of these new Brazilians soon gravitated to the cities, where they became the owners, managers, and workers in the new industries. The attitudes of the planters—who controlled the state government—also affected the rate of industrial growth. In São Paulo, to a greater extent than in other parts of Brazil, plantation owners tended to invest a portion of their profits in other business ventures, chiefly banking and commerce. Even before the outbreak of war in Europe, however, some of them had begun to invest directly in manufacturing, blurring the lines between the rural aristocracy and the aspiring urban, industrial middle class. As a result, little or no social stigma was attached to industry, and state leaders were sympathetic to some of the views of industrialists. Thus, São Paulo had a suitable political climate for industry, wealth for investment, an ample and efficient labor supply, and a large, affluent, and accessible domestic market. The state was in an excellent position to fill the industrial gap caused by the interruption of trade with Europe during World War I.

The social structure of Brazil proved remarkably resistant to change during the half-century that witnessed abolition, massive immigration, rapid urbanization, the rise of industry, and the transition from monarchy to republic. A few safety valves were provided to avert explosion before 1920, but these benefitted only the more fortunate. The traditional social pyramid was distended to make room for the industrial leaders who had forced their way to the top, and the ranks of the urban middle class were expanded to include sons of immigrants who had managed to acquire a secondary education. For the most part, however, the ex-slaves, the recently arrived European farm workers, and the growing numbers of factory workers, both immigrant and native-born, were expected to be content with their lot. Although slavery gave way to wage or contract labor, the position and role of the rural lower class remained substantially unchanged by abolition or the establishment or the republic. The political revolution did enfranchise several thousands of Brazilians in the cities, but 95 per cent of the population was still barred from direct participation in the political process. The patterns of patriarchal society persisted because both the rural aristocracy and the educated, urban elite of lawyers, physicians, and merchants shared the values of that society. Under the republic, as under the empire, they successfully resisted significant social change through their control over law-making and law-enforcing agencies and over education.

As a practical matter, the expansion of educational opportunities, particularly at the primary level, during the first three decades of the republic out-paced the growth in population, adding to the pressures for social change. In the waning years of the empire well under 3 per cent of the population was attending schools at all levels, even though by law public primary education was free, and in some provinces compulsory. The law, however, was ignored almost entirely in the rural areas and received little more than lip service in the cities and towns, for few men in public life were convinced of the desirability of formal education for the lower orders. In any case, there were never enough funds or qualified teachers to provide facilities for universal primary training. In a nation of some 14 million people there were only 7500 elementary schools offering instruction through the fourth year to about 260,000 pupils. This meant that for every thousand children of school age, 864 received no schooling at all. Moreover, only a small percentage of those who started the first year completed the fourth grade. At the secondary level there were about 300 public schools attracting upwards of 12,000 students. In addition, 4000 students were enrolled in private secondary schools in Rio de Janeiro, and there may have been an equal number in private institutions in the provincial capitals. Higher education was limited to two medical schools, two law schools, one school of engineering, and a school of mines, with a combined enrollment under 2500. Vocational schools were rare. Instruction beyond the elementary grades was heavily classical, with the emphasis on rhetoric, literature, and the liberal arts. Clearly, in practice, formal education was a privilege for the few who were destined to become the leaders of society and government.

The men who rose to national prominence with the establishment of the republic were products of the traditional educational system. By and large they were satisfied with the nature and purpose of the instruction provided in the secondary and professional schools, and made little serious effort to modify it, beyond adding a few courses in the sciences and opportunities for advanced training in commerce and agriculture. Under the republic those who were educated past the primary level continued to constitute an intellectual elite, although the ranks of this privileged group were considerably expanded. By 1910, about 8000 students were attending professional courses, while some 30,000 were enrolled in 298 private and 29 public secondary schools throughout Brazil. Half of these schools, and more than half of the students, were found in the Federal District and the states of Minas Gerais, São Paulo, and Rio Grande do Sul. A decade later the number of advanced and secondary school students—still concentrated in the larger cities—had risen to perhaps 12,000 and 50,000 respectively.

There was much less complacency about the state of elementary education among the new leaders of Brazil in 1889, although they were not agreed on the urgency of educational reform. The minority of doctrinaire Republicans—many of whom were newspapermen—were convinced that the republican system of government required a literate, informed citizenry, and that this could best be assured through universal primary education. The positivists among them further insisted on the need for wide dissemination of "practical" scientific training. These views—which coincided with the opinions of industrialists seeking a skilled, literate labor force, and with the ambitions of the European immigrants, who prized formal education as the key to upward social mobility for their children—were reflected in the directives of the short-lived national ministry of education. The federal Constitution of

February 1891, however, left the responsibility for primary education largely to the individual states. Consequently, increases in the number of schools and in school enrollments were greatest in central and southern Brazil—in the industrial urban areas and in rural communities settled predominantly by immigrants from Europe. In some of the latter, instruction was entirely in the mother tongue of the immigrants. While the rate of progress was much slower in the northern and northeastern states than in the southern parts of the country, elementary school enrollments increased steadily in every region of Brazil. In 1910 there were more than 11,000 primary schools with an enrollment of nearly 566,000 pupils. By 1920 enrollments exceeded 1,250,000. The dreams of the early Republicans had not yet been fulfilled, for most rural districts still had no schools, and only one-fourth of the adult population was literate in 1920. Nevertheless, in the preceding three decades, while the national population was doubling, the number of pupils in elementary schools had increased almost fivefold.

This situation contributed to the so-called "social question," which arose out of the frustrated aspirations of the urban working class. The immigrants from Europe and the native-born Brazilians who flocked to the new factories in the cities expected to improve their lot and that of their children. Increasingly, working-class parents sent their sons, and even daughters, to school in the belief that a smattering or more of education would entitle them to a higher economic and social status. Occasionally these ambitions were realized, but more often they were not, for relatively few pupils went beyond the elementary level. The great majority received less than two years of formal instruction, barely sufficient to make them literate. This might qualify them for employment on a newspaper or in a store, but it did not assure them economic security or entry into a higher social class.

The concept of generalized social mobility developed slowly in Brazil, for it ran counter to the country's heritage of authoritarianism and a stratified society. Moreover, the leaders of the young republic had no desire to upset the traditional social order, and they seem not to have realized that federal and state programs to expand the public school system might well have that result. Although they had, in effect, opened a Pandora's box by increasing educational opportunities in a land where education was considered a privilege, they refused to accept the logical consequences of their own actions. It had always been possible for men of exceptional talents and abilities to rise in the social scale in Brazil, but the ruling group was surprised and appalled that the sons of manual laborers and others who performed demeaning tasks should aspire to higher social, economic, and political positions merely because they had been to school for a short time. In its view, education for the lower orders was intended to make them better workers, not to fill them with pretensions to rise above their station. Those who took advantage of their schooling to protest against the status quo should, therefore, be regarded as dangerous subversives seeking to destroy the established order.

The fears of the ruling group were not without foundation. Under the republic many members of the urban working class came to feel that drastic, even violent changes were necessary to bring them a better life. Not only did thousands of youths attempt individually to escape the poverty and social stigma of the lower class by remaining longer in school, but some radicals were calling upon workers to unite as a class and to use their collective strength to secure a larger share of the fruits of their labor. Almost invariably the most effective advocates of labor unions, strikes, boycotts, and demonstrations were men who had received some primary training in Europe or in the new schools in Brazil. Rarely did a man with secondary education concern himself with the plight and protests of wage earners. After 1900, such protests became commonplace, particularly in São Paulo, which had the largest concentration of foreign-born in the industrial labor force. For this reason the political authorities usually attributed discontent among workers to foreign agitators.

There was much to protest against, even though the conditions of industrial labor had been improving somewhat since the last decades of the empire. Under the republic it was no longer possible to find examples of the kind described in 1876, when Brazil's largest cigarette factory was manned chiefly by orphan children, who received room, board, clothing, primary education, and instruction in music during a three-year apprenticeship, and thereafter "wages corresponding to their aptitude." Such situations, smacking of indentured servitude, were incompatible with the new attitudes toward the role of the state in education. But child labor was still common after the turn of the century, for children could be legally employed from the age of twelve. They received lower wages than were paid to men or women. In the small shops and processing plants, which comprised the great majority of all industrial establishments, employers and employees frequently worked side by side. The close personal relationship partially offset discontent over long hours and subsistence pay. The large mills and factories, however, were fortress-like buildings directed by foremen, with armed guards to keep the gates locked except at the beginning and end of the working day. The hours of labor ranged from nine or nine and a half for certain skilled craftsmen, such as typesetters and cabinet makers, to upwards of sixteen hours for street cleaners and garbage collectors. Bakers, barbers, and retail merchants kept their shops open until noon on Sundays, but most other businesses observed Sunday as a day of rest. Wages were adequate to pay for food, rent, and clothing for a small family, but did not permit luxuries or savings. Larger families ordinarily required two or more breadwinners. No provision was made by industry or the state to protect workers against loss of income during periods of unemployment or in old age.

There were no labor unions in Brazil until after the establishment of the republic. In the first years of the republic the national government sponsored the formation of trade unions among transportation and port workers in Rio de Janeiro, apparently as instruments to control labor votes. These organizations were recognized by the regime, but they remained under political leadership and were largely ineffective in securing benefits for their members. As a practical matter, workingmen's clubs and mutual benefit societies provided the only form of social security available to urban labor. They were formed by employees in the same factory or trade, or, more often, by immigrants from the same village or province in Europe. Such voluntary associations enjoyed legal status, but were not accepted by employers or political authorities as competent to bargain on behalf of workers in labor disputes. Some of these formed the basis for incipient labor unions after 1900.

Two distinct trends in the last quarter of the nineteenth century had a direct bearing on the kind of labor movement that developed in Brazil before 1920. These were the revolution in communications that swept Brazil into the orbit of European news media, and the flood of immigrants that brought tens of thousands of literate foreign-born workers into the urban labor force. All the major news events in Europe, including political disturbances and labor agitation, were reported daily to the Brazilian reading public in Portuguese, Italian, and German. The working class was well informed on when, where, and how the common people in Europe protested against conditions similar to those in Brazil. It is not surprising that some were inspired to emulate European critics of the old order. This was particularly true of a minority of the immigrants. Their numbers included Italian socialists, Spanish syndicalists and anarchists, and German social democrats, whose colleagues in Europe before 1914 were calling for the violent overthrow of existing governments and the establishment of some sort of workers' paradise. Brazilian radicals differed over tactics and the precise form of the regime to be created, but agreed that labor must be mobilized for political action. The attainment of immediate material gains for the working class was only a first step toward the long-range political objective. Under the circumstances, the most active labor organizers were the most radical politically. Consequently, trade unionism in Brazil was equated with subversion and political violence, and was dealt with accordingly by the political authorities. Strikes were regularly suppressed by force. Trouble makers were blacklisted by employers, and agitators were rounded up periodically by the police. Immigrants among them were deported and the native-born were jailed or sent to work on the railroad—popularly known as the "road of death"—then being pushed through hostile Indian territory in Mato Grosso.

Despite the disservice to the labor movement by political extremists, which made all workers' associations suspect before the law, the number of trade unions increased rapidly after 1900. The first national labor conference was held in 1906, and a national labor confederation was formed as a political party in 1912. It claimed to speak for all urban workers, but exerted no discernible influence in national, state, or municipal politics. Significantly, only two so-called "general strikes" occurred before 1920, and both were clearly non-political. The first, in 1907, forced a reduction in the working day, while the second, a decade later, was a spontaneous outburst against wartime inflation and the soaring cost of living. Virtually all industrial employers were obliged to grant higher wages. With these two exceptions, the labor movement was unable to overcome the taint of subversion that clung to it. Nor was it able to persuade Brazil's leaders to modify the labor policy of the republic, which was often summed up in the cryptic expression, "the social question is a question for the police." In the 1920's it was to become a question for the army, and a cause for revolution.

Chapter 7 • The Industrial Revolution

The growth of industry has been the most striking phenomenon in the economic development of Brazil since 1920, dwarfing the accomplishments of the preceding fifty years. Although the national economy is still heavily dependent upon the export of a few agricultural commodities, Brazil has become the most industrialized country of Latin America. It ranks ahead of Mexico in range and volume of industrial production and leads all other Latin American republics by a widening margin. The transformation of the Brazilian economy in the course of a long generation did not follow a consistent, irreversible pattern. Rates of progress varied from year to year and from one branch of industry to another. In each decade some established concerns failed to adjust to changing circumstances and some new initiatives were stifled as new obstacles arose to impede industrialization. These included the revival of foreign competition in the 1920's, the economic depression and war that successively engulfed the Western world from 1929 to 1945, and soaring inflation and recurrent political unrest within Brazil in the postwar period. Yet, with the perspective of half a century it is possible to discern continuing trends and to assess the positive impact of domestic and international crises on the pace and direction of industrial expansion.

The rise of industry in Brazil after 1920 could not fail to encourage and reflect sweeping changes in the urban social structure and to affect the balance of political power between urban and rural areas. Confined, as it was, almost entirely to the larger cities and towns, industrialization was both a cause and effect of rapid urban growth. In the five decades ending in 1970 millions of migrants from the countryside swarmed into the cities, drawn in part by the lure of jobs in shops, mills, and factories. Whether or not their hopes for a better life were realized, the migrants were immediately absorbed into the money economy, thereby enlarging the domestic market for processed goods and manufactures. Under this sustained stimulus Brazil's industrial base expanded many times over, primarily as a result of new firms entering the field. Between 1920 and 1960 the number of plants increased more than eightfold, to over 110,000, and continued to rise. By 1970 the population had more than trebled over the 1920 figure, and the industrial labor force in Brazil had expanded by seven times to exceed 3 million, or about 3.5 per cent of the national population. The growth of industry also contributed to a massive increase in the urban electorate and to a sharp rise in the political influence of both employers and workers in the industrial centers. Since the 1930's the growing ranks of owners and directors of industry have comprised an effective pressure group with a major voice in the formulation of national economic policies, while in the period of open politics from 1945 to 1964 industrial workers—who by and large were literate, and thus qualified to vote—were a crucial, and at times decisive, element in Brazilian elections.

These aspects of the Brazilian industrial revolution may be measured in material terms. But perhaps more significant than the physical growth of Brazil's industrial capacity is the profound shift it represented in attitudes toward the importance of industry to the nation. Within a single lifetime the goal of an industrialized economy was converted from an impractical dream into a national objective. Few Brazilians in 1920 were prepared to insist that inefficient, war-born

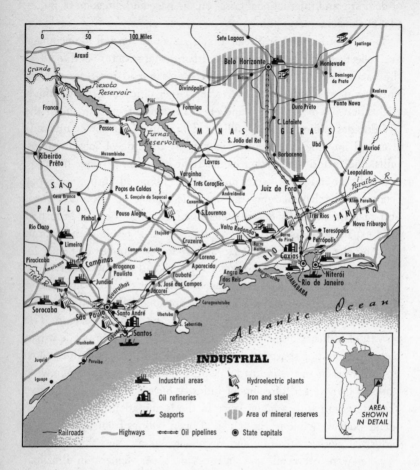

processing and manufacturing industries were vital to the economic life of the republic. It was still widely held as common sense that Brazil should exploit its natural advantages to produce tropical commodities which could be exchanged for industrial products from abroad. Desirable as national industries might be, they must justify their existence economically, and should not be promoted at the expense of agriculture. In sharp contrast, since World War II dependence upon agricultural exports has generally been decried as a major deterrent to economic development, while a high degree of industrial self-sufficiency has come to be almost universally accepted within Brazil as indispensable to the well-being of the population and the state.

The reversal of popular and official opinion about the relative merits of agriculture and industry was a result of the continuing reappraisal of Brazil's economic policies since the depression era. Traditionally, national economic policies had been based on the twin assumptions that Brazil would receive compensatory prices for its chief exports and that it would have easy access to the products of European and North American industries. Although world market conditions fluctuated considerably from year to year, these assumptions had usually proved valid before 1914—particularly after the adoption of the coffee valorization plan—and they seemed sound once more as the world returned to normal in the 1920's. Both, however, were undermined and discredited by the series of crises after 1929, which exposed the vulnerability of the Brazilian economy to any interruption in the established pattern of foreign commerce or deterioration in the terms of trade. During the depression decade the catastrophic drop in the market value of primary products pulled Brazilian foreign exchange earnings far below the level required to maintain the customary volume of imports. The economy had not yet recuperated from this blow when World War II imposed even greater restrictions on foreign trade. In spite of high prices for all Brazilian exports, the shortage of shipping and the conversion of European and United States industries to military production in the war years forced a further drastic curtailment in Brazilian imports of industrial raw materials and finished goods. And after a brief respite in the immediate postwar period, world market prices for Brazil's leading exports entered a long decline in relation to the cost of manufactured articles. With the terms of trade operating against Brazil, the nation's leaders felt increasingly obliged to turn to the printing press and to heavy foreign borrowing in an effort to sustain economic development at rates demanded and expected by the Brazilian people.

The drive to build an industrial economy in Brazil was accompanied and reinforced at every stage by the growth of economic nationalism. The interaction between the two processes was so complete that they cannot be fully distinguished from one another. On the one hand, economic nationalism—nurtured by the adversities that increased Brazilian awareness of the value of national industries—provided emotional or psychological justification for creating and protecting such industries. On the other hand, each new addition to the country's industrial capacity added to the intensity and scope of nationalistic fervor, which by the 1960's had become virtually synonymous with patriotism in Brazil.

For the most part the evolution of economic nationalism as a broad, coherent, and vital force in Brazilian life dates from the Vargas era after 1930. Earlier, in the decade of the 1920's, its advocates had been drawn mainly from two small sectors of society. One was the dedicated minority of intellectuals and political figures with a grandiose vision of Brazil's future. The other was comprised of local industrialists seeking to preserve their hold on the domestic market. Their effectiveness was limited, for their proposals ran counter to the deeply ingrained internationalism of the educated elite and to the willingness of informed Brazilians generally to acknowledge the important role played by foreigners in the national economy. Under the circumstances, response to the xenophobic appeals inherent in nationalism was not widespread and could only be aroused when the public was convinced that alien interests threatened the national patrimony. This situation was illustrated in the treatment of three issues affecting industry in Brazil in the 1920's. The economic nationalists generated enthusiastic and effective popular approval for their campaign to prevent foreign control and exportation of Brazil's iron ore reserves. Yet, even while the anti-foreign campaign was under way, there was no strong objection on nationalistic grounds to the creation of a new steel industry within the country, almost entirely by foreign firms. Nor were Brazilian food processors and manufacturers of consumer goods—who were widely blamed for the rising cost of living—able to elicit public sympathy for their demands to restrict foreign competition with existing industries.

Economic nationalism and industrialization spread rapidly under the double impact of the world depression of 1929 and the revolution of

1930 that brought Getulio Vargas to power. As chief of state for fifteen years Vargas did more than any individual to promote these trends, presenting industry as the panacea for Brazil's economic ills and resorting frequently to nationalistic appeals to win support for his regime and its programs. In his hands economic nationalism was a highly effective political tool used with calculated effect. This, however, did not mean a frontal attack on the plantation economy or an end to the long-standing Brazilian ambivalence toward foreigners. Vargas himself rarely indulged in the shrill xenophobic outbursts that he tolerated from extreme nationalists. He and his associates took it for granted that Brazil must have industries to provide the goods no longer available from overseas, but recognized that in order to achieve this goal—to lessen dependence on foreign sources of supply—it was necessary to import the essentials for industrial growth. Without foreign capital, technology, and machinery, the economy would stagnate at a subsistence level. Therefore, the rural export sector could not be abandoned, for it had to earn the foreign exchange needed to subsidize the expansion of industry. The nationalistic solution to the economic crises of the 1930's and 1940's was to enhance the regulatory powers of the state over the economy. Under Vargas the central government exercised greater control over Brazil's export trade and imposed fairly rigid standards of selectivity for imports. Luxury items were heavily taxed while incentives were offered for the importation of machines to make machines. The results were soon evident. By 1938 industrial production in Brazil was 60 per cent greater by value than the combined output of livestock and agriculture. The culmination of Vargas's industrialization program was the establishment of the national iron and steel plant at Volta Redonda, which began operations after he left office.

The postwar division of the world into developed and underdeveloped nations added a new dimension—and a large new vocabulary—to economic nationalism in Brazil. To a greater extent than ever before industry was equated with power and prestige in international circles, while production of foodstuffs and raw materials for export was associated with "colonial" economies. Measured by these criteria, Brazil was clearly underdeveloped, despite the gains registered by Brazilian industry since 1930. Ardent nationalists came increasingly to attribute this situation to exploitation by industrial powers, the United States above all, and to insist that Brazil would not have true political independence until it had achieved economic independence as well. At the same time, they asserted that the United States had a moral obligation to help Brazil narrow the economic gap between the two countries.

The drive to industrialize the economy was intensified after World War II, but the objective was broadened to include development of the entire economic base—physical, financial, and human. The shift of attention to the so-called "economic infrastructure" was evident in the SALTE plan of the late 1940's, a five-year plan of government investments to promote rapid development in the fields of health, food, transportation, and power.* The magnitude of the problems to be resolved in these areas seemed to call for unprecedented quantities of foreign capital and a co-ordinated program of development under the direction of the central government. Thereafter, the state assumed an increasing amount of responsibility for economic planning and participated more directly in the national economy, investing heavily in hydroelectric projects, highway construction, and even in the production of some durable consumer goods. A substantial part of the new investment was obtained from foreign loans. But even as foreign public and private investments mounted in Brazil, there was a growing clamor to bar foreigners from vital sectors of the economy. The nationalists held that strategic natural resources and public utilities should be controlled by the state. Under the spur of an intensive nationalistic campaign, a national petroleum monopoly was established in the early 1950's, and proposals for similar monopolies on the development of electrical power and nuclear energy were vociferously debated. In the early 1960's most foreign-owned telephone and electric companies were nationalized. This trend was checked by the revolution of 1964, which revealed the bitter split among the people of Brazil over the role of the

---

* SALTE is derived from the first letters of the Portuguese words *Saúde, Alimentação, Transporte e Energia* meaning health, food, transportation, and power.

foreigner and the state in the economy. The trend toward rapid industrialization continued without serious interruption, however, for in
spite of deep divisions over the methods by which this goal should be
achieved, there was general agreement about the need for broad economic development. In the 1970's Brazilians of every political persuasion were convinced that an industrial economy was essential to
protect the country against the vagaries of world markets for primary
products and to assure Brazil a significant role in the community of
nations.

The evolution of this attitude—and of the rising aspirations of the
Brazilian people—may be seen in an examination of the actions of native entrepreneurs, laborers, government, and foreign capital in selected
areas of the economy since 1920. During each decade the bases were
laid for further growth and diversification of the economy, and for an
increasingly nationalistic approach to the problems of economic development.

The decade of the 1920's was a difficult one for national industry in
Brazil. Even though expansion of the urban population and periodic
increases in import duties permitted industrial production to rise by
over 40 per cent in real value between 1920 and 1929, the number of
industrial firms appears to have dropped substantially, and their share
of the national market declined from wartime levels. With the return
of world peace, the prewar pattern of international trade was largely
restored. Foreign purchases of Brazilian processed foods, fabrics, semi-
manufactures, and ores dwindled, while, in the aggregate, sales of Brazil's traditional exports surpassed records established before 1914. At
the same time manufacturers in Europe and the United States resumed
normal peacetime operations and by 1923 were once more flooding
Brazil with consumer goods. This situation, favorable to commercial
houses and to producers of agricultural and pastoral commodities, made
it virtually impossible to attract new, large-scale Brazilian investments
to the manufacturing sector, where risks appeared greater and profits
less certain than in agriculture. In 1927 the total production of Brazilian industries was nearly 60 per cent less by value than that of the
nation's plantations and ranches. In the state of São Paulo, which now

accounted for well over one-third of Brazil's industrial output, the growing disparity between the interests of merchants and manufacturers was exposed in 1928 when the latter withdrew from the venerable Commercial Association to form their own body, the São Paulo Center of Industries. The new organization collected and disseminated information requested by its members, lobbied on behalf of industry before the state and federal governments, and engaged in an active propaganda campaign extolling the benefits that a strong national industry would bring to the people of Brazil. As long as coffee sales were high, however, providing the exchange to pay for imported manufactures, local industrialists had little success in persuading the public to buy Brazilian-made items in preference to the more prestigious foreign products.

Although the domestic consumer goods industry received little public or official support in the 1920's, there were occasional indications of concern over the weakness of the nation's industrial base. An undercurrent of dissatisfaction with the economic backwardness of Brazil ran through the waves of popular discontent that were directed primarily against political and social grievances during the middle years of the decade. Even those who argued that Brazil should not attempt to compete with more advanced countries in the manufacture of products requiring a high level of technological development came to feel that Brazilians were neglecting opportunities to establish basic industries well within the competence of local entrepreneurs and the labor force. The full extent of Brazil's natural resources was not known, but clearly the republic was more bountifully endowed with industrial raw materials than many of the countries from which it imported finished articles of all kinds. It seemed anomalous that a heavily forested nation should import wood pulp and newsprint for its publishing industry. It seemed unreasonable that the country's only cement plant, established during the war years, should fail at a time when Brazil was importing hundreds of thousands of tons of cement each year for building construction. Above all, public attention was drawn to the fact that Brazil, with untold reserves of iron ore, manganese, and coal, was unable to meet its own modest needs for iron and steel.

Such anomalies, of course, had long existed in the Brazilian economy and had provoked sporadic outbursts by government leaders, economic nationalists, and some members of the business community. No consensus had been reached about the proper way to develop basic industries, nor was there agreement now, but after World War I the problem began to receive fairly consistent attention in the press and in political debate. Successive federal administrations, concerned not to disturb the prosperous export economy, were nonetheless willing to provide long-term tax exemptions on imported machinery and equipment to qualified firms seeking to develop new industries based on Brazil's natural resources. The government normally preferred to leave the initiative and financing to private capital, foreign or domestic. Potential investors, however, usually urged the state to guarantee them a protected national market, insisting that Brazilian companies could not survive unless tariffs were imposed to raise the price of competing foreign manufactures. Thus, the question was ultimately reduced to whether or how much tariff protection local producers should receive. Significantly, there were few serious proposals that the federal government itself should participate directly in industrial enterprises.

The response of the government to demands for the protection of the various national industries depended on which industry was being considered. Official attitudes were influenced not only by the size and strategic importance of the individual industry and the potential market for its products, but also on occasion by the amount of political pressure and popular interest its proponents could muster. In the absence of strong political pressure and clearly articulated public opinion, the federal authorities appear to have weighed their action in terms of its impact on the budget and the balance of trade. When tariff protection could be expected to result in a decline in imports—and a consequent loss of revenue from customs—the request was usually denied. On the other hand, if the domestic market was thought to be growing sufficiently to permit an increase in import duties without adverse effect on foreign suppliers or customs receipts, the demands of local producers might be met, wholly or in part.

The range of alternatives acceptable to the national executive and the congress was illustrated in their decisions affecting the wood pulp, cement, and steel industries. In the first two instances, public opinion was not a significant factor. It proved difficult to generate widespread enthusiasm for a native wood pulp and paper industry among a population that was largely illiterate or even among the small core of intellectuals, who comprised the most influential sector of the reading public. The latter generally preferred foreign, chiefly French, writings over Brazilian publications. As long as the demand for paper remained small and men of letters continued to look abroad for intellectual stimulus, local pulp and paper producers received no significant assistance from the government. The modest growth of the industry during the 1920's and after was achieved in the face of sustained foreign competition, as Brazil continued to meet most of its requirements in this area through imports. In the case of cement, neither the general public, the building contractors, who were the principal consumers, nor the construction workers—the least skilled and the least sophisticated politically of the urban labor force—displayed marked concern over the foreign origin of this prime building material. Nonetheless, since the market for cement was expanding, import duties were raised to shelter the industry newly established in 1926. The action, which led to higher prices for cement throughout Brazil, was rationalized on the grounds that domestic production would represent some savings of foreign exchange and that the higher tariff would enhance government revenues. Such reasoning proved sound, at least over the short run, for Brazilian production increased more than sevenfold between 1926 and 1929, while imports during the same period were rising by more than one-third. In 1929 foreign sources still accounted for about 85 per cent of the cement consumed in Brazil.

The relative calm in which the debates over the wood pulp and cement industries were conducted was replaced by a climate of intense emotionalism when the steel question was raised. This issue generated more heat and less light than any other related to Brazil's economic development between World War I and World War II. Moreover, the controversy delayed the establishment of a large, integrated steel industry for two decades, and ultimately paved the way for the central government to enter the steel business as the largest producer in the nation.

From the beginning the steel issue was a political issue, involving state and regional rivalries, matters of national defense, fears of a foreign monopoly over a major national resource, and vociferous commentary in the press and other public forums. Under the circumstances the development of the steel industry was rarely considered in strictly economic terms. Nor was it surprising that those engaged in the heated discussion in the 1920's were unable or unwilling to distinguish between two related but separate aspects of the question—the manufacture of iron and steel in Brazil on the one hand, and the exportation of iron ore from Brazil on the other. The insistence upon finding a single solution to this dual problem contributed to the persistent discord over iron and steel.

As a practical matter there was general agreement that Brazil must have the capacity to meet its own needs for most grades of iron and steel. The difficulty lay in deciding where and by whom the mills should be built. The federal administration placed a high priority on the expansion of the industry, and as early as 1918 was authorized by congress to make substantial loans to companies willing to erect plants capable of producing 50,000 tons per year. The authorization contained no restrictions against foreign firms legally registered under Brazilian law. No giants of the industry were attracted to Brazil by this provision, but beginning in 1921 several small firms entered the field. Their mills were located chiefly in southern Minas Gerais, where charcoal was used as fuel to reduce native ores, and in São Paulo, where steel was produced in electric furnaces from scrap and imported pig iron. Production soared from under 5000 tons to 91,000 tons annually during the 1920's, but despite this dramatic expansion the national industry still supplied less than one-fifth of the domestic market for iron and steel products at the end of the decade.

The search for a solution to the steel issue was complicated by serious problems of transportation, fuel, and power, as well as by contradictory opinions about the extent and quality of Brazil's iron and coal reserves. While it was accepted that Brazil possessed large deposits of high grade ore and substantial quantities of coal, these were located in widely separated areas sparse in population and lacking adequate transportation facilities or developed sources of electric power. Estimates of the size of Brazil's iron deposits varied widely and were subject to frequent upward revision during the 1920's and 1930's. At the same time it was believed that the poor quality of Brazilian coal made it unsuitable for coke and hence of little value for steelmaking, an attitude that persisted even after the utility of the coal had been demonstrated. But even if Brazilian coal were used, there remained the problem of bringing ore and fuel together at an economical çost. Any scheme to resolve the question had to include provisions for the construction of railroads and power plants. The coal interests, and nationalists who demanded that the steel industry be entirely free from dependence on foreign supplies, urged the installation of one mill near the coal mines to serve the growing market for iron and steel in southern Brazil. Their main proposal, however, called for tidewater mills near the major consuming centers of Rio de Janeiro and São Paulo. Such mills could receive ore by rail from Minas Gerais and coal by ship from Santa Catarina. Those who approached the question primarily from an economic point of view also recommended tidewater sites, but held that the steel plants should use superior imported coal obtained in exchange for exports of iron ore.

The latter proposal was vigorously resisted on nationalistic grounds. The extreme nationalists maintained that large-scale exports of iron ore would merely enrich foreign exploiters and leave Brazil with holes in the ground, as had occurred during the gold-mining era in the eighteenth century. The political leaders of Minas Gerais encouraged this view and used it for their own purposes. They mistakenly assumed that world iron reserves were rapidly being exhausted and that foreign steel producers would soon be obliged to meet Brazil's terms for ore that was increasing in value with every passing year. While not opposed to modest sales of ore abroad—which they regarded as a generous gesture by Brazil to nations whose deposits were dwindling—they insisted that the establishment of a major steel manufacturing industry in Brazil must precede arrangements for massive ore exports.

The spokesmen for Minas Gerais further insisted that the large steel complex be installed near the iron mines, and refused to approve any proposal to the contrary. This position was dictated by their hope and belief that the steel industry would attract other industries to the state, enabling Minas Gerais to keep pace with the economic growth of São Paulo.

The chief target of the nationalistic attack was Percival Farquhar, a North American engineer and tycoon who proposed a master solution to Brazil's iron and steel problem in 1919. Farquhar headed the Itabira Iron Ore Company, Ltd., which was financed by United States, British, and German capital. His company owned large ore deposits in the iron-rich Itabira range in Minas Gerais and controlled the rail outlet through Espírito Santo to the Atlantic. Farquhar planned to refurbish and re-route the railroad and to construct a new port in order to export up to 5 million tons of ore annually to steelmakers in Europe. This was his principal concern, but to make the proposal palatable to Brazilian authorities he also agreed to install an integrated iron and steel mill with a capacity of 150,000 tons. The mill, to be located in the Rio Doce Valley in eastern Minas Gerais, would use imported coking coal brought to Brazil in the company's fleet of ore transports. The entire operation would be controlled by the Itabira Iron Ore Company, giving it a commanding position in Brazil's infant steel industry. That position seemed assured when the administration of President Epitácio Pessoa approved the Farquhar plan by awarding a formal contract in 1920.

Despite such early promise, the Itabira project never materialized. Resistance by the Minas Gerais state government in the 1920's and the world economic depression after 1929 combined to make the contract a dead letter, even though it remained in force for more than two decades. The plan, economically sound under the wage and price structure of the day, was vulnerable to any drastic rise in taxes. The company enjoyed exemptions from federal import duties on essential equipment and raw materials but had no assurance against future prohibitive increases in the state export tax on iron ore. Under the circumstances, Farquhar's foreign backers withheld financial support until a guarantee could be secured from the state of Minas Gerais. This proved to be a major obstacle. Artur Bernardes, the governor of Minas Gerais from 1918 to 1922 and president of Brazil from 1922 to 1926, insisted the contract must first be revised, asserting that the company was seeking a de facto monopoly over ore exports through the Rio Doce Valley. The revision of the federal contract and the elaboration of a separate agreement with the state government took eight years to complete. Then, before Farquhar could arrange suitable financing, the collapse of the international money market eliminated any real possibility that the project would be inaugurated. By the late 1930's, when the international situation again seemed favorable, sentiment in Brazil had moved much closer to a nationalistic solution to the steel problem.

Ardent nationalists have since elevated Artur Bernardes to the stature of a national hero for thwarting a scheme that could have placed control of Brazil's iron and steel in foreign hands. While there is no doubt about Bernardes's opposition to the Itabira Iron contract, this interpretation distorts his views and greatly exaggerates the strength of xenophobia in Brazil during the 1920's. Neither Bernardes nor his successors as governor of Minas Gerais opposed the participation of foreign capital, per se, in the industrial development of the state and the nation. In the final analysis, Farquhar's plan was blocked because it was too ambitious and seemed likely to create a monopoly, not because he and his company were foreign.

Even while the controversy over the Itabira Iron contract was raging, foreign private capital was, in fact, assuming a major role in the emerging steel industry. Brazilians with capital to invest in iron and steel works usually turned to European companies for financial as well as technological support. Some small firms were entirely owned by Brazilian investors, but mixed-capital ventures controlled by foreign interests were more common. The prime example was the Belgo-Mineira steel company in Minas Gerais, the earliest and largest of the new firms established in the 1920's. It included politically important Brazilians among its stockholders, but was dominated by the Belgian-Luxemburg holding company, ARBED, with extensive interests in steel manufacturing throughout Europe. Belgo-Mineira remained the leading company in the field until the founding of the national steel corporation at Volta Redonda during World War II.

Foreign capital made its most notable contribution to Brazil's industrial development in the 1920's in the expansion of electric power facilities. In the decade ending in 1930 the amount of electricity generated in Brazil more than doubled, to about 700,000 kilowatts. This growth was due overwhelmingly to the activities of two foreign consortiums. The Rio and São Paulo Light and Traction group, financed by Canadian, British, and United States capital, supplied all the electricity consumed in the Rio de Janeiro-São Paulo-Santos area. Most of the other large communities of Brazil were served by local branches of *Empresas Elétricas Brasileiras,* wholly-owned subsidiaries of American and Foreign Power, a private corporation with headquarters in the United States. Brazilian entrepreneurs were notoriously reluctant to risk capital in public utilities. Thus, the availability of electric power, which increasingly governed the rate of industrial expansion in Brazil, was heavily dependent upon the decisions of foreign managers and stockholders.

The economic growth of Brazil in the 1920's took place in a climate of social ferment, reflecting a poorly defined sense of unrest that found sporadic expression in violence. In retrospect it is apparent that the root of the trouble was the inability of Brazil's tradition-bound political leadership to respond to the changing needs and aspirations of the growing urban, commercial-industrial society. As shown above, federal and state administrations were willing to assist private capital in certain areas of economic development, but they tolerated change only to the extent that it complemented the established rural economy and did not pose an added burden on official revenues. They accepted fatalistically that the prosperity of the nation would continue to depend upon the sale of foodstuffs and raw materials to foreign markets. But even here Brazil's leaders preferred stability to expansion. To increase agricultural exports it was necessary to provide access to new lands in the interior, but beyond adding a few miles of paved highways near the coastal cities the governments of the 1920's did little to extend the transportation network. A start was made on a system of motor roads, but rail facilities were allowed to deteriorate. Fiscal considerations—a strong currency and a balanced budget—took precedence over development, even of the traditional economy. Outside the coffee zone transportation in Brazil in 1930 was no better, and in some areas was more difficult, than it had been a decade earlier.

Although the economic bases of the unrest of the 1920's now appear self-evident, this source of the widespread social malaise was not clearly discerned at the time. Thus, few purely economic issues were included among the numerous and often contradictory remedies proposed by various disaffected groups in urban society. Brazilian artists and writers sought relief in a declaration of cultural independence from Europe and dedication to the search for national or regional themes in painting, music, and literature. Others looked to political solutions for social problems, striking out against immediate, tangible grievances. A handful of communists, socialists, and anarchists harangued the city working class, calling for revolution, and were themselves harrassed by the police. Labor strikes were ordinarily suppressed. Port and railroad workers succeeded in gaining a few social security benefits, such as a vacation period and limited retirement provisions, but the expanding labor movement as a whole remained unorganized, unprotected, and without voice or influence in political circles.

The most serious political protest was led by younger officers of the army, the so-called *tenentes*, or lieutenants, who rebelled in Rio de Janeiro in 1922 and in São Paulo two years later. The second uprising culminated in the dramatic twenty-seven-month march through the backlands of Brazil by army rebels under Captain Luiz Carlos Prestes. The attempt to ignite a nation-wide revolt failed, however, because the rural populace was politically inert, and the police were able to keep restive urban groups in check. The *tenentes*, nonetheless, contributed to the growing awareness of the need for economic and social change by focusing public attention on shortcomings of the Old Republic in these areas. Many of their proposals, moreover, were soon to be incorporated into the program of the successful Vargas revolution of 1930.

Although the *tenentes* attempted to seize power by violence, and thus could reasonably claim to be political revolutionaries, they actually sought to reform rather than to destroy the established system. This was particularly true of their proposals in the economic sphere. For that reason their economic reform platform, which may be gleaned from

their scattered and highly generalized pronouncements on the urgency
for change, was at least as significant for what it omitted as for what it
contained. Like the civilian and military leadership in Brazil in the
1920's the young officers had a simplistic view of economic issues. They
tended to regard economic problems largely as problems of fiscal policy
or law enforcement. They denounced profiteering and tax evasion by
merchants and industrialists as violations of existing laws. They seemed
to agree on the desirability of industrial development, but implied that
this would come when state and local governments provided suitable
incentives. In this vein, their only specific recommendation for economic reform was a tax measure to give municipal governments larger
revenues and greater autonomy in fiscal matters. There was a hint of
xenophobia in the demand "to castigate the defrauders of the national
patrimony"—a category which could embrace citizens and aliens alike
—but the *tenentes* did not advocate exclusion of foreigners from the
economic life of the nation. Their program contained no overt expressions of anti-foreignism and no direct assault on private capital,
foreign or domestic. They issued no demand for sweeping agrarian reform, no call to nationalize public utilities or natural resources, and no
suggestion that the federal government should displace private enterprise in basic industries. Such views, which were to become commonplace in later decades, were still too radical to be accepted by the only
organized force in Brazil willing to fight for social and economic reform in the 1920's.

A new chapter in the economic history of Brazil opened with the
decade of the 1930's. Even before the crash of the New York stock
market, which signaled the beginning of the world economic depression in October 1929, the traditional export economy was facing its
gravest crisis in more than two centuries. The second bumper coffee
crop in as many years wrecked the government's valorization program,
throwing unprecedented quantities of coffee onto the market and
forcing prices into a precipitous decline. Lesser export commodities encountered equally critical market conditions as the depression deep-
ened. The impact on state and national revenues and on the nation's

credit rating was disastrous. The political repercussions were felt in the revolution of October 1930 that broke the power of the rural oligarchy and placed Getulio Vargas in office as chief of state, a position he was to hold for fifteen years. This sequence of events—so catastrophic for the established economic and political order—ushered in a new era of growth and progress for Brazilian industry.

Various factors coincided to bring about the revolution of 1930. Clearly, the world economic depression exacerbated a difficult political situation by making it impossible for the regime to satisfy the financial demands of its most important constituents, the coffee planters of São Paulo. As in 1889, many large landowners, who were the political bosses of their districts, quietly withdrew support from the government and refused to come to its aid in time of peril. A basic underlying cause was the growing impatience of the urban population over the government's inability or unwillingness to alleviate the political and social inequities that had given rise to the protest movements of the 1920's. The disaffection of the landowners and unrest in the cities were not sufficient in themselves to topple the Washington Luiz administration, but they provided an ideal climate for those plotting a violent solution to the political impasse.

The March 1930 presidential election severely strained the political system that had functioned efficiently for more than thirty-five years. Since 1894 the outgoing president had usually picked his successor, who was then elected—by fraud if need be—by the majority of the state Republican party organizations throughout the nation. No opposition candidate had ever reached the presidency of Brazil. A key element of this system was the understanding between the Republican parties of São Paulo and Minas Gerais, which together controlled about 40 per cent of the small Brazilian electorate. Except under unusual circumstances, the presidency alternated between these two states. It was the turn of Minas Gerais to supply the new president in 1930, but Washington Luiz broke with established practice by selecting a fellow Paulista, Governor Julio Prestes, as the administration candidate. Minas Gerais then joined the opposition Liberal Alliance, which presented Governor Getulio Vargas of Rio Grande do Sul and Governor João

Pessoa of Paraíba, respectively, for the presidency and vice presidency of the republic. As the symbol of opposition, Vargas attracted the support of reformers, revolutionaries, and disgruntled politicians from all parts of Brazil. The reforms for which the *tenentes* had fought in vain were incorporated into the Liberal Alliance platform and given wide publicity during the campaign, but again to no avail. When the congress in May announced the victory of Julio Prestes—who was thus slated to take office on November 15—many of Vargas's followers were convinced that the political and social changes they sought could only be achieved by force of arms. Vargas, however, while not excluding the possibility of revolution, seemed willing to abide by the results of the election.

The spark that ignited the revolution was the assassination of João Pessoa in June 1930. Vargas's supporters, believing that Pessoa's death had been ordered by the regime, could no longer be restrained. With apparent reluctance, Vargas agreed to lead the revolutionary movement. After several months of thinly veiled preparations, which the government ignored, the revolution broke out in Paraíba, Minas Gerais, and Rio Grande do Sul on October 3. Former *tenente* Juarez Távora led dissident army elements in the Northeast, quickly seizing control of state capitals as far south as Bahia, while from Pôrto Alegre rebel forces under Lieutenant Colonel Góis Monteiro proceeded with little resistance along the rail line to São Paulo. On October 24, with full-scale hostilities imminent on the São Paulo border, the military high command in Rio de Janeiro deposed Washington Luiz and ordered the army to lay down its weapons in order to avert a fratricidal conflict. Getulio Vargas assumed full power as provisional president on November 3, 1930, and immediately began to deal with the political, social, and economic problems that had overwhelmed the Old Republic.

In certain respects the economic crisis in Brazil in the early 1930's was similar to that in 1914. A major upheaval affecting Brazil's principal trading partners disrupted the usual pattern of international commerce, severely limiting Brazilian access to foreign markets. But while in 1914 the blow to the economy had been short-lived, and was followed by a period of soaring demand and prices for Brazilian products, in the first years of the world depression foreign markets remained tight and prices continued their downward plunge. Unable to dispose of its goods abroad at normal prices and in the customary amounts, Brazil could not sustain the previous level of imports. Between 1929 and 1932 Brazil's overseas trade fell 37 per cent by volume and 67 per cent by value. Such a drastic cut in foreign exchange earnings made it impossible for the new government to maintain either the schedule of service on the foreign debt or the exchange value of Brazilian currency. The foreign exchange rate of the *milréis* reached a new low, thus causing a sharp increase in the domestic price of all imported items. For example, the cost of French books and periodicals to readers in Brazil quadrupled within three years. At the same time, as a result of internal price stability and industrial growth, the purchasing power of the currency remained relatively constant with respect to articles produced in Brazil. In these circumstances, consumers were under greater pressure than ever before to substitute Brazilian processed goods and manufactures for long familiar foreign products.

The process of industrialization in Brazil—already stimulated by the deteriorating international economic situation—was further accelerated by direct and indirect assistance from the Vargas administration. In order to husband precious foreign exchange income, as well as to increase revenues from customs, the regime raised import duties on luxuries and responded to the pleas of Brazilian manufacturers for additional tariff protection on many essential consumer goods. By 1933 import duties had reached their highest point since 1910, averaging 39 per cent of the cost of imports sold in Brazil. Thereafter, tariff barriers were again lowered until they averaged 19 per cent in 1940. The greatest reductions, however, were on raw materials and semi-manufactures imported for processing in Brazilian industries.

Industrial expansion was also encouraged by official actions taken to support other areas of the national economy. The new government promptly assumed regulatory powers over coffee production; it reorganized the national coffee institute, fixed minimum price scales, and severely limited acreage under cultivation. Similar agencies were subsequently created for sugar, cacao, and other plantation crops. These measures were designed to protect agricultural producers against the full shock of the economic depression and to prevent widespread unemployment among plantation workers. The immediate policy objective was achieved, and a great deal more, although it seems unlikely that federal authorities anticipated the beneficial effects of the agrarian price support program on the urban economy. The establishment of a guaranteed minimum price for coffee, for example, enabled the majority of planters to escape financial ruin and to keep most of their employees on the payroll. This was only the first step in a complex process, however. Much of the federal subsidy to agriculture soon found its way into the commercial-industrial sector, as many growers either abandoned agriculture altogether or diversified their holdings by shifting some investments into urban enterprises. At the same time a substantial proportion of the plantation workers migrated to the cities to swell the ranks of the industrial labor force. But whether they found employment in town or stayed in the rural areas, such wage earners remained in the money economy as an important part of the domestic market for national products.

The consequences of governmental intervention in the agrarian economy were most apparent in São Paulo, which was both the leading coffee producer and the manufacturing center of the nation. During the 1930's the output of processing and manufacturing plants shot up rapidly, while coffee production gradually declined. The most impressive demonstration of the growth of the industrial park in São Paulo was provided in the so-called "Constitutionalist Revolution" of 1932, when for three months the people of the state, relying entirely upon their own resources, sustained a major military campaign against the combined forces of the federal government and neighboring states.

Less dramatic evidence of industrial development—largely, but not exclusively in São Paulo—may be seen in national production figures for electric power, cement, industrial chemicals, and steel during the 1930's. Facilities for generating electricity were expanded by 1940 to a capacity of more than 1,100,000 kilowatts, of which 60 per cent was located in the São Paulo area. The increase was due chiefly to the installation of new hydroelectric plants by the two large foreign-owned consortiums. Cement production, which had stood at only 87,000 tons in 1930, when 384,000 tons were imported, exceeded 700,000 tons in 1940, to account for 98 per cent of the cement consumed in Brazil. The production of industrial chemicals, almost non-existent at the beginning of the depression, began to take on importance after the middle of the decade. The manufacture of caustic soda, for example, doubled from 13,000 tons in 1936 to nearly 27,000 tons two years later, when approximately the same amount was imported. During the same period production of sulfuric acid rose from negligible quantities to about 50,000 tons annually, sufficient to meet the domestic demand. With regard to the iron and steel industry, output increased steadily from about 90,000 tons in 1929 to about 150,000 tons—roughly half the volume of imports—a decade later. Moreover, by the late 1930's Brazil had begun to export some processed and semi-processed iron products to other South American countries.

During the depression decade foreign capital assumed a broader and more direct role than it had previously played in the expansion of consumer goods industries in Brazil. The Vargas administration encouraged the public to buy Brazilian products rather than imported articles, but it did not insist that all manufacturing within the country be financed and directed by Brazilian citizens. Thus, when tariff barriers and exchange difficulties impeded competition from abroad, many foreign firms sought and obtained authorization to erect branch factories in Brazil. In this way foreign corporations were able to enlarge their share of the internal market and could continue to supply much of the demand for light manufactures and processed goods in Brazil. Some accepted Brazilian partners or stockholders, but for the most part the branch plants in Brazil were merely extensions of the parent companies in the United States or Europe. The presence of such companies occasionally delayed the entry of purely national firms into certain areas of manufacturing. Nonetheless, the foreign-owned enterprises contributed immediately and over the long run to the development of the industrial economy by adding to the volume and variety of articles produced within the country, by opening new markets for Brazilian raw materials, and by increasing employment opportunities for the local labor force and for the small group of Brazilians prepared to fill managerial positions. Frequently they introduced new manufacturing methods and skills. Invariably the branch plants served in effect as training schools, where instruction was provided in techniques of industrial production and management perennially in short supply in Brazil. A large proportion of the owners, managers, and foremen of Brazilian industrial concerns founded after World War II first gained experience in industry as employees of foreign companies operating in Brazil in the 1930's.

Although foreign-owned factories were conspicuous in the industrial complex of São Paulo and the Federal District, national firms continued to comprise the great majority of the total in Brazil and to employ the bulk of the industrial workers throughout the country. The industrial census of 1940 listed 49,418 establishments with 781,185 workers and other personnel. This represented nearly a threefold increase over the respective figures for 1920. During the same period the value of industrial production in current prices rose more than six times. São Paulo alone now accounted for about 29 per cent of the plants, nearly 35 per cent of the industrial labor force, and over 43 per cent of the value of industrial production in Brazil. The Federal District and the states of Rio Grande do Sul, Minas Gerais, Rio de Janeiro, and Pernambuco ranked next in descending order of importance. Together with São Paulo they were responsible for over three-fourths of the employment and output of processing and manufacturing industries in Brazil. Food processing was still the leading branch of industry, producing slightly over one-third of the total by value. It was followed closely by textiles and clothing, which supplied just under a third of all Brazilian industrial products. Another 10 per cent was contributed by mining, refining, and metallurgy. The production of chemicals and pharmaceuticals, lumber and wood products, building materials, and paper accounted for most of the remaining industrial activities in Brazil in 1940.

The expansion of the industrial labor force considerably outstripped the growth of the population as a whole. Between 1920 and 1940, while the number of Brazilians was increasing by half, the proportion engaged in industry roughly doubled, from under 1 per cent to nearly 2 per cent of the national population. The most rapid numerical growth occurred during the decade of the 1930's.

The position and prestige of industrial labor was greatly strengthened by the Vargas government, which looked to the working class for much of its political support. One of the first acts of the revolutionary regime, in November 1930, was the creation of a labor ministry, to which the existing secretariats of industry and commerce were attached. The latter had long been directed by the minister of agriculture, but Brazil had never before had a cabinet position concerned chiefly with labor matters. Beginning in 1931 the government issued a rash of decree-laws, extending to Brazilian workers many of the rights and privileges that laborers in other countries had attained only after prolonged struggle. The right to form trade unions and to engage in collective bargaining with employer organizations—under the aegis of the ministry of labor—was granted. Job security after ten years of employment was guaranteed. The eight-hour day, six-day week, and paid annual vacations were established as the norm for most categories of commercial employees and workers in industry. Maternity benefits and child care were provided for women employees. Restaurants and low cost food stores were opened by the new social security institutes in the larger cities. New standards of health and safety in places of employment were imposed. In 1934 it became mandatory for employers to staff at least two-thirds of all positions with Brazilian citizens, and in 1936 the ministry of labor was given authority to set minimum wages throughout the country. In addition, the Vargas government established an elaborate system of labor courts to adjudicate disputes between workers, or trade unions, and employers. The right to strike, specifically guaranteed by the Constitution of 1934, was widely used until the establishment of the authoritarian *Estado Novo* (New State), which banned both strikes and lockouts. All other labor benefits, however, were preserved by the dictatorship. Ostensibly, these applied to wage earners everywhere in Brazil, but in practice they did not extend to rural workers and domestics—who constituted about 85 per cent of the national work force. Under Vargas, therefore, the urban working class was a privileged minority. In many respects the industrial labor force comprised an elite group within that minority. Although industrial workers clearly did not enjoy unrestricted freedom of action, they were acknowledged as a vital segment of the economy and society, and were given access, through the labor ministry, to the highest counsels of government.

A new period of crisis and challenge for the Brazilian economy began with the outbreak of World War II in 1939 and persisted until peace was restored six years later. Although the full impact was not felt until Brazil was drawn into the conflict in 1942, hostilities between the country's major European trading partners disturbed the pattern of exports, caused interruptions in the flow of essential imports, and forced a critical reassessment of the growth of national industries in the 1930's. In the light of Brazil's wartime needs it was soon evident that the preceding decade had not been one of unrelieved economic progress on all fronts. In fact, important sectors of the economy had been badly neglected, and even those that had registered remarkable gains were still dependent upon imported fuels and raw materials.

Outstanding among the areas of neglect were maritime and railroad transportation. Despite recurrent nationalistic protests against the cost and inconvenience of foreign carriers, the Vargas administrations had made no attempt to create a trans-Atlantic merchant fleet. As in the past, all of Brazil's international trade was transported in foreign bottoms, many of which now flew belligerent flags and were subject to the hazards of naval warfare. Nor had the government taken effective measures to maintain the standards of its coastal fleet, which was the only regular passenger and freight service operating along much of the Brazilian seaboard. At the same time the nation's railway needs were largely ignored. While the number of passengers and the volume of merchandise moved by rail had increased during the decade, the facilities were never equal to the demand. Some rail lines had been taken over by the state and others remained in private hands, but in most instances the nature of the management had little bearing on the quality of service, for the Vargas regime refused to provide for adequate upkeep and modernization of the equipment by authorizing substantial rate increases or by granting large subsidies. The federal administration was reluctant, moreover, to divert public funds from politically prestigious urban projects in order to build important new sections of railroad lines. The long-discussed link between Minas Gerais and Bahia, to join the separate rail networks of northern and southern Brazil, was not finished until 1949. As a practical matter, only 1250 miles of track—about one-seventeenth of the mileage in operation at the end of the decade—were added in the 1930's, chiefly as extensions of strategic routes to remote frontier posts. The glaring inadequacies of coastal and overland transportation helped to perpetuate the dispersal of small, inefficient industrial plants throughout the occupied sections of the country. It was no coincidence that the phenomenal industrial growth of the 1930's had occurred in the São Paulo region, which enjoyed the finest transportation facilities in Brazil.

The neglect of railroads was partially offset by increased attention to newer forms of transportation and communications in Brazil. Commercial aviation—introduced on a limited basis in the late 1920's— spread rapidly. During the decade after 1930 ten Brazilian and foreign companies inaugurated regularly scheduled flights over some 140,000 miles of air routes between major cities and to many otherwise virtually inaccessible interior communities. The airlines not only provided fast passenger and mail service but, because of their speed over long distances, also developed a significant air freight traffic in articles of relatively high unit value. There was a comparable improvement in surface transportation as the highway system was expanded to more than 150,-000 miles in the same period. Over half of the highway mileage and three-fourths of the 225,000 motor vehicles in Brazil in 1940 were located in the Federal District and the states of São Paulo, Minas Gerais, and Rio Grande do Sul, although in every state trucks and buses were penetrating rural areas formerly served only by pack animals. But while aviation and motor transport were signs of economic progress—and were universally hailed as such in Brazil—they could not fully compensate for the lack of an efficient railroad system. Their increased use, moreover, heightened Brazil's dependence upon foreign trade and foreign technology. All the highway construction machinery, every airplane, every motor vehicle, and every drop of fuel to power them had to be imported and paid for in foreign exchange. In 1940 such items, including fuel and equipment for railroads and coastal vessels, accounted for one-fourth the value of all imports into Brazil.

Brazil's fuel problems, which still have not been satisfactorily resolved, attracted increasingly critical attention during the Vargas administrations. Most of the debate centered on the development of the nation's coal resources, first to provide a substitute for the firewood and charcoal widely used in transportation and industry, and second to reduce or eliminate the need for coal imports. Little, if any, progress was made in the first area, and considerable resistance was encountered in the second, for the relatively low caloric value and high ash content of native coal, and the remoteness of the mines from consuming centers, made it less suitable and more expensive than the imported product. Nevertheless, in 1931, under the stimulus of economic depression on the one hand and rising nationalism on the other, the government strengthened the position of the coal-mining industry by requiring that imported coal be used only in mixture with Brazilian coal. Annual production rose steadily from about half a million tons in that year to 2 million tons in 1947. Self-sufficiency was not achieved, but Brazilian mines have consistently supplied from half to two-thirds of the coal consumed in the country since 1940.

The increasing consumption of gasoline and fuel oil in the 1930's soon led to demands for the establishment of a national petroleum industry to free Brazil from dependence on foreign suppliers. Even though a modest and intermittent prospecting program by federal geologists had failed to turn up convincing signs of petroleum, vociferous nationalists insisted that Brazil was floating on a sea of oil, and that only the blindness of the nation's leaders and the cupidity of the international oil companies had delayed its proper development and use. By 1938 the Vargas government could no longer ignore such pressures. In that year the National Petroleum Council was founded and charged with discovering and exploiting oil deposits in Brazil. The search was intensified, but with disappointing results. One minor oil strike was made in Bahia in 1939, but prevailing opinion held that the field was too small to justify the expense of intensive exploitation. In any case, essential equipment and technical assistance were in extremely short supply during World War II. Thus, throughout the war years and after, Brazil continued to rely almost exclusively on imports to meet its growing needs for petroleum and petroleum products.

Brazil's entry into World War II focused public and official attention closely on weaknesses in the national economy. The German submarine offensive disrupted transportation along the Brazilian coast, effectively isolating the North and Northeast from the rest of the country. At the same time, fuel shortages forced a drastic reduction in rail and truck traffic in the central and southern states. Despite these handicaps, the nation was called upon simultaneously to increase exports of strategic minerals and other raw materials for the Allied war effort, and to expand industrial production for the home market to fill the gap left by the curtailment of exports from the United States. The first objective was achieved, and some progress was made toward the second goal as well, but for the remaining years of the war Brazilian consumers were obliged to forego many processed goods and manufactures to which they had become accustomed. Most of the limited cargo space that could be allotted for imports into Brazil was reserved for coal, in order to keep essential transportation and electric power facilities in operation.

A careful review of Brazil's economic needs in 1942 revealed that the nation was not wholly self-sufficient in a single major branch of industry. Although established firms in such areas as cotton textile manufacturing and food processing could, and did, expand output substantially by employing more workers and operating old equipment at full capacity, they could not obtain new machinery, for imports were virtually cut off, and Brazil lacked the basic industries to produce its own. At the root of the problem was the severely limited production of industrial chemicals and metals, which, in effect, determined the kind and number of new manufacturing activities that might be introduced. It was discovered, for example, that the chemical industry—which had been nearly adequate to meet the prewar demand—was geared to imports of sulfur and nitrates. These were no longer available in quantity from abroad, and the substitution of local raw materials was being delayed by transportation shortages within Brazil. The situation was somewhat less critical in the metallurgical industry, but even here Brazilian producers had customarily relied upon imports for heavy machinery, furnaces, and some pig iron for steelmaking. In spite of Brazil's enormous mineral resources, the national industry accounted for no more than 35 per cent of the domestic consumption of iron and steel in the early 1940's.

Even before Brazil was drawn into the global conflict, the Vargas regime had adopted a bold program to increase steel production dramatically, but the results were not felt until after the war. During the late 1930's it explored various proposals involving large investments by foreign steel companies but eventually rejected all of them in favor of a new state enterprise, the National Steel Company, founded in 1941. In the next five years the company completed construction of a huge integrated iron and steel complex at Volta Redonda in the Paraíba Valley, inland from Rio de Janeiro and roughly midway between the iron mines of Minas Gerais and the chief steel market in São Paulo. The Volta Redonda plant had an initial capacity of 300,000 tons per year—double the combined output of all the private steel mills in Brazil —and was designed to be expanded ultimately to a million tons or more by the installation of additional blast furnaces. The mill was unique in using coke prepared at the site from Brazilian and imported coal. In case of necessity it could operate, although less efficiently, on native coal alone. By-products from the coking process contributed to the growth of the postwar chemical industry. The principal novelty of the Volta Redonda experiment, however, was the preponderance of public capital, both domestic and foreign, in its financial structure. Although Brazilian private citizens were encouraged to invest, the response was cool. Thus, the government retained controlling interest and supplied most of the funds for construction of the plant. The dollar costs of imported materials and technological assistance were met by a series of loans from the Export-Import Bank in Washington. These reached $45 million by 1946, and the investment by the Brazilian government brought the total to well over $100 million when the mill began operations in that year. The periodic expansion of facilities at Volta Redonda has since raised the full investment many times over, and has permitted the National Steel Company to remain by far the largest producer of iron and steel in Brazil.

Since 1941 Volta Redonda has been hailed correctly as a major victory for economic nationalism in Brazil and as the first important breakthrough by advocates of direct state participation in the economy. With equal justification it could also be regarded as a victory for traditional diplomacy and a temporary setback to political nationalism, since Volta Redonda could be launched only with foreign co-operation. Except for the objections of highly placed nationalists, a steel mill comparable to that at Volta Redonda could have been built in Brazil by private foreign capital at any time after World War I. As a state-operated enterprise, however, it was not feasible until the early years of World War II, when the Brazilian government was able to finance the domestic costs of the project, and when the international situation was propitious. Vargas left little doubt that he would turn to Germany if the United States did not co-operate in his steel venture. Previously, the United States had consistently opposed public loans for state development of industries traditionally reserved to private capital, but it was now willing to modify this policy in order to check the spread of Axis influence in Brazil. It seems likely, moreover, that the decision by the United States government was motivated in large part by its desire to establish military bases in northern Brazil, along the air route to Africa. The steel issue and the question of air bases were the subjects of concurrent but separate negotiations between the two governments in 1940 and 1941. Vargas's agreement to lease the bases to the United States before either country had entered the war was without precedent in Brazilian history, and left his regime vulnerable to criticism for surrendering a portion of the national sovereignty. It must be regarded as part of the price Vargas was willing to pay to achieve his overriding goal—the national iron and steel mill at Volta Redonda.

In the postwar era Brazil has experienced remarkable economic growth, with industry expanding much faster than other sectors of the economy. In fact, since 1945 the range and rate of industrial expansion have greatly surpassed the accomplishments of all the preceding years. Many factors contributed to this end. The increase in industrial production was, of course, a logical consequence of building on foundations laid down earlier. It was also a response by native and foreign capital to the explosive growth of the urban population, and thus of the domestic market, as well as a reaction to recurrent foreign exchange shortages. Finally, rapid industrialization was both an objective and a result of direct intervention by the state in the national economy. The latter technique, ordinarily identified with the Vargas regimes before 1945, has actually been used far more extensively by postwar administrations.

During the fifteen-year reign of Getulio Vargas the state set priorities, allocated foreign exchange, and regulated both employer and labor organizations—it established and enforced the ground rules for economic development. For the most part, however, the government did not itself engage in business activities but left the problems and profits of industrial growth to private initiative. A few rail lines, which the government operated consistently at a deficit, and the steel mill at Volta Redonda were the principal exceptions to this practice.

The end of World War II brought abrupt changes to Brazil, as the ruling groups reacted sharply to the defeat of totalitarianism abroad and to the enforced economic austerity of the war years. For a time, Vargas and much that he represented were rejected. The avowedly totalitarian *Estado Novo* was replaced by a democratically elected government under a new constitution which guaranteed personal liberties, encouraged social mobility, and reaffirmed the rights of property and private enterprise. The new government abolished numerous federal regulatory powers and simply ignored others. It was not possible, however, to ignore the force of economic nationalism; thus, the National Steel Company—the industrial showpiece of the dictatorship and symbol of Brazil's economic progress—was retained as a government corporation. Nonetheless, the main trend of the new economic policies was in the other direction. For example, the government lifted all restrictions on the availability and use of foreign exchange. It was apparently assumed that the free play of market forces among a free people in a political democracy would ensure economic development and prosperity.

Such optimism seemed justified in 1945, for despite serious obstacles Brazil's industrial base had expanded significantly during the war, and the public had come to accept many new domestic products. The wartime ban on imports had permitted Brazil to amass large foreign exchange credits which could now be used to finance long-postponed imports of industrial equipment and machinery. And the rising market for Brazilian exports in the immediate postwar period suggested that this situation might persist indefinitely, continuing to provide a favorable balance of foreign exchange for imports, debt servicing, and the remittance of profits by foreign companies operating in Brazil. As in the past, it was accepted as a fact of life that the rate of economic development would be determined ultimately by the volume and value of the country's export trade.

The results of the new policies were disappointing to the advocates of private enterprise and were denounced as disastrous by outspoken economic nationalists. Within three years the backlog of foreign exchange reserves was virtually exhausted, and it was evident that the refurbishing and expansion of the industrial base was not proceeding as rapidly as expected. In the absence of selective criteria for imports, much of the delayed income from wartime exports was lavished on conspicuous consumption of luxuries long missing from the local market. As soon as the automobile industries of Great Britain and the United States returned to normal, the streets of Rio de Janeiro crawled with Jaguars and Cadillacs. But the source of the difficulty was not the unrestrained selfishness and greed of the wealthy few. The prodigal spending spree affected all levels of urban society and involved a broad range of consumers' goods, yet it produced relatively little tax revenue or other benefits for the nation. The process was facilitated by internal inflation and an outmoded tariff schedule, which together canceled the effect of customs as a barrier to imports. Another contributing factor was the artificially high exchange value of the *cruzeiro,* which reduced the cost of imported articles below that of comparable Brazilian manufactures. At the same time, the overvaluation of the currency raised the price of Brazilian goods in world markets, thus causing a sharp drop in the level of exports and a consequent decline in new foreign exchange earnings.

As the euphoria of the early postwar period dissipated, the Dutra administration found it advisable to abandon its laissez-faire economic policy and to restrict the movement of goods and capital to and from Brazil. In order to preserve the nation's dwindling credit balances and to protect national industries from undue foreign competition, federal authorities in mid-1947 instituted a system of foreign exchange licensing which established a scale of priorities for imports according to need. At one extreme, such necessities as medicines and fertilizers could be imported in unlimited amounts. At the other extreme, articles similar to those already produced in Brazil might be excluded altogether. The change had the desired effect of speeding industrial growth, but this, in turn, aggravated another serious problem—the soaring demand for public services and utilities. The availability of electric power, transportation, and communications had remained almost stationary during the war years, and, despite some expansion of facilities after 1945, was now inadequate even in the most favored areas of the country. The high rate of economic growth could not long be sustained unless prompt measures were taken. Under these circumstances the Dutra government initiated a program of state-directed economic planning and assumed major responsibility for strengthening the economic infrastructure.

The nature and extent of the shift in government policy were revealed by two interrelated activities launched in 1948. One of these was a joint venture by the governments of Brazil and the United States to survey and project the development needs of major sectors of the Brazilian economy. The first of a series of economic surveys in postwar Brazil, it was designed to recommend a co-ordinated program of private and public investments that would eliminate bottlenecks to economic progress and promote balanced development of natural resources. Even more ambitious was the SALTE plan, an administration proposal for a vastly accelerated schedule of federal investments over a five-year period in areas vital to economic growth but relatively unattractive to private capital. These included fisheries, livestock, and some phases of agriculture; public health; rail, highway, and water transportation; and, petroleum and electric power. Although the SALTE plan was substantially modified by congressional action, and was thoroughly revised by the new regime in 1951, its fundamental premise was not questioned. State planning and massive federal intervention in the economic life of the nation have been accepted as basic attributes of government by every administration in Brazil since 1948.

The SALTE plan embraced both traditional and extraordinary public works programs which contributed directly or indirectly to the expansion of industry in Brazil. Many of these were already under way when the plan was announced. Highway building, for example, received special attention, as more than twenty new projects, including an all-weather road from Rio de Janeiro to Salvador, were brought under its aegis. The largest and most novel project, however, was the construction of a hydroelectric plant at the Paulo Afonso Falls of the São Francisco River between Bahia and Alagôas. It was probably the greatest innovation of the Dutra regime, for it marked the first entry by the federal government into an area of the economy that had been the exclusive domain of private capital. The hydroelectric power project was patterned after the Volta Redonda experiment in organization and concept. The new enterprise was designed to supplement, but not to displace, the privately operated power companies in the area. The construction and management of the plant was undertaken by a mixed-capital corporation, the São Francisco Hydroelectric Company, in which the central government held a majority of the shares. The purchase of generators and other equipment abroad was financed by foreign loans. The Paulo Afonso power plant, which had a generating capacity of 120,000 kilowatts when inaugurated in 1955, was designed for long-range expansion to more than a million kilowatts so that it could continue to meet the growing needs for electricity in northeastern Brazil.

The census of 1950 provided graphic evidence of the impact of the war and the postwar boom on industrialization in Brazil during the 1940's. In every major category the increases for the ten-year period equalled or surpassed those of the preceding two decades. The value of production, as measured in current prices, rose nearly sixfold. The number of industrial establishments grew by more than two-thirds, to 83,703, while the industrial labor force expanded by almost half a million persons, to 1,279,184—an increase of over 63 per cent. Workers in industry now represented about 2.5 per cent of the national population. The concentration of industrial activities in the central and southern regions continued unabated, with the largest gains recorded in the state of São Paulo, which contained more than a fourth of the industrial plants, employed about four of every ten factory workers, and accounted for nearly half of all industrial production in Brazil. As in 1940 the Federal District and the states of Minas Gerais, Rio Grande do Sul, and Rio de Janeiro ranked next after São Paulo. Pernambuco, while declining in national standing, remained significant as a regional industrial center. In 1950 these six areas supplied about nine-tenths of the output of Brazilian industries and employed 80 per cent of the industrial laborers.

Changes in the pattern of industrial activities between 1940 and 1950 were reflected in the relative decline of foodstuffs and textiles—from two-thirds to about half of all production by value—and in the growing importance of metallurgy, refining, and the manufacture of machinery and equipment for the electrical, transportation, and communications industries. The production of chemicals and pharmaceuticals, lumber and wood products, building materials, and paper kept pace with the over-all expansion of the industrial sector during the decade. The physical growth of Brazil's industrial facilities—and incidentally of its cities—could be seen in the fact that the construction industry employed nearly one-tenth of the industrial work force and accounted for more than 5 per cent of the output of industry in Brazil in 1950.

The transformation of Brazilian industry, which was just getting seriously under way at the time of the 1950 census, proceeded rapidly over the next few years. Between 1948 and 1953, for example, while the output of consumers' goods was increasing by little more than a third, production of capital goods rose 77 per cent by volume. The most impressive gains were registered in the manufacture of steel, rubber goods, and cement. The trend reflected a large influx of private foreign capital into the manufacturing sector—usually in partnership with Brazilian investors—and the expanding role of the government in the development of basic industries.

The decade of the 1950's opened with a resurgence of economic and political nationalism throughout Brazil that exposed negative aspects of the postwar boom. The rise in nationalistic sentiment had been intensified by the emergence since 1945 of a dozen political parties which played upon the hopes and frustrations of the urban electorate in their competition for a mass following. All urged the voters to voice their protests at the polls. And protest they did, for despite the unprecedented expansion of the economy—and of the industrial sector in particular— the production of goods and services had lagged behind soaring popular aspirations for a better life. Not only had conditions failed to improve for the bulk of the population, but inflation and the rising cost of living regularly outran modest increases in income for workers and employees in government, commerce, and industry. In 1950 living standards for wage earners and salaried persons generally were lower than they had been in the last years of the dictatorship. The point was hammered home incessantly by politicians who drew inspiration from Getulio Vargas.

Under the circumstances, in the general elections of October 1950 Vargas was swept back into power on the votes of workers, bureaucrats, businessmen, and nationalists of all classes, who looked to him to produce a painless formula for economic prosperity and national greatness. Any possibility that he might somehow be able to satisfy such great expectations was eliminated by the election of a congress comprised in the majority of moderates and conservatives. Nonetheless, his electoral victory was widely interpreted as a mandate for a more statist economic policy and as evidence of a new, more aggressive spirit of nationalism abroad in the land.

The new nationalism coupled demands for accelerated economic growth with insistence upon untrammeled sovereignty for the Brazilian nation. The chauvinism implicit in the nationalistic campaigns of earlier decades was now overt and blatant. In the heated debate over the proper role of foreigners and foreign capital in Brazil in the early 1950's, a vociferous minority of ultra-nationalists sought to explain the imbalances and shortcomings of the economy as the result of a plot by alien interests to keep Brazil economically weak and politically subservient. Foreign-owned power companies, for example, were charged with extracting huge profits from the public and then deliberately refusing to provide adequate service in order to delay industrialization in Brazil. Relatively few informed persons were yet prepared to accept such distorted charges without question, but there was growing acceptance of the idea that foreigners should be excluded from basic sectors of the economy. Some supporters of this view merely wished to reserve public utilities and the nation's subsoil resources for development by domestic private capital, but others argued that the state should have sole responsibility for areas so vital to national security.

The nationalist campaign touched every sector of the economy but aroused the strongest support, and stiffest opposition, over the petroleum issue. The intensity of the public response was a clear indication of the importance of oil to Brazil's continued economic development. In the early 1950's Brazil was spending on the order of a quarter of a billion dollars each year for petroleum imports, while consumption of oil was rising faster than that of any other imported commodity. Something had to be done, for the oil field operated by the National Petroleum Council in Bahia met only 2 per cent of the nation's needs for crude oil, and the limited facilities of government-owned and private refineries could process only 5 per cent of the petroleum products consumed in Brazil. Distribution was handled by foreign oil firms, which also held inactive contracts for exploration and the construction of refineries. Starting from the premise that Brazil had untold reserves of petroleum which the foreign companies refused to search out and develop, ultra-nationalists waged a sustained drive in the press and congress for legislation to make the entire oil industry a state monopoly. While their communist-inspired slogan, "The Oil Is Ours," elicited enthusiastic endorsement from the populace, they lacked the political strength to impose their full program on the congress. The result was a compromise which secured most of the nationalistic objectives but failed to eliminate foreign and native oil companies altogether. A new mixed-capital corporation, *Petrobrás,* was established in October 1953 with an absolute monopoly over all aspects of the industry except distribution and refining. Thus, private capital might continue to operate existing facilities and to expand its activities somewhat in the petrochemical field, in competition with the state. The anti-foreign bias was so strong, however, that naturalized Brazilians and native-born citizens married to foreigners could not own shares in *Petrobrás.*

The political climate which encouraged economic nationalism changed abruptly following the overthrow and suicide of Getulio Vargas in August 1954. Men of more orthodox economic views dominated the successor administration under President João Café Filho. Although they were not prepared to reduce the role of government in the national economy, they felt the power of the state should be employed to promote greater participation by domestic and foreign private capital. The shortage of foreign exchange was one of the serious obstacles restricting imports of essential equipment for Brazil's manufacturing industries. To meet this problem, early in 1955 the new regime authorized the importation of complete sets of machinery without exchange cover, provided the exporter took payment in shares of the company that purchased the machinery. This procedure, which persisted through the rest of the decade, greatly stimulated the flow of capital goods and technology into Brazil and the formation of business partnerships between Brazilian and European or United States firms. It was instrumental in the introduction of the complex of parts and assembly plants for the new automobile industry after 1956.

The most remarkable surge of economic growth yet recorded in Brazil occurred during the five-year administration of Juscelino Kubitschek, who took office in January 1956. Appealing to the Vargas legend and promising "fifty years of progress in five," Kubitschek presented himself as an ardent nationalist but called for a vast expansion of investment in the private as well as public sector of the economy. He had no fear of foreign capital which supplemented Brazilian development efforts. His campaign platform consisted of some thirty production goals —largely in manufacturing and basic industries—with special attention to electric power, transportation, and foodstuffs. His audacity and confidence captured the imagination of the Brazilian people. This factor, and uninterrupted political stability, contributed to the substantial success of his economic program. The construction of Brasília, the new capital on the interior plateau, lent added urgency to his plans to create a network of inter-regional highways. Kubitschek completed about 11,000 miles of new roads and highways, for an increase of 80 per cent between 1955 and 1960. He expanded Brazil's merchant fleet to first rank in Latin America. During his term steel production rose from just over 1 million tons to nearly 2 millon tons annually. Brazil became self-sufficient in the production of cement, with about 4.5 million tons per year. Kubitschek gave full support to *Petrobrás,* which expanded petroleum production in the Bahian oil field by thirteen times and doubled the nation's refinery capacity to 100,000 barrels per day. New hydroelectric projects increased installed generating capacity from 3 million kilowatts to about 5 million kilowatts by 1960, while construction was started or authorized on projects to add another 3 million kilowatts in the next five years. Moreover, by 1960 Brazilian manufacturers were turning out much of the equipment required by the power industry.

In each of these areas Kubitschek was building on bases established during earlier regimes. The creation of a national automotive industry, however, was almost entirely the result of policies adopted by his government. Prior to 1956 several foreign companies operated automobile and truck assembly plants in Brazil, but only one firm, the government-owned National Motors Factory, produced trucks largely from locally manufactured components. The Kubitschek administration employed a variety of incentives, including an absolute ban on imports of competing motor vehicles, to induce ten foreign automobile companies to begin manufacturing their products in Brazil. Initially, half of the component parts were to be Brazilian-made. The proportion had risen to 80 per cent by weight in 1960, when the industry produced over 130,000 cars, trucks, and utility vehicles. The automotive industry became the symbol of the new level of sophistication achieved by the manufacturing sector in Brazil under Kubitschek.

The impressive growth in Brazil since 1950 was reflected statistically in the industrial census of 1960. As measured in current prices, production increased more than ten times in ten years, although inflation accounted for much of the added value. A better indication of the expansion of industry could be seen in figures on the growth of the industrial plant and labor force, which rose by one-third and 40 per cent, respectively, during the decade. In 1960 there were 110,339 industrial establishments employing 1,796,857 persons. São Paulo continued throughout the 1950's to pull ahead of the rest of the nation as a manufacturing center, accounting for almost a third of the plants, upwards of half of the industrial workers, and 55 per cent of the output of all Brazilian industries. The growing importance of southern Brazil was seen in the rise of Paraná to sixth rank, displacing Pernambuco in number of plants and value of production. As in 1950, over 80 per cent of the industrial personnel were found in the top six states, which supplied nearly 90 per cent of the industrial production of Brazil. Foodstuffs and textiles declined in relative importance but remained the leading branches of industry. The processing of food and beverages supplied just over one-fourth of Brazil's industrial output by value in 1960, while textiles and wearing apparel accounted for about 16 per cent of the total. Chemicals and pharmaceuticals, which still contributed about a tenth of the value of Brazil's industrial products, had been surpassed by metallurgy and the processing of non-metallic minerals, with 15 per cent, and by manufacturing of machinery and of equipment for the electrical, transportation, and communications sectors, with 14 per cent. The most rapid growth in these categories occurred during the Kubitschek years.

The material accomplishments of the Kubitschek administration cannot be refuted. The price of progress, however, was high, and the full cost was not realized until after Kubitschek left office. The illusion of prosperity was maintained in part by frequent emissions of new money, which contributed to steady inflation and a threefold rise in the cost of living between 1955 and 1960. At the same time, the lavish expenditure of funds on crash projects seemed to encourage an unusual degree of corruption and inefficiency in public office at all levels. And finally, his heavy foreign borrowings imposed a schedule of debt repayments that was to plague Kubitschek's successors.

The extent of these difficulties was not immediately apparent as the decade of the 1960's began. In fact, in the prevailing climate of optimism it was widely assumed that Brazil's industrial economy would soon achieve a self-sustaining level at which growth would continue almost automatically. This vision was rudely shattered, however, and confidence in the future was virtually destroyed by a dramatic change in the economic and political environment. Within four years the high rate of economic growth was first checked and then reversed, foreign sources of public and private capital dried up, the flight of domestic capital from Brazil reached serious proportions, and about one-fourth of the industrial labor force was unemployed. The most important of the many factors contributing to this situation was xenophobic nationalism on the one hand and spiraling inflation on the other. Together they produced a climate of extreme political tension inimical to economic development.

Virulent nationalism was revived in the presidential campaign of 1960 and was further stimulated by the policies of the Quadros and Goulart administrations. Jânio Quadros won the presidency in 1960 as a reform candidate who vowed to sweep away waste and dishonesty in government while pursuing a completely "independent" foreign policy. To reduce Brazil's heavy economic dependence upon the United States, he sought not only closer commercial ties with western Europe and Latin America, but new markets and financial aid in the communist camp as well. This policy met with general approval throughout Brazil, but his decision to resume diplomatic relations with the Soviet Union and the communist nations of Europe, and to send the vice president on a state visit to Communist China, aroused fears among Brazilian propertied groups and the military. These were exposed in the political crisis that followed Quadros's abrupt resignation in August 1961, after only seven months in office. Vice President João Goulart, a labor-leftist, was believed to be much too radical to hold office as president. Civil war was narrowly averted by a compromise that permitted Goulart to assume the presidency of a parliamentary government in which his powers were severely limited. For the next sixteen months, until the presidential system was restored by a national plebiscite in January 1963, all economic questions were subordinated to politics as Goulart engaged in an uninterrupted demagogic campaign to build a popular following. Feeling that he owed his office to the support of ultra-nationalists, Goulart did nothing to curb their exuberance. A wave of anti-foreignism swept across the country, and extremists demanded the prompt nationalization of all foreign firms exploiting Brazil's natural resources or providing public utilities. They prevailed in Rio Grande do Sul, where the state government had taken over foreign-owned power and telephone companies.

Following the plebiscite in 1963 it was hoped that Brazil would return to political peace and economic progress. Goulart announced a three-year plan for over-all economic and social development that was to provide a 7 per cent annual increase in national income for the remainder of his term. The plan, devised by highly qualified economists, was both politically and economically feasible, and could have been a positive contribution to Brazil's industrial growth. But it offered no immediate relief to the urban masses beset by soaring living costs and did not satisfy the rural lower class, then beginning to agitate for land reform in the countryside. Bowing to pressure from these two groups, Goulart sacrificed his plan to the exigencies of politics. As political polarization and economic decline continued unchecked, Goulart resorted increasingly to nationalistic demagogy in appeals for popular backing. His announcement of a partial agrarian reform and nationalization of privately-owned petroleum refineries—designed to secure such support—led directly to the middle-class revolt that drove him from office on April 2, 1964.

Monetary inflation of such magnitude that it jeopardized Brazil's political and social institutions was the overriding economic problem of the early 1960's. Brazilians were slow to recognize the danger, however, for inflation was endemic in the economy and had long been regarded

as an inevitable—perhaps desirable—condition of economic development. Brazil's experience during the postwar period, when striking
economic growth was accompanied by an annual inflation of about 17
per cent, seemed to justify this view. In fact, it was strengthened by
the continued expansion of the industrial sector at nearly 10 per cent
yearly through 1961, although the cost of living had shot up more than
40 per cent in 1959 and rose between one-quarter and one-third in each
of the next two years. It was widely believed, moreover, that any steps
taken to curb inflation must necessarily have deleterious effects on the
nation's economic progress. Nationalist extremists even denounced proposals for fiscal stability as evidence of an anti-national plot to retard
Brazil's economic growth and emergence as a major power. In these
circumstances, the Goulart regime made no effort to control the situation. But by late 1962 it was apparent that inflation itself was becoming a primary deterrent to economic development. In that year the rate
of industrial growth dropped below 8 per cent, while the cost of living
rose by more than half. The trend reached alarming proportions in
1963, when industrial expansion was a mere .2 per cent, and the cost
of living spiraled to 80 per cent. During the first three months of 1964
living costs were rising at the rate of 144 per cent per year, and there
was no relief in sight. The political repercussions could no longer be
contained.

The revolution that overthrew the Goulart administration marked a
major turning point in recent Brazilian history. It brought the armed
forces to power for the first time in the twentieth century and placed
responsibility for national decision-making in the hands of men with
an innate distrust of partisan politics and professional politicians. In
the years since 1964 there has been a progressive erosion of civilian authority in Brazil. More than a thousand legislators and bureaucrats
deemed corrupt or subversive by the regime have been deprived of
public office and political rights, and the instruments of democratic
government have been reshaped to reduce the freedom of action of the
electorate and its representatives. At the same time, through a series of
"Institutional Acts" subsequently incorporated into the constitutions of
1967 and 1969, power has been concentrated increasingly in the execu-

tive branch at the expense of the legislature and judiciary, and in the national government at the expense of the states and municipalities. One of the consequences of the revolution of 1964 has been to give Brazil a strong central administration, determined and able to carry out coherent, long-term programs of national development without serious hindrance from congress or public opinion.

With respect to the economy, the revolution transferred control of the nation to men who shared many of the views of the urban, industrial middle class, including faith in the virtues of private enterprise. At the same time, the officers who assumed political leadership were imbued with the technocratic, developmentalist concepts of the National War College, which emphasize the need for careful planning and coordination of economic programs. In these circumstances, the administrations since 1964 have held it the duty of the state to give the private sector appropriate policy guidance, investment opportunities, tax curbs on its avariciousness, and an adequate infrastructure of power, fuels, transportation, and basic industries to support an expanding economy. In adhering to such policies, the post-1964 regimes have engaged in economic planning at the national level to a much greater extent than ever before in Brazil, and have made the state the major investor in the economy. The government's massive investments have been confined primarily to those areas of the economic infrastructure deemed vital to national security or unattractive to private capital. The fields of agriculture, manufacturing, and most aspects of mining and the processing of raw materials have been left to private initiative. The combination of private enterprise and state planning has given rise to what is frequently described as the "Brazilian miracle" of sustained, rapid economic growth.

But economic progress did not come quickly or easily to Brazil. Under Marshal Humberto Castello Branco, who succeeded President Goulart in April 1964, three years were required to check the downward trend and lay the basis for economic recovery. The Castello Branco administration recognized the economic and fiscal crisis as the principal problem facing the nation, and created the Ministry of Planning to devise and coordinate measures to cope with the situation. The post was entrusted to Roberto Campos, one of Brazil's foremost economists, who prescribed a policy of austerity in order to reduce inflation gradually, to eliminate balance of payments deficits and restore Brazil's credit rating abroad, and to channel larger public investments into the economic infrastructure. In pursuit of these goals the central government drastically curtailed credit, slashed imports, removed subsidies from such consumer items as wheat and gasoline, closely controlled wages, and imposed a sweeping tax reform. Even though highly unpalatable to the public, and protested as overly severe by bankers, planters, and industrialists, the program was successful in restoring a favorable climate for economic growth. One of the chief economic indicators, monetary inflation, was held to 91 per cent in 1964, and thereafter was progressively reduced to about 66 per cent in 1965, to 41 per cent in 1966, and to 30 per cent in 1967. The impact of the government's policies could also be measured in the growth of the gross national product, which had fallen to 1.6 per cent in 1963. It rose to about 4.5 per cent in 1966, when the national product was equivalent to $28 billion, and reached 5 per cent the following year. The national income was calculated at $315 per capita in 1967, although there were gross inequities in its distribution among sectors of society and geographic regions of Brazil. By March 1967, when Castello Branco transferred power to President Artur da Costa e Silva, the economic crisis had been largely overcome. Significantly, much of the progress registered in such sectors as electric power, transportation, and basic industries resulted from completion of projects initiated by the Kubitschek administration seven years earlier.

Comparatively vast sums of capital in domestic currency and foreign exchange were required to finance the government's economic program. To obtain such funds the Castello Branco administration relied heavily upon increased tax receipts, foreign investments, and new loans. One of its first acts was a revision of the personal and corporate income tax structure, raising the rates, tightening collection procedures, and providing stiff penalties for tax evasion. The number of contributors quintupled, and receipts rose at an even faster pace. But substantial, long-term expansion of the tax base depended upon increasing economic productivity and the market for Brazilian goods. The regime imposed low ceilings on wages and salaries, in part to hold down production costs and thereby accelerate capital accumulation by employers. The administration also used its fiscal powers to encourage growth of the domestic market and the export trade. Special tax favors were conceded to exporters of industrial products, and each firm was allowed to cancel up to half of its annual income tax if it invested a comparable amount in a new or branch plant in one of the underdeveloped regions of Brazil. The same incentives were offered to Brazilian firms and to the foreign corporations that flocked into the country once political stability was assured. The Northeast and to a lesser extent the Amazon region were the principal beneficiaries of the program to create regional industrial centers and bring hundreds of thousands of Brazilians into the money economy. In the area of foreign trade favorable balances, as a result of bumper crops in 1965 and the growth of industrial exports in 1965 and 1966, enabled Brazil to pay outstanding commercial debts, to renegotiate and resume regular servicing of foreign loans, and to borrow new large sums abroad. By 1967 Brazil's foreign debt stood at $670 million, and its credit rating with international lending agencies was excellent.

President Costa e Silva brought a different tone to national leadership with his promise to "humanize the Revolution," but in office he pursued essentially the same economic policies as his predecessor. His administration raised wages and salaries, although by less than the rate of inflation, and pegged subsequent increases to rises in the cost of living, thereby perpetuating the loss of real income suffered by labor since 1964. The government did relax some of the restrictions on credit for investors and diverted a somewhat larger portion of national revenues into the areas of education, housing, and public health, but the infrastructure continued to absorb the lion's share of the budget. Shortly after taking office, Costa e Silva announced a three-year plan which included commitments to double the output of the Volta Redonda steel mill to 2.5 million tons, make Brazil self-sufficient in the processing of petroleum products, and increase electric power generating capacity from eight to eleven million kilowatts by 1970. The latter target involved the expansion or construction of twenty-six electric power plants at a cost equivalent to $2 billion. The fact that the central government could pledge such heavy expenditures was a measure of the economic recovery Brazil was experiencing. The favorable trends continued. Inflation ranged from 30 per cent to 22 per cent during the two and one-half years of the Costa e Silva regime, while in 1969 the national product grew by 9 per cent and the value of exports surpassed $2 billion for the first time in the nation's history. But Costa e Silva did not live to see these and other results of his economic program, which exceeded most of its objectives. Incapacitated by a stroke, he was succeeded by General Emílio Garrastazu Médici, whom congress elected in October 1969 for a term ending in 1974.

From the outset President Médici had the advantage of governing a nation that enjoyed unprecedented economic prosperity. The gross national product rose by nearly 10 per cent, to $37 billion, in 1970, and the national income was $385 per capita. Two years later the national product and per capita income were on the order of $45 billion and $460, respectively. In these circumstances, without adversely affecting economic growth, the Médici administration was able, on the one hand, to intensify efforts to contain inflation—holding it below 20 per cent in 1971 and 16 per cent in 1972—and on the other hand, to increase the purchasing power of labor by allowing wages to rise faster than the cost of living. By the same token, the government could devote a major portion of its budget to areas of social welfare without reducing investments in the basic economy. During 1970 the Médici administration announced two ambitious, interrelated plans for social and national integration, designed to unite all the regions and people of Brazil, economically, physically, and emotionally, into one great nation able to assume its future role as a world power.* These were long-range goals that called for extensions of the developmental programs launched under the two preceding regimes, but with higher priorities assigned to the needs of society and to the effective occupation of the national territory. The first phase of Médici's integration program—the trans-Amazon highway and related colonization projects

* The social integration program is discussed in Chapter 8.

in the North—captured the public imagination and took on the nature of a national crusade, in much the same fashion as had the construction of Brasília in the 1950's.

The impact of the state-directed developmental programs of the post-1964 administrations in Brazil is subject to continuing reassessment, but some positive and negative results seem likely to persist. The most difficult to gauge is the cost in terms of political frustration and freedoms suppressed, although dissent has been minimal since 1970. Proponents of the government reiterate the hope that the Brazilian people will come to prefer the present political system. In strictly material terms, Brazil's economic growth has been spectacular. In no comparable span in the nation's history has the economy grown so rapidly or affected so large a part of the country and its people. Brazil is by far the most prosperous nation in Latin America and, after Japan, has the highest sustained rate of economic expansion in the world. It also has one of the highest levels of foreign indebtedness. Between 1967 and 1971 Brazil's foreign debt increased by five times, to $3.3 billion, and continued to grow after that date. Few Brazilians are concerned about the country's ability to repay its loans, but some voices have been raised to protest the heavy concentration of foreign capital in the economy. There have been remarkable increases in production in all fields of economic activity, particularly in the industrial sector. Moreover, the efforts of successive regimes to spread industry to the outlying regions have contributed to substantial increases in output and employment in all areas of Brazil. Yet, the gap between the previously industrialized South and the rest of the country appears to have widened. The total industrial labor force, for example, expanded from less than two million to well over three million between 1960 and 1970. The proportion of industrial workers employed in the South rose by more than 1 per cent, and in São Paulo alone by .5 per cent, during that period. With regard to the distribution of income among the various sectors of Brazilian society, the disparity is even greater. In 1960 one-fifth of the population received over half of the national income. A decade later this group enjoyed over 63 per cent of the income. There is no question that the rich in Brazil have become much richer since the revolution of 1964. Nevertheless, because the total economy has expanded at an unprecedented rate, each sector of the population that shares in the money economy now enjoys a higher real income than it did before the 1964 revolution.

Several basic characteristics of Brazilian industry have been obscured by the tremendous expansion of the industrial base in the past half-century. Outstanding among these is the heavy concentration on the production of primary necessities, because of the limited purchasing power of the great majority of the Brazilian people. Food and beverages still account for the greatest proportion of industry, followed by textiles and clothing. As late as 1960 these categories made up more than 40 per cent of the plants, labor force, and output of industry in Brazil. The relatively simple level of production is also reflected in figures on the size of industrial firms. The average plant employs sixteen persons. The average is misleading, however, for 83 per cent of all industrial concerns in Brazil have fewer than ten employees, and two-thirds of the plants are operated by four persons or less, including the owner and members of his immediate family. These proportions are found in São Paulo as well as in less progressive states of Brazil. Their small size may help to explain the ephemeral life of many individual concerns, which disappear as the result of bankruptcy or mergers in the intervals between industrial censuses. In 1920 and 1940, for example, only about 10 per cent of the firms tabulated had been in existence for more than twenty years. This trend appears to have continued to the present. But, significantly, a study of the twenty-nine largest Brazilian companies reveals that the majority were formed before World War I. Another prominent tendency, usually associated with small companies, applies in Brazil to industrial organizations of all sizes. This is the strong preference for individual ownership or partnerships rather than a corporate business structure. While this pattern is beginning to break down, many of the large industrial complexes are still essentially family enterprises. Yet, despite these characteristics, which are more typical of "underdeveloped" than of "developed" economies, the transformation of industry is the basis for the growing conviction among Brazilians that their country is destined soon to escape the ranks of underdeveloped nations.

Chapter 8 • The New Society

Explosive numerical growth, mobility, and restiveness are the principal characteristics of modern Brazilian society. In fifty years the number of people in Brazil has more than tripled, and the rate of increase is expected to remain well above the world average through the rest of this century. Although much of the population is harnessed to the land and to the traditional social structure, the exodus from the countryside continues unabated. In larger numbers than ever before, rural Brazilians are flocking to the cities, to swell the ranks of the urban lower class and to fill the vacuum left by the minority moving upward in the social scale. There they become active participants in the economic and political life of the nation, and are exposed to needs and opportunities non-existent in the outlying regions. While the rural populace generally is quiescent, the urban dwellers are insistent in their demands for a bigger share of the rewards offered by an industrial economy, and are less willing than their forebears to accept further delays with patience. For the great majority, however, the sheer pressure of population on limited resources thwarts their aspirations for a better life and adds a note of frustration that occasionally erupts into violence. Ironically, this volatile situation, which no Brazilian administration can ignore, is a measure of the progress made in the fields of health, education, transportation, communications, and living standards since 1920. In a real sense the new society is the most dynamic and promising product of the industrial revolution in Brazil.

The population explosion, which is at once a primary cause and a direct effect of social change in contemporary Brazil, is not a recent phenomenon. Since the waning years of the empire the people of Brazil have been accustomed to absorbing millions of new residents each decade, and have come to regard such growth as normal and desirable evidence of national progress. The current boom, however, is without precedent in Brazilian history, both in the high rate of increase and in the fact that it results almost entirely from natural growth. The following table based on the corrected returns of periodic national censuses shows the over-all rate of expansion since 1872:*

POPULATION OF BRAZIL, GROWTH RATES, 1872-1970
(population in thousands)

Year	Total	Increase	Per Cent Increase Over Previous Census	Per Cent Increase In Twenty Years
1872	10 099			
1890	14 199	4 100	40.59	
1900	17 984	3 785	26.69	53.08
1920	27 404	9 420	52.37	52.37
1940	41 114	13 710	50.02	50.02
1950	51 944	10 830	26.34	
1960	70 992	19 048	36.67	72.67
1970	93 204	22 212	31.29	79.43

Sources: *Anuário Estatístico do Brasil, 1958*, p. 21; *1971*, p. 39.

It is significant that since 1940, without massive immigration, the population of Brazil has been growing faster than it did in the heyday of immigration before World War I. In the sixty years ending in 1940 the population rose by half or more every two decades, while it more

* Before 1950 Brazilian census returns erred as much as 10 per cent. The rounded revised figures are given in the table above. The original returns showed the following totals: 9,930,478 (1872); 14,333,915 (1890); 17,438,434 (1900); 30,635,605 (1920); and 41,236,415 (1940). Calculations for 1970 are based on preliminary data.

than doubled in total amount between 1940 and 1960. In the 1880's and 1890's immigration accounted, respectively, for about one-fifth and one-third of the increase. During the first twenty years of this century roughly one of every six new Brazilians was foreign-born. The proportion dropped to about 9 per cent, or one in eleven, after 1920, and to only slightly more than 2 per cent in the years following 1940. The downward trend continued through the decade of the 1960's, when the annual net increase in popoulation exceeded 2 million, of whom fewer than 20,000 on the average were immigrants.

The phenomenal growth of population provides both a stimulus and an obstacle to the rapid economic development that has become a national aspiration in Brazil. It is widely accepted—virtually as an article of faith by Brazilian nationalists—that the stature and well-being of the country depend upon a constant increase in numbers. The addition of more than 2 million new citizens each year must be viewed as an advantage by a society that has always suffered from a shortage of manpower. For the first time in their history the Brazilian people can expect to see the day when there will be enough men and women at hand to till the empty fields and attend the myriad of other tasks required in a developing economy. The increase in population that expands the labor pool, moreover, automatically enlarges the internal market, thereby serving as further incentive for the growth of industry and commerce. At the same time, larger numbers in themselves are expected to bring greater recognition to the nation and allow Brazil to play a more important role in international affairs. The growth cycle, thus, is seen as an upward spiral which leads inevitably to higher levels of employment, productivity, and prosperity at home and to enhanced prestige and influence abroad.

Even the most dedicated optimists acknowledge, however, that these goals will not be achieved overnight, because of the irreducible time lag between the birth of a child and his entry into the labor force. Since natural increase rather than adult immigration accounts for substantially all of the current annual increment in population, a rise in numbers cannot be translated immediately into greater productivity or power. On the other hand, there is necessarily an immediate correlation between expansion of the young, dependent segment of society and mounting pressure on national resources. In these circumstances, despite a moderate expansion of the work force, the availability of goods and services is not adequate to satisfy the urgent needs of a growing population and to support a general rise in living standards simultaneously. Thus, the very population explosion that seems to assure national development is a continuing impediment to its attainment.

The excess of youths and children over those of working age is a long-standing problem in Brazil. More than half of all Brazilians enumerated in periodic censuses in this century have been under twenty years of age, and children below fifteen have consistently comprised over 40 per cent of the total. For nearly fifty years these proportions remained fairly constant, tending to fluctuate downward slightly. Since the 1940's, however, the juvenile population has grown precipitously, raising the problem to the magnitude of a crisis. The period of peak growth to date occurred in the decade ending in 1960, when the increase in the number of persons under age ten was more than double that of any other age group. Returns from the 1970 census indicate that the rate of demographic growth declined somewhat during the 1960's, but it is not clear whether the change represents more than a temporary deviation from the established upward trend. In any event, by 1970 there were as many Brazilians under ten years of age as there had been in the entire population of the republic in 1920, while the under-twenty category was nearly as large as the total population in 1950. The following table shows the relative strength of various age groups in the Brazilian population between 1900 and 1970.

POPULATION OF BRAZIL BY AGE GROUPS, 1900-1970
(in percentages)

Age	1900	1920	1940	1950	1960	1970
0-4	17.21	14.99	15.60	16.11	15.97	14.91
5-9	15.04	14.94	13.96	13.52	14.48	14.27
10-14	11.83	12.76	12.92	12.14	12.22	12.52
15-19	10.68	13.77*	10.78	10.59	10.19	10.95
20-29	17.35	15.10*	17.39	17.57	16.22	16.06
30-59	23.86	24.20	25.10	25.61	26.03	26.00
over 60 & unknown	4.03	4.24	4.15	4.46	4.89	5.29

* Persons 20 years of age are included in the 15-19 age group.
Source: *Anuário Estatístico do Brasil, 1965*, p. 35; *1971*, p. 48.

It seems paradoxical that the population explosion in Brazil has taken place and is continuing without a rise in the birth rate. In fact, the birth rate, which has always been high, declined from an estimated 46 per thousand in 1900 to 45 per thousand in the 1950's, and then dropped sharply to about 38 per thousand by 1970. During most of that period high levels of mortality, especially among infants, largely off-set the natural increase in population. At the beginning of the century at least one-fourth of all babies born in Brazil died within their first year from parasites and diseases that also took a heavy toll of older children and adults. The average life expectancy was well under forty years. This situation was gradually ameliorated by the improved health and sanitation practices that were introduced into the larger cities before World War I and into many rural areas after 1930, appreciably reducing the incidence of epidemic diseases. Between the early 1900's and the 1940's the over-all death rate fell from about 26 per thousand to approximately 20 per thousand. The truly dramatic change, however, has occurred since the end of World War II, chiefly as a result of the widespread use of antibiotics, which not only have enabled the great majority of infants to survive childhood but have extended the life span of the adult population as well. By 1960 the mortality rate had dropped to 12 per thousand, and life expectancy had risen to 55 years. A decade later the death rate was under 10 per thousand, and life expectancy was 57 for men and 61 years for women. Both trends are expected to continue as the benefits of modern medicine are made available to an ever larger proportion of the population.

Data such as these are useful for measuring social change within Brazil and for comparing certain aspects of Brazilian society with those of other nations. However, sweeping generalizations about the plight or progress of the Brazilian people based on national averages are usually misleading, no matter what criterion may be selected as a gauge. The distinctions noted previously between the economically advanced and backward sections of the country—between modern and archaic Brazil —apply with equal force to Brazilian society. To be meaningful, generalizations about society in Brazil must be qualified to clarify which Brazil is being considered, for there are great discrepancies between regions, between urban and rural areas within regions, and between social classes in a single city or rural district. Virtually the entire range of social conditions and types known in Europe and Spanish America can be found in contemporary Brazil, from the well-fed, well-schooled, white urban sophisticates of the international jet set to the impoverished, unlettered, dark-skinned country folk scratching a brief existence from the soil in squalor and isolation.

Nonetheless, while avoiding the pitfalls of oversimplification, and allowing for the inevitable exceptions, a few valid observations may be made about conditions of life in the various geographic regions and among different sectors of society in Brazil. As a general rule, birth and death rates are lower and life expectancy and levels of literacy and income are higher in the South than in the Northeast, in Amazonia, or in the frontier zones of the Center-West. The full spectrum is encountered in the East. By the same token, it is generally true that living conditions are relatively more favorable in the cities and towns than in the countryside, even in regions that rank below the national averages. It is equally true, however, that the residents of some rural counties in southern Brazil have a higher standard of living, as measured in terms of diet, health, and longevity, than all but the favored few in the leading cities in the Amazon Valley and the Northeast. An indication of the gap between regions may be seen in the range of life expectancy from one state to another. In 1950, when the national average was under forty-four years, the average life span varied from only thirty-six years in Mato Grosso and thirty-eight years in Pará, to forty-nine years in Santa Catarina and São Paulo, and fifty-three years in Rio Grande do Sul. Almost certainly, moreover, the range was greater, then as now, between social classes and ethnic groups than between states. The present life span of the modern, thoroughly Europeanized middle and upper classes of the cities of southern Brazil probably approaches the biblical three score years and ten, while the average life expectancy of the lower class mixed-bloods and Negroes crowded into the squalid slums of the northeastern capitals is still only about thirty-five years. These are the extremes, but it is accepted as a fact of life throughout Brazil that the ill-fed, ill-clothed, ill-housed, illiterate members of society are more apt to be Negroes and mulattos—who are concentrated heavily at the bottom of the social scale—than Brazilians of predominantly European, Levantine, or Japanese extraction. Mulattos and other mixed-bloods, who are the fastest growing element in the population, have the highest rate of birth, while the Negroes, who comprise a shrinking proportion of the population, and actually decreased in numbers between 1940 and 1950, have the highest infant mortality rate and shortest life expectancy of any ethnic group in Brazilian society.

At the beginning of the century there was much greater equality, in terms of health, among the people of Brazil. It mattered little whether a Brazilian-born family lived in the North or South, was rich or poor, white or colored, urban or rural. The quality of housing and clothing might vary according to climate and the family's financial circumstances, but Brazilians of all social classes in all regions ate substantially the same inadequate diet, produced about the same number of children per family, and died at an early age of the same diseases. Physicians and medical facilities were few and of limited help against the scourges of yellow fever, smallpox, malaria, and intestinal parasites that attacked rich and poor alike. Life, if anything, was more hazardous in the cities than on *fazendas* in the interior, where the incidence of communicable disease was lower. Only among a few well-traveled wealthy families and in the immigrant communities in the South did something approaching contemporary European health standards prevail.

By the 1920's the traditional pattern had undergone a revolutionary change in the large cities that were rapidly being modernized. In less than a quarter-century mosquito-borne diseases had been eliminated or controlled, public water and sewerage systems had been reconstructed and extended to new suburbs and working-class districts, permitting higher levels of health and comfort, and a sustained information campaign had made public health a matter of common knowledge and concern among urban dwellers. The latter trend was reinforced in Rio de Janeiro and cities to the South by the demands and example of the large immigrant population. Immigrants also influenced living conditions by expanding the Brazilian diet to include a broad variety of vegetables, grains, and special dishes long familiar in Italy and central Europe. Wherever they settled in substantial numbers restaurants were opened and truck gardening was introduced. By and large these developments, which did not generally affect the rural population, were shared by all residents of the cities regardless of wealth or station.

The various groups in urban society did not benefit equally from significant innovations in the field of medicine that enabled physicians to prevent or cure many of the maladies common in Brazil. For the first time affluence became a decisive factor in determining the health and longevity of individual Brazilians. Those who could afford the cost of medical attention could now protect themselves from diseases that were still decimating the poorer classes. Under the Vargas administrations after 1930 an attempt was made to carry these benefits to the common people by opening free clinics in the cities and establishing mobile public health units to serve some rural zones, but such services could reach only a small minority of the populace. In these circumstances it is understandable that the sections of the country with the highest levels of economic development, and therefore with the highest per capita income, continued to have a generally healthier citizenry than did the traditional, less developed areas of the nation.

The distance between regions and classes, moreover, either remains unchanged or is increasing. Although over-all health standards are rising in Brazil, the uneven pace of modernization has tended, over the long term, to perpetuate or to widen the gap between traditional and progressive sectors of the nation and its people. The outlying rural areas have yet to feel the impact of advances in health sciences and services in Brazil, and even in the most advantaged urban areas dramatic fluctuations in health conditions may occur from one year to the next.

These patterns may be seen in the infant mortality rates of the cities of São Paulo, Rio de Janeiro, Belém, and Recife since the late 1930's. São Paulo long maintained the lowest rates, with an average of 138 infant deaths per thousand live births between 1939 and 1941, as against 86 in the late 1940's and 63 in the early 1960's. By 1969, however, the rate had risen again to 84. Recife regularly recorded much higher levels, with figures of 272, 244, 146, and 165, respectively. The reversal of the trend was actually sharper than these data suggest, for in 1970 the infant death rate soared to 206 in Recife. Rio de Janeiro followed somewhat the same pattern, but with less striking deviations, while in Belém the infant mortality rate first dropped, then rose again, and thereafter declined erratically to reach the lowest average among the four cities. Significantly, the proportion of infant deaths was identical in Rio de Janeiro and Belém in the 1939-41 period, when 159 per thousand were reported. A decade later the average had fallen to 111 in Belém and to 97 in the national capital. By the early 1960's the rate was 78 in Rio de Janeiro, but it had climbed to about 140 in Belém. The reversal of the downward trend in the Amazon city revealed the unavoidable deterioration of social conditions when the expansion of urban facilities, employment opportunities, and food supply fail to keep pace with a continuous, heavy influx of population. Improvements in these areas, despite sustained migration into Belém, largely accounted for the drop in the infant mortality rate to 107 in 1968 and only 52 in 1969. Rio de Janeiro registered rates of 49 and 53 in these years. The increase in the rate of infant mortality in Rio de Janeiro and São Paulo in the late 1960's was above all a reflection of the great difficulty in achieving a permanent improvement in the deplorable living conditions under which hundreds of thousands of slum dwellers existed in the two largest and most modern cities of Brazil.

Situations such as this, which involve so many individual family tragedies, have not deterred the growth of cities in Brazil. One of the most far-reaching and rapidly accelerating transformations in Brazilian society in this century—perhaps more fundamental than the population explosion itself—has been the shift from rural to urban areas. For the most part this change has taken place since 1940, and has assumed truly impressive dimensions only since 1950. At the beginning of the century Brazil had no city with a million inhabitants. Rio de Janeiro with 811,000 residents was in a class by itself, for the second city, São Paulo, still boasted fewer than 250,000. By 1920 Rio de Janeiro had passed the 1-million mark and São Paulo was approaching 600,000. The two cities contained as many people as all other state capitals combined. Many residents of these communities were not, properly speaking, city dwellers, for persons living in rural districts within the municipal boundaries were also included in the tabulations. The census of 1920 did not distinguish between them, but it is probable that the urban segment then constituted less than 20 per cent of the population of Brazil, or roughly 5 million persons. As late as 1939 Brazilians still described their country as one of the most rural in the world. The 1940 census, however, modified that view, showing that 31 per cent of the Brazilian people—nearly 13 million—lived in "cities" of all sizes. Thereafter, the trend toward urbanization gained momentum. The proportion of urban residents rose steadily to 36 per cent—about 19 million—in 1950, to 45 per cent—approximately 32 million persons—in 1960, and to almost 53 million, or 56 per cent of all Brazilians in 1970. In five decades, while the national population multiplied by about three and a half times, the urban sector increased tenfold.

Two distinct trends may be noted in the pattern of urban growth in Brazil. First is the proliferation of new communities with relatively small populations. Since 1950 the number of cities and towns has increased by more than one hundred per year on the average. This reflects a comparable rise in the number of counties (*municípios*), which to a large extent is a product of internal migration rather than demographic growth. Every county seat, regardless of size, is a "city" by virtue of its politico-administrative function. In addition, every town (*vila*), including those with less than 200 inhabitants, is considered "urban" for

CITIES AND TOWNS IN BRAZIL, 1970

Size	Number of Cities	Per Cent of Cities	Urban Population	Per Cent of Urban Population
Under 1000	4079	52.07 ⎫	1 748 830	3.30 ⎫
1001-2000	1316	16.80 ⎪ 91.68	1 871 560	3.54 ⎪ 21.41
2001-5000	1241	15.84 ⎪	3 899 127	7.37 ⎪
5001-10,000	546	6.97 ⎭	3 810 647	7.20 ⎭
10,001-50,000	537	6.85	13 234 114	25.02
50,001-1,000,000	110	1.40	15 569 491	29.42
Over 1,000,000	5	0.07	12 771 015	24.15
Total	7834	100.00	52 904 744	100.00

Source: *Sinopse Preliminar do Censo Demográfico, VII Recenseamento Geral—1970, BRASIL,* pp. 39, 92-95.

census purposes, even though the vast majority are mere hamlets or villages displaying few of the amenities or other characteristics of urban places. Thus, as the preceding table indicates, in 1970 more than half of the cities and towns of Brazil had fewer than 1000 residents, and communities of under 10,000 persons comprised over 90 per cent of the total. Together they accounted for only about one-fifth of the urban population of Brazil, or less than the combined total for the metropolitan areas of São Paulo and Rio de Janeiro. The proliferation of small towns and cities is continuing, but their rate of growth is below the national average and well under that of the urban population as a whole.

The second, more significant trend in urbanization in Brazil is the continued growth of the larger cities. Nearly a third of the Brazilian people now live in 115 cities of 50,000 or more inhabitants, as opposed to 22 per cent of the national population in 68 cities of this size in 1960. The long-term pattern for twelve of the leading cities of Brazil is shown in the table below. It reveals clearly that São Paulo and Rio de Janeiro have long dominated the urban scene. São Paulo, in particular, has undergone spectacular growth, increasing more than tenfold in half a century, while Rio de Janeiro roughly quadrupled in numbers. Each, moreover, is now the hub of a sprawling metropolitan area, with over 8 million persons in Greater São Paulo and more than 7 million

GROWTH OF SELECTED MUNICIPALITIES, 1900-1970
(population in thousands)

Municipality	1900	1920	1940	1950	1960	1970
São Paulo	240	575	1 326	2 198	3 852	5 979
Rio de Janeiro	811	1 158	1 764	2 377	3 307	4 316
Belo Horizonte	13	56	211	353	693	1 255
Recife	113	238	348	525	797	1 084
Salvador	206	283	290	417	656	1 027
Pôrto Alegre	74	179	272	394	641	903
Fortaleza	48	79	180	270	515	873
Belém	97	236	206	255	402	642
Curitiba	50	79	141	181	361	624
Brasília (Federal District)	–	–	–	–	142	538
Niterói	53	86	142	186	245	330
Manaus	50	76	106	140	175	314

Source: *Anuário Estatístico do Brasil*, 1965, p. 34; 1971, p. 42.

in Rio de Janeiro and its environs in 1970. But while these two giants continue to expand prodigiously in absolute numbers, the rate of increase has begun to decline in São Paulo, and since 1960 has dropped below the national average in Rio de Janeiro. This change has been more than offset, however, by the mushrooming of towns on the periphery of the great metropolitan agglomerations, and by the sustained growth of already large cities in various states. Three of the latter passed the one million mark in the decade ending in 1970. These are Belo Horizonte, Salvador, and Recife, which grew by more than three-fourths, one-half, and one-third, respectively, between 1960 and 1970. During the same period nine cities surpassed 200,000 population. There are now 19 cities in the 200,000 to 1,000,000 range, and another 36 with more than 100,000 residents.

To a large extent these fast-growing cities are industrial communities concentrated in the South and East, for urbanization in Brazil has tended to go hand in hand with the spread of industry. Between 1960 and 1970 the highest urban growth rate in the nation was recorded in Mauá, an industrial satellite of São Paulo, which exploded from 14,000 to 102,000. Garulhos, another working class suburb of São Paulo, grew by 185 per cent in the same years to 222,000 population, while Nova Iguaçú, near Rio de Janeiro, experienced an increase of 148 per cent, to reach 333,000 population and become one of the fifteen largest cities in Brazil. These are outstanding examples, but throughout the industrial suburbs of Rio de Janeiro and São Paulo demographic expansion by 80 per cent or more in a decade is the norm which many cities exceed by a wide margin. Therefore, it is not surprising that almost half of the increase in the urban population of Brazil since 1960 has taken place in the heavily industrialized states of Guanabara, Rio de Janeiro, and São Paulo.

Nonetheless, it is significant that no area of Brazil has escaped the urbanization process. In fact, eight capitals of states and territories that still have essentially agricultural or pastoral economies grew at a faster rate than the urban population as a whole in the 1960-70 period. These include Goiânia, which tripled in size to 370,000 inhabitants, Macapá, Cuiabá, Manaus, Rio Branco, Pôrto Velho, São Luís, and Fortaleza. The latter, with 530,000 urban residents in 1970, is the largest city in this group; the smallest is Rio Branco, capital of Acre, with 34,500 population. Urban expansion in the outlying areas of Brazil is not confined solely to the administrative capitals. The distant territories of Roraima and Fernando de Noronha are the only ones with a population under 20,000. Each of the other territories has a city of this size or larger, and all the states except Acre and Amazonas boast three or more. The movement into the cities and towns of the North, Northeast, and Center-West is largely a response to developmental programs fostered by the national government. The phenomenal growth of the Federal District, which had over half a million urban residents in 1970, reflects the increasing concentration of government functions in Brasília and the impact of the inter-regional highways that converge on the inland capital.

Historically, the cities of Brazil have drawn a large proportion of their inhabitants from outlying areas. Until recent decades, however, because of the difficulty of land transportation over long distances, the bulk of the newcomers to all Brazilian cities were from the immediate hinterland or from overseas. While the data are not precise, it appears that the number of residents of Brazilian cities and towns grew about three times as fast as the population at large from 1920 to 1940. More detailed census returns indicate that in the three decades ending in 1970 the rate of urban growth was about twice that of the population as a whole. Since the demographic base was constantly expanding, the number of people involved rose dramatically year after year. In absolute terms the increase in the urban sector—on the order of 40 million— was as great as the entire population of Brazil in 1940, and at least half the increase has occurred since 1960. Even when allowance is made for higher levels of health, and thus for a greater excess of births over deaths in the cities than in the countryside, it is apparent that natural increase cannot account for the sustained rapid expansion of the urban sector over the past several decades. Foreign immigration into Rio de Janeiro and São Paulo remained statistically impressive in the 1920's, but even then did not materially affect the boom in other large cities. Since the early 1930's, because they constitute a much smaller proportion of the total than formerly, the foreign-born have not contributed significantly to urban growth anywhere in Brazil. Clearly, the urban population explosion resulted from the increasing displacement of the rural population to the cities and towns of Brazil.

The surging growth of cities at the expense of rural areas is evidence of a restlessness among the Brazilian people in recent years akin to the spirit of adventure and the search for greener pastures that lured the *bandeirantes* across the heartland of South America in the seventeenth century. Treks of comparable distance—by truck from Rio Grande do Sul to Goiás, Mato Grosso, and Rondônia; by boat from Ceará to the upper reaches of the Amazon Valley; and by all manner of conveyances from the far corners of the republic to Rio de Janeiro and São Paulo—are familiar in the annals of this century. And like the *bandeiras* of old, migration within Brazil today is largely voluntary. Nonetheless, despite the nomadic heritage from the past, the modern migrant has little in common with the proud *bandeirante* of colonial days. In the first place, internal migration in Brazil is occurring on a far larger scale than ever before. In 1950 one of every ten Brazilians had moved at least once from the state of his birth. The proportion has surely risen sharply since that date, to reach a much higher figure in a single generation than the total for all foreign immigration into the country since 1822. Migration now also frequently involves the resettlement of entire families, as well as single men and women of various classes, and much of it is directed toward the cities rather than the *sertão*. In Rio de Janeiro in 1950 nearly 950,000 residents, of whom over half were women, were from other parts of the country. They represented more than 40 per cent of the population of the city. At the same time well over a million natives of other states were residing in the state of São Paulo. The movement of population, moreover, seems to reveal no consistent pattern, for it is taking place simultaneously in various directions. The industrialized areas of the South have received the largest contingents, chiefly from the East and Northeast, but there are strong counter currents from the South to the East and Center-West and from the Northeast into the North and Center-West, as well as a great deal of movement from place to place within individual states and regions.

A substantial part of the intra-state and intra-region migration, particularly in the Northeast, is of the seasonal or periodic variety that has given rise to the stereotype of the drought-driven *sertanejo* that recurs in the literature and folklore of Brazil today. The popular image is one of a humble squatter or tenant farmer from the backlands of Bahia or Ceará trudging with his family on foot, or perched perilously atop an overloaded truck, bound for more hospitable climes where he will seek work until it rains again in the *sertão*. This picture is a composite of the hundreds of thousands of drought victims who have been forced to abandon their homes within the past hundred years. It was such unfortunates who peopled the remote rubber camps in the Amazon before 1914, and cleared the forested cacao zone of southern Bahia in the first three decades of this century. More recently, in drought years they have fled by the thousands along the São Francisco River or the Rio-Bahia highway in search of fertile soils to the south. Currently, many rural families from the interior of the Northeast are flocking to the virgin forests of central Maranhão, while others are establishing themselves in the newly opened lands bordering the highway from Brasíla to Belém. By and large, however, refugees from the drought have neither the stamina nor the means to journey so far. Out of preference and necessity they look for a haven in the nearest coastal town or plantation zone, usually within their own state. Many do, indeed, return to the *sertão* at the earliest opportunity, but even more adapt to their new situation and remain in or near the urban areas. Popular belief to the contrary, most Brazilian migrants do not return to their point of departure, for the bulk of them are seeking a change of social status or way of life in moving to another geographic region.

Comparatively few migrant families from the Northeast or other technologically backward rural areas move directly to the larger industrial cities of the South and East. Census returns for 1950 and recent sociological studies in Rio de Janeiro and São Paulo suggest that the shift of population has followed a more complex pattern. Ordinarily, the displaced squatters, drought victims, or ambitious young *sertanejos* who try their fortune in these regions first settle in rural sectors. Single men and women may go directly to the big city, but the heads of families usually become *colonos* or ranch hands doing the only kind of work they know. Such employment is readily available to them because much of the local labor force has already succumbed to the lure of the city or the prospect of better conditions in a progressive plantation area. In due course, after acquiring a few new skills, the migrants may move on to another rural district where wages are higher and schools are perhaps closer at hand for their children. Again they take the place of workers who have moved to town. It is a continuous process, with new arrivals from outlying regions displacing native sons or earlier migrants who in turn proceed to Rio de Janeiro, São Paulo, or other urban centers. The number of intermediate stages varies greatly from one family to another, but it may well require two generations, or even three for a migrant family to make the transition from a *roça* in Ceará to a mill or factory in a southern city.

The great mobility of the Brazilian people is a phenomenon of recent origin, which dates for the most part from the 1930's and has achieved major proportions only since World War II. In a real sense it is a product of the continuing revolution in transportation and communications throughout the Western world in this century. The most important material changes contributing to the migratory current in Brazil has been the introduction of motor vehicles, chiefly trucks and buses, and the opening of roads to accommodate them. Since the early 1920's when some of the larger cities were linked by all-weather roads, and increasingly since the mid-1930's national and state administrations and a majority of the municipal governments have undertaken extensive road-building programs, to give Brazil today a network of more than 650,000 miles of roads and highways. There was a comparable increase in the number of motor vehicles from a few thousand in 1920 to about three million in 1970. Significantly, there was no substantial change in the size of the railway network, which has remained under 25,000 miles. From the beginning the bulk of the motor roads and vehicles had been found in the economically advanced sections of the country, but some trucks had penetrated all states and territories and before 1930 pioneer bus lines were operating in most of the coastal states. Commercial aviation, which was introduced in the 1920's, has served to tie distant reaches of the nation closer to the populated centers than ever before. Air travel, however, because of its high cost, has had only peripheral impact on internal migration. In this respect, the airplane in Brazil has made a more vital contribution in the field of communications.

Both transportation and communication services were improved by the new motor roads that were pushed into the interior in the 1920's and after. While they were designed initially as access roads to speed the movement of ranch, plantation, and mine products to markets on or near the coast, they served equally well as exit routes, even for those who had to travel on foot. They also helped to give formerly remote and isolated sectors of the population greater awareness of developments in the urban centers and other parts of Brazil. The movement of people in both directions, in itself, increased the exchange of information between the coast and the *sertão*. Moreover, the relative ease of transportation improved the postal service somewhat, and there was a small but significant increase in the distribution of newspapers and magazines from the larger cities among readers in the smaller inland communities. In sum, the expansion of the network of motor roads brought large areas of rural Brazil under the political, economic, and cultural influence of the state and national capitals, and made it more difficult for the people of interior communities to resist the forces of change that had been at work in the coastal cities since the last quarter of the nineteenth century.

This development—uniformly hailed as progress in the cities—was fully recognized and deplored by much of the traditional leadership in the *sertão*. Here, old-fashioned *coronéis,* or colonels, whose power stemmed usually from land ownership and almost absolute control over a submissive and dependent lower class tied to them by bonds of custom, family, and godparenthood had long ruled their respective areas in a quasi-feudal manner in exchange for periodic delivery of votes in state and national elections and occasional armed support for political bosses in the state capital. They did not welcome innovations that might weaken their autonomy or disturb the apathy of their followers. For similar reasons the numerous outlaw bands in the interior resisted the road-building programs that would extend the effective range and authority of police forces based in the state capitals. Nowhere was the reaction of these two groups more clearly evident than in the interior of the northeastern states, where local political leaders and bandits joined together in the late 1920's to oppose the penetration of roads and new ideas. At times they were allied with contingents of the national army and state police fighting against the rebel army column led by Luiz Carlos Prestes, who was trying in vain to arouse the rural populace to social revolution. At other times they attacked their former allies, assaulting engineer battalions assigned to road construction projects in the Northeast. Not until after the political revolution of 1930 and the capture of the most infamous of the bandit chieftains in 1934 was it safe for highway crews to work in the northeastern *sertão* without armed protection.

The roads and motor transportation made it possible for rural Brazilians to travel in greater numbers, but did not assure that they would do so. Except during periods of severe drought or other calamity, when it was necessary to migrate in order to survive, large-scale migration did not occur in Brazil until improvements in communications permitted the rural populace to compare their situation with that of people in other parts of the country. Newspapers, magazines, and letters from friends who had moved to a different area may have provided a basis for comparison by those who could read, but they did not affect the mass of illiterates. For them the radio and motion pictures probably awakened a sense of dissatisfaction with conditions at home and increased their awareness of greater opportunities elsewhere. Radio broadcasting, which has expanded tremendously since the first stations were inaugurated in the early 1920's, has served both as a vital cultural link between the coast and the towns and villages of the interior and as an agent of change in the traditional areas of the country. By the late 1930's there were nearly 100 stations bringing news, music, advertising, and politics to virtually every community served by electricity. All stations were joined into a single network for the weekly *Hora do Brasil* program, in which Getulio Vargas expounded on the progress of his administration and insisted that the old ways not only could but must be changed. The cost of the bulky, expensive radio receivers was offset by the installation of loudspeakers in public plazas of every market town in the Northeast, East, and South, and in numerous communities in the North and Center-West. Such installations have continued and are now commonplace in towns of the interior, but since the early 1960's a much larger audience has been reached by the inexpensive transistor radios carried by rural and urban Brazilians of all economic levels. By 1970 there were about a thousand radio stations scattered across Brazil. Over half were located in the South and more than a quarter of them in the East. The national government is encouraging the establishment of stations in frontier regions reached chiefly by broadcasts from neighboring countries, for Brazil's political leaders recognize the radio as an important vehicle for the cultural integration of the Brazilian people.

The motion picture has spread almost as widely as the radio. By the 1930's cinemas had been set up for at least weekly showings at modest prices in small towns where electric power was available, if only for a few hours in the evening. Although the films, chiefly from Hollywood or Europe, were intended solely as entertainment, they opened new vistas for simple people who had seldom ventured more than a few miles from their birthplace. In these circumstances it is perhaps not surprising that rural migrants moving from traditional to more modern areas of Brazil have often had an unrealistic vision of what to expect in their new home.

Even though internal migration has become a prominent, and apparently permanent, characteristic of Brazilian society since the 1920's, relatively little is known about the specific motives that have impelled ever increasing numbers of people to break with established routine and familiar surroundings. Obviously, in periods of drought, floods, or other natural disasters, the basic drive for self-preservation has accounted for much of the migratory movement, but at other times the decision to migrate appears to have been made for more prosaic reasons, both material and intangible. On the one hand, the migrants seek to escape from a situation that a smattering of education or exposure to new ideas has taught them to regard as intolerable. In all likelihood the monotonous routine of life in the interior—a condition accepted by their forebears as normal and inevitable—has been the most important single factor encouraging young men and women to leave their native district. On the other hand, the lure of steady jobs and a money income serves as an immediate inducement to migrate. Beyond such a practical consideration, however, is the vision of excitement and activity of life in "progressive" areas of Brazil. For a people who equate progress and modernity with movement and describe a quiet, uneventful community as decayed, this is a major consideration.

Comparatively few migrants to the cities are well equipped to cope with the complexities of urban existence, but the low rate of return to the countryside suggests that on the whole they have not been disillusioned by the new experience. The great majority gravitate to the sprawling—and frequently picturesque—slums that have become part of the urban scene in Brazil in this century. Even here, however, despite the overcrowding and squalor, their situation is usually an improvement over the one they have left behind. The poorest slum shacks are no worse than the hovels occupied by much of the rural lower class. The lack of sanitary conveniences is not lamented by families that have never known them, while the availability of running water from a public tap or fountain only a few blocks away may be regarded as a luxury. Moreover, there may be electricity for the lights, radio, or even television—symbols of great affluence to persons from traditional rural Brazil—that are now within their reach. At the same time slum dwellers, like other urban residents, have access to the public health agencies, schools, and other government-financed services, as well as sports, festivals, and many peculiarly urban forms of public entertainment. Their children can, and often do, attend primary school, if only for a few hours during the day. Above all, they become part of the hustle and bustle of the city, of the *"movimento"* that can only be found where large numbers of people live and work in close proximity.

The migrant must usually pay the price of anonymity for the real and presumed advantages of urban existence. By moving to city or town he cuts himself off from the basic sources of social stability in the two-class structure of rural Brazil. These are his personal relationships with the extended family on the one hand, and with a powerful protector, or *patrão,* on the other. Rarely does an entire clan transfer intact to the same urban center. The migrant, thus, is deprived of the frequent contacts and mutual assistance of cousins, in-laws, and godparents that are an indispensable feature of society in traditional areas. The loss is minimized if other members of the family have accompanied or preceded him, but in any case the adjustment to the crowded city life is often a lonely and difficult one.

The absence of a *patrão* may pose an even greater problem for the new arrival, who is left to his own devices in the search for food, lodging, employment, and a sense of identity. In the rural areas the *patrão* is a person of property and influence who provides employment, a plot of land for cultivation, small loans or other favors, and intercedes as necessary on behalf of his lower-class client before representatives of the law and local or state governments. He may also act as godparent to one or more of the client's children. In exchange for such favors, received or anticipated, the client gives his loyalty, labor, and perhaps his vote at election time. Before 1930—and even today in some remote areas of the *sertão*—the client might also serve as an armed retainer of the *patrão* in clashes with squatters, bandits, other landowners, or rival politicians. The *patrão*-client relationship, while highly exploitive, is still a highly personal one which preserves the individual dignity of both parties. There is no equivalent of the *patrão* in urban Brazil. The recent migrant, nonetheless, almost invariably expends a great deal of energy seeking a substitute. Single women, who are most often employed as domestics, frequently attempt to attach themselves to the family of their employer. The men, both single and heads of families, whose first employment is apt to be as unskilled construction workers, look to their foreman, a trade union official, a member of the bureaucracy, or perhaps a local politician as a benefactor and shield against the anonymity and impersonalism of the city.

In the city, as in the rural sectors of modern Brazil, migrants from the traditional areas have usually entered at the bottom of the social scale, not only adding to the size of the lower class but also, in part, replacing others who have risen to a higher social status. This is not to say that all migrants are simple, unlettered country folk, for Rio de Janeiro—and to a lesser extent São Paulo, Belo Horizonte, and Pôrto Alegre—have regularly attracted substantial numbers of successful and ambitious middle-class youths, politicians, businessmen, and intellectuals from distant parts of the nation. But for the most part the newcomers to the large industrial cities have been functionally illiterate and untrained for the specialized roles required in an industrial society. In these circumstances, the chance to improve their social condition has depended largely upon their acquisition of skills and attitudes not highly valued in the rural districts from which they came.

Upward mobility, which has always been possible, although not always encouraged in Brazil, was greatly accelerated by the simultaneous processes of industrialization and urbanization that have gained momentum steadily in the South and East since World War I. It is significant that in locations where urbanization has occurred without considerable industrial growth the social structure has changed much more slowly than in heavily industrialized areas. The new urban industries themselves have been primary agents of social mobility, for by teaching managerial and technological skills to members of the middle and lower classes, respectively, they have opened the way for advancement by both groups to more remunerative and more prestigious positions.

Wealth earned in industry or in commercial extensions of industrial enterprises—wholesale merchandising, export-import trade, and banking—has permitted many sons of middle-class families to move into the upper middle class. In some instances, prosperous young industrialists have married into the established upper class, or have joined the ranks of what may be called a new upper class, whose elite status derives from financial holdings rather than land and inherited position. Seldom, however, does a person from the lower class manage to reach the top of the social pyramid. The "rags to riches" phenomenon is not unknown in Brazil but is extremely rare, and in this century has been associated more often with foreign-born immigrants than with native Brazilians.

The industrial worker who achieves a position as a foreman or key technician in a complex manufacturing process thereby achieves a measure of elite status within the working class. Since competition for his services is keen, he may move from one concern or industry to another in response to offers of higher pay and fringe benefits that give him greater material comforts than are enjoyed by most members of the lower middle class. If he has the appropriate combination of income, educational background, and personal inclinations, he may acquire some middle-class values, although as long as he earns his livelihood by manual labor he will not be accepted as a member of the middle class.

Other avenues for moving from the lower to the middle class, or upward within the middle class, are sports, the arts, the civil bureaucracy, and less frequently, politics, and the armed forces. As in the United States, professional athletes are drawn from all social strata, but tend to come largely from the lower and lower middle classes. The few who gain nationwide and perhaps international stature as stars of Brazil's national game—soccer (futebol)—command high salaries and public esteem that enable them to overcome the limitations of their social background. The leading artists, too, in the fields of drama, music, and the plastic arts enjoy a privileged status and freedom to move at ease in all social circles, even though their professional earnings may be lower than those of the outstanding athletes. The artists, as a group, are more apt to be of middle-class origin, but representatives of all social sectors may be found among them.

Government service has traditionally been the principal form of respectable employment of a large segment of the Brazilian middle class. A position as a public functionary at any level confers a degree of prestige out of all proportion to the modest stipend it carries. As a practical matter, it has been customary for government employees to accumulate two or more appointments, or to combine these with other appropriate employment, in order to earn an adequate income. But for individuals schooled to regard physical labor as suitable only for slaves or menials, it is far preferable to subsist as a petty government official than to work with one's hands. Until 1930 the expansion of the bureaucracy appears to have barely kept pace with the growth of the population. Relatively few persons from the lower class were able to rise socially by this route, for the available posts were passed back and forth, according to the fortunes of politics, between substantially the same established middle-class families that had held them for generations. Following the revolution of 1930, however, old political patterns were disrupted and the government assumed increasing responsibility for the economic and social welfare of the nation and its people. In these circumstances there has been a multifold increase in the number of municipal, state, and federal employees, and, consequently, in the opportunities for new elements to enter government service. For more than four decades now, any Brazilian who has completed secondary school, and many with even less formal training, has usually been able to claim a position in the bureaucracy, and with it middle-class standing.

In the Brazilian tradition political leadership has ordinarily been regarded as the prerogative of the upper and upper middle classes. In most instances the men who have achieved prominence in state and national politics have been university graduates—the so-called *bacharéis* —from well-known families, whose entry into public life was facilitated by wealth, social position, and connections in official circles. On occasion men without such advantages, but gifted with oratorical and administrative talents, have made a political career their road to fame and fortune. The 1930 revolution opened the way for scores of men in this category, while opportunities for the emergence of self-made political leaders were further increased by the adoption of an open, multi-party system in 1946. The handful of Japanese-Brazilians in the postwar state and national legislatures were products of this system, although the process has not been limited to representatives of any single region or ethnic minority. Juscelino Kubitschek and Jânio Quadros, who rose from the lower middle class through municipal and state office to the presidency of the nation, are outstanding examples of men for whom social advancement has been one of the rewards of political success.

The armed forces, and particularly the army, in Brazil have served in a limited fashion as an avenue for social mobility. The officers of the military establishments are generally considered to be middle class, but this observation is based as much on the nature of the military institution in Brazil as on the social origins of the men themselves. Regardless of their family background, the officers become or remain middle class by virtue of their training and the positions they hold. Thus, a military career has rarely proved attractive to young men from upper class families. The navy provides a partial exception to the rule, for it has the reputation of being socially the most elite of the services, and in the nineteenth century drew its officers chiefly from the upper rungs of society in the coastal areas. For the past two or three generations, however, the naval officer corps appears to have been comprised largely of sons of navy families. No branch of the service attracts significant numbers of officer candidates from the civilian middle or lower middle classes in the industrial areas of Guanabara, São Paulo, and Minas Gerais, where alternative opportunities for material and social advancement are plentiful. A disproportionately high percentage of army officers are drawn from Rio Grande do Sul—where a third of the force is garrisoned—and from Mato Grosso and the northeastern states. Although the evidence is not conclusive, it appears that men of working-class origin have been entering in somewhat larger numbers since the 1930's, but sons of officers still constitute a large percentage of the newly commissioned lieutenants each year. The principal obstacle long faced by aspirants to a military career was admission to one of the secondary schools maintained by the armed forces, for only graduates from these schools could expect to enter the service academies. Partly to overcome this problem and partly to ensure a steady influx of new officer candidates, the academies have now been opened to a limited number of graduates of non-military high schools as well. Advancement through the academies is based on merit, and subsequent promotion through the middle grades is usually routine. There seems to be no conscious discrimination on the grounds of social origin, race, or color, except that few Negroes qualify for admission to the officer corps, and fewer still attain positions of command.

No element in Brazilian society has chosen a career in the non-commissioned ranks as a means of attaining higher social status. In part this is due to the limited opportunities, but even more it reflects the low esteem in which enlisted men are held by the public. The rank and file of Brazil's conscript army spend less than one year in uniform, are poorly paid, and receive little respect from the civilian population. Tours of duty are longer in the navy and air force, but otherwise there is little to distinguish the sailor or airman from the common soldier. Non-commissioned officers are volunteers. Army corporals rarely serve more than two years. Sergeants usually hold career appointments, but a large percentage resign after a few years of service. In the postwar period, and especially since 1960, efforts have been made with only moderate success to improve morale and to encourage a career mentality among non-commissioned officers, who possess or acquire technological skills in short supply in Brazil.

The Church in Brazil has not been an important institution for social mobility, although the parish clergy, drawn in good part from the lower class, enjoys middle-class status. In the colonial period and well into the nineteenth century, propertied families often encouraged sons or daughters to seek a clerical vocation in order to demonstrate or to preserve the family's social position. In this century, however, a clerical career is respected but not highly esteemed by any class in Brazilian society. Paradoxically, the seminaries have usually been well attended, because their students receive a sound education, but relatively few graduates opt to become priests. The Church has never attracted enough vocations within Brazil to meet its needs for parish priests and teachers.

The qualities and accomplishments required of the individual moving upward in Brazilian society vary according to the career or profession he selects, but all avenues of social mobility—except for certain areas of sports and entertainment—demand at least some formal education. Ex-President Kubitschek, for example, was educated as a physician before he entered politics, while Jânio Quadros began his public career as a secondary school teacher. Among a people who have traditionally considered schooling the privilege of the elite, those who have attended school are invariably accorded higher status than those who have not. While there is no exact correlation between educational level and social level, by and large the more formal training the individual receives, the higher he may rise on the social scale. The university graduate does not automatically enter the upper class, but he may do so if he satisfies the other criteria for membership in that class. As a general rule, completion of secondary school (*colégio*) or normal school assures one of middle-class standing regardless of family background or social origin. Graduation from commercial, industrial, or agricultural schools at a comparable level confers less prestige, but still distinguishes the student clearly from those whose education terminated at an earlier stage. Literacy, which is usually not retained unless the student has had more than two years of primary schooling, is the indispensable minimum requirement for social advancement even within the lower class in the modern areas of Brazil. Commercial and industrial society places a premium not only on the ability to read and write, but also on the cultural values instilled by the educational process. Members of the illiterate mass of the population—sometimes described as an infra-lower class—have no real chance to change their social condition unless they learn to read and write.

The rising rate of social mobility since 1920 reflects a substantial increase in educational opportunities for the Brazilian people. In 1920, when elementary school enrollments for the entire nation were on the order of 1,250,000, little more than one-fifth of the children between ages seven and fourteen were attending school. At the secondary level, where enrollments probably did not exceed 50,000, the proportion of active students in the potential school population was about one in eighty. And the 12,000-odd students in various advanced courses represented only a tiny fraction of their age group. About two-thirds of the elementary school pupils and a higher percentage of the post-primary students were in the Federal District, São Paulo, Minas Gerais, and Rio Grande do Sul, which were even then the most heavily industrialized areas of the country. Matriculations generally ran somewhat ahead of population growth during the 1920's, but the distribution of students by state and educational level changed little if at all.

By 1932 there were about 2,275,000 students at all levels in Brazil, of whom slightly over 2 million were enrolled in the primary grades.

The situation changed rapidly after the revolution of 1930, especially at the secondary and advanced levels. The influence of the rising urban middle class was evident in the assumption by the federal government of direct responsibility for training personnel for commerce and industry. To a much greater extent than ever before, education was used to promote economic growth and, incidentally, social change. Hundreds of small technical schools offering instruction in basic subjects and specialized training in various trades provided a form of secondary education to students who did not aspire to enter a university. Whether operated by federal agencies, the states, or by private enterprise, such schools conformed to standards established by the new ministry of education. This ministry also initiated a dramatic development in the structure of higher education in Brazil, encouraging the consolidation of separate faculties into universities. Brazil's first university, that of Paraná, founded in 1912, had been joined in 1920 by the University of Rio de Janeiro. The University of São Paulo was created as a state institution in 1934, and the University of Brazil was founded by the federal government in the city of Rio de Janeiro in 1938. The proliferation of universities has since continued at an accelerating rate. In the mid-1940's there were five; by 1950 there were eight; by the mid-1960's the total had risen to more than thirty, with at least one in each state; and by 1970 there were sixty or more universities in Brazil, of which about a third had opened their doors in the preceding two years.

The change in educational policies and the expansion of school facilities were accompanied by rising student enrollments. By 1940 primary school matriculations had increased to about 3 million. At the same time there were nearly 200,000 students in the regular secondary and normal schools, and perhaps as many more in a variety of specialized courses and training programs. The university student population exceeded 20,000 in a national population of more than 40 million. By 1950 the elementary schools were attracting over 5 million pupils, the secondary schools of all kinds had a total registration of 1 million, and there were some 40,000 university students. The persistence of these trends was revealed in the school census of 1964, which showed more than 9 million children attending elementary schools, upwards of 2 million in secondary schools, and 144,000 in the universities and other institutions of higher learning in Brazil. Six years later the figures had risen to 12 million, 4 million, and 430,000, respectively. The five states of Guanabara (the former Federal District), São Paulo, Minas Gerais, Rio Grande do Sul, and Rio de Janeiro accounted for about half of the primary school enrollments, over 60 per cent of those in secondary schools, and more than two-thirds of the university matriculations. The contrast with the situation in 1920 was enormous. In half a century there had been some diffusion of students geographically throughout Brazil and a striking increase in their numbers, both absolutely and as a proportion of the total population. While the national population rose by about three and one-half times between 1920 and 1970, the over-all school population was expanding by twelve and one-half times, increasing from one in every twenty-one Brazilians to about one in five.

Rates of growth varied tremendously among the three categories of student enrollments. The number of elementary school pupils increased almost tenfold, to comprise 17 per cent of the population of Brazil in 1970, as opposed to only 4.6 per cent fifty years earlier. By comparison, the eightyfold expansion in the ranks of secondary school students was staggering, even though much smaller numbers of students were involved. Less than .2 per cent of the Brazilian people were attending secondary schools in 1920. Five decades later over 4 per cent of the population were so engaged. The number of students in institutions of higher learning increased by some thirty-five times, and rose from a mere .04 per cent of the population in 1920 to .46 per cent in 1970. At the same time it is highly significant that the university student contingent actually shrank in relation to the size of the secondary school population. In 1920 there were about four students at the secondary level for each one enrolled in advanced courses. By 1970 the proportion was about ten to one.

The widening gap between the university and secondary school stu-

dent populations points up two fundamental characteristics of education in Brazil. One is the growing attraction of the technical and professional courses that have been introduced for students who plan to
terminate their formal instruction at the secondary level. The second
is the persistence of institutional and other barriers that greatly restrict
the number of students who are permitted to enter the university each
year. Every Brazilian administration since the 1930's has recognized
the fact that the nation does not produce enough technicians to meet
the needs of the economy and society in a technological age, and has
sought to resolve the problem by encouraging new institutions offering specialized training at the high school level. Until recently, however, very little has been done to modify the basic system of formal education in Brazil or to change the elitist concept of the university as a
sort of civilian academy to train the select few in the traditional professions and gentlemanly arts.

Under the system of education that evolved in Brazil after 1930,
most universities were free and public, and the standard curriculum
in the lower schools was designed to prepare students for admission to
a university. Nonetheless, it proved nearly impossible for the student
who attended only public schools to attain this goal. The primary
schools, predominantly tax-supported institutions operated by the
states or municipalities, usually did not offer more than four years of
instruction. Ordinarily, the student required at least five years of primary training in order to pass the entrance examination for admission
to secondary school, but the so-called "supplementary schools," offering instruction in the fifth and sixth grades, were seldom found outside the larger cities. As a practical matter, therefore, most students
had to enroll with a tutor or in a private school for the fifth year. The
standard secondary pattern included the four-year *ginásio* followed by
three years of *colégio,* or normal school from four to seven years. *Gi-
násios* and *colégios* were usually private, although there was at least
one state- or federally-supported school in each category in every state
in Brazil. Normal schools, which are located in all states and territories, might be public or private institutions. Any combination resulting in seven years of secondary education might qualify the student to

take the fiercely competitive university entrance examination. Less than half of the qualified applicants were normally admitted to the university. No provision was made for those who were refused entrance but not adequately prepared for alternative careers.

This system of formal education is now undergoing great change, although its external structure is still much in evidence in Brazil. The Ministry of Education, which determines curricula at all levels of instruction, has divided the educational process into eight years of compulsory primary training, four years of intermediate instruction, and four years of university. Moreover, successful completion of the primary cycle entitles the student to admission to secondary school without further examination. The curricula in the elementary grades remain much as before, but the intermediate courses must include a substantial offering of mathematics and basic sciences. The use of laboratories is another innovation in teaching practices at the secondary level. The standard college-preparatory courses are still available, but intermediate school students may also choose from a variety of alternative course patterns that will prepare them for careers in industry, agriculture, commerce, or other "practical" activities. The public universities are no longer free, but admissions are still controlled by the entrance examination. The student, however, has the option of choosing among a growing list of courses and disciplines. Well over half of all university students continue to enroll in medicine, law, and the humanities, although increasing numbers of them are studying agriculture, architecture and design, economics, engineering, mathematics, and the basic sciences.

The phenomenal strides Brazil has made in the area of public and private education in recent decades obscures the fact that more people than ever before are denied access to formal education of any kind. Every Brazilian constitution since 1934 has stipulated that all citizens have a right to a primary education, which shall be free and compulsory. Nonetheless, in the face of sustained rapid population growth, it has never been possible to enforce these provisions, even in the largest and wealthiest urban centers. Thus, Brazil is confronted with the paradox that while the rate of illiteracy has declined steadily—from about

65 per cent of those over age fifteen in 1920 to about 39 per cent of those over age five in 1970—the number of people who cannot read has increased. In the earlier year approximately 17 million Brazilians over seven years of age were illiterate. Fifty years later the corresponding figure has risen to more than 30 million. This situation arises from the fact that schools are still relatively few and attendance is infrequent in the rural areas, hamlets, and villages that contain about half of the population of Brazil. Three-fourths or more of the children not attending school live in rural districts. Conditions, moreover, are only slightly better in the cities, where the public elementary schools offer two, and sometimes three or even four, sessions per day. There are simply not enough teachers and classroom facilities to accommodate all potential students. In 1964, for example, more than 40,000 children of primary school age in Rio de Janeiro, and over 100,000 in the city of São Paulo, were not in school. These included some children who had never entered school, those who had completed the primary grades but were unwilling or unable for scholastic or financial reasons to continue formal study, and a much higher proportion of ex-students who had dropped out along the way.

The great majority of students who enroll at each level do not complete the course at the end of the year. It has been observed that among a school generation—all children and youths from age seven to twenty-two—about 14 per cent either do not enter school or fail to finish the first year. Thereafter, the drop out rate rises spectacularly. Less than half complete two years of primary training, and little more than one-quarter finish the fourth year, which is the most advanced grade available in much of the country. Only about half of these enter secondary school, and less than 4 per cent of the school-age population graduate. Again, roughly half of this reduced group enrolls in a university or comparable institution, because of rigid entrance examinations. Proportionately more university students complete their course of studies, but the number who graduate still constitute barely more than 1 per cent of their school generation.

The educational situation varies considerably from one region to another. Some parts of modern Brazil compare favorably with the countries of Latin Europe, while the more traditional regions rank with the least developed countries of the Western Hemisphere. By and large there are more schools and teachers and fewer illiterates in the cities than in the rural sections throughout the country. By the same token the heavily urbanized, industrial areas generally enjoy a much more favorable situation than the traditional, predominantly rural-oriented regions of the North and Northeast. In 1970, for example, when 61 per cent of Brazilians over age five could read and write, 83 per cent of the inhabitants of the states of Guanabara and Rio de Janeiro were literate, as were 82 per cent of those in São Paulo and the Federal District. Urban literacy rates were even higher, approaching 90 per cent in the cities in Guanabara and São Paulo, and averaging over 85 per cent in cities throughout Paraná, Santa Catarina, and Rio Grande do Sul. By contrast, in that same year only half the residents of the Northeast were literate, and in the rural areas only one person in three could read and write his own name. Both the number and percentage of literates are increasing in all sections of Brazil, but over the years the gap between the modern and traditional areas has progressively widened.

To date the most ambitious, if as yet inconclusive attempts to reverse this trend and to incorporate a larger portion of the rural population into the modern sector have been made outside the formal education structure. In the late 1950's, reflecting the rising politico-social ferment of the times, various governmental, private, and church agencies launched crash programs to combat illiteracy among Brazilians of voting age. For the most part their immediate aim was to enable rural adults to meet minimum literacy requirements as voters. Special attention was directed toward the populace in rural zones near the large cities of the Northeast. With few exceptions, such programs were cancelled after the revolution of 1964 because of their radical political content. The adult literacy campaign was revived in 1970, however, by the central government, with the creation of a new agency, the Brazilian Literacy Movement (*Mobral*). Its goal was to provide a five-month course of instruction in basic reading and writing skills to every illiterate Brazilian between the ages of twenty and thirty-five. By the end of 1972 over 7 million students had entered the program, of whom perhaps half became functionally literate. A small percentage of the graduates was subsequently enrolled in a one-year primary education course. The literacy campaign reaches nearly every *município* in Brazil and has had some impact in rural areas, but its principal successes have been registered among slum dwellers and recent migrants to the larger cities.

The accomplishments and shortcomings of both the regular school system and the literacy campaigns are direct reflections, on the one hand, of the higher practical and prestige value attached to formal education in the more progressive, up-to-date sectors of the society and economy, and, on the other, of the great difficulty in persuading qualified teachers to live and work in rural communities. Even such incentives as *Mobral* and the law that requires graduates of rural normal schools to teach at least one year in a rural school before accepting an appointment in the city have had little effect in locating teachers permanently in rural districts. Beyond these difficulties lie such pervasive matters as the overwhelmingly urban outlook of educational planners and the relative poverty of the states and municipalities in the less developed regions of the country. As has always been the case, the rural student, regardless of age, who wants more than the bare rudiments of a primary education must move to town.

The improved educational opportunities in the cities, coinciding with rapid urbanization and economic development to accelerate social mobility in Brazil since 1920, have had a discernible effect on popular attitudes toward race and color. While Brazilians historically have been more tolerant than other peoples in the Western Hemisphere of efforts by Negroes and mulattos to improve their social status, it is only in the past two generations that they have had to put their much vaunted ethnic democracy to sustained test. Previously, as long as society remained fairly static, with nearly all persons of color restricted to the lower class, and as long as a considerable majority of the Negro population remained in the rural plantation zones where changes occurred slowly if at all, social mobility was the infrequent exception rather than the rule. The rare mulatto, or even rarer Negro, who combined sufficient ambition, education, native talent, and sheer luck to rise in the social scale, could be tolerated as evidence of the lack of racial discrimination in Portuguese America. Such persons were usually absorbed into the small urban middle class without incident, but could aspire to no higher station. The abolition of slavery in 1888 removed all legal barriers to the social mobility of ex-slaves and the descendants of slaves, in much the same fashion as the Emancipation Proclamation had done in the United States twenty-five years earlier, but it produced no immediate change in social conditions. Nor did the shift to the republican form of government in 1889 offer any reason to expect that colored Brazilians in large numbers would henceforth receive more generous treatment than their counterparts in North America.

The present situation in Brazil, in which Negroes and mixed-bloods of partial Negro ancestry may ordinarily rise socially as far as their talents and accomplishments will take them, is largely a product of the period since World War I. Obviously, this striking change in circumstances owes much to the long-standing proclivity of Brazilians generally to judge others on their individual merits rather than on the basis of color or ethnic origin. But the rapid progress Brazilian society has made toward full racial democracy in the past half-century is equally the result of fortuitous trends on two separate levels, economic and intellectual.

The steady increase in opportunities for employment in urban commerce and industry has provided the material base for upward social movement. The hordes of rural migrants—chiefly persons of mixed blood—drawn to the cities after 1920, and particularly since 1940, in response to the demand for urban labor have proved capable of performing all tasks for which they were suitably trained. Those who have attained positions of responsibility have usually been accorded commensurate social status. In this regard undoubtedly the greatest advantages of the colored Brazilians have been their numerical superiority and the absence of an entrenched, white labor force with ingrained feelings of racial superiority. There has been no organized opposition to their advancement in the job market or in the social structure. The practical impossibility of barring persons of color from any field of employment was reflected in Brazilian law following the 1930 revolution. The decree of 1934, for example, requiring that at least two-thirds of the employees of each business concern must be Brazilian citizens was designed in part to guarantee the rights of colored workers excluded from employment by foreign-owned public utility companies. Discrimination on ethnic grounds was not a serious problem in Brazilian-owned establishments. Even the descendants of immigrants from countries in which racial bigotry is common appear to have acquired a typically Brazilian attitude toward race and color.

This cultural adaptation is evidence of the second, and more pervasive trend, which has supplied theoretical justification for social integration in Brazil in recent decades. Since the late 1920's the writings of Artur Ramos, Gilberto Freyre, and numerous other scholars have emphasized the positive contributions of the Negro to Brazilian culture and society. Such studies, often revealing extensive research and penetrating analysis, have tended to glorify and romanticize the Brazilian tradition of harmony between races. Freyre has gone further, suggesting that the people of Brazil are in the process of developing a new amalgam of the human species uniquely suited for tropical civilization. Gradually, and after sometimes acrimonious debate among Brazilian intellectuals, these scholarly endeavors have been accepted as valid reinterpretations of Brazil's social history, and have been passed on by educators as veritable articles of faith to new generations of students for whom slavery and other forms of racial injustice are only unfortunate traits of a long-dead past. Ever larger numbers of school children —of varying shades and hues—learn that racial democracy is a peculiarly Brazilian characteristic in which they can and should take great pride. The scholars, thus, have not only argued cogently for even broader tolerance and co-operation between Brazilians of different ethnic origins, but have contributed directly toward the attainment of that goal. The general acceptance of their views has not radically altered the real social condition of the bulk of the population, but it assures all qualified Brazilians substantially equal access to the avenues of social mobility. Awareness of this fact has permitted Brazilian so-

ciety to undergo a continuing social revolution for more than four decades without racial violence, truly an extraordinary accomplishment in
a world beset by racial tensions.

In addition to schools and scholars, a broad range of other institutions were engaged, directly or indirectly, continuously or intermit-
tently, in promoting social change in Brazilian cities during the past
several decades. Chief among these were the public press, government-
directed labor unions, and, until 1965, the political parties. They ca-
tered to the burgeoning urban population—including both lower and
middle classes—whose views, hopes, and ambitions had usually been
ignored or frustrated by the old-line political leadership before 1930.
At different times, according to the form of government in vogue at
the moment, each provided a forum for the exchange of ideas and a
channel of communications between the people and their leaders. Under the *Estado Novo* (1937-45), when partisan politics were suspended and the public press was subdued, the labor unions, official
broadcasts, and government-sponsored publications served as the principal agents for both indoctrination and social change. To a lesser extent this situation has developed again since the revolution of 1964.
Before 1937, and intensively after the return to unbridled, competitive
politics in 1945, the opposition parties and the administration, through
its control over trade-union activities, appealed to the urban voters,
promising them effective democracy, personal dignity, and a larger
share of the products of an expanding economy. One immediate result
was to raise public expectations for a better life to unreasonable
heights. Another was to reinforce the prevailing view that prompt
fulfillment of such aspirations was the responsibility of the federal government. Furthermore, each promise and each inevitable delay were
exposed and exacerbated by the partisan press, which was seldom constrained by the mild provisions against libel and incitement in Brazilian law. But whether in opposition or in support of the regime, each
agency remained a fervent advocate of Brazilian nationalism, which
carries with it implicit faith in social, economic, and national "progress." Under the impact of this incessant barrage, by the early 1960's
more than half the population was caught up in the ferment of peace-

ful social revolution, continued economic development, and soaring nationalistic aspirations—a process described by participants of diametrically opposed political views as the Brazilian Revolution.

Until about 1960 this revolution remained well within the bounds of established Brazilian institutions and practice. It was exclusively an urban process. Except for isolated outbursts of collective exasperation over deficient public transportation and occasional brief shortages of foodstuffs, revolutionary violence was entirely rhetorical. Despite rising inflation, wholesale tax evasion by the public, and extensive corruption in public office, the pace of economic expansion was sufficient to meet the most pressing needs of the growing population of the cities. The bulk of the rural populace remained apathetic, since the more restless and ambitious were drawn off in the migration to urban areas. Brazil appeared to be following a course of rapid evolutionary change that was still moderate enough to allow time for adjustment, thereby obviating the need for social or political upheaval.

This situation deteriorated abruptly in the early 1960's, when the rate of inflation surpassed that of economic growth, provoking advocates of conflicting panaceas to demand ever more drastic political remedies, ranging from the imposition of a military dictatorship on the one hand to the establishment of a people's republic on the other. There was no agreement about the source of Brazil's difficulties, which were attributed variously to communist subversion, subservience to foreign capital, political corruption, the ambition and ineptness of the president, and to a general lowering of the standards of public morality. In the midst of the furor and confusion over political drift and economic stagnation, the urban ferment was being carried to the rural areas by zealous, and often opportunistic, political organizers who called for sweeping agrarian reform and extension of the franchise and labor laws to illiterate plantation workers as the solution to the nation's economic, social, and political dilemmas. By law, in 1962, farm workers were given the right to organize and engage in collective bargaining. Consequently, several rural trade unions were formed, chiefly in the states of Pernambuco and São Paulo. As proposed, however, the other reforms ran counter to existing constitutional provisions, jeopardized one of the fundamental bases of private property in Brazil,

and threatened to destroy the precarious political balance between urban and rural areas. When the president himself took up the cry, and
simultaneously sought the backing of the military rank and file, the
armed forces and the propertied groups coalesced into a spontaneous
political force. Convinced that compromise was no longer feasible, the
army in March 1964 deposed the constitutional regime and took power
in the name of the revolution, vowing to return Brazil to the path of
order and progress.

Since March 1964 the views of Brazil's military leaders have been
paramount in shaping national policies affecting all segments of the
society and economy. Although before 1964 the armed forces had not
exercised power in this century, the officers feel particularly well qualified to direct the course of national affairs during a period of institutional crisis. Since the early days of the republic they have considered
themselves the guardians of national institutions, and intervened on
behalf of civilian factions on half a dozen occasions between 1930 and
1961, when those institutions seemed in jeopardy. As citizens conscious of the national heritage—which includes few military figures
of political prominence—they share the common belief that ideally a
civilian-directed, representative government is preferable to other systems. At the same time, as professional soldiers who take pride in their
efficiency and order, they have little respect for the ineffective—and, in
their view irresponsible and self-serving—politicians, who required
their steadying hand at frequent intervals. In their own eyes the
officers have several distinctive characteristics not commonly found
among civilian politicians in postwar Brazil. They are honest. They
are experienced administrators. Their loyalty to the nation is beyond
question, and they have a keen sense of identity with the republic, as
the form of government established in Brazil by the armed forces.
Above all, they feel they have a uniquely national perspective on national problems because they are drawn from all parts of the country
and in the course of their career serve for extended periods in each of
the various geographic regions. This, they believe, sets them apart
from the politicians, who are essentially representatives of state or
local interests.

Thus, in power, the military struck first at subversion and corruption, barring from the political process all elected and appointed officials judged disloyal or dishonest, and impressing upon the survivors of the purge the need for complete probity in public office. Stern measures were taken to remove politics from labor and student organizations, which had become hotbeds of political agitation by the early 1960's. Much of the form of democratic, republican rule that had been known in Brazil was preserved, even while its spirit was stifled. Lacking faith in the ability of the Brazilian people to choose their elected representatives wisely, the new regime instituted a succession of changes that served to insulate it increasingly from the electorate. The plethora of squabbling, pragmatic parties was abolished in 1965 and replaced the following year by two parties—created by the government without grass roots support—which henceforth would supply all candidates for public office throughout Brazil. The range of acceptable dissent was narrowed to exclude radicals of the right and left. Moreover, the indirect election of the president was made a permanent feature of the new system, and the election of governors by the state legislatures was introduced as the practice to be followed for an indefinite period. The congress, state governorships, and legislatures remained predominantly in civilian hands, but those in military office retained the power of decision on all matters of high policy. In this area top priority was given to restoration of the economy. The need for social reforms was recognized, but subordinated to the urgency for economic recovery.

A great deal of the economic progress recorded by the administrations of Humberto Castello Branco (1964-67) and Artur da Costa e Silva (1967-69) was achieved at the expense of urban workers and the salaried middle class. In its determination to check the soaring wage-price spiral, the central government forbade unauthorized increases in the wages of labor and the salaries of government employees. It also imposed partial price controls, but removed subsidies from key consumer goods, which were allowed to find their own price level. Periodic adjustments of the minimum wage regularly lagged behind rises in the cost of living. The result was a steady loss of purchasing power for the millions of workers whose income was pegged to the minimum wage set by the Ministry of Labor. At the same time, most strikes were prohibited, and the majority of established labor leaders were replaced by "interventors," who took over the leadership of the trade unions until their members could elect new officers acceptable to the government. From the point of view of the regime, organized labor simply could not be permitted to obstruct the course of national development. The Castello Branco administration largely ignored expressions of public discontent with government policies, but Costa e Silva sought to "clarify" public opinion in order to persuade the working class that the unpalatable sacrifices imposed upon it were temporary and in the national interest.

Much the same attitude prevailed in official circles toward the rural populace. Although rural labor legislation remained on the books, and some elderly plantation workers in São Paulo eventually received retirement benefits, most of the northeastern farm organizations withered when their organizers were purged as political subversives. Church efforts to arouse the social, and perhaps political, consciousness of the rural lower class were also looked upon with suspicion. Constitutional obstacles to land reform were removed and a moderate agrarian reform bill was enacted into law by the national government, but implementation proceeded slowly. Brazil's leaders appeared to feel that the pre-1964 social unrest in the rural areas had been artificially stimulated, and that pressure for agrarian reform would subside as new industries raised economic levels and provided employment opportunities for the depressed lower classes in the outlying regions.

Both the Castello Branco and Costa e Silva administrations attempted to meet the pressing needs of society by expanding established social services. The results were modest, at best, in the areas of public health and housing, but notable advances were registered in the field of education. Mounting student protests, which exploded into violence in 1968, obscured the fact of substantial increases in the budget for education, particularly at the secondary school and university levels. A significant innovation was the distribution of thousands of high school scholarships by the Labor Ministry to the children of trade union members, who could not otherwise have gone beyond a primary education. All in all, university enrollments rose by two and one-half times and secondary school matriculations nearly doubled between 1964 and 1969. In contrast, the expansion of health services available to the working public and unemployed barely exceeded the rate of demographic growth. The combination of natural population growth and continued migration into the cities also intensified the serious housing shortage, especially for the millions of slum dwellers in the large industrial centers. In fact, the deficit in housing for the urban lower class actually increased during the Castello Branco term, even though the National Housing Bank provided long-term loans for home purchases to wage earners and tens of thousands of new units were constructed. Costa e Silva's three-year plan set a goal of about 1,400,000 new working class residences, but only half that number were completed by 1970. There were no government programs to provide better housing for the rural populace. Not until 1970 did the government turn its attention fully to the social problems of the lower and middle classes.

The administration of Emílio Garrastazu Médici, which took office in October 1969, was the first one in more than a decade in Brazil with both the means and determination to launch a major assault on the most glaring social problems of the nation. While maintaining the drive for material development, the new regime recognized the urgent need to develop Brazil's human resources as well. Acknowledging that "the economy is going well, but the people fare badly," Médici reordered the priorities of his predecessors and called for a substantial diversion of funds to meet the needs of urban and rural society. In 1970 he announced coordinated programs of national and social integration which would absorb 18 per cent of the gross national product during the remaining years of his term. The national integration program is concerned above all with the opening and settlement of the territorial expanse of the interior of Brazil. It is a long-term project that will in due course provide employment, land, and participation in the money economy to much of the rural populace, while effectively incorporating vast, presently unoccupied reaches of the *sertão* into the nation. The social integration program, designed to raise the material, cultural, and technological level of Brazilian society, affects both urban and rural areas. A special feature of the program is a form of social security, paid by employers into a national fund and available to employees before retirement to cover specified large expenses, such as the purchase of a home. The social policies of the Médici administration also provide for successive increases in wages and salaries above the rate of inflation, expansion and extension of established social services, and a thorough revision of the school system. Early in his term Médici assigned top priority and a major share of the budget to education. His administration pledged a total investment equivalent to $5 billion in education between 1971 and 1974, in order to reduce adult illiteracy to a modest level and to equip an increasing proportion of the Brazilian people to cope with the challenges of a modernizing, industrializing nation in a technological age.

Few civilians in Brazil could be expected to be in complete accord with the order of priorities assigned to national goals by the military-dominated regime, or with the specific measures employed to attain them. Nevertheless, there is basic agreement between the uniformed services and the civilian population over fundamental assumptions about the nature and destiny of Brazil and over broad, long-range national objectives. Continued social mobility and racial integration are taken for granted by all parties, although supporters of the post-1964 administrations would stress that upward social mobility should be achieved through education, as a result of personal effort, rather than through political action designed to lower the barriers between classes. The men in power since 1964 emphasize the role of private enterprise in economic development, but all agree that some state planning and strong regulatory powers by the federal government are necessary to prevent wasteful exploitation of natural resources and other abuses by private capital. Regardless of their immediate political views, civilians and soldiers share a common vision of the future, in which there will be equality, dignity, and plenty for all the people in a Brazil which enjoys untrammeled independence and the respect of the community of nations.

Political Chronology

I. COLONIAL PERIOD

1493   Papal division of newly discovered and undiscovered areas between crowns of Portugal and Castille gives Portugal primacy over coast of Africa and lands to the east.

1494   Treaty of Tordesillas gives Portugal a claim to the eastern portion of the as yet undiscovered continent of South America.

1500   Pedro Alvares Cabral, en route to India, discovers and claims Brazil for Portugal. The new possession is known variously as Santa Cruz and Ilha da Vera Cruz.

1501-30   Amerigo Vespucci and others explore the coastline of Brazil. The dyewood trade is established. Occasional squadrons sent to expel Breton "interlopers" from the Brazilian coast.

1532   First Portuguese colony in Brazil founded at São Vicente by Martim Afonso de Souza.

1534   The captaincy system is introduced. Brazil is divided into hereditary captaincies granted to a dozen donatories.

1549   The first governor-general, Thomé de Souza, establishes the capital of Brazil at Bahia. The first Jesuits reach Brazil.

1551   The Bishopric of Brazil is created, with its center at Bahia.

1554   The founding of a Jesuit school, the Colégio de São Paulo de Piratininga, marks the beginning of urban settlement at São Paulo.

1555-67   A French colony, Antarctic France, is established at Guanabara
           Bay by an expedition under the command of Admiral Villega-
           gnon. It is destroyed and the French are expelled after two cam-
           paigns, during which the settlement at Rio de Janeiro is founded
           (1565) by the Portuguese.

1580   The Portuguese and Spanish crowns are united under Philip II
           of Spain.

1604   The India Council, patterned after the Spanish Council of the
           Indies, is created in Lisbon to prepare laws and supervise the
           administration of Brazil and other parts of the Portuguese em-
           pire. The name is later changed to Overseas Council (1642)
           and Department of Marine and Overseas (1736).

1612-16   In a flurry of colonial rivalry the French found the town of São
           Luiz do Maranhão (1612), which is taken by the Portuguese
           (1615), who establish Belém (1616) as a base of operations
           against French, Dutch, and English footholds in the Amazon
           delta.

1621   The State of Maranhão (including Ceará, Maranhão, and Pará)
           is established.

1624   The Dutch attack Bahia.

1630   The Dutch capture Pernambuco and begin the conquest of
           northeastern Brazil.

1637-39   Expedition led by Pedro Teixeira establishes Portugal's claim to
           the Amazon basin.

1640   Restoration of the Portuguese monarchy under João IV of the
           House of Bragança. The first viceroy appointed to Brazil.

1648   The first permanent settlement in Paraná is founded at Parana-
           guá.

1654   The Dutch are expelled from Brazil.

1658   The first permanent settlement in Santa Catarina is founded at
           São Francisco do Sul.

1680   Colônia do Sacramento is founded by the Portuguese, across the
           estuary from Buenos Aires, beginning a century and a half of
           armed rivalry for control of Uruguay and access to the River
           Plate.

1709   Creation of the captaincy of São Paulo e Minas de Ouro, to
           establish royal authority in the mining area of Minas Gerais.

1720-63   A series of administrative reorganizations reflect the settlement
           of the gold-mining regions in central Brazil and expansion to the
           south. Minas Gerais separated from the captaincy of São Paulo
           (1720); military garrison established at Rio Grande (1737);

Santa Catarina, including Rio Grande do Sul, separated from the captaincy of São Paulo (1738); dismemberment of São Paulo completed with elevation of Goiás and Mato Grosso to captaincy status and transfer of remaining territory to the jurisdiction of governor at Rio de Janeiro (1748); re-creation of the captaincy of São Paulo, and transfer of the capital of the viceroyalty of Brazil from Bahia to Rio de Janeiro (1763).

1750   The Treaty of Madrid between Portugal and Spain recognizes Portuguese possessions west of the line of Tordesillas, introducing the principle of *uti possidetis* in settling boundary disputes between the colonies of the two powers.

1752-54   The last of the hereditary captaincies revert to the crown.

1759   The Jesuits are expelled from all Portuguese territories in America.

1777   The Treaty of San Ildefonso between Portugal and Spain fixes, in rough outline, the present boundaries of Brazil, confirming Portuguese possession of the Amazon basin and Spanish possession of Uruguay.

1789   The *Inconfidência Mineira* in Vila Rica marks the first abortive attempt to establish a republic in Brazil. The chief plotters are exiled and their leader, Tiradentes, is executed (1792).

1808   The royal court moves from Lisbon to Rio de Janeiro, which becomes the capital of the Portuguese empire. The ports of Brazil are opened to trade with all friendly nations.

1810   Anglo-Portuguese treaty extends preferential commercial rights in Brazil to Great Britain.

1815   Brazil is elevated to the status of kingdom co-equal with Portugal.

1816   Prince Regent Dom João becomes King João VI, of Portugal, Brazil, and Algarves. Luso-Brazilian troops conquer Uruguay, which is incorporated (1821) into Brazil as the Cisplatine Province.

1817   Revolt with republican overtones is suppressed in Pernambuco.

1821   João VI returns to Portugal leaving his heir, Dom Pedro, as regent in Brazil.

II. THE EMPIRE

1822   Declaration of Brazil's independence (September 7) by Prince Regent Dom Pedro, who becomes Emperor Pedro I.

1824   First Brazilian constitution proclaimed. United States recognizes Brazilian independence.

1825   Portugal and Great Britain recognize Brazilian independence.

1825-28   War with Argentina. Uruguay is established as an independent republic.

1827   Commercial treaty with Great Britain. Brazil agrees to abolish African slave traffic within three years.

1831   Abdication of Pedro I in favor of his five-year-old son.

1831-40   Brazil is governed by a series of regents. The regency period, in effect, is an unsuccessful experiment with republican rule.

1834   Promulgation of the Additional Act, the only major amendment to the constitution of 1824, enlarges provincial autonomy.

1835-45   The Farroupilha Revolt in Rio Grande do Sul rages for a full decade. Its failure helps to assure the continued political unity of Brazil.

1840   Dom Pedro II is proclaimed emperor at age fourteen (July 23).

1844   Brazil denounces the treaty with Great Britain. Anglo-Brazilian relations deteriorate rapidly because of rising imports of Negro slaves into Brazil.

1850   The Queiroz Law (September 4) abolishes the African slave traffic to Brazil.

1852   Brazil intervenes in Argentina to assist in the overthrow of Rosas.

1865-70   The War of the Triple Alliance pits Brazil, Argentina, and Uruguay against Paraguay, which continues until the death of Paraguayan dictator Solano López.

1870   First Republican Manifesto is published.

1871   The Rio Branco Law, or Law of Free Birth, provides for the gradual extinction of slavery in Brazil.

1885   The Saraiva-Cotegipe Law frees all slaves over age sixty.

1888   The Golden Law is signed by Princess Regent Isabel (May 13), abolishing slavery without compensation to slave owners.

1889   The army, under Marshal Deodoro da Fonseca, deposes the emperor and proclaims the republic (November 15).

III.   THE REPUBLIC

1891   The first constitution of the republic of the United States of Brazil is promulgated (February 24). Provisional President Fonseca is replaced by Vice President Floriano Peixoto (November 23).

1893-95   The government is victorious in a civil war sparked by naval opposition to the Peixoto administration.

1894   The first civilian president, Prudente de Morais, of São Paulo, assumes office (November 15). His term marks the beginning of the so-called "Old Republic" (1894-1930) in which the administration candidate is invariably elected.

1910   Heated presidential campaign between opposition jurist Ruy Barbosa and Marshal Hermes da Fonseca is fought over the issue of militarism in government.

1917   Brazil enters World War I as an Allied power (October 26).

1922   Military unrest, signaling the beginning of the *"tenentista"* movement, breaks out with the revolt (July 5) of younger officers at Fort Copacabana in Rio de Janeiro.

1924-27 A military uprising in São Paulo (July 5, 1924) is followed by the march of the Prestes Column through the interior of Brazil. The attempt to ignite a popular revolution fails.

1930   Getulio Vargas, the defeated candidate for the presidency, seizes power (November 3) at the head of a revolutionary movement. A provisional government is established.

1932   The Constitutionalist Revolution (July 9-September 29) in São Paulo is suppressed by the federal government.

1934   The second republican constitution is promulgated and Vargas is elected president by the congress (July 16).

1935   Communist-led revolt within the army in Natal and Rio de Janeiro is suppressed after bloody fighting (November 24-27).

1937   A coup d'etat establishes the authoritarian *Estado Novo* (New State), with Vargas as dictator-president (November 10). On the same day a previously drafted constitution is promulgated.

1942   Brazil enters World War II as a member of the Allied forces (August 22).

1943   A secret but widely disseminated *Manifesto Mineiro*, drafted by opposition leaders in Minas Gerais, calls for a return to democratic government.

1944   The Brazilian Expeditionary Force takes part in the Italian campaign.

1945   Vargas is removed from power by military coup d'etat (October 29); open representative government is restored; War Minister Eurico Gaspar Dutra is elected president (December 2).

1946   The fourth constitution of the republic is promulgated (September 18).

1950   Vargas is returned to the presidency by election (October 3).

1954   An air force officer is killed (August 5) in an assassination attempt against opposition newsman Carlos Lacerda, touching off the final crisis of the Vargas regime; military leaders demand

Vargas's resignation (August 22); Vargas commits suicide (August 24); Vice President João Café Filho assumes power.

1955   Juscelino Kubitschek is elected president and João Goulart is elected vice president (October 3); War Minister Henrique Lott leads coup d'etat (November 11) to guarantee election results.

1956   Kubitschek and Goulart are installed in office (January 31).

1960   Capital of Brazil is transferred from Rio de Janeiro to Brasília (April 21). Jânio Quadros and João Goulart are elected president and vice president, respectively (October 3).

1961   Quadros resigns unexpectedly (August 25); over military protests, Goulart is installed as president (September 7); the parliamentary system of government is introduced to curb Goulart's powers.

1963   By national plebiscite (January 6) the presidential system of government is restored.

1964   Civilian-military revolution (March 31-April 2) deposes Goulart; First Institutional Act (April 9) establishes new revolutionary regime and authorizes purge of leftists and corrupt officeholders; Marshal Humberto Castello Branco elected president by congress (April 15).

1965   Second Institutional Act (October 27) revises political party structure.

1967   The fifth constitution of the republic, incorporating changes introduced by the revolutionary government, is promulgated (January 24); General Artur da Costa e Silva is inaugurated as president (March 15); Castello Branco dies in air crash (July 18).

1968   University student riots in Rio de Janeiro suppressed by police and army troops (June); Fifth Institutional Act (Dec. 13) initiates the "revolution within the revolution." Habeas corpus is suspended, and the government is given discretionary powers to remove dissidents from political office. Congress adjourned indefinitely.

1969   Costa e Silva suffers massive stroke, and power is assumed by the three military cabinet ministers (Aug. 31); U.S. Ambassador Elbrick kidnapped by terrorists (Sept. 3) and released in exchange for 15 political prisoners (Sept. 6); death penalty decreed for crimes of subversion and revolutionary war (Sept. 10); military high command selects Gen. Emílio Garrastazu Médici as next president of Brazil (Oct. 6); revised constitution promulgated (Oct. 17); congress reconvened (Oct. 22) and elects Médici and Admiral Augusto Rademaker as president and vice-president, respectively, (Oct. 25) for term ending March 15, 1974. Médici and Rademaker take office (Oct. 30). Costa e Silva dies (Dec. 18).

1970 Médici assert Brazil's sovereignty over 200-mile territorial sea (March 25); administration party (ARENA) elects 21 of 22 state governors (Oct. 3).

A Selective Guide to the
Literature on Brazil

The bibliographical guide is designed primarily to suggest additional sources for the general reader who may wish to delve more deeply into topics touched upon in this study. It is intended to be illustrative of the range of materials available rather than an exhaustive listing of works on Brazil. The guide is divided into six broad categories. Over-all, and within each section, general works and works in English precede more specialized studies and works in Portuguese or other languages. The first section includes only representative items in English by North American, European, and Brazilian authors. These are followed by travel accounts, largely but not exclusively in English, with emphasis on the period since 1822. The section dealing with histories of Brazil is arranged chronologically, while the sections on the society and economy focus principally on themes developed in this volume. The final section provides an indication of the major bibliographies, periodicals, and newspapers indispensable for serious research into the social and economic history of Brazil. No attempt has been made to incorporate the voluminous periodical literature on Brazil, or to include the recent flood of publications on Brazilian politics.

I. REPRESENTATIVE WORKS IN ENGLISH

Easily the most readable and informative brief account of Brazilian society today is *An Introduction to Brazil* (rev. ed., New York, 1971) by Charles Wagley, who views the conditions and aspirations of the various social classes objectively and sympathetically. A penetrating, subjective assessment of the evolution of Brazilian society and its values by a leading Brazilian scholar is José Honório Rodrigues, *The Brazilians, Their Character and Aspirations* (Austin, 1967). A somewhat more clinical approach prevails in T. Lynn Smith, *Brazil: People and Institutions* (4th ed., Baton Rouge, 1971), which assesses the origins, heritage, and actions of the Brazilian people from the point of view of a rural sociologist. Since it first appeared in 1946, Smith's study has been the standard work on this subject. A perceptive journalistic account of the pressures for social and political change in the 1960's is *Brazil on the Move* (New York, 1963) by John Dos Passos. *Brazil, the Infinite Country* (New York, 1961), by William L. Schurz, deals clearly and imaginatively with the interaction between Indians, Europeans, and Negroes, and their adjustment to the environment over the entire span of Brazilian history. The most authoritative study of Brazilian geography is Preston James, *Brazil* (New York, 1946). The anthology edited by Eric N. Baklanoff, *New Perspectives of Brazil* (Nashville, 1966), includes essays on the economy, society, politics, geography, religion, and culture of the Brazilians. Similar in format but broader in content are T. Lynn Smith and Alexander Marchant, eds., *Brazil: Portrait of Half a Continent* (New York, 1951), and Lawrence F. Hill, ed., *Brazil* (Berkeley and Los Angeles, 1947), which may still be read with profit by the layman and specialist alike. British interpretations of Brazil may be found in Harold V. Livermore, ed., *Portugal and Brazil* (London, 1953).

Acute observations by foreigners impressed with the progress and promise of Brazil before and during the first world war reveal the persistence of fundamental social and economic problems, and provide a gauge for measuring the rate of change in Brazil in this century. Among the more useful studies in this respect are Pierre Denis, *Brazil*, translated by Bernard Miall (London, 1914); C. S. Cooper, *The Brazilians and Their Country* (New York, 1917) and appropriate chapters in James B. Bryce, *South America: Observations and Impressions* (London, 1912), and Georges E. B. Clemenceau, *South America Today: A Study of Conditions, Social, Political, and Commercial in Argentina, Uruguay and Brazil* (London, 1911).

The history of Brazil from discovery to the present is synthesized in E. Bradford Burns, *A History of Brazil* (New York, 1970). The reader interested in the color and pageantry of Brazilian history as recorded by contemporaries will wish to consult the same author's *A Documentary History of Brazil* (New York, 1966), which contains excerpts in English translation from key documentary sources for the centuries from 1494 to 1964. Much of the story of the territorial expansion of Brazil in the colonial period is related in Richard M. Morse, ed., *The Bandeirantes, the Histori-*

cal Role of the Brazilian Pathfinders (New York, 1965). The excitement
of the eighteenth-century gold rush, and the impact of the mining era on
colonial society are stirringly told in C. R. Boxer, *The Golden Age of Brazil,
1695-1750* (Berkeley and Los Angeles, 1962). A. J. R. Russell-Wood provides insight into various segments of society in the colonial capital in his
*Fidalgos and Philanthropists, the Santa Casa de Misericordia of Bahia,
1550-1775* (Berkeley and Los Angeles, 1968). A detailed examination of
the problems of colonial administration and war on the southern frontier
is found in Dauril Alden, *Royal Government in Colonial Brazil* (Berkeley
and Los Angeles, 1968), while some of the same themes are treated from
a regionalist viewpoint by Moysés Vellinho in *Brazil South, Its Conquest
and Settlement* (New York, 1968). A brief sketch of Brazilian history is
included in J. A. Camacho, *Brazil: An Interim Assessment* (London,
1952), while a standard Brazilian text covering the period 1500-1930 is
available in João Pandiá Calógeras, *A History of Brazil*, translated and
edited by Percy A. Martin (Chapel Hill, 1939; reissued, New York, 1963).
The translator has added a narrative account of events in the 1930's, which
may be supplemented by Jordan M. Young, *The Brazilian Revolution of
1930 and the Aftermath* (New Brunswick, 1967), and Thomas E. Skidmore, *Politics in Brazil, 1930-1964* (New York, 1967). The history of the
republic is presented in José Maria Bello, *A History of Modern Brazil,
1889-1964*, translated by James L. Taylor, with a new concluding chapter
by Rollie E. Poppino (Stanford, 1966).

Few biographies of prominent Brazilian figures have yet appeared in
English. Sérgio Corrêa da Costa reviews the agitated life of Pedro I in
Every Inch a King, translated by Samuel Putnam (New York, 1950).
Pedro II is the hero of Mary W. Williams's uncritical *Dom Pedro the
Magnanimous, Second Emperor of Brazil* (Chapel Hill, 1937). The two
emperors and their families are the subjects of Bertita Harding's popularized account, *Amazon Throne; the Story of the Braganzas of Brazil* (In-
dianapolis, 1941). The life and times of Brazil's pioneer industrialist are
treated in Anyda Marchant's *Viscount Mauá and the Empire of Brazil*
(Berkeley and Los Angeles, 1965). Carolina Nabuco has recaptured much
of the aura of society, politics, and diplomacy of the late empire and early
republic in the biography of her father, *The Life of Joaquim Nabuco,* translated and edited by Ronald Hilton, *et al.* (Stanford, 1950). The outstanding Brazilian diplomatist, the Baron Rio Branco, is the central figure in
E. Bradford Burns, *The Unwritten Alliance: Rio-Branco and Brazilian-
American Relations* (New York, 1966). John W. F. Dulles has provided a
biography of the dominant political personality of twentieth-century Brazil
in *Vargas of Brazil* (Austin, 1967).

Scholarly works by Brazilian authors are increasingly available in English translation. The basic study of the culture of Brazil since colonial times, providing a solid background for further reading in social and intellectual history, is Fernando de Azevedo's monumental *Brazilian Culture,* translated by William Rex Crawford (New York, 1950). Without question the best known Brazilian writer in the United States is Gilberto Freyre, whose theories on the blending of races and cultures in the slave-holding plantation society of tropical Brazil have affected nearly every area of Brazilian studies since the appearance of *Casa grande e senzala* (Rio de Janeiro, 1933). While Freyre is seldom constrained by chronological limits, this classic, translated by Samuel Putnam as *The Masters and the Slaves; a Study in the Development of Brazilian Civilization* (New York, 1946; 2d ed., 1956; abridged ed., 1964), deals primarily with the colonial era. In the same vein, but concerned chiefly with the nineteenth century, is *The Mansions and the Shanties; the Making of Modern Brazil,* edited and translated by Harriet de Onís, with an introduction by Frank Tannenbaum (New York, 1962). Freyre carries essentially the same theme into the early twentieth century in his *Order and Progress. Brazil from Monarchy to Republic,* edited and translated by Rod W. Horton (New York, 1970). These works presume a great deal of knowledge about Brazilian history and culture on the part of the reader. The uninitiated should begin with *New World in the Tropics* (New York, 1959), an expanded and revised version of Freyre's *Brazil, An Interpretation* (New York, 1945), which was written originally in English to explain Brazil and the Brazilians to the North Americans. José Honório Rodrigues is interested in many of the same questions as Freyre, but gives a different emphasis and a sharper focus on the current situation in his *Brazil and Africa,* translated by Richard A. Mazzara and Sam Hileman, with an introduction by Alan K. Manchester (Berkeley and Los Angeles, 1965). Glimpses into the evolution of Brazilian attitudes toward themselves and their nation are presented in E. Bradford Burns, ed., *Nationalism in Brazil, a Historical Survey* (New York, 1968). The colonial origins of contemporary Brazilian institutions are dealt with in masterful fashion by Caio Prado Júnior in *The Colonial Background of Modern Brazil,* translated by Suzette Macedo (Berkeley and Los Angeles, 1967). Celso Furtado, an outstanding economist with a keen sense of history and a flair for clear prose, has provided equally valuable perspective on the Brazilian economy in *The Economic Growth of Brazil, A Survey from Colonial to Modern Times,* translated by Ricardo W. de Aguiar and Eric Charles Drysdale (Berkeley and Los Angeles, 1963). The current socio-political ramifications of many of these same questions are considered in Octavio Ianni, *Crisis in Brazil* (New

York, 1970), and Hélio Jaguaribe, *Economic and Political Development. A Theoretical Approach and a Brazilian Case Study* (Cambridge, 1968). The reader will be intrigued by the explanation of the differences between Brazil and the United States, in terms of the backgrounds and motivations of the early settlers, offered by Clodomir Vianna Moog in *Bandeirantes and Pioneers*, translated by L. L. Barrett (New York, 1964). Carl N. Degler provides a comparison of the institution of slavery in the two countries in *Neither Black nor White: Slavery and Race Relations in Brazil and the United States* (New York, 1971), while Florestan Fernandes examines the position of the Negro in Brazil since the abolition of slavery in his *The Negro in Brazilian Society*, edited by Phyllis B. Eveleth (New York, 1969).

Only a small portion of the wealth of Brazilian literature has yet been brought within reach of English-language audiences, although new titles are being translated every year. Much of the pioneer work in the field was done by Samuel Putnam, whose translation of Euclides da Cunha's *Os sertões* (Rio de Janeiro, 1902), the modern Brazilian classic, was published as *Rebellion in the Backlands* (Chicago, 1944). Guides to the literature of Brazil are Manuel Bandeira, *Brief History of Brazilian Literature* (New York, 1958), Erico Veríssimo, *Brazilian Literature, An Outline* (New York, 1945), and Samuel Putnam's *Marvelous Journey. A Survey of Four Centuries of Brazilian Writing* (New York, 1948). The latter is perhaps the finest compilation of its kind in any language. The principal trends in Brazilian literature since the 1920's are examined in John Nist, *The Modernist Movement in Brazil* (Austin, 1967). Among the earlier Brazilian novelists whose works have appeared in English, Machado de Assís is well represented with *Eitaph of a Small Winner*, translated by William L. Grossman (New York, 1952); *The Psychiatrist and Other Stories*, translated by William L. Grossman and Helen Caldwell (Berkeley and Los Angeles, 1963); and *Dom Casmurro*, translated with introduction by Helen Caldwell (New York, 1953; Berkeley and Los Angeles, 1966). Brazil's leading novelist today, Jorge Amado, has had numerous works published in English translation. Most useful for their exposition of manners and mores in Bahia are *Gabriela, Clove and Cinnamon*, translated by James A. Taylor and William L. Grossman (New York, 1962), and *Shepherds of the Night*, translated by Harriet de Onís (New York, 1967).

II. TRAVEL ACCOUNTS

Many of the most fascinating accounts of Brazil have been written by foreign visitors who commented on the significant commonplaces that usually escaped mention by their Brazilian contemporaries. Over the full span of Brazilian history such accounts provide a wide range of information, from social customs of the various peoples of the colony, empire, or republic to technical aspects of the operation of plantations, ranches, and mines. For the late colonial period and much of the imperial era they are often a ready source of statistical data on commerce, slavery, and the slave trade. With rare exceptions the finest treatises on the flora, fauna, and mineralogy of Brazil have been written by visiting foreign scientists. Many travel accounts appeared originally in English, and others have been translated into English from French or German editions, but a complete listing would have to include works in all European tongues as well as Arabic and Japanese. By and large, those that best illustrate important aspects of the Brazilian past have been published in Portuguese translation. The bulk of these have appeared since 1839 in the *Revista do Instituto Histórico e Geográfico Brasileiro* or, since 1932, in the Brasiliana series of the *Biblioteca Pedagógica Brasileira*.

In point of time the earliest visitor to leave a written record of his impressions of Brazil was Pero Vaz da Caminha, scribe of the Cabral expedition of 1500. His letter to the king may be found in English translation in William B. Greenlee, ed., *The Voyage of Pedro Alvares Cabral to Brazil and India* (London, 1938), and Charles David Ley, ed., *Portuguese Voyages, 1498-1663* (New York, 1947). An excerpt from the latter edition also appears in E. Brandford Burns, *A Documentary History of Brazil*. The full text is available in Portuguese in Pero Vaz da Caminha, *Carta a El Rei D. Manuel* (São Paulo, 1963). Of the subsequent voyages of exploration along the Brazilian coast, the most readable and complete account is Pero Lopes de Souza, *Diário da navegação de Pero Lopes de Souza de 1530 a 1532* (2 vols., Rio de Janeiro, 1927), which presents details of the entire expedition. Hans Staden, an early German visitor, has left an exciting memoir of life in São Vicente and among the Indians of Brazil in the mid-1500's. First published in German in 1567, Staden's story has gone through numerous editions and translations. The reader may wish to consult *Hans Staden, the True Story of his Captivity*, translated and edited by Malcolm Letts (London, 1928).

French efforts to establish colonies in Brazil in the sixteenth and seventeenth centuries are recalled in memoirs which include invaluable data on the habits, languages, and environment of the aboriginal inhabitants of Antarctic France and Maranhão. They are not available in English. The earliest is André Thevet, *Les singularitez de la France Antarctique* (Paris, 1558). The standard version of Thevet's work is the annotated edition by Paul Gaffarel (Paris, 1878). Jean de Léry observed native customs and the process of French settlement on Guanabara Bay in *Histoire d'un voyage fait en la terre du Brésil* (La Rochelle, 1578). The most recent Portuguese translation, by Sérgio Milliet, appeared as *Viagem à terra do Brasil* (São Paulo, 1961). Two Capuchin priests, Claude d'Abbeville and Yves d'Evreux, left memorable accounts of the French and their Indian allies in Maranhão from 1612 to 1614. The definitive version of d'Abbeville's *Histoire de la mission des peres capvcins en l'isle de Maragnan et terres circonuoisines* (Paris, 1614) is the facsimile edition with preface by Capistrano de Abreu and glossary by Adolfo Garcia (Paris, 1922). Evreux' *Voyage dans le nord du Brésil fait durand les années 1613 et 1614* (Paris, 1615) was republished with introduction and notes by Ferdinand Denis (Leipzig, 1864).

The British also visited Brazil both in peace and war throughout the colonial period. Most of the accounts of voyages of exploration have appeared in the Hakluyt series. Lancaster's raid on Pernambuco in 1595 is recorded in William Foster, ed., *The Voyage of Sir James Lancaster to Brazil and the East Indies, 1591-1603* (London, 1940). William Dampier's monthlong sojourn in Bahia in 1699 is related in *A New Voyage Round the World* (London, 1927). George Anson, who called at Santa Catarina in 1740 on the first leg of his voyage around the globe, has left a graphic description of its fortifications and defenders as well as general notices about the discovery of gold and diamonds in Brazil. His maps and commentaries may be found in Richard Walter, ed., *Anson's Voyage Round the World* (London, 1928). John Barrow recorded his impressions of Rio de Janeiro in *A Voyage to Cochinchina in the Years 1792 and 1793* (London, 1806). One of the last of the colonial period accounts by a British visitor, with excellent descriptions of daily life in Bahia, is Thomas Lindley's *Narrative of a Voyage to Brazil* (London, 1805).

The Amazon and its peoples are described romantically in the report of its first European visitor, Francisco de Orellana, in H. C. Heaton, ed., *The Discovery of the Amazon,* translated by Bertram T. Lee (New York, 1934), and more realistically in George Edmundson, ed., *Journal of the Travels and Labours of Father Samuel Fritz in the River of the Amazons between 1686 and 1723* (London, 1922).

With the transfer of the royal court from Lisbon to Rio de Janeiro in 1807-08, Brazil was opened to virtually unrestricted travel by the citizens or subjects of friendly foreign powers. A large number of accounts by British commercial agents are part of the legacy of this period. Moreover, at the close of the Napoleonic Wars in Europe, King João VI invited a large artistic mission, chiefly from France, whose members have left a rich heritage of impressions in prose and paintings, while the royal marriage uniting the Houses of Bragança and Hapsburg in 1817 brought a number of scientific expeditions from Austria and Bavaria to Brazil. Their observations were eventually published in German and in most instances also appeared in French and English. In sheer volume the number of travel accounts for the years 1808-22 probably exceeds the total for the three centuries of the colonial era.

For the most part the British were concerned about commercial opportunities in the country. Thomas Ashe encouraged the expansion of trade in the area and assessed Brazil's wealth with voluminous statistical information in *A Commercial View and Geographical Sketch of the Brazil in South America* (London, 1812). In the same year John Mawe, the first foreigner authorized to inspect the diamond-mining area, published his *Travels in the Interior of Brazil* (London, 1812). It is an unrivaled source of information on the society and economy of Minas Gerais at the end of the colonial period. Henry Koster, who resided and traveled extensively in the Northeast from 1809 until his death in 1820, was one of the most perceptive observers ever to write on Brazil. His *Travels in Brazil* (London, 1816) comprise an indispensable document on the social, economic, and political history of the region. John Luccock, a British merchant, explored economic prospects in Brazil and the River Plate in *Notes on Rio de Janeiro and the Southern Parts of Brazil Taken During a Residence of Ten Years in the Country from 1808 to 1818* (London, 1820). Henry Chamberlain described Rio de Janeiro in *Views and Costumes of the City and Neighborhood of Rio de Janeiro* (London, 1822). Extremely valuable for its insights into court life and feminine society at the time of Brazilian independence is Maria Graham's *Journal of a Voyage to Brazil and Residence There During the Years 1821, 1822, 1823* (London, 1824). The author's own, well-annotated copy of this edition together with notes of her return voyage to Brazil in 1824 were translated and edited by Américo Jacobina Lacombe as *Diário de uma viagem ao Brasil* (São Paulo, 1956). The Scottish nobleman, Thomas Cochrane, Earl of Dundonald, served as commander of naval forces in both the Chilean and Brazilian wars for independence. His impressions are recorded in Thomas Dundonald, *Narrative of Service in the Liberation of Chile, Peru, and Brazil* (2 vols., London, 1859). Volume II is devoted to Brazil, with special attention to the campaign in the North. Robert Walsh, chaplain of the British legation in Rio de Janeiro, gives detailed comments on politics and society in the capital and on the difficulties of travel to Minas Gerais in *Notices of Brazil in 1828-1829* (2 vols., London, 1830). His observations on the size and composition of the population of Rio de Janeiro and on the slave traffic are among the most useful sources on these subjects during the reign of Pedro I.

The classic travel accounts of Brazil on the eve of independence were written by Augustin de Saint-Hilaire, a member of the French artistic mission from 1816 to 1822. An indefatigable botanist, Saint-Hilaire visited every province in the vast triangle between Espírito Santo, Goiás, and Uruguay, keeping minute records of all that he observed. The *Segunda viagem do Rio de Janeiro a Minas Geraes e a São Paulo, 1822,* translated by Afonso de E. Taunay (São Paulo, 1932), is one of at least eight accounts of his travels to appear in Portuguese. At the other extreme is Jean Baptiste Debret, who published only one record of his fifteen years (1816-31) in Brazil. Translated by Sérgio Milliet as *Viagem pitoresca e histórica ao Brasil* (2 vols., São Paulo, 1940), it is nonetheless a primary source on the Indians of Brazil and on aspects of everyday life in Rio de Janeiro. Debret's many superb paintings and sketches constitute a veritable photographic record of Brazil under João VI and Pedro I. Numerous other paintings, drawings, and lithographs by contemporaries of Debret and Saint-Hilaire have been reproduced in Brazil in connection with the fourth centenary of Rio de Janeiro in 1965.

The outstanding work by German travelers to Brazil after 1808 is the collaborative effort by Johann B. von Spix and Karl F. P. von Martius, of which a substantial part was published in English as *Travels in Brazil, 1817-1820* (London, 1824). The full text is available in German and in Portuguese translation. Although, as naturalists, Spix and Martius were concerned chiefly with flora and fauna, their curiosity embraced everything they observed. Their commentaries on the life of the people they met in Rio de Janeiro and its hinterland, in the Northeast, and in the Amazon provide the ingredients for social and economic history of the period. An erstwhile companion of Spix and Martius, Johann Emmanuel Pohl, who traveled extensively in Minas Gerais and Goiás, has left a valuable account of his wanderings in *Reise im Innern von Brasilien . . . in den Jahren 1817-1821* (2 vols., Leipzig, n. d.). The Vienna edition of 1832 was translated as *Viagem ao interior do Brasil empreendida nos anos de 1817 a 1821* (2 vols., Rio de Janeiro, 1951). Prince Maximilian von Wied-Neuwied, who journeyed overland from Rio de Janeiro to Ilhéus collecting zoological specimens, has contributed a fundamental, copiously illustrated work on forest Indians. The first part of his travel account appeared in English as *Travels in Brazil in 1815, 1816, and 1817* (London, 1822).

After the opening of Brazilian ports in 1808 occasional accounts of Brazil were published by North American visitors, including officials, merchants, travelers en route to the Pacific or Far East, and later, explorers and Protestant missionaries. The early accounts dealt primarily with trade. The most useful of this kind is the report by the first United States consul at

Bahia, now available in a bi-lingual edition as Henry Hill, *A View of the Commerce of Brazil [Uma visão do comércio do Brasil em 1808]*, translated by Gilda Pires, with notes by Luís Henrique Dias Tavares (Rio de Janeiro, 1964). In a similar vein is John M. Baker, *A View of the Commerce between the United States and Rio de Janeiro* (Washington, 1838), which includes interesting comments on the ice trade between the two countries. Perceptive commentary on social customs and race relations in Rio de Janeiro are found in Rev. C. S. Stewart's *A Visit to the South Seas, in the United States Ship Vincennes, during the Years 1829 and 1830* (London, 1832). The same author provides the basis for comparison in his lengthy description of Rio de Janeiro more than two decades later in *Brazil and La Plata; the Personal Record of a Cruise* (New York, 1856). Lieutenant Charles Wilkes has preserved the record of an ambitious undertaking in *Narrative of the United States Exploring Expedition during the Years 1838, 1839, 1840, 1841, 1842* (5 vols., New York, 1856). The sections dealing with Brazil are included in Volume III. The North American who closely approximated Henry Koster in his ability to capture the essence of the Brazilian way of life was Thomas Ewbank, whose *Life in Brazil* (New York, 1856) is a remarkable document on the people and institutions of Rio de Janeiro at the mid-century. The observations of one of the first missionaries to Brazil are presented in Daniel P. Kidder, *Sketches of a Residence and Travels in Brazil* (2 vols., Philadelphia, 1845). Better known for its sectarian bias is the later volume that Kidder wrote with J. C. Fletcher, *Brazil and the Brazilians* (Philadelphia, 1857), which offers interesting views on social and economic institutions in the interior of Brazil.

Kidder's attitude of superiority was far surpassed by that of the French Count Suzannet, who traveled overland from Rio de Janeiro to the North in the 1840's. His incisive, and invariably uncomplimentary, comments on the economy and culture of the empire during a time of political turmoil are, however, a vital source of information on the period. His account was relatively unknown until its publication in Portuguese as *O Brasil em 1845*, translated by Márcia de Moura Castro, with introduction by Austregésilo de Athayde (Rio de Janeiro, 1957). More kindly toward the Brazilians, and unique for its detailed observations of areas seldom seen by foreigners, is the account by the English botanist, George Gardner, *Travels in the Interior of Brazil* (London, 1846). Richard F. Burton, the British vice consul at Santos, has provided perhaps the most readable and exciting memoir of travel and exploration in the Brazilian *sertão* in his *Exploration of the Highlands of Brazil; with a Full Account of the Gold and Diamond Mines* (2 vols., London, 1869).

The lure of the Amazon attracted foreign explorers and scientists throughout the nineteenth century. Wilkes visited the river sea in the 1830's. J. E. Warren's *Para* (New York, 1851) includes valuable com-ments on the residents of the great valley. William Lewis Herndon and Lardner Gibbon descended the river from its headwaters to the sea in 1851-52. The record of the expedition is contained in their *Exploration of the Valley of the Amazon, Made under Direction of the Navy Department* (3 vols., Washington, 1854). The Wallace-Bates expedition in 1848 produced two notable studies of value to the historian and social scientist as well as to the natural scientist: A. R. Wallace, *Travels on the Amazon and Rio Negro* (London, 1853); and Henry W. Bates, *The Naturalist on the River Amazons* (2 vols., London, 1863; 2d ed., 1864; reissued in one volume, with introduction by Robert L. Usinger, Berkeley and Los Angeles, 1962). The Thayer expedition of 1865-66 also resulted in two useful and interesting accounts. The personal recollections of Professor and Mrs. Louis Agassiz are found in *A Journey in Brazil* (Boston, 1868), while the professional aspects of the expedition are recorded in Louis Agassiz, *Scientific Results of a Journey in Brazil* (Boston, 1870).

A substantial majority of the travel accounts written during the second half of the nineteenth century deal with economic development or colonization. One of the most useful sources of information and commentary on the economy, with particular attention to the introduction of railroads, is the series of accounts by William Hadfield, *Brazil, the River Plate, and the Falkland Islands* (London, 1854); *Brazil and the River Plate in 1868* (London, 1869); *Brazil and the River Plate 1870-76* (London, 1877). Ballard S. Dunn, who was seeking a haven for emigrants from the United States following the defeat of the Confederacy in the Civil War, wrote *Brazil, the Home for Southerners* (New York, 1866). It is a good source on slavery and economic life in Brazil during the Paraguayan War. John Codman, *Ten Months in Brazil* (Boston, 1867), is rich in information on coffee plantations in the province of Rio de Janeiro, the Paraguayan War, and North American immigration into Brazil. Oskar Canstatt's *Brasil: a terra e a gente, 1871,* translated by Eduardo de Lima Castro (Rio de Janeiro, 1954), was published originally in German. It deals with German immigrants in Brazil as well as with general conditions during and immediately after the Paraguayan War. The German colonies in southern Brazil were also described by Michael G. Mulhall, a British journalist in Buenos Aires, in *Rio Grande do Sul and Its German Colonies* (London, 1873). The chief value of the book, however, is found in Mulhall's introductory comments on the economic state of Brazil. The prospects for British settlers were pointed out in T. P. Bigg-Whither, *Pioneering in South Brazil* (2 vols., London, 1878). Conditions in the Northeast and the Amazon in the 1870's are graphically portrayed in Herbert H. Smith's *Brazil, the Amazons and the Coast* (New York, 1879). Smith provides the finest available first-hand report of the great drought beginning in 1877. H. C. Dent, *A Year in Brazil* (London, 1886), is particularly useful for the data it provides on slavery and the abolition movement. Social change and economic conditions during the final decades of the empire and first decades of the republic are described in Frank Bennett, *Forty Years in Brazil* (London, 1914).

In the twentieth century foreign visitors to Brazil have tended to focus on the coffee and rubber industries, on the exotic appeal of one of the world's last frontiers, and more recently on Brazil's promise as an emerging world power still struggling to overcome the inertia of underdevelopment. Early examples of the first type are Manuel Bernárdez, *Le Brésil, sa vie, son travail, son avenir* (Buenos Aires, 1908), by an Argentine journalist; William D. Boyce, *Illustrated South America* (Chicago and New York, 1912), a popularized account which includes an excellent description of the American colony at Vila Americana in São Paulo; and Joseph F. Woodruffe, *The Upper Reaches of the Amazon* (London, 1914), which recounts the adventures of a rubber gatherer. Theodore Roosevelt's recollections of a hunting trip in the wilds of Brazil, *Through the Brazilian Wilderness* (London, 1914), is useful for its revelations about Colonel Rondon and the Brazilian Indian Service. L. E. Elliott's *Brazil: Today and Tomorrow* (New York, 1917) is a mine of information on the agricultural and industrial economy. William H. Koebel, *The Great Southland: The River Plate and Southern Brazil of Today* (New York, 1920) draws interesting contrasts between Brazil and Argentina. Konrad Guenther, *A Naturalist in Brazil: The Flora and Fauna and the People of Brazil,* translated by Bernard Miall (London, 1931) provides an authoritative account of agriculture and folk customs in the interior of the Northeast. Stefan Zweig, whose *Brazil, Land of the Future,* translated by Andrew St. James (New York, 1941) combines a historical sketch with personal observations, fell in love with the country and could find nothing discouraging or unpleasant to write about it. For all its romantic bias, his book, which presents a detailed travelogue of the settled areas, interprets Brazilian culture through the impressions of a sensitive artist. Claude Lévi-Strauss, another sensitive observer, provides a frank but sympathetic portrayal of the plight and prospects of the Amerindians of Brazil in *World on the Wane* (London, 1961). And John Dos Passos's *Brazil on the Move,* which was listed above, might also be included as a travel account by a foreign visitor concerned for the problems and promise of Brazil's national development.

III. HISTORY

A. *General*

The only general history of Brazil from 1500 to the present available in English is Burns's *A History of Brazil,* mentioned above. Calogeras's *A History of Brazil* provides uneven coverage to 1930, and Américo Jacobina Lacombe, *Brazil: A Brief History,* translated by W. A. R. Richardson (Rio de Janeiro, 1954) is a clear and succinct outline. Bailey W. Diffie, *Latin American Civilization: Colonial Period* (Harrisburg, 1945; reissued, New York, 1967) includes a masterful synthesis, while Harry Bernstein, *Modern and Contemporary Latin America,* Part III (New York, 1965) offers a continuous history of Brazil from the eighteenth century to the present. The classic English-language history of colonial Brazil to 1808 remains Robert Southey, *History of Brazil* (3 vols., London, 1810-19). Two anthologies that seek to draw on the entire span of Brazilian history to explain the recent past are Eric N. Baklanoff, ed., *The Shaping of Modern Brazil* (Baton Rouge, 1969), and Henry H. Keith and S. F. Edwards, eds., *Conflict and Continuity in Brazilian Society* (Charleston, S.C., 1969).

The most productive and influential historian of nineteenth-century Brazil was Francisco Adolfo Varnhagen, Viscount of Pôrto Seguro. His *História geral do Brasil,* with notes by Capistrano de Abreu and Rodolfo Garcia (7th ed., 6 vols., São Paulo, 1962), is the standard comprehensive account of Brazil from discovery to independence. Varnhagen heavily emphasizes administrative and diplomatic history. To date the most exhaustive study of Brazilian history is José Francisco de Rocha Pombo, *História do Brasil* (10 vols., Rio de Janeiro, 1906-1910), which ranges in time from the pre-Portuguese period to the first decade of the republic. Pedro Calmon, *História do Brasil* (5 vols., São Paulo, 1939-56; illus. ed. 7 vols., Rio de Janeiro, 1959-61) combines primary documents with skillful synthesis of secondary sources. His *História social do Brasil* (3 vols., São Paulo, 1937-39) is excellent. The monumental *História da Companhia de Jesus no Brasil* (10 vols., Lisbon and Rio de Janeiro, 1936-50), edited by Serafim Leite, S. J., is based primarily on manuscripts by members of the Society of Jesus in Brazil. Leite's work, however, should not be regarded solely as a history of the Jesuit Order in Brazil, or as religious history, but rather as social history in the broad sense.

The most recent, and in some respects the most ambitious project for a multi-volume history of Brazil is Sérgio Buarque de Holanda, ed., *História geral da civilização brasileira* (São Paulo, 1960-   ). To date seven volumes, including two on the colonial period and five on the empire, have appeared. These differ from the general histories cited above in being the work of various authorities commissioned to prepare detailed monographic contributions in the areas of their specialty. The contributors include historians, economists, and sociologists, the majority of whom are associated with the University of São Paulo. The *História geral da civilização brasileira* has already become an indispensable reference for serious study of Brazilian economic, social, and cultural history.

B. Discovery, Exploration, and Settlement

The drama of Portuguese maritime expansion and the discovery of Brazil has been well told in English in Bailey W. Diffie, *Prelude to Empire: Portugal Overseas before Henry the Navigator* (Lincoln, 1961); Samuel E. Morison, *Portuguese Voyages to America in the Fifteenth Century* (Cambridge, 1940); Edgar Prestage, *The Portuguese Pioneers* (London, 1933); and C. R. Boxer, *Four Centuries of Portuguese Expansion, 1415-1825* (Johannesburg, 1951): Pero Magalhães de Gandavo, a sixteenth-century resident of Brazil, provided abundant data on the size and location of Portuguese settlements in the first history of the colony in 1576, which is available in English as *Histories of Brazil* (2 vols., New York, 1922). Alexander Marchant also deals with early settlements along the Brazilian seaboard in his *From Barter to Slavery: the Economic Relations of Portuguese and Indians in the Settlement of Brazil, 1500-1580* (Baltimore, 1942), while documents on penetration of the *sertão* by Paulistas in the seventeenth and eighteenth centuries may be found in translation in *The Bandeirantes,* by Richard M. Morse. Still the finest synthesis in English of the process of exploration and settlement in the colonial period is Roy Nash, *The Conquest of Brazil* (New York, 1926).

There is a vast literature in Portuguese on the discovery and occupation of Brazil. Each of the general histories cited above devotes considerable attention to these subjects. The basic published source of documents on the discovery is Carlos Malheiro Dias, ed., *História da colonização portuguêsa do Brasil* (3 vols., Pôrto, 1924). A scholarly review is presented by Jaime Cortesão in *Os descobrimentos portugueses* (2 vols., Lisbon, 1959-61). The same author considers the possibility of a pre-1500 discovery of Brazil in *A política de sigilo nos descobrimentos* (Lisbon, 1960). Gabriel Soares de Souza's *Tratado descriptivo do Brasil em 1587,* with notes by Francisco Adolfo de Varnhagen (3d ed., São Paulo, 1938), which is also available in Spanish as *Derrotero general de la costa del Brasil* (Madrid, 1958), supplements the work of Pero Magalhães de Gandavo with significant detail about settlement patterns in the plantation zone of the Northeast. Afonso de Escragnolle Taunay's *História geral das bandeiras paulis-*

tas (11 vols., São Paulo, 1924-50) is the most comprehensive work on the contribution of the *bandeirantes* to the territorial expansion of Portuguese America. In *Rapôso Tavares e a formação territorial do Brasil* (Rio de Janeiro, 1958) Jaime Cortesão examines the career of an explorer who carried the flag of Portugal from Rio Grande do Sul to the Andes. Capistrano de Abreu's *Caminhos antigos e povoamento do Brasil* (Rio de Janeiro, 1930) is an erudite and imaginative interpretation of the conquest of the *sertão*, with emphasis on the North and Northeast, while the finest monographic treatment of the subject for Brazil as a whole is Basílio de Magalhães, *Expansão geográfica do Brasil colonial* (São Paulo, 1944).

C.   Colonial Period to 1808

All of the general histories listed above deal extensively with the colonial era. Among works in English Southey's *History of Brazil,* Diffie's *Latin American Civilization: Colonial Period,* and C. R. Boxer's *The Golden Age of Brazil* may be supplemented by monographs such as Luiz Edmundo da Costa, *Rio in the Time of the Viceroys,* translated by Dorothea H. Momsen (Rio de Janeiro, 1936), which describes the colonial capital in the eighteenth century, and by a series of studies of seventeenth-century Brazil by C. R. Boxer. The latter include his *A Great Luso-Brazilian Figure: Padre Antônio Vieira, S. J.,* 1608-1697 (London, 1957); *The Dutch in Brazil,* 1624-1654 (Oxford, 1957); and *Salvador de Sá and the Struggle for Brazil and Angola,* 1602-1686 (London, 1952).

Of the contemporary accounts the reader should consult Pero Magalhães de Gandavo, cited above, Frei Vicente do Salvador, *História do Brasil,* 1500-1627 (São Paulo, 1918; 5th ed., 1965) and João Antônio Andreoni [pseud. André João Antonil], *Cultura e opulência do Brasil* (São Paulo, 1923; Salvador, 1950, 1955; São Paulo, 1963, 1967). Frei Vicente was the first to criticize the Portuguese in Brazil for "scratching along the shore like crabs." Andreoni's work, which first appeared in 1711, was promptly banned to avert undue foreign interest in the newly discovered gold mines. It is perhaps the most lucid observation of the society and economy of colonial Brazil. Andreoni reflects the prosperity and optimism prevalent in Brazil at the opening of the eighteenth century. More pessimistic in tone are the earlier sermons and letters of Father Vieira, who frequently despaired of the future of Brazil. His works are found in Antônio Sérgio and Hernani Cidade, eds., *Padre Antônio Vieira: obras completas* (12 vols., Lisbon, 1951-54). Vieira casts a glaring light on the chronic economic depression and the weaknesses of the social order in seventeenth-century Brazil.

Vieira is also an excellent source on the Dutch attempt to conquer and hold an empire in the Northeast. This episode has attracted a great deal of attention from historians on both sides of the Atlantic. For an introduction to the subject the reader may wish to consult Boxer's *The Dutch in Brazil, 1624-1654;* José Antônio Gonsalves de Mello, *Tempos dos flamengos, influência da ocupação holandêsa na vida e na cultura do norte do Brasil* (Rio de Janeiro, 1947); and Hermann Wätjen, *Das Holländische Kolonialreich in Brasilien* (Gotha, 1921), which is also available in Portuguese as *O domínio colonial holandês no Brasil,* translated by Pedro Celso Uchôa Cavalcanti (São Paulo, 1938).

The standard works on colonial government are Caio Prado Júnior, *The Colonial Background of Modern Brazil,* and Dauril Alden, *Royal Government in Colonial Brazil,* both cited above. They may be supplemented by Max Fleuiss, *História administrativa do Brasil* (2d ed., São Paulo, 1925), which is based on official documents of the colonial, imperial, and early republican regimes, and by Marcos Carneiro de Mendonça, *O Marquês de Pombal e o Brasil* (São Paulo, 1960). Mendonça includes a nearly complete compilation of the decrees and other pronouncements sponsored by the famous prime minister in his quarter-century-long campaign to reform the colonial administration. An excellent social and economic history, which also sheds a great deal of light on governmental practices throughout the colonial period is Thales de Azevedo, *Povoamento da cidade do Salvador* (Salvador, 1950; 2d ed., São Paulo, 1955).

The history of the Amazon has been told in more than a dozen works by Arthur Cézar Ferreira Reis. The reader should consult his *Súmula de história do Amazonas* (Manaus, 1965) for an outline and bibliography of the field. Of particular value for the colonial period are Edson Carneiro, *A conquista da Amazônia* (Rio de Janeiro, 1956), and Mathias C. Kiemen, *The Indian Policy of Portugal in the Amazon Region, 1614-1693* (Washington, 1954).

D. *Kingdom and Empire, 1808-89*

The history of Brazil from 1808 to 1889 has not been well covered in English, but Brazilian writers have concentrated heavily on the period. The quality of their works ranges from superlative scholarship to trite romanticism, with a considerable preponderance of the latter, since the deceptively placid reign of Pedro II has been recalled as the "good old days" by many Brazilians of the twentieth century. C. H. Haring, *Empire in Brazil, a New World Experiment with Monarchy* (Cambridge, 1958) is a first-rate introduction and summary. For the role of the crown, the reader should review the biographies of Pedro I and Pedro II by Corrêa da Costa and Mary W.

Williams listed above. The transition from colony to nation is presented in *History of Brazil* (London, 1836) by John Armitage, a British merchant in Rio de Janeiro, who was a witness of much that he described. Armitage's work, which deals with events from the arrival of the Portuguese court in 1808 to the abdication of Pedro I in 1831, is often regarded as an extension of Southey's classic account of the colonial era. The position and influence of the British in Brazil is the subject of Alan K. Manchester's *British Preëminence in Brazil: Its Rise and Decline* (Chapel Hill, 1933). It focuses largely on commerce and on the slave traffic. Richard Graham examines British influence on Brazil in the period following abolition of the slave traffic in *Britain and the Onset of Modernization in Brazil, 1850-1914* (Cambridge, 1968). Lawrence F. Hill approaches some of the same materials from the United States point of view in *Diplomatic Relations between the United States and Brazil* (Durham, 1932). P. H. Box, *The Origins of the Paraguayan War* (2 vols., Urbana, 1929), remains the basic study in English of the bloodiest and most costly war in Brazilian history. The impact of new ideas in the postwar years, contributing to the fall of the empire in 1889, is discussed in Richard Graham, ed., *A Century of Brazilian History since 1865* (New York, 1969), and João Cruz Costa, *A History of Ideas in Brazil*, translated by Suzette Macedo (Berkeley and Los Angeles, 1964). The final chapter in Haring, *Empire in Brazil*, and the introductory chapters in José Maria Bello, *A History of Modern Brazil, 1889-1964*, provide excellent analyses of the causes of the overthrow of the monarchy and establishment of the republic.

In Portuguese the basic study of the empire is *O império brasileiro* (São Paulo, n. d.) by Manoel de Oliveira Lima, whose *Dom João VI no Brasil, 1808-1821* (2 vols., Rio de Janeiro, 1909) is still the leading history of the years spent by the Portuguese court in Rio de Janeiro. The lives of the founding fathers of the Brazilian empire are recounted in laborious detail in Octávio Tarquinio de Sousa, *História dos fundadores do império do Brasil* (10 vols., Rio de Janeiro, 1957). Heinrich Handelmann, *Geschichte von Brasilien* (Berlin, 1860), translated by Lucia Furquim Lahmeyer as *História do Brasil* (Rio de Janeiro, 1931), is a scholarly synthesis of colony, kingdom, and the first quarter-century of the empire. It is particularly useful for its comments on German immigration into Brazil to the mid-nineteenth century. A Marxist interpretation of Brazilian history from 1500 to 1889, but with emphasis on the imperial era, is Leôncio Basbaum, *História sincera da república, das origens a 1889* (2d ed., São Paulo, 1962). Basbaum concentrates heavily on economic and social trends. A fine synthesis of the politico-administrative history of Brazil from discovery to the latter years of the empire is José Maria da Silva Paranhos Júnior, the Baron Rio

Branco, "Esquisse de l'histoire du Brésil," which appeared in F. J. de Santa Anna Nery, ed., *Le Brésil en 1889* (Paris, 1889). It may be regarded as the official history of Brazil at the time of publication. The regime Rio Branco described was being undermined even as he wrote. The finest account of the rise of republicanism in Brazil is George C. A. Boehrer, *Da monarquia à república: história do partido republicano do Brasil, 1870-1889* (Rio de Janeiro, 1954). The influence of Positivism, which permeated much of the republican movement, is examined in Ivan Lins, *História do positivismo no Brasil* (São Paulo, 1964). Joseph L. Love deals with both Positivism and the republican party organization in southern Brazil in *Rio Grande do Sul and Brazilian Regionalism, 1882-1930* (Stanford, 1971). The role of the armed forces in the demise of the empire has been dealt with in several studies by Nelson Werneck Sodré, most recently in his *História militar do Brasil* (Rio de Janeiro, 1965). The classic interpretation of the decline and fall of the monarchy is Francisco José de Oliveira Vianna, *O occaso do império* (São Paulo, 1933). A somewhat more penetrating analysis is found in Heitor Lyra, *História da queda do império* (2 vols., São Paulo, 1964).

E. Republic

Few historians have attempted general surveys or syntheses of events in Brazil since the founding of the republic. For the most part the story has been told in political terms in memoirs, biographies, published records of various presidential administrations, and in monographs devoted to a single topic or a limited time span.

Of works in English, Bello, *A History of Modern Brazil, 1889-1964* is the only one covering the entire period in detail, while Bernstein, *Modern and Contemporary Latin America* includes a fine review of the republic in brief compass. The earlier accounts—Calógeras, *A History of Brazil* (1939), and the historical sections in Hill, *Brazil* (1947) and Smith and Marchant, *Brazil: Portrait of Half a Continent* (1951)—interpret the chief development from 1889 to date of publication. Skidmore's *Politics in Brazil* and Young's *The Brazilian Revolution of 1930* are primarily concerned with political trends after 1930, and Baklanoff's *New Perspectives of Brazil* deals only with the years since 1945.

A fundamental element of social history is developed in Robert J. Havighurst and J. Roberto Moreira, *Society and Education in Brazil* (Pittsburgh, 1965), which traces the evolution of educational policies and attitudes toward public education from the waning years of the empire to the present. An overview of the emergence of the middle class and the role of the armed forces in the nineteenth and twentieth centuries may be found in the chapters on Brazil in John J. Johnson, *Political Change in Latin America* (Stanford, 1958) and *The Military and Society in Latin America* (Stanford, 1964). Works that concentrate on the role of the military in the republic include Werneck Sodré's *História militar do Brasil,* cited earlier. and June E. Hahner, *Civilian-Military Relations in Brazil, 1889-1898* (Columbia, S. C., 1969). Alfred Stepan, *The Military in Politics, Changing Patterns in Brazil* (Princeton, 1971), focuses on the post World War II period, while Ronald M. Schneider, *The Political System of Brazil: Emergence of a "Modernizing" Authoritarian Regime, 1964-1970* (New York, 1971), deals primarily with the current scene.

Herman G. James, *Brazil after a Century of Independence* (New York, 1925) is a basic contemporary account of the so-called "Old Republic," expressed largely in terms of political institutions and public finance. An uncritical but useful biography of a leading statesman during the first three decades of the republic is Charles W. Turner, *Ruy Barbosa: Brazilian Crusader for the Essential Freedoms* (New York, 1945). A superb account of Padre Cícero, one of the most powerful of the backland political bosses during the Old Republic, may be found in Ralph della Cava, *Miracle at Joaseiro* (New York, 1970). Getulio Vargas, who dominated the political scene in Brazil for twenty-five years, is the subject of Ernest Hambloch, *His Majesty the President* (London, 1935), and Karl Loewenstein, *Brazil under Vargas* (New York, 1942). Both were written while Vargas was in power. A short journalistic appraisal of the man and his times is included in Tad Szulc, *Twilight of the Tyrants* (New York, 1959), while Vargas appears as a social revolutionary in Robert J. Alexander, *Prophets of the Revolution* (New York, 1962). The developmental policies of the Vargas regimes are examined in John D. Wirth, *The Politics of Brazilian Development, 1930-1954* (Stanford, 1970). Some of the urgency for social change in postwar Brazil is caught in Irving L. Horowitz, *Revolution in Brazil* (New York, 1964), useful as a compilation of extremist views but remarkably uneven in quality. Far more valuable for its effort to penetrate the underlying social and economic sources of political unrest is Celso Furtado, *Diagnosis of the Brazilian Crisis,* translated by Suzette Macedo (Berkeley and Los Angeles, 1965).

The history of republican Brazil is usually divided into two parts, before and after the 1930 revolution. Brazilian writers generally focus on one or the other. Edgard Carone, *A primeira república* (São Paulo, 1969), falls into the first category. Glauco Carneiro, *História das revoluções brasileiras* (2 vols., Rio de Janeiro, 1965), and João Cruz Costa, *Pequena história da república* (Rio de Janeiro, 1968), give about equal attention to both periods. Another is Leôncio Basbaum, who devotes Volume II of his *História sincera da república* (2d ed., São Paulo, 1962) to the Old Republic, and Volume III (São Paulo, 1962) to the years since 1930.

The political history of the Old Republic can be gleaned from the wealth of memoirs and biographies. Oustanding examples are Afonso Arinos de Mello Franco, *Um estadista da república* (3 vols., Rio de Janeiro, 1955), and Brígido Tinoco, *A vida de Nilo Peçanha* (Rio de Janeiro, 1962), which between them span the years from the 1890's to the mid-1930's. The importance of regional politics in the Old Republic is stressed in Love's *Rio Grande do Sul and Brazilian Regionalism, 1882-1930.* By far the most perceptive account of grass-roots politics before 1930 is the now-classic *Coronelismo, enxada e voto* (Rio de Janeiro, 1948) by Víctor Nunes Leal. Juarez Távora, one of the leaders of the *tenente* movement, has left a chronicle and analysis of the socio-political protest by young army officers in the 1920's in his *A guisa de depoimento sôbre a revolução brasileira* (2 vols., Rio de Janeiro, 1927-28), while the social inequities of the Old Republic are recounted from the point of view of an urban labor organizer in Everardo Dias, *História das lutas sociais no Brasil* (Rio de Janeiro, 1962).

For many Brazilians the contemporary period begins with the Vargas revolution of 1930, although recent scholarship is calling attention to the origins of that revolution in the social ferment of the 1920's. One of the more ambitious such efforts is being undertaken by Hélio Silva. Twelve volumes of his *O ciclo de Vargas* (Rio de Janeiro, 1964-   ) have appeared to date. An early, and still sound interpretation of the 1930 revolution is Barbosa Lima Sobrinho, *A verdade sôbre a revolução de outubro* (São Paulo, 1933). A somewhat different view, by the man who led Vargas's march on the capital in 1930 and suppressed the São Paulo revolt in 1932, is presented in General Pedro Aurélio de Góis Monteiro, *A revolução de 30 e a finalidade política do exército* (Rio de Janeiro, 1934). The anti-Vargas revolt in São Paulo has elicited a large bibliography, of which a representative example is Euclydes Figueiredo, *Contribuição para a história da revolução constitucionalista de 1932* (São Paulo, 1954).

Vargas did not write an autobiography, but *A nova política do Brasil* (11 vols., Rio de Janeiro, 1933-47) constitutes an official biography of his first three administrations (1930-45). This collection is a compilation of his public statements and programs during fifteen years in office. After his death, Alzira Vargas do Amaral Peixoto published *Getúlio Vargas, meu pai* (Rio de Janeiro, 1960), which reflects her dual role as his affectionate daughter and personal secretary. In sharp contrast is Affonso Henriques, whose *Vargas, o maquiavélico* (São Paulo, 1961) was expanded to three volumes as *Ascensão e queda de Getúlio Vargas* (Rio de Janeiro, 1966).

Henriques's bitterly critical study is both a biography and an appraisal of the Vargas era. Biographies or memoirs of each of the men who succeeded Vargas in power have been published in Brazil. The most useful for its revelations of political and social change after 1930, and for the light it sheds on the last Vargas administration, is João Café Filho, *Do sindicato ao Catete* (2 vols., Rio de Janeiro, 1966).

A highly sophisticated re-examination of trends since 1930 in the light of the 1964 revolution is Fernando Pedreira, *Março 31: civis e militares no processo da crise brasileira* (Rio de Janeiro, 1964). Much more ambitious in probing the imperial and even colonial past of Brazil for the roots of present social and economic problems, are Octavio Ianni, *Política e revolução social no Brasil* (Rio de Janeiro, 1965); Nelson Werneck Sodré, *Introdução à revolução brasileira* (Rio de Janeiro, 1958); and José Honório Rodrigues, *Aspirações nacionais* (Rio de Janeiro, 1963), *Conciliação e reforma no Brasil* (Rio de Janeiro, 1965), and *Interêsse nacional e política externa* (Rio de Janeiro, 1966).

IV. THE SOCIETY

Among the general works in English on the society of Brazil, Fernando de Azevedo, *Brazilian Culture,* and Gilberto Freyre, *New World in the Tropics,* provide the colonial and imperial background, while Charles Wagley, *An Introduction to Brazil,* and T. Lynn Smith, *Brazil: People and Institutions,* concentrate primarily on the current scene. Penetrating insights into Brazilian practices and attitudes toward race, family, and religion are presented in Thales de Azevedo, *Social Change in Brazil* (Gainesville, 1962). Hernane Tavares de Sá offers less scholarly, but delightful sketches of the manners and mores of his countrymen in *The Brazilians: People of Tomorrow* (New York, 1947).

An excellent contemporary statement on the society and economy of Brazil at the end of the imperial era is F. J. de Santa Anna Nery, ed., *Le Brésil en 1889* (Paris, 1889). A view of the traditional rural lower class in Brazil today may be found in Allen W. Johnson, *Sharecroppers of the Sertão; Economics and Dependence on a Brazilian Plantation* (Stanford, 1971). The urban *vs.* rural and modern *vs.* traditional dichotomies of Brazilian society in the twentieth century are examined from different points of view in Portuguese by Roger Batside, *Brasil, terra de contrastes* (Rio de Janeiro, 1959); Jacques Lambert, *Os dois Brasís* (Rio de Janeiro, 1959); Florestan Fernandes, *Mudanças sociais no Brasil* (São Paulo, 1960); and Manuel Diégues Júnior, *Regiões culturais do Brasil* (Rio de Janeiro, 1960). The relations of Europeans with persons of other races has been a matter of concern to writers on Brazil since the arrival of the first Portuguese. C. R. Boxer discusses this subject in the light of the world-wide experiences of the Portuguese over four centuries in *Race Relations in the Portuguese Colonial Empire, 1415-1825* (London, 1963). Marvin Harris considers the Brazilian situation in hemispheric context in his *Patterns of Race in the Americas* (New York, 1964). Charles Wagley, ed., *Race and Class in Rural Brazil* (Paris, 1952) examines the persistence of established patterns among rural Brazilians. In a real sense, all the works of Gilberto Freyre deal with relations between races in Brazil or other parts of the Portuguese world. It is the principal theme of his *O mundo que o português criou* (Rio de Janeiro, 1940). The classic of Brazilian literature, Euclides da Cunha's *Rebellion in the Backlands,* is also an excellent analysis of a peculiarly Brazilian ethnic amalgam, the *sertanejo* of the Northeast.

The present generation of sociologists in Brazil has produced some interesting studies questioning long-held assumptions about race and social mobility. Typical of these are Florestan Fernandes and Roger Bastide, *Brancos e negros em São Paulo* (2d ed., São Paulo, 1959), and Fernando Henrique Cardoso and Octavio Ianni, *Côr e mobilidade social em Florianópolis* (São Paulo, 1960). Thales de Azevedo provides both his own expert observations and a summary of recent Brazilian scholarship in *Cultura e situação racial no Brasil* (Rio de Janeiro, 1966).

Contact between Europeans and Amerindians in Brazil began with the arrival of Cabral and has continued without interruption to the present. The nature and range of such contacts are indicated in numerous documents in E. Bradford Burns, ed., *A Documentary History of Brazil,* and in the multi-volume general histories of the country. Alexander Marchant, *From Barter to Slavery,* describes the evolution of social as well as economic relationships between colonists and aborigines during the sixteenth century, while Mathias C. Kiemen weighs the contradictory claims of colonists and clergy on the Indians in the seventeenth century in *The Indian Policy of Portugal in the Amazon Region, 1614-1693.* Charles Wagley, *Amazon Town: A Study of Man in the Tropics* (New York, 1953) is a detailed study of the way of life of a people largely Indian in blood but no longer Indian in culture. The standard work in Portuguese on Indian slavery and other forms of servitude is Agostinho Marques Perdigão Malheiro, *A escravidão no Brasil; ensaio histórico-jurídico-social* (3 vols., Rio de Janeiro, 1867; 2d ed., 2 vols., São Paulo, 1944). Volume I deals exhaustively with the question of Indian servitude.

Over the past century and a half far more attention has been directed toward the Negro in Brazil, with particular emphasis on the issues of slavery and slave traffic. The reader interested in this vast topic may begin with

Florestan Fernandes's *The Negro in Brazilian Society*, listed above; Artur Ramos, *The Negro in Brazil* (Washington, 1951); Donald Pierson, *Negroes in Brazil, A Study of Race Contact at Bahia* (Chicago, 1942; 1967); or Eduardo Octávio da Costa, *The Negro in North Brazil* (New York, 1940). There is a great deal of information on slavery and the traffic in Celso Furtado, *The Economic Growth of Brazil*, and José Honório Rodrigues, *Brazil and Africa*. João Pandiá Calógeras, *A History of Brazil*, is interesting for earlier estimates of the volume of the slave trade. Also useful for their comparative treatment of slavery in various countries of the hemisphere are Frank Tannenbaum, *Slave and Citizen, the Negro in the Americas* (New York, 1947); David Brion Davis, *The Problem of Slavery in Western Culture* (Ithaca, 1966); and, Carl N. Degler, *Neither Black nor White: Slavery and Race Relations in Brazil and the United States* (New York, 1971).

Virtually every foreign visitor to Brazil before 1850 commented on the slave traffic, and travel accounts of the empire after that date provide a wealth of information about the institution of slavery and about the abolition movement. Particularly valuable in these respects are John Mawe, *Travels in the Interior of Brazil* (1812); John Luccock, *Notes on Rio de Janeiro . . . 1808 to 1818* (1820); R. Walsh, *Notices of Brazil in 1828 and 1829* (1830); C. S. Stewart, *A Visit to the South Seas . . .* (1833); Thomas Ewbank, *Life in Brazil* (1856); D. P. Kidder and J. C. Fletcher, *Brazil and the Brazilians* (1857); and H. C. Dent, *A Year in Brazil* (1886). A leading abolitionist's view of the abolition movement is reflected in Carolina Nabuco, *The Life of Joaquim Nabuco*. Recent scholarly and revisionist assessments of the last years of slavery in Brazil are Robert Conrad, *The Destruction of Brazilian Slavery, 1850-1888* (Berkeley, Los Angeles, London, 1972), and Robert Brent Toplin, *The Abolition of Slavery in Brazil* (New York, 1972).

The second volume of Perdigão Malheiro's *A escravidão no Brasil* is devoted to Negro slavery and the position of the Negro in Brazilian society in the 1860's. Another basic contemporary account is Aureliano Cândido Tavares Bastos, *Cartas do solitário* (Rio de Janeiro, 1862; 3d ed., São Paulo, 1938), which is a key document on the final days of the slave trade and on the condition of slaves in Brazil. Among the leading histories of Brazilian slavery written in the twentieth century are Evaristo de Morães, *A escravidão africana no Brasil* (São Paulo, 1933); Afonso de E. Taunay, *Subsídios para a história do tráfico africano no Brasil* (São Paulo, 1941); Maurilio de Gouveia, *História da escravidão* (Rio de Janeiro, 1955). Regional, and somewhat revisionist studies by modern Brazilian sociologists include Fernando Henrique Cardoso, *Capitalismo e escravidão no Brasil meridional. O negro na sociedade escravocrata do Rio Grande do Sul* (São Paulo, 1962), and Octavio Ianni, *As metamorfoses do escravo; apogeu e crise da escravatura no Brasil meridional* (São Paulo, 1962).

Voluntary immigration into Brazil has stirred relatively less interest than the imports of slaves from Africa. T. Lynn Smith, *Brazil: People and Institutions* contains a fine summary and description of immigration since 1884. Fernando Bastos de Avila, S. J., *Economic Aspects of Immigration: the Brazilian Immigration Problem* (The Hague, 1954), considers the questions of immigration and colonization in the postwar years, as does Margaret Bates, ed., *The Migration of Peoples to Latin America* (Washington, 1957). The adjustment of the Japanese immigrant to Brazilian society is discussed briefly in Yukio Fujii and T. Lynn Smith, *The Acculturation of Japanese Immigrants in Brazil* (Gainesville, 1959), and in greater depth in Hiroshi Saito, *O japonês no Brasil; estudo de mobilidade e fixação* (São Paulo, 1961). Vicenzo Grossi, *Storia della colonizzazione europea al Brasile e della emigrazione italiana nello stato di S. Paulo* (Rome, 1905) is excellent for the colonial period and the nineteenth century. Firsthand accounts of Italian immigration into southern Brazil are included in Fidélis Dalcin Barbosa, ed., *Semblantes de pioneiros; vultos e fatos da colonização italiana no Rio Grande do Sul* (Pôrto Alegre, 1961). German colonization is reviewed in Max Tavares d'Amaral, *Contribuição à história da colonização alemã no vale do Itajaí* (São Paulo, 1950), and in Emilio Willems, *Aculturação dos alemães no Brasil* (São Paulo, 1946).

All of the general works on society in Brazil today deal with the questions of internal migration and the growth of cities. Again, the most useful studies in English are Wagley, *An Introduction to Brazil,* and T. Lynn Smith, *Brazil: People and Institutions.* Richard M. Morse presents a biography of Brazil's largest city in *From Community to Metropolis* (Gainesville, 1958), while a radically different perspective appears in Carolina Maria de Jesus, *Child of the Dark,* translated by David St. Clair (New York, 1962), a vivid but depressing account of life in a São Paulo slum. Urbanization in the same city is dealt with from still another angle in Warren Dean, *The Industrialization of São Paulo* (Austin, 1969). For an introduction to the literature in Portuguese the reader should consult Nestor Goulart Reis Filho, *Contribuição ao estudo da evolução urbana do Brasil, 1500/1720* (São Paulo, 1968), and Geraldo de Menezes Cortes, *Migração e colonização no Brasil* (Rio de Janeiro, 1958). Two more specialized studies, Pedro Pinchas Geiger, *Evolução da rêde urbana brasileira* (Rio de Janeiro, 1963), and Paul Israel Singer, *Desenvolvimento econômico e evolução urbana* (São Paulo, 1968), examine the process of urbanization in the twentieth century in a few Brazilian cities.

V. THE ECONOMY

There are few general works on Brazilian economic history in any language. Many of the more useful studies in English have already been mentioned above in another context. The finest introduction to the subject is Celso Furtado, *The Economic Growth of Brazil* written for the non-specialist. An earlier work, still useful for its description of the colonial economic system, is João F. Normano, *Brazil, a Study of Economic Types* (Chapel Hill, 1935). Caio Prado Júnior, *The Colonial Background of Modern Brazil* presents a great deal of material on the economy in the late eighteenth and early nineteenth century, while Bailey W. Diffie, *Latin American Civilization: Colonial Period* succinctly reviews economic developments throughout the colonial era.

Numerous works deal with a shorter time span or with a specific aspect of the colonial economy. Alexander Marchant's *From Barter to Slavery: The Economic Relations of Portuguese and Indians in the Settlement of Brazil, 1500-1580* provides a detailed examination of the brazilwood trade and the beginnings of the sugar plantation economy. C. R. Boxer describes the agricultural economy of northeastern Brazil in *The Dutch in Brazil*, and recreates the gold and diamond cycles in *The Golden Age of Brazil, 1695-1750*. Visitors to Brazil after 1808 supply the most satisfactory descriptions of economic activities at the end of the colonial period. These include Henry Hill's *A View of the Commerce of Brazil [Uma visão do comércio do Brasil em 1808]*; John Mawe's graphic account of the diamond industry in *Travels in the Interior of Brazil*; a British merchant's view in John Luccock, *Notes on Rio de Janeiro and the Southern Parts of Brazil Taken During a Residence of Ten Years in the Country from 1808 to 1818*; and the thorough reporting on exports from Rio de Janeiro in Johann B. von Spix and Karl F. P. von Martius, *Travels in Brazil, 1817-1820*.

The best single work on the colonial economy is Roberto C. Simonsen, *História econômica do Brasil, 1500-1820* (2 vols., São Paulo, 1937; 4th ed., 1962), although for certain details José Gabriel de Lemos Britto, *Pontos de partida para a história econômica do Brasil* (São Paulo, 1939) is more informative. Highly regarded is Caio Prado Júnior, *História econômica do Brasil* (São Paulo, 1945; 7th ed., 1962), which presents a Marxist interpretation of Brazil's economic development. These may be supplemented by João Dornas Filho, *Aspectos da economia colonial* (Rio de Janeiro, 1958); Ivan Pedro de Martins, *Introdução à economia brasileira* (Rio de Janeiro, 1961); Heitor Ferreira Lima, *Formação econômica do Brasil (período colonial)* (Rio de Janeiro, 1961); and Luís Amaral's substantial *História geral da agricultura brasileira* (3 vols., São Paulo, 1939-40).

An indication of the complexities of colonial commerce may be found in Alice P. Canabrava, *O comércio português no Rio da Prata, 1580-1640* (São Paulo, 1944), and in Jerônimo de Viveiros, *História do comércio do Maranhão, 1612-1895* (2 vols., São Luís, 1954). The great majority of the documents surviving from the colonial period deal in one way or another with economic matters. The oustanding one is João Antônio Andreoni [André João Antonil], *Cultura e opulência do Brasil,* first published in 1711. The complaints of the planter class at the end of the colonial era are forcefully presented in Rodrigues de Brito, *A economia brasileira no alvorecer do século XIX* (Salvador, n. d.). The impact of the new economic policies introduced by Dom João is studied in Manoel Pinto de Aguiar, *A abertura dos pôrtos do Brasil* (Salvador, 1950).

The broad sweep of Brazil's economic development since independence is dealt with in some of the general works listed above. Again, travel accounts are excellent, if often impressionistic sources. Diplomatic and consular reports by British and American representatives in Brazil are an almost inexhaustible fount of data, particularly on commerce and agricultural production, while full details on various aspects of the economy are provided in occasional publications of the Brazilian government, such as *The Empire of Brazil at the Universal Exhibition of 1876 in Philadelphia* (Rio de Janeiro, 1876). The basic study of the close trade and financial ties between Brazil and Great Britain in the nineteenth century is Alan K. Manchester, *British Preëminence in Brazil: Its Rise and Decline.* It may be supplemented by *Viscount Mauá and the Empire of Brazil,* Anyda Marchant's biography of the great industrialist and financier whose success depended largely upon ready access to British capital, and by Richard Graham's *Britain and the Onset of Modernization in Brazil, 1850-1914.* Stanley J. Stein focuses on two vital areas of the economy in *Vassouras: A Brazilian Coffee County, 1850-1900* (Cambridge, 1957), and *Brazilian Cotton Manufacture: Textile Enterprise in an Underdeveloped Area* (Cambridge, 1957).

These and other themes have been examined by Brazilian students of national economic development. The definitive study of the growth of the coffee industry is Afonso de E. Taunay, *História do café no Brasil* (15 vols., São Paulo, 1939-43), but the reader may glean the highlights of the story as it pertains to the state of São Paulo in Sérgio Milliet, *Roteiro do Café* (São Paulo, 1946). Alice P. Canabrava examines a boom period in the cotton industry in *O desenvolvimento da cultura do algodão na província de São Paulo, 1861-1875* (São Paulo, 1951). The Amazon rubber boom is the subject of Richard Collier's *The River That God Forgot* (London, 1968). Raul de Góes traces the historical development of Brazilian merchant associations in *A Associação Comercial no império e na república* (Rio de Janeiro, 1955), and Oliver Onody provides copious details about the inflationary process in *A inflação brasileira* (1820-1958). The most useful contemporary account describing the state of the economy at the close of the empire is F. J. de Santa Anna Nery, ed., *Le Brésil en 1889.* The rise of industry and the evolution of national policies toward industrialization are carefully treated in Nícia Vilela Luz, *A luta pela industrialização no Brasil, 1808-1930* (São Paulo, 1961). It is strongest on the period since the establishment of the republic.

This study may be supplemented in English by Roberto C. Simonsen, *Brazil's Industrial Revolution* (São Paulo, 1939); José Jobim, *Brazil in the Making* (New York, 1943); and Brazil, Ministry of Foreign Affairs, *Brazil, 1943: Resources and Possibilities* (Rio de Janeiro, 1944). These are excellent sources of information on the growth of manufacturing industries under the republic, and especially after 1930. The somewhat jaundiced view of Brazil's potential as an industrial nation reflected in Henry W. Spiegel, *The Brazilian Economy: Chronic Inflation and Sporadic Industrialization* (Homewood, Ill., 1949) is balanced by the note of optimism in George Wythe, *et al., Brazil, an Expanding Economy* (New York, 1949). In the decade 1944-54 three binational economic missions provided a veritable mine of data on Brazil's economic infrastructure. This material may be found in Morris L. Cooke, *Brazil on the March—A Study in International Cooperation. Reflections on the Report of the American Technical Mission to Brazil* (New York, 1944); *Report of the Joint Brazil-United States Technical Commission* (Washington, 1949); and *The Development of Brazil. Report of the Joint Brazil-United States Economic Development Commission* (2 vols., Washington, 1954-55). The role of private foreign capital and entrepreneurship in the development of Brazil's natural resources is pointed up in Charles A. Gauld, *The Last Titan, Percival Farquhar, American Entrepreneur in Latin America* (Stanford, 1964). Lincoln Gorddon and E. L. Grommers analyze the experiences of several North American firms in Brazil in *United States Manufacturing Investment in Brazil, 1946-1960* (Boston, 1962), while a single corporation is examined in Theodore Geiger and Liesel Goode, *The General Electric Company in Brazil* (New York, 1961). The role of state planning for industrial expansion is examined in relation to the steel industry in Werner Baer, *The Development of the Brazilian Steel Industry* (Nashville, 1969), and for both steel and petroleum in Wirth's *The Politics of Brazilian Development, 1930-1954.* An excellent work which provides an over-all view is Howard S. Ellis, *The Economy of Brazil* (Berkeley and Los Angeles, 1969).

The Brazilian situation has been examined in the light of general theories of economic development in Simon Kuznets, *et al.*, *Economic Growth: Brazil, India, Japan* (Durham, 1955); Albert O. Hirschman, *Journeys toward Progress: Studies of Economic Policy-Making in Latin America* (New York, 1963); Stefan H. Robock, *Brazil's Developing Northeast: A Study of Regional Planning and Foreign Aid* (Washington, 1964); Celso Furtado, *Diagnosis of the Brazilian Crisis*, translated by Suzette Macedo (Berkeley and Los Angeles, 1965); and Hélio Jaguaribe, *Economic and Political Development. A Theoretical Approach and a Brazilian Case Study.*

In the postwar years the industrial economy has been a favorite topic of Brazilian writers, who have examined it from many points of view. Heitor Ferreira Lima, *Evolução industrial de São Paulo (esboço histórico)* (São Paulo, 1954), reviews São Paulo's rise to pre-eminence. Clovis de Oliveira shows the politico-military significance of industry in São Paulo in the early 1930's in *A indústria e o movimento constitucionalista de 1932* (São Paulo, 1956). Others have considered the social problems of industrialization. Typical of such studies are Pedro Rache, *O problema social-econômico do Brasil* (Rio de Janeiro, 1946), and Manuel Diégues Júnior, *Industrialização, urbanização, imigração* (Rio de Janeiro, 1962). João Albertino Rodrigues, *Sindicato e desenvolvimento no Brasil* (São Paulo, 1968), deals with the structure of the urban industrial labor movement from about 1900 to the revolution of 1964. The institutional approach is followed in Anapio Gomes, *Radiografia do Brasil* (Rio de Janeiro, 1955), which is an analysis of the role of state enterprises in Brazil's economic development. Mario Henrique Simonsen explores a persistent postwar financial problem in *A experiência inflacionária no Brasil* (Rio de Janeiro, 1964). The administration that took power in 1964 published a substantial body of economic studies which combine application of economic theories to the Brazilian situation with justification of the government's economic polities. Particularly useful are two reports by the Ministério do Planejamento e Coordenação Econômica, *Programa de ação econômica do govêrno, 1964-1966* (2d ed., Rio de Janeiro, 1965), and *O programa de ação e as reformas de base* (2 vols., Rio de Janeiro, 1965). Finally, an encyclopedic catalog of Brazil's industrial resources and the current status of their development may be found in successive editions of Hugo Schlesinger, *Geografia industrial do Brasil* (São Paulo, 1952). The most useful such volume, however, appeared in English as a publication of the Brazilian Embassy, *A Survey of the Brazilian Economy, 1965* (Washington, 1966).

VI. BIBLIOGRAPHIES AND PERIODICALS

Each of the general works and many of the specialized studies listed above contain excellent bibliographies of writings on Brazil. The reader can locate additional sources over a broad range of scholarly disciplines in the annual *Handbook of Latin American Studies* (Cambridge, 1936-51; Gainesville, 1951-   ). The most complete guides in English to historical studies on Brazil are R. A. Humphreys, *Latin American History: A Guide to the Literature in English* (London, 1958); the American Historical Association's *Guide to Historical Literature* (New York, 1961); Stanley J. Stein, "The Historiography of Brazil, 1808-1889," *Hispanic American Historical Review*, XL, No. 2 (May 1960); and E. Bradford Burns, "A Working Bibliography for the Study of Brazilian History," *The Americas*, XXII, No. I (July 1965). Brazilian studies figure prominently in Charles C. Griffin, ed., *Latin America: A Guide to the Historical Literature* (Austin, 1971). The reader should also consult the periodic supplements to the American Universities Field Staff, *A Select Bibliography: Asia, Africa, Eastern Europe, Latin America* (New York, 1960; 1961; 1963; 1965), and Harry Bernstein, *A Bookshelf on Brazil* (University of the State of New York, Albany, 1966, mimeograph), which include other subjects as well as history.

The following are of interest to the specialist: New York Public Library, *Dictionary Catalog of the History of the Americas* (28 vols., Boston, 1961); University of California, The Bancroft Library, *Catalog of Printed Books* (22 vols., & index, Boston, 1964); and Harvard University Library, *Widener Library Shelflist, Nos. 5 and 6, Latin America and Latin American Periodicals* (2 vols., Cambridge, 1966).

S. A. Baytich, *Latin America, A Bibliographical Guide to Economy, History, Law, Politics, and Society* (Coral Gables, 1961), which is a particularly valuable source for legal studies, lists well over a hundred bibliographic and reference works that pertain to Brazil. Older, but still useful is C. K. Jones, *A Bibliography of Latin American Bibliographies* (Baltimore, 1922; 2d ed., Washington, 1942). These may be supplemented by the *Inter-American Review of Bibliography* (Washington, 1951-   ). A literary guide is provided in J. M. Topete, *A Working Bibliography of Brazilian Literature* (Gainesville, 1957). The basic reference work on Brazilian Indians is Julian H. Steward, ed., *Handbook of South American Indians* (6 vols. & index, Washington, 1946-59). An introduction to studies of the economy of Brazil may be found in Harvard University, Bureau for Economic Research, *The Economic Literature of Latin America* (2 vols., Cambridge, 1935-36), and Tom B. Jones, *et al.*, *A Bibliography on South American Economic Affairs: Articles in Nineteenth-Century Periodicals* (Minneapolis, 1955). Both reference materials and current articles on the Brazilian economy appear in the United Nations Economic Commission for Latin America, *Economic Survey of Latin America* (New York, 1948-   ), while statistical data may be found in University of California at Los Angeles, Center of Latin American Studies, *Statistical Abstract of Latin America* (Los Angeles, 1955-   ).

Guides to periodical literature are Irene Zimmerman, *A Guide to Current Latin American Periodicals* (Gainesville, 1961); Columbus Memorial Library, *Index to Latin American Periodical Literature, 1929-1960* (Boston, 1961); and Columbus Memorial Library and New York Public Library, *Index to Latin American Periodicals* (Boston, 1961-   , quarterly).

In Portuguese the *Manual bibliográfico de estudos brasileiros* (Rio de Janeiro, 1949), edited by Rubens Borba de Moraes and William Berrien, is by far the most complete bibliography on Brazilian history and other subjects. For the most part it includes items published through 1945. Moraes's *Bibliographia brasiliana* (2 vols., The Hague, 1949) is a thorough work on rare books about Brazil published from 1504 to 1900, and works by Brazilian authors published abroad before 1822. Both bibliographies include travel accounts in various languages. Additional references to this topic may be found in Afonso de E. Taunay, *Visitantes do Brasil colonial* (2d ed., São Paulo, 1938), and in Cândido de Mello-Leitão, *Visitantes do primeiro império* (São Paulo, 1934), and *O Brasil visto pelos ingleses* (São Paulo, 1937). An annotated bibliography on the 1964 revolution is provided by Amaury de Souza, "Março ou Abril?" *Dados,* Vol. 1 (1966).

Brazil's leading historiographer, José Honório Rodrigues, offers interpretations of the methods and approaches to historical writing in Brazil, periodization of Brazilian history, and comments on Brazilian historians in his *Teoria da história do Brasil* (São Paulo, 1949; 2d ed., 2 vols., 1957) and *História e historiadores do Brasil* (Rio de Janeiro, 1965). The student of the colonial period should also consult his *Brasil: período colonial* (México, 1953); *Historiografía del Brasil: Siglo XVI* (México, 1957); and *Historiografía del Brasil: Siglo XVII* (México, 1963), which appeared in Spanish under the auspices of the Pan American Institute of Geography and History. Nelson Werneck Sodré, *O que se deve ler para conhecer o Brasil* (Rio de Janeiro, 1945; 2d ed., 1960), which includes works in a wide variety of fields, is useful for the layman interested chiefly in the national period. The best guide to current publications in all fields is *Boletim Bibliográfico Brasileiro, Revista dos Editôres* (Rio de Janeiro, 1954-   , monthly).

The American student interested in the history of Brazil will wish to acquaint himself with the back files and current issues of several scholarly journals. Outstanding among these is the *Hispanic American Historical Review* (Baltimore, 1918-22; Durham, 1926-   , quarterly). Other leading historical journals are *Mid-America* (Chicago, 1918-   , quarterly), *The Americas: A Quarterly Review of Inter-American History* (Washington, 1947-   ), and the *Luso-Brazilian Review* (Madison, 1964-   , semi-annually), which does not limit its offerings to history. Articles on slavery, the African slave traffic, and the history of the Negro in Brazil may be encountered from time to time in the *Journal of Negro History* (Lancaster & Washington, 1916- , quarterly). *The Journal of Inter-American Studies and World Affairs* (Gainesville, 1959-64; Coral Gables 1964- , quarterly) and its accompanying Latin American monograph series (1959-62) include studies on a broad range of subjects. Economic history and current economic developments are dealt with in *Inter-American Economic Affairs* (Washington, 1947- , quarterly). Political background and current trends are discussed in several journals of political science, such as the *Political Science Quarterly* (Boston, 1886-), and *Western Political Quarterly* (Salt Lake City, 1948-). Outside the United States the *Revista de Historia de América* (México, 1938- , now semi-annually) carries occasional articles on the history and historiography of Portuguese America.

Over the past century and a half there has been a vast number of ephemeral periodicals in Brazil devoted to the study of the history, society, and economy of the nation. At present most of the universities and nearly all state historical societies issue at least occasional journals. The leading historical journal is the *Revista do Instituto Histórico e Geográfico Brasileiro* (Rio de Janeiro, 1839- , now semi-annually). The *Revista de História* (São Paulo, 1959- , quarterly) is a valuable source of articles and reviews on colonial and imperial history. Probably the finest political science journal in Latin America is the *Revista Brasileira de Estudos Políticos* (Belo Horizonte, 1957- , semi-annually). Current and basic studies of the Brazilian economy may be found in the monthly publication of the Getúlio Vargas Foundation, *Conjuntura Econômica* (Rio de Janeiro, 1947-). The social sciences are treated in *América Latina* (Rio de Janeiro, 1958- , quarterly) published by the United Nations Centro Latino Americano de Pesquisas em Ciências Sociais; and in the *Revista Brasileira de Ciências Sociais* (Belo Horizonte, 1961 , semi-annually). A publication designed to appeal to intellectuals in all fields of study is *Dados* (Rio de Janeiro, 1966- , semi-annually). For general coverage of current social, economic, and political events—and not infrequently for articles of historical significance—the reader should consult *O Cruzeiro* (Rio de Janeiro, 1929- , weekly); *Manchete* (Rio de Janeiro, 1953- , weekly); *Visão* (São Paulo, 1952–June 1957, bi-weekly; July 1957- , weekly); and *Veja* (São Paulo, 1968- , weekly).

Although press coverage of Latin American events has increased substantially in the United States in recent years, *The New York Times* is still the only daily newspaper that can be expected to provide the minimum news essential to keep the North American reader informed about major developments in Brazil. The *Christian Science Monitor* is an excellent source for occasional special reports on Brazilian topics. Of the hundreds of newspapers published in Brazil, the few that attempt national coverage and are of both current and research value to the specialist include the *Estado de S. Paulo* of São Paulo, and *Jornal do Comércio, Jornal do Brasil,* and *Correio da Manhã* of Rio de Janeiro.

Tables

I. BRAZIL: DISTRIBUTION OF INDUSTRIAL PRODUCTION BY STATE (1907-60)*

State	1907 Per cent	1920 Per cent	1940 Per cent	1950 Per cent	1960 Per cent
Amazonas [with Acre, Rondônia, Roraima]	2.0	0.1	0.2	0.2	0.4
Pará [including Amapá]	2.7	1.1	0.8	0.5	0.5
Maranhão	0.7	0.7	0.3	0.3	0.3
Piauí	0.1	0.2	0.1	0.06	0.1
Ceará	0.4	0.8	0.6	0.7	0.7
Rio Grande do Norte	0.1	0.6	0.5	0.5	0.5
Paraíba	0.4	1.1	1.1	1.0	0.7
Pernambuco	4.0	6.8	4.6	4.1	2.8
Alagôas	1.0	1.6	1.0	0.8	0.5
Sergipe	0.6	1.2	0.5	0.4	0.2
Bahia	3.2	2.8	1.3	1.3	1.9
Minas Gerais	4.8	5.5	6.7	7.2	6.0
Espírito Santo	0.1	0.7	0.4	0.7	0.3
Rio de Janeiro	6.7	7.4	4.9	5.9	6.5
Federal District [Guanabara]	33.1	20.8	19.0	13.9	9.6
São Paulo	16.5	31.5	43.5	47.5	54.8
Paraná	4.9	3.2	2.1	2.9	4.0
Santa Catarina	2.0	1.9	1.8	2.4	2.2
Rio Grande do Sul	14.9	11.0	9.8	8.8	7.1
Mato Grosso	0.5	0.2	0.3	0.2	0.3
Goiás	0.2	0.1	0.2	0.4	0.4

* José Jobim, *Brazil in the Making* (1943), p. 96; *Anuário Estatístico do Brasil, 1958*, p. 84; *1964*, pp. 83-4.

2. BRAZIL: DISTRIBUTION OF INDUSTRIAL LABOR FORCE BY STATE
(1920-69)*

State	1920	1940	1950	1960†	1969†**
Acre	22	175	211	296	
Amazonas [including Rondônia,. Roraima]	636	3 413	4 034	4 476	10 469
Pará [including Amapá]	3 033	10 595	10 654	11 775	21 641
Maranhão	3 575	6 425	8 757	11 042	6 534
Piauí	1 175	1 590	1 913	3 072	5 009
Ceará	4 717	7 859	17 352	16 504	33 901
Rio Grande do Norte	2 146	4 879	12 034	10 967	11 533
Paraíba	3 295	13 210	26 215	14 387	17 959
Pernambuco	22 248	57 327	76 483	60 297	88 978
Alagôas	7 930	12 563	22 143	16 529	21 301
Sergipe	7 708	11 438	14 532	11 761	14 063
Bahia	16 698	23 361	35 719	35 352	88 001
Minas Gerais	18 848	74 267	111 513	114 211	230 411
Espírito Santo	1 109	4 066	7 214	7 582	26 756
Rio de Janeiro	20 714	45 483	78 631	90 833	164 596
Federal District [Guanabara]	56 229	123 459	171 463	137 923	347 407
São Paulo	85 466	272 865	488 633	647 244	1 450 451
Paraná	7 295	20 451	40 086	55 364	125 114
Santa Catarina	5 367	21 015	44 526	57 656	112 719
Rio Grande do Sul	24 661	60 908	99 945	104 763	252 437
Mato Grosso	557	4 349	3 712	5 949	21 036
Goiás	244	1 487	3 355	5 003	17 421
Federal District [Brasília]					45 342
Total	293 673	781 185	1 279 184	1 422 986	3 113 079

* *Anuário Estatístico do Brasil, 1958*, p. 82; *1964*, p. 91; *1971*, pp. 515-536.
† The figures for 1960 and 1969 do not include owner-operators or members of their families, employed without remuneration.
** No data are available for the state of Acre and the territories of Amapá, Rondônia, and Roraima in 1969.

3. BRAZIL: DISTRIBUTION OF INDUSTRIAL ESTABLISHMENTS BY STATE
(1920-60)*

State	1920	1940	1950	1960
Acre	10	34	48	150
Amazonas [including Rondônia, Roraima]	69	212	260	367
Pará [including Amapá]	168	666	909	1 278
Maranhão	90	703	1 005	2 430
Piauí	56	164	388	1 187
Ceará	295	789	2 572	2 223
Rio Grande do Norte	197	593	1 123	1 158
Paraíba	253	737	1 398	1 146
Pernambuco	496	1 877	3 490	3 599
Alagôas	367	687	1 139	1 566
Sergipe	307	743	1 300	1 882
Bahia	511	1 766	3 910	5 929
Minas Gerais	1 248	6 224	10 620	12 259
Espírito Santo	77	984	1 752	1 608
Rio de Janeiro	496	2 405	3 539	4 534
Federal District [Guanabara]	1 541	4 169	4 916	5 306
São Paulo	4 157	14 225	23 303	36 129
Paraná	623	2 264	3 460	6 403
Santa Catarina	793	2 847	4 753	5 906
Rio Grande do Sul	1 773	6 557	12 751	12 582
Mato Grosso	26	402	444	1 098
Goiás	16	370	623	1 599
Total	13 569	49 418	83 703	110 339

* *Anuário Estatístico do Brasil*, 1958, p. 82; 1963, pp. 92-100; 1964, p. 83.

4. BRAZIL: DISTRIBUTION AND SIZE OF INDUSTRIAL ESTABLISHMENTS (1960)*

Number of Industrial Establishments

State/ Territory	Total Plants	Number of Personnel per Plant									Not Declared
		1-4	5-9	10-19	20-49	50-99	100-249	250-499	500-999	1 000+	
Rondônia	55	24	20	7	2	2					
Acre	150	124	21	5							
Amazonas	305	149	65	43	35	6	3	2	1		1
Roraima	7	4	2		1						
Pará	1 211	751	243	128	52	28	8	1	1		
Amapá	67	43	8	6	5	2	1	1	1		2
Maranhão	2 430	1 724	538	122	31	5	1	6	1		2
Piauí	1 187	1 005	129	38	12	2	1		1		
Ceará	2 223	1 432	490	188	78	15	7	7	1		
Rio Grande do Norte	1 158	796	187	78	63	21	11	1		1	5
Paraíba	1 146	710	268	91	46	16	12	1	1		
Pernambuco	3 599	2 379	666	249	152	46	55	28	12	7	5
Alagôas	1 566	1 289	161	54	23	10	14	5	4	2	4
Sergipe	1 882	1 569	217	48	25	8	5	2	6		2
Bahia	5 929	4 753	711	252	123	42	30	12	2		4
Minas Gerais	12 259	9 402	1 492	609	391	148	97	41	24	10	45
Espírito Santo	1 608	1 292	192	67	42	2	10	3			
Rio de Janeiro	4 534	3 116	653	299	198	102	75	41	25	11	14
Guanabara	5 306	2 318	1 101	775	598	256	168	55	15	14	6
São Paulo	36 129	22 876	5 046	3 251	2 531	1 011	727	311	128	67	181
Paraná	6 403	4 201	1 019	643	343	105	44	14	2	2	30
Santa Catarina	5 906	4 137	895	433	255	92	44	18	11	6	15
Rio Grande do Sul	12 582	9 187	1 451	822	637	253	118	29	19	3	63
Mato Grosso	1 098	779	202	69	33	9	6				
Goiás	1 599	1 281	215	68	20	7	3				5
North	1 795	1 095	359	189	95	38	12	3	1		5
Northeast	13 309	9 335	2 439	820	405	115	100	48	19	12	16
East	31 518	22 450	4 366	2 050	1 377	558	385	154	72	39	67
South	61 020	40 401	8 411	5 149	3 766	1 461	933	372	160	78	289
Center-West	2 697	2 060	417	137	53	16	9				5
Total	110 339	75 341	15 992	8 345	5 696	2 188	1 439	577	254	129	378
% of National Total		(68.28%)	(14.49%)	(7.56%)	(5.16%)	(1.98%)	(1.30%)	(0.52%)	(0.23%)	(0.11%)	(0.34%)

* Anuário Estatístico do Brasil, 1963, pp. 92-100.

5. BRAZIL: DISTRIBUTION OF INDUSTRIAL PLANTS, PERSONNEL, AND
PRODUCTION BY STATE AND REGION (1960)*

State/Region	Per Cent of Industrial Plants	Per Cent of Industrial Personnel	Per Cent of Industrial Production
São Paulo	32.73	46.09	54.82
Guanabara	4.80	9.92	9.63
Rio Grande do Sul	11.40	7.46	7.15
Rio de Janeiro	4.10	6.09	6.54
Minas Gerais	11.11	7.78	5.99
Paraná	5.80	3.80	3.98
Pernambuco	3.26	4.00	2.77
Santa Catarina	5.35	3.87	2.21
Bahia	5.37	2.78	1.88
% of Nat'l Total	83.92	91.79	89.97
North	1.62	1.11	0.86
Northeast	12.06	8.90	5.67
East	28.56	27.92	24.57
South	55.30	61.23	68.16
Center-West	2.44	0.82	0.72
Total	99.98	99.98	99.98
	Number of Industrial Plants	Number of Industrial Personnel	Value of Industrial Production (Cr$ 1,000)
Brazil	110,339	1,796,837	Cr$1,186,933,228

* *Anuário Estatístico do Brasil*, 1963, pp. 92-100; 1964, pp. 83-91.

Index